ALSO BY WARREN HINCKLE

Guerilla-Krieg in USA (with Steven Chain and David Goldstein)

If You Have a Lemon, Make Lemonade: An Essential Memoir of a Lunatic Decade

The 10-Second Jailbreak: The Helicopter Escape of Joel David Kaplan
(with Eliot Asinof and William W. Turner)

The Richest Place on Earth: The Story of Virginia City and the Heyday
of the Comstock Lode (with Frederic Hobbs)

The Fish Is Red: The Story of the Secret War Against Castro
(with William W. Turner)

Gayslayer!: The Story of How Dan White Killed Harvey Milk
and George Moscone & Got Away with Murder

The Big Strike: A Pictorial History of the 1934 San Francisco General Strike

The Agnos Years: 1988–1991

Deadly Secrets: The CIA-Mafia War Against Castro and the Assassination of JFK
(with William W. Turner)

Who Killed Hunter S. Thompson?
The Picaresque Story of the Birth of Gonzo

Ransoming Pagan Babies

Ransoming Pagan Babies

The Selected Writings of Warren Hinckle

Edited by Emmerich Anklam and Steve Wasserman

HEYDAY, BERKELEY, CALIFORNIA

The essays and articles in this book originally appeared, sometimes in slightly
different form, in the following publications: *The Argonaut*, *City of San Francisco*, *Frisco*,
Ramparts, the *San Francisco Chronicle*, the *San Francisco Examiner*, and *Scanlan's Monthly*.
Grateful acknowledgment is made to Guy Stilson for permission to reprint articles
which were originally published in *Ramparts* magazine.

Library of Congress Cataloging-in-Publication Data is available online.

Endpapers: front, Warren Hinckle arrested in the *San Francisco Chronicle* newsroom
for walking his dog, Bentley, without a leash, February 1985. Photograph by Eric
Luse, *San Francisco Chronicle*/Polaris. Used by permission; back, Illustration by
Robert Crumb drawn for *San Francisco Examiner* cardboard rack cards on newspaper
stands promoting Warren Hinckle's new column, 1985. Used by permission.

Cover Design by Ashley Ingram
Printed in Saline, Michigan, by McNaughton and Gunn

Orders, inquiries, and correspondence should be addressed to:
Heyday
P.O. Box 9145, Berkeley, CA 94709
(510) 549-3564, Fax (510) 549-1889
www.heydaybooks.com

10 9 8 7 6 5 4 3 2 1

Contents

Acknowledgments

This book is dedicated to Warren James Hinckle III.

While in high school in Erie, Pennsylvania, I became intrigued by the writings in *Ramparts* and *Scanlan's* magazines, which opened my eyes to a world I had never imagined. Little did I know that I would one day meet the creative force behind these journals and become his partner for over nineteen years. Warren was the love of my life, my partner through thick and thin, and always encouraged me to be me. I will forever miss him and be thankful for our time together.

Ransoming Pagan Babies became a reality thanks to Heyday's Steve Wasserman, publisher and executive director, who was hired by Warren in 1975 to help edit *City* magazine and who later helped research Warren's book on Castro and the CIA, *The Fish Is Red*. Steve had long yearned to publish a collection of Warren's writings and proposed it to Warren in the months before his passing and received his permission to do so. He then came to me with the project shortly after Warren's death. I was only too happy to give him my blessing.

Thanks to Emmerich Anklam of Heyday, who found the editorial key that turned a stack of sallies and columns and essays into a monument to Warren's brilliant and often game-changing writing, muckraking zeal, and rollicking lust for life; and to the entire publishing team at Heyday: truly it takes a village.

To John Briscoe, Warren's longtime friend, and my friend in need, who helped make this publication possible through his generosity, I will be eternally grateful.

Thanks also to Guy Stilson, legal custodian of *Ramparts* rights and permissions, for granting reprinting of various articles from that remarkable publication. And a grateful acknowledgment to Warren's daughters, Pia and Hilary, and to his son, Warren Hinckle IV, for their enduring love for him.

After an amazing run with life, Warren's health took an unexpected hit. His medical team at St. Mary's Medical Center in San Francisco treated him with respect, kindness, compassion, and dignity.

Thanks to the family and friends who stood by both of us through the most trying of times and held us together with both laughter and tears.

Finally, I especially want to acknowledge the dear friends without whom I would be lost:

Janet McKinley and George Miller for standing beside us when we needed it most: George for his generosity of spirit as he and Warren solved the world's problems, ranging from politics to football, and Janet for being my friend, confidant, and sous-chef.

And, of course, our dog Delilah, who steadfastly sat by his side waiting for the crumbs.

Linda Corso
San Francisco
November 2017

The
Narrow
Door

Ransoming Pagan Babies

*T*HERE IS SOMETHING to be said for the disadvantages of Catholic education, at least as it was in San Francisco of the logy, foggy fifties. For one thing, in grammar school I learned about ransoming pagan babies. We had to save our dimes to ransom the poor unbaptized creatures of China. To facilitate the financial aspect of this spiritual transaction, we purchased savings certificates—watermarked in the fuzzy purple of the nuns' hectograph machine and resembling somewhat Blue Chip Stamps—which were popularly known as "Pagan Baby Stamps." When we had accumulated sufficient markers, we were assured that a yellow pagan baby of our choice would receive a Catholic baptism. We also got to name it, with a saint's name, of course. It cost five dollars to ransom a boy, and three dollars for a girl. The good Sisters explained that girls came cheaper, since the Chinese routinely drowned girls at birth like baby kittens, because there were so many of them. This led to considerable discussion about the relative value of boys and girls, and provoked a compromise, arranged by the nuns, which was widely considered a bargain: for ten dollars we could ransom one boy and two girls.

The Catholic umbrella under which I grew up shaded a vacuum-sealed, middle-class, and unflinchingly white ghetto. We all went to Catholic schools and our parents paid their dues and regularly received the sacraments, as did we kids, but it was more routine than a leap of faith. The church seemed everywhere, Authority incarnate, yet it didn't really connect. It was authority largely without terror. The church I knew was not the Church of Savonarola, nor of James Joyce—it was too settled and comfortable to summon the fire and brimstone for Stephen Dedalus–type retreats. The priests who weren't stuck in the confessional box on Saturdays put on Pendleton sport shirts and went off to play golf at the Irish Catholic Olympic Club. Our confessors did scare us a little by warning we could lose our minds and maybe even our hair if we touched ourselves, but suggested that if we pulled hard on an ear it would dispel temptation. Naturally we tugged our ears, but otherwise the operating principle was to accept everything the church taught while paying as little attention to it as possible. Thus we went to Mass on Sundays and sinned on Mondays and went to confession on Saturdays so we could receive Communion on Sunday and be in a state of grace to sin again on Monday.

I came to accept the church for the tinsel, lazy, corrupt, and at the same time appealing thing that it was. During those gray and quiet years, the church was like some pervasive closed system dominating an endless science fiction novel, wherein it seemed the fate of the mutinous among us to do continuous dubious battle against it; there was great fun in the rum of rebellion, and we fought on in the not unpleasant expectation of losing. Changing the church was no more real than changing the ocean.

This background ill prepared me for the liberal Catholic reformers with whom I became involved in the early sixties. I was astonished to find that there were Catholics abroad who actually thought that unyielding institution was going to improve itself and thereby improve the world. Most of the reformers I encountered had not endured sixteen years of Catholic education as I had, but had escaped to prep school and secular colleges far removed from the bad breath and pimples of the workaday church.

I found it difficult to believe that these earnest people were attempting to make a blushing bride of that fine old whore, the church. While these reformers were shocked to discover how materialistic the Vatican really was, I had learned in grammar school that profitable money-changing was the natural condition of the priestly calling. Our pastor used to stand in front of the altar during collections at Christmas Mass and exhort the faithful to "make it a green Christmas." The reformers were freshly aglow with the illuminating theological proposition that the church was as much human as divine; I knew that was the truth back in the third grade the first time I heard a nun fart.

I later watched the priests cream these well-meaning liberals: Lions 14, Christians 0. The odds were lopsided from the start. Just as the tougher, peasant Stalin made a better revolutionary than the more bourgeois and intellectual Bolsheviks, these starry-eyed Catholic reformers with their idealized view of the church were no match for the crafty and possessive priest-Pachucos who gave out karate chops instead of blessings. Most of the young priests who rushed to the aid of the reformers were likewise clobbered and have long since left the church, along with a goodly percentage of the reformers. They succeeded in vulgarizing the Mass and making some other niggling reforms, and then drifted off to various new enthusiasms—Anglicism, agnosticism, even astrology— leaving confusion in their wake, like little kids taking apart some gigantic radio set to improve the reception, then tiring of the project but not knowing how to put the set back together. These thwarted reformers then became bitter at the church for doing what came naturally to preserve the monolith. The difference in my expectations of the Church of Rome and that of many of the liberal intellectual Catholics of the early sixties was that of sixteen years in Catholic schools, which were susceptible to all the analogies of *Stalag 17*.

[CATHOLIC REFORM SCHOOL]

My Catholic education taught me never to trust a priest—under or over thirty. They became quite vicious if one threatened their sense of authority or in any way profaned their pride, which I was constantly doing. Here they had given up their lives in the service of God, got up at five every morning to say Mass, and wore lousy black gabardine slacks that itched, and had tossed their sex lives in the wastebasket and, goddamnit, they expected the laymen-serfs to click their heels and pay proper respect.

My four years in Catholic high school were a boot camp in guerrilla warfare against overweening authority. I served my sentence at Riordan High School, a newish cement-walled institution that served as sort of a respectable Catholic reform school for the children of lower-middle-class San Francisco Italian and Irish families and was otherwise distinguished by having been named after an archbishop who had been killed by a train.

The student body was a monstrous assembly of truants who enjoyed committing battery on the men who had consecrated their bodies to God. The unenviable title of the worst of our bad lot was generally considered a toss-up between myself and another student, who had the unpleasant habit upon boarding a streetcar of unzipping his pants and urinating in the fare box. In the World War II epics popular at the time, John Wayne always painted tiny Japanese suns on the fuselage of his plane each time he bagged a Zero. Similarly, the lads of Riordan maintained a running box score on how many religious we were able to send down in flames.

Our teachers were the Brothers of Mary, an uninspired religious order whose ranks held the usual number of failed hedonists and sexual malcontents. The brothers, who preferred red double-breasted black business suits to the more traditional clerical robes, were on the spectrum of religious vocation between the dull gray of the consecrated eunuch and the purple glory of the priesthood. In addition to the vows of poverty, chastity, and obedience, they took an additional vow, that of special devotion to the Blessed Virgin Mary, an inamorata they referred to with some intimacy as the "BVM." The order was like a religious displaced-persons camp of grade four and lower civil servants.

The all-male Riordan student body was warned about the physical dangers of public high schools, not the least of which was the hazard of bloody Kotex that shameless Protestant and Jewish girls were said to drop carelessly on dark stairways. Our contact with the outside world was largely limited to mandatory special pleading to the Lord to free Cardinal Mindszenty from an atheistic holding cell in Hungary, and reading about contemporary events in the brown pages of a jejune publication called the *Junior Catholic Messenger*, which featured front-page photos of the eminent Catholic junior senator from Wisconsin, Joseph McCarthy, buzzing about the Senate subway doing God's work in Washington.

Catholic high school proved an excellent place to learn the nature of bureaucracy and the fine art of bamboozling. I gained access to the school sherry supply and discovered the wonderful world of banquets and cocktail parties, the entrance to which could be gained by creating sundry committees, letterheads, and other artifacts of eleemosynary hoodwinkery. I and my childhood buddy, a kindred musketeer named Gerry Davalos, got happily drunk every Saturday afternoon excepting Advent and Lent by putting on our good suits and walking into strange wedding receptions in the Catholic catering halls of the Sunset District, where we pretended that we were the groom's relations to the bride's people, and vice versa.

WHILE THUS BEING EDUCATED, I discovered that I was a print junkie. I made the school newspaper my personal fiefdom to indulge my insatiable craving for the joys of printing plants—clunking linotypes spitting out words of metal, Ludlow machines creating veritable milky ways of headlines in type fat and thin, hissing stereotype machines, ill-mannered printers cursing instructively. For me, no secrets of science or metaphysics were comparable to that miraculous process whereby words were transported from your head through a typewriter to a typesetter into metal artfully arranged, which produced a printed page. If there was a heaven, it had to have a composing room. The printing plant over which I first lusted was a squat green building on the wrong side of Market Street called the Garrett Press, which produced shoppers and dreary house organs. (I began putting out newspapers there when I was thirteen and was still at it nearly two decades later at *Ramparts*, which, to keep me amused, published two newspapers, one of them a daily.)

I had found my place in the sun in this dark, dingy printing plant which I thought of as King Solomon's Mines. I would stand bent over the makeup forms for hours on end, drunk with the ordeal. I became ecstatic when, in violation of all union rules, I was allowed to handle a piece of hot type. The hours I spent in the company of printers came to exceed those in the classroom, and gave me quite a different view of the universe than that afforded by the Brothers of Mary. I spent my spare time and money on pilgrimages to the out-of-town newspaper stands, which were located between skid row and the red-light district. I would step obliviously over the bodies of winos and dodge around hookers to reach the delicious racks of stale newspapers, and come away burdened with as many copies as my money could buy of the *New York Daily News,* the defunct *Los Angeles Daily News,* and its also dead-and-gone successor the *Mirror;* at the time I had a crush on tabloids.

Often at night I traveled to Mecca, which was the rundown sports department of the *San Francisco Examiner,* where a kindly, drunken old Hearst deskman would let me stand around and drool over the teletype machines. My traveling companion in these excursions was my high school sports editor, a burly football player named Jim Clifford, who had the reasonably balanced view of our journalistic calling that it came somewhere after football and girls. One evening as we stood watching the teletypes pound and ring in the news a slight incident occurred that was illustrative of where my head was at this point in young manhood. A copyboy dumped off several copies of the advance "bulldog" news section of the Sunday paper, printed early to be trucked off to the boonies and filled with undated features about trout fishing in Alaska and publicity stills of aspiring Swedish starlets with their titties showing.

"Jez-zus, look at that!" Clifford said, staring at a large front-page photograph of a girl with a cleavage as deep as the Grand Canyon. But all I noticed was the unusual red headlines in a typeface the conservatively made-up *Examiner* normally reserved for world wars.

"Wow, that's really something," I replied to the salivating Clifford. "That's beautiful! Can you imagine running 60-point Cheltenham italic in red ink?"

Clifford gave me a very strange look, and all the way home on the streetcar that night he read the sports section in silence, occasionally glancing up to stare at me as if I were some sort of nut.

The Brothers of Mary were so delighted to be rid of my person that they made me the valedictorian, a gesture they had cause to regret when I delivered an X-rated speech. I took at least one of them over the wall with me. He was a beanstalk-tall and scarecrow-thin friar with a mordant sense of Christianity, one Brother Nunes, a high-speed talker with a clapped-out sinus that occasioned his voice to come out his nose with the pitch and whine of a jet engine. Brother Nunes was constantly taking hits off a Vicks inhaler, a habit he claimed I drove him to by my didos on the school paper, which he had the unwelcome detail of moderating. He described himself as hounded by the furies of Irish Catholic teenage journalists *manqués*. My coconspirator in driving the good brother to burn his black gabardines was Dan O'Neill—who in the sixties became the *enfant terrible* cartoonist at the *San Francisco Chronicle*, the creator of the comic strip *Odd Bodkins*, syndicated in some three hundred papers while he was still in his early twenties. He was fired at the peak of his popularity for outrageously inserting Morse code obscenities and recruiting messages for the Irish Republican Army in his strip, and thereafter went underground in Belfast, where he drew propaganda comic strips for the IRA. After letting the two of us loose in the world, Brother Nunes quit.

[EYEBALL TO EYEBALL WITH THE JESUITS]

At various times during the checkered decade past I have been called licentious, a profligate, an adventurer, a sensationalist, a wastrel, a capitalist guerrilla, a boozer, a corporate wrecker, a degenerate, a wheeler-dealer, and a pirate, among other things.

There exist sufficient grounds for most of those appellations that they could be regarded as faint praise unto the truth, which is that all I am now or may be considered to be I owe to the Jesuits.

Jesuit college education was a continuing Congress of Wonders, at times approaching the delirium of a mushroom sect. One professor spoke confidentially of undertaking scientific experiments in support of the little-known theory of Justinian that homosexuality was the cause of earthquakes. Theology units were earned by becoming versed in the finer points of religious etiquette, such as if one's gums were bleeding one could swallow the blood and still receive Communion without breaking one's fast, but if one cut one's finger one could not suck it, finger blood apparently being of a different theological type than gum blood. The instruction concerning women seemed peculiar even in that insensitive time of the mid-fifties—women were worthy to receive Communion on their tongues, but no other part of their anatomy could come into contact with the Host; the rules were different for men. If a woman lay dying and for some ungodly reason had to be anointed on the mouth, her lipstick must be first wiped off or else the sacrament of Extreme Unction, like vaccination under the wrong conditions, might not take.

Seniors were required to take a Last Chance course in the Catholic dos and do nots about sex; when, on occasion, a married student, as none others could dare to speak on the subject for fear of scandal, would raise a practical objection to the explicit instructions, such as how could a priest know what gives with sexual foreplay, the answer would invariably come, in the manner of the Jesuits, in another question: Did a doctor have to endure cancer in order to treat it?

Sex seemed to be the only exception to the general principle of plasticity characteristic of the Jesuit approach to moral and religious absolutes. Their Hard Line on carnality led them, historically, to some extremes, such as removing the stairs to Madame de Pompadour's apartment so as to render more difficult the entrance of Louis XV to her bedchamber, for which, among other peccadillos, they were kicked out of court.

In addition to such mandatory instructions in theology, the Jesuits insisted that their students at the University of San Francisco, locally known by the call letters USF, learn about "the warped logic of Lenin." This study came under the academic category of political science, and everyone was required to take Poli Sci 140: "The Philosophy, Dynamics and Tactics of International Communism." The text for the course was J. Edgar Hoover's *Masters of Deceit,* and the FBI director was said to be kindly disposed toward the Jesuit Fathers for unloading so many thousands of copies right there in the USF bookstore.

The ringmaster of Political Science 140 was Raymond T. Feeley, S.J., a bulldog-faced padre known as the "waterfront priest" for his activities in the thirties on the labor-strife-torn San Francisco docks in the cause of anticommunism and responsible Catholic unionism, a phrase some of Father Feeley's critics translated as meaning pro-management.

Father Feeley was a tough man, said to have single-handedly tossed several Reds into the chill waters of San Francisco Bay. He stared a good deal when in the classroom, constantly peering up and down the rows of wooden chairs as if he expected to find a red herring underneath. He called the attendance roll in a way that made you feel you should answer "Not Guilty" instead of "Present." We took notes from a scratchy recording of the "confession" of Whittaker Chambers. Our guest professors included an exiled Russian Jesuit named Urusov and the visiting Irish Catholic heads of the intelligence units called "Red Squads" in metropolitan police departments.

Father Feeley's lectures ran red with the blood of Bolshevik history. He established a peculiar sense of authority by never referring to the great figures in Russian history by their common political names, reverting instead to their original Russian names, enunciating each syllable as if it were one count in an indictment:

Not Stalin, but *Jos-if Vis-sar-iono-vich Dju-gash-vi-li.*

Not Lenin, but *Vla-dim-ir Ill-ich Ul-yan-ov.*

Those four Ivory Tower years were therefore spent in a sort of Charlie Chaplin waltz, learning what I was forced to learn to stay in the place, then unlearning it from the original sources. Those academic activities I carried on in my spare time, most waking hours being devoted to play-ing with the school newspaper, the *Foghorn*, and its necessary corollary of engaging in guerrilla warfare against the Jesuits. I had but one eye so I was excused from the fangs of the Reserve Officers Training Corps, known otherwise as ROTC. (My left eye had been blanked out in an automobile accident when I was eight.)

I, nevertheless, received plenty of military training in actual combat with the Jesuits.

WHEN YOU ARE ON THE OFFENSIVE against them the Jesuits work man-to-man rather than employing a zone defense. The Jesuit assigned to do me in was the Reverend Francis A. Moore, the dean of students, a tall, sun-tanned, cobra-eyed Jesuit with the stock smile of a hired assassin.

Moore did not like me, possibly because of an unfortunate incident in Corvallis, Oregon, in 1957, when I threw up all over him. I was drunk as only a college freshman can get, wandering aimlessly in the bowels of a basketball stadium, when two sportsmen from the rival college asked if I wanted some créme de menthe; I thought that was terrific of them and slugged the green substance down, which turned out to be liquid hand soap. This inconvenienced a number of USF rooters shortly after, when I staggered into the crowded stands and became violently ill. One of the unfortunate few within range was the dean of students, who I doubt ever forgave me that vile cascade of green slime and vomit down his black back. He threw the book at me for the putative crime of being drunk and disgraceful in a public rooting place.

That was the first—but the only one that stuck—in a relentless string of prosecutions and entrapments, the others of which I somehow escaped in the cliffhanger tradition of "Daredevils of the Red Circle"—a stubborn pin left standing in a twenty-four-hour Jesuit bowling alley. I survived attempted firings, suspensions and expulsions, and, those failing or being preempted, Jesuit threats and attempts to use the lend-lease of the civil authorities for the prosecution of various offenses to the commonweal, such as arson. An impartial observer of this extended combat once likened the relationship between the dean of students and me as that of Cardinal Richelieu to D'Artagnan—but if the truth be told we were both more Lady de Winter.

The dean especially held against me the matter of the Jesuit president's niece, a flower of Irish Catholic girlhood whom I dated during my stormy career as Casey Crime Photographer at USF, which courtship Father Moore apparently assumed made it more difficult to whip me at the pillory lest she get upset; he was outraged, wrongly considering it a high card of knavery on my part, refusing to accept the relationship for the coincidence of honest affection that it was. His loathing rose to a new boiling point on the occasion, in the midst of an especially dull news week, when my friend Brennan Newsom and I burned down a wooden guardhouse protecting the entrance to the campus—all so I would have something to headline in the *Foghorn,* which I then edited.

I produced an inflammatory front-page editorial denouncing the arsonist as having no respect for private property and called upon the dean of students to get off his ordained duff, find the maniac responsible, and "root this evil from our midst." I recommended expulsion for the guilty party. The dean knew, by intuition and stool pigeons, that I had done it, but he had no proof; the San Francisco Police arson inspectors only added fuel to his slow burn when, at his suggestion, they asked me my whereabouts at the time of the crime, and I replied that I had spent the night with the president's niece.

At the age of eighteen I fell into the practice, having somewhere read that Gogol used to write in taverns, of working in bars, a habit of industry that I have maintained with religious consistency since. There is little in the job description of an editor that cannot be accomplished in a good saloon. Such tasks as reading, thinking, editing, interviewing, writing, laying out pages, conferring with colleagues, and general plotting and inventing lend themselves to the calming environment of a proper pub, particularly as opposed to the busywork, artificiality, social climbing, and general beadledom of an office. You can be telephoned at a bar if people must, but the distance from an office discourages trivia; and, as you are escaping the tyranny of your own institution, you can tell the bartender to say that you have left; a professional bartender is an infinitely more effective liar than the most efficient secretary. I have consequently maintained offices for the necessary evils that they encompass but have gone to them as infrequently as possible; over the years I have been the more productive, if in some dry minds the more notorious, for it.

The Jesuits recklessly struck down a technical improvement I had ordered—the installation of a telephone extension from the university switchboard to a bar I frequented some ten blocks distant. I retaliated by sawing up Father Moore's favorite table, a round rostrum of golden wood at which he sat in kangaroo court judgment of truant students, fashioning from the remains a horseshoe-shaped copy desk for the *Foghorn* office. I was indignant that these black pimpernels of the pope would deign to be holier-than-thou about my right to drink. I vowed to spill as much Jesuit liquor as was humanly possible, and launched a blitzkrieg against temperance by a series of soirees, conferences, and dinners on campus to which I invited important citizens of the town whose favor the Jesuits curried, so the Fathers could not but acquiesce in the serving of drinks. The result each time was that the staff of the student paper got thoroughly swacked. Such activities led to my becoming known, in an analogy not always used in a completely complimentary sense, as the Elsa Maxwell of USF.

The grandest party of all was hosted at Jesuit expense when I turned the *Foghorn* into a daily newspaper. It was a surprise party for the Jesuits, as they did not know it was happening. I had laid cunning plans to make the paper a daily, keeping them strictly to myself, as does a prisoner on Devil's Island an escape plan. This was a politic thing to do as even those minority Jesuits favorably disposed to me considered me a young Dr. Strangelove of journalism.

So I secretly wrote an inch-thick white paper explaining the new daily publishing schedule in which, in the sacred tradition of white papers, I rationalized the increased work load as actually less work for everyone. For security, I had that classified document printed and bound at Stanford University Press and sent the bill to the Jesuits. I distributed it after dark to a clandestine gathering of the newspaper staff a week before Daily Day, all reporters pledging not to let it fall into any Jesuit hands. I wrote a press release—"New Era of Journalism at USF; *Foghorn* Becomes First Catholic College Daily Newspaper in U.S."—and handed it to the university publicity man with exact instructions on how to distribute it to the news media. Carl Nolte, the flack, was a former *Foghorn* man so I thought I could trust him. But he turned out a journalistic Judas and sent the press release to the dean for approval.

The morning the first edition was secretly scheduled to go to press I called Nolte to see if the announcement had gone out on time. The flack admitted that he had shown it to Father Moore, and that Father Moore had ripped it up. "He said you're not going daily," Nolte said. "He said you didn't get permission, and he's not going to let you do it, anyway." I began screaming in the general direction of the receiver, banging it on the table with such fury that the instrument broke in half and further communication was thereby ended, so I never did get to tell Nolte what I thought.

When I could walk again, I went directly to the nearest bar and composed a telegram announcing the daily publication of the *Foghorn*, which I sent to every newspaper in the state. I then sent out another telegram to various judges and city officials, prominent alumni, former *Foghorn* editors, and a goodly number of San Francisco reporters who would cross the Sahara itself for a free drink, inviting them all to a grand party that night to celebrate the *Foghorn* becoming a daily newspaper. I also invited many congressmen and senators in Washington, who of course would not come, but I knew someone on their staff would draft a routine telegram of congratulations. I told every Jesuit with whom I was on speaking terms to come to a party, neglecting to say what for.

Father Moore walked belatedly into the campus banquet hall that night and found it as packed as a Breughel people-scape with drunken newspapermen, students, Jesuits, San Francisco politicians, and fat-cat alumni, all raising toasts and singing hosannas to the grand event of the *Foghorn* becoming a daily. Six girls wearing white T-shirts with "DAILY FOGHORN" emblazoned across the front—and otherwise skimpily costumed in the tradition of the old Paris *Herald Tribune* newsgirls—were dancing through the crowd distributing copies fresh off the press of the next morning's edition of the *Foghorn,* with red headlines across the top of the front page: "CITY'S FOURTH DAILY IS BORN."

I walked up to Father Moore and handed him two telegrams of congratulations—from Vice President Richard Nixon and Senator John F. Kennedy. He looked pale and I suggested he break his fast and have a drink.

The next day the San Francisco newspapers all carried editorials congratulating the University of San Francisco on its great journalistic leap forward. It was a great victory for the doctrine of *fait accompli.*

ONCE AN EXHAUSTED STUDENT JOURNALIST, his eyes smallpox red from lack of sleep, his grade-point average dropping below the freezing point, asked me a question about newspaper frequency. He wanted to know why—as USF offered no journalism courses and gave no academic credit or relief for long unpaid volunteer hours spent working on the newspaper—just why did I want to go daily when everyone was already half-dead from the ball-busting effort of producing a weekly?

I understood at that moment why General Patton slapped the crying soldier. I restrained my reply to a single decibel answer: "Why? You fool, I'll tell you why. Because it's more fun!"

It seems that I am possessed at times of an ungovernable tendency to increase the pace and frequency of things. This has to do with many activities in life, including mischief, and, of course, publishing. I have made of quarterlies, monthlies: of monthlies, biweeklies; and of weeklies, dailies. I once, in an emergency, put out my college yearbook in six weeks, start to finish, as the editor of record had fallen into a fearful lethargy and had done nothing all year save hold meetings, finally resigning and hiding himself in a closet; I found that to be a cheering crisis and volunteered to produce it in the six weeks before school ended.

The mechanics of the metamorphosis of the *Foghorn* from weekly into daily were outlandishly simple: the weekly newspaper was six standard garbage-can-liner-sized pages; I divided that whole into several parts—tabloid-sized pages suitable for emptying a small vacuum cleaner bag. The daily was therefore actually no more than the same substance as the weekly, yet by certain manipulations of format and frequency and saying it was so, it was now a daily. (Years later, when I told Howard Gossage this, he pointed out that I had without realizing it hit upon one of his fundamental principles: "Never mistake the thing promoted for the thing itself.")

This particular daily was supposed to come out three times a week—sometimes it came out four times, sometimes twice, occasionally once. I defended the semantics involved by citing that bible of the newspaper industry, *Editor and Publisher*, which luckily listed fourteen colleges as having daily newspapers that came out three times weekly—but that was largely a dodge. I have never been too impressed by the arbitrary cycles of publication frequency, which by and large have a deleterious effect on content. In the five years I edited *Ramparts*, there was only one year when we actually published twelve times in twelve months. I often held an edition to get an important story so that by the time the April issue was ready to come out it would be nearly May, so we would "lose" April. I was forever writing notices to our subscribers from "the little man who runs our computer," informing them that their subscriptions would be extended as we had just "lost" another month. This practice gained *Ramparts* some important stories it would otherwise have lost but drove librarians to frenzy; they were always writing to ask where was April, and I would write back and say never to worry, that April was May, a simple enough metaphysic that they often failed to comprehend. (The entire dating game on magazines is a phony, anyway. If you subscribe to *Esquire*, it will come in the mail in the beginning of May but be dated June. That insanity is largely to accommodate illiterate newsstand dealers, who have become accustomed over the years to throwing away anything with an honest date; a May magazine in May is considered "stale.")

THE STRANGE THING called the *Daily Foghorn* was a monster frog in a small pond, causing distraction and disruption of those things the Jesuits held dear. Their nice Catholic college paper was transformed into a freak of Hearst proportions: "Sunday a.m." extras, weekday "5 a.m." extras, banner headlines in type suitable for the sinking of the *Titanic*, vitriolic front-page opinions, special editions, magazine supplements, exclusives in red ink, incessant and bitchy editorial crusades.

Jesuits picking up their campus paper read such headlines as "VIRGINIA CITY PRIEST ASSAULTS 47-YEAR-OLD WOMAN POLIO VICTIM" … "ROTC GENERAL ATTEMPTS TO STRANGLE STUDENT" … "DOROTHY DAY ASKS: WHO BAPTIZED CAPITALISM?" The school newspaper paid scant attention to the school, its pages filled with Herblock cartoons and AP stories such as "NAPOLEON MEMOIRS SOLD." (The *Foghorn* needed an AP wire as it did a jackhammer, but I installed one, to Jesuit dismay, as I have always had a fondness for teletypes—the kind that some men have for ladies' shoes or subway turnstiles.)

I assigned myself to cover the 1960 Winter Olympics in Squaw Valley, where I had a ball telegraphing front-page stories night press rate collect and otherwise ran the newspaper for two weeks via long-distance telephone and telegraph from the bar at a ski lodge.

One Halloween I stole the entire press run of the S.F. State College newspaper, thereby inspiring Father Moore to attempt to have grand theft charges brought against me. The administration constantly tried to cut off the *Foghorn*'s funds so as to bring this rollercoaster to a halt, and I was forever staying up nights drafting financial reports and revised budgets to stymie their attempts at sabotage. Near graduation, the dean of students sent me a bill for some $13,000, which he claimed was the *Foghorn* deficit, which I must personally pay before receiving my grades.

I had to get the famous barrister Jake Ehrlich to threaten the Society of Jesus with a lawsuit before I could get my transcript.

The *Daily Foghorn* had a short life. As soon as I left, the Jesuits busted it in rank back to a weekly.

[From *If You Have a Lemon, Make Lemonade:
An Essential Memoir of a Lunatic Decade,* 1974]

The Mad Organist of the Comstock*

THE LATE SILVER-SPOONED boulevardier Lucius Beebe, whose appreciation of the Irish in general was less than overwhelming but who curtsied to wealth in any robe, tells a story in *The Big Spenders* that captures the rash spirit of Virginia City in its boom days. Two Irish bonanza kings-to-be, John Mackay and his partner-in-muck, Jim Fair, trekked the 250 miles from San Francisco across the High Sierra to the windswept wasteland of the Comstock and came over the pass hungry and tired to behold below them the twenty-four-hour exercise in bacchanalia that was the mining town of Virginia City. Mackay reached in his pocket to find it empty and asked Fair if he had any money on him.

"Here's four bits; it's the only money I have in the world," Fair replied.

Mackay took the coin and sent it spinning into the Nevada sagebrush deep down the hillside.

"Whatever did you do that for, John?"

"So we can arrive like gentlemen."

When Mackay died some forty years later, his secretary told the press it was impossible to estimate his employer's fortune within $20 million. And Mackay's granddaughter married Irving Berlin.

Virginia City was once the richest place on earth. It has been as productive as a sucked egg since its silver mines petered out in the 1880s, but so fabulous were the fortunes produced and the manner of their spending and squandering so superlative that it burns through the fog of historical memory as a Cinderella city, a real-life, uniquely American Camelot devoted to the questionable art of conspicuous consumption. The Golconda from the deep mines of the Comstock changed the face of the West, enriched the North in the Civil War, built San Francisco into a Pacific Paris, laid the Atlantic cable, founded the Hearst newspaper

*Coauthored with Frederic Hobbs

empire, introduced Shanty Irish to the Court of St. James and the bou-
doirs of the Vanderbilts, spawned the first environmentalist, created
frontier Medicis and uncommon Scrooges, and fattened the lean meat
of the American dream with the carbohydrate of success stories about
lumpen mining stock speculators who struck it rich—butter salesmen
wandering around in morning coats and cleaning ladies scrubbing floors
with diamond-encrusted hands.

Seventy-five years after all this had happened and Virginia City had
become for all practical purposes save the collecting of tourists' pennies
a ghost town, the aforementioned Lucius Beebe, oenophile and unre-
pentant Edwardian, chugged across the country in his private railroad
car, puffed up the steep, winding twenty-mile road separating Virginia
City from the plastic of Reno, and settled down in the mountain city for
the rest of his unnatural life.

I knew Beebe when we were both writing for the *Chronicle*, San Francisco's daily funny paper. Beebe was as snobbish as a pewter pitcher of
martinis and as brittle as a frozen Hershey bar. A woman came up to
him at a cocktail party and complained about some department of the
Chronicle. Beebe slapped her with his eyes. "Madam," he said, "I write for
the *Chronicle* but I never *read* it."

Beebe had foaled café society in an acidulously snobbish column
in which he covered the upper classes for the *New York Herald Tribune*.
Beebe was one of their number but, in the words of Hilaire Belloc,
"Like many of the upper class, he loved the sound of smashing glass."
He played high-stakes cat's cradle in the thirties and forties in the velvet
bomb shelters of 21 and Morocco, the Turkish baths of the Biltmore,
and the magnificent zoo of Bleeck's Artists and Writers Restaurant (formerly Club), a hard-drinking newspaper joint where the great and the
demented took daily Communion. At Bleeck's a daft barkeep scattered
cracked corn to an imaginary flock of chickens behind the ice bins while
Stanley Walker, the *Herald Tribune*'s great city editor, proclaimed cirrhosis of the liver as the occupational disease of the journalist, and Gene
Fowler, the biographer of John Barrymore, announced that money is
for throwing off the back of trains. A constant ornament of existence in
the expensive watering holes of Manhattan, Beebe became known from
Antoine's in New Orleans to Locke-Ober's in Boston as "Mr. New York"
(Walter Winchell called him "Luscious Lucius"), and his lordly walking

around was so conspicuous that one critic described him as "a sort of sandwich board for the rich."

It was therefore an object of considerable consternation among the well-to-do when Beebe in 1950 pulled up stakes in New York with the abruptness of a vampire vanishing at dawn and moved to Virginia City, Nevada. Few could understand why. There was some speculation that it was due to Beebe's oft-stated belief that one should leave a party while it was still good. The fact was that Beebe had at last found a town worthy of his excesses. When Lucius went to bed at night he knelt to pray that the twentieth century, which he considered a "street accident," would go away before he waked. The wooden-boardwalked Old West mountain city of Virginia contributed little to the distinction between fantasies and reality, and there Beebe was able to act out a life of nineteenth-century manners, amorality, distinguished letters, alcoholism, and howling personal journalism of the day of the code duello. Beebe walked around town in a clawhammer coat and a wide-brimmed black hat and the natives never gave him a second glance.

Western historian Oscar Lewis once said Nevada was "the wishing well of the nation." People come to Nevada from the forty-nine other states to pitch their pennies in the three-eyed fountains of Las Vegas and Reno and await the clatter of coins that substitutes for their dreams coming true. Lucius Beebe's dream of the good life in the amiable tradition of Nero materialized in the thin mountain air six thousand feet above Reno. He delighted in the fact that Virginia City maintained twenty saloons—that with only 650 men, women, and children in town. Lest the pinched-face statisticians of Alcoholics Anonymous find such numbers inexplicable, it should be explained that the fifties, despite the club-footed attempts of social historians to paint them a uniform gray, were actually fun-loving years for the middle classes, and those salmon inclined toward frolic would stream uphill from Tahoe and Reno to Virginia City and environs where prostitution and most anything else was legal. The Comstock natives, a tough eggs-and-Tabasco-sauce lot, minded their own business and expected visitors to follow their example. The confiscatory personal income tax is unknown in Nevada, and the state in Beebe's time, and now, remains uniquely the last wide-open space in the United States, a combination of Old West individualism and turn-of-the-century Southern California entrepreneurism.

Nevada enshrined gambling and made divorce a family business; the Sagebrush State legalized acupuncture when it was still a Chinese word, and recently approved a fountain-of-youth drug, Gerovital, which is as popular in Europe as Lydia Pinkham's but barred elsewhere in the United States by the Food and Drug Administration; and Nevada *loved* Laetrile.

In this citadel of anything goes, Beebe lived out his last fifteen years in a condition of life that the legendary *Harper's Bazaar* editor Henry Sell described as "expensive cheerfulness," which was, for all its ostentation, productive. Beebe with his partner and lifetime companion, Chuck Clegg, cranked out an impressive string of books on Western Americana in which they indulged an unbridled love affair with the train. As railroad historians, Beebe and Clegg did for the High Iron what Macaulay did for the Whigs, and when they departed Virginia City during the inclement months they traveled about in a sultan's splendor in a private railway car named after the town and equipped with a fireplace, Turkish bath, and other voluptory amenities.

The visiting great—Cole Porter, restaurateur Dave Chasen, barrister Jake Ehrlich—would drop by Beebe and Clegg's Virginia City newspaper office to share the cup that cheers while throughout the country professors of journalism looked in horror on Beebe's magnificent resuscitation of the Virginia City *Territorial Enterprise,* the frontier newspaper where Mark Twain cut his editorial teeth. Beebe as publisher was a sort of Mad Organist of the Comstock, composing hydrophobic editorials against packaged breakfast cereals, digit dialing (Virginia City had crank-down phones), Billy Graham, zippers on men's pants, the American Newspaper Guild, woman's suffrage, TV dinners, the once-a-day mail delivery, the *Christian Science Monitor,* nuclear fission, Bobby Kennedy, one-ounce martinis, and the jet airplane—which the editorialist when he was in wine referred to as a "cartridge of death." These and other opinions were expressed at considerable length in Beebe's memorable form of the essay, which disdained periods and even semicolons, and exhibited even less regard for the paragraph.

Beebe's Baron Munchausen tastes notwithstanding, his newspaper was a classic of its kind, a black lotus late blooming out of the mud of barroom journalism. Its excessive tone was perfectly consistent with the history of Virginia City, which is in all facets a history of excess.

During the bonanza decades on the Comstock, select horses had silver shoes, highwaymen gallantly treated their victims to champagne and truffles while they robbed them, and Mark Twain's *Enterprise* escalated the nineteenth-century journalistic tradition of crime hoaxes by publishing science-fiction hoaxes as news—by some accounts it was the first science fiction published in America.

The Comstock maintained a perverse balance sheet where every excess or debit deed had its positive side as an asset, recognized as such or not, of the times. The excesses of the *Enterprise* of the bonanza years gave birth to the laughter of genius. The excesses of Beebe's *Enterprise* served to remind one of what a dreary manufacturing business the news business has become. There was once in American journalism an adventurous sense of going down to the sea in ships, of doing business in great waters, and of course doing this under the influence of strong waters. Reporters used to spend as much time in the saloon as the city room, and the liveliness of journalism seems to have benefited from the general insobriety of the profession. The newshounding and -hening of greatness past combined wit and fortitude with unabashed rascality, the practical joke with the people's crusade. It was as forthright and natural as soldiers talking bawdy one moment and displaying great courage in battle the next. Beebe for a time picked up the warble of Western journalism, individualistic, eccentric, and melodious even when off-key, which had reached its pitch during the forty years the *Denver Post* was run by Fred Bonfils and Harry Tammen like a three-ring circus, with the reporters kept in saloons and whorehouses until the ringmasters brought them on stage to perform. Bonfils and Tammen ruled the Rockies from a flaming-red partner's room with a globe of the world and a shotgun on prominent display; in their wacky, cash-and-carry way they uncovered the Teapot Dome scandal and didn't even consider it a public service.

Such personal journalism is now, alas, one with the Kelvinator and the Edsel. Lucius Beebe in his salad days in the Virginia City *Territorial Enterprise* did one and all a favor by reminding us that journalists as well as mortals can be fools, but damn interesting ones.

ONE NIGHT DURING a fierce wind and rainstorm on the Comstock, Lucius Beebe found Mr. T-Bone, his beloved Saint Bernard, staring intently into the storm as if trying to make out something in the dim distance. That night and for a week thereafter the Saint Bernard would not leave Beebe's side, following him everywhere. Beebe realized later that the dog was trying to tell him something: it was going to die. Mr. T-Bone died a week after the storm. Beebe wrote in his grief: "That night in the storm he heard a call from somewhere far off, something that only a dog could hear, and he sensed it on the storm wind that came down from the north where he had been born. A long, atavistic call from beyond the realm of senses and beyond his memory of puppyhood. He knew it then and wanted to tell me, and I never understood. It breaks my heart that I was so stupid and insensible."

Like many men who do not overly care for their fellow man, Lucius Beebe loved animals. He said that the huge Saint Bernard was one of the major forces in shaping his life, along with Jack Daniels whiskey and the *Herald Tribune* stylebook. When his dog died, Beebe wanted to die with it, to sit in eternity like the man and the dog in Thurber's famous drawing, facing west alone against the astral horizon of the stars, both no longer of this earth. Beebe and Clegg sold the *Enterprise* the year of Mr. T-Bone's death, in 1960. Without Beebe's pen the paper slowly sank back into the grave from whence he had resurrected it. Beebe continued to live part of the year in Virginia City until he died suddenly, of a heart attack, on February 4, 1966. Chuck Clegg attempted mouth-to-mouth resuscitation, but it was too late.

Wolcott Gibbs in a *NewYorker* profile of Beebe said that, in the words of the song popularized by Ethel Merman, "Beebe had class, with a capital K." Which is also to say, slightly crass class. The same epitaph could well be written for Virginia City. Every character in the spellbinding history of Virginia City overdid, in the direction of the outlandish. Virginia City's luck was of colossal proportions and so were its mistakes. It was never very good at being good, but when it was, it was very, very good, and when it was bad, it was so bad it was enchanting. The story of Virginia City could in many ways be taken as a brief for the Manichaean nature of man, or for the more commonplace observation about man's ability to do good and evil simultaneously.

Virginia City has always brought out the worst in people in a way that made it their best.

[From *The Richest Place on Earth:*
The Story of Virginia City and the Heyday of the Comstock Lode, 1978]

The Hobo Won't Bum Around

*T*HE THIRD STREET DRAWBRIDGE floated gray and black in a watery dawn. Underneath, a white-bearded man poked around in the rubble of his past. He was looking for hobos. Winos, he said. All there is, is winos. There's no hobos in San Francisco anymore. He kicked an empty bottle of Ripple into the green slime along the tumbled-down banks of the urban canal and climbed puffingly up the slope and around the Cyclone fence that is there to keep people out. He was tall and slightly stooped. Above a beard that would do a Macy's Santa proud his red face was lined and stained with the alkali of sixty-five years on the road. His lively blue eyes had the impatience of restless souls awaiting a transfer from a used body. He is called, simply, Hobo. That is both his name and his game. He will be seventy-five next month. He is one of the last of his kind.

THE TOWN PUMP WAS ANYTHING BUT DRY at six-thirty in the morning. When we walked in people were standing around drinking screwdrivers and watching firemen stomp out a mattress fire in a hotel across the street at 18th and Mission. A one-armed guy in a red shirt and overalls had come in early to practice his pool game. Hobo ordered a hot water and brandy. He took a short red-and-white straw from his coat pocket and put it in the drink. He sipped the booze through the straw. He does this every time he has a drink, which is not on rare occasions. "Have you ever seen an old man sitting in a bar with his chin whiskers all dripping from drinking whiskey?" he says. "Disgusting. Use a straw and you don't dribble. I want to get away from what happens to old men."

Hobo thinks his parents were missionaries. He was born in China during the Boxer Rebellion and orphaned by it. He became "a foster-child of the U.S. government" and was brought to America in 1908, an anonymous blond boy consigned to an orphanic one-more-bowl-of-porridge hell in East Coast Tudor mansions. That was seventy years ago. He ran away at fourteen and has been on the road ever since. Barely a decade has passed that he hasn't spent time in San Francisco—in the twenties seen from a view window in Alcatraz, where he did a hitch for giving the World War I military induction the raspberry ("Hell, I was born in one goddamn war and that was enough"); in the thirties delivering bootleg pints around North Beach for the legendary prohibitionist Doc Pucinelli; in the fifties hanging out with the beats and in the sixties with the hippies in the Haight. For years Hobo was a sidewalk fixture at Enrico's, composing instant poems for the tourista for a buck or whatever the traffic would bear. But always he would break away to wander, a motion as essential to him as spinning to a top.

Now he was back in San Francisco again, and we were going to Third Street, under the drawbridge, to see if hobos were still camping there, as he remembered they once had. But there were no traces. Hobos, he said, don't drink Ripple. "These days, it's getting harder to find a real hobo than a buffalo," he said.

HOBO WAS FURIOUS OVER A RECENT ARTICLE in the *New York Times* describing the mole-like winter existence of broken-down men who lived in giant steam tunnels below Grand Central Terminal and ate by scavenging on the Midtown streets. The offending article had freely used "hobos" as a synonym for "derelicts," a crime the headline writer had compounded in 36-point type.

Hobo said the *New York Times* didn't know a hobo from a hole in the ground. In the first place, hobos in the east always go south for the winter to Louisiana or Florida to sell programs at Hialeah. Hell, those weren't hobos—they were bums! Bums, said Hobo, are constitutional do-nothings and know-nothings who exist by begging and stealing to buy cheap booze: winos are a subgenus of bum, familiar to San Francisco. Hobos are by contrast nice of property, although mostly portable property. They never beg or thieve but always "find a way to make a piece of change" or work for barter for food or services. A hobo will often work for a month or two and then go on the road with his stash and live like a king. Why, books have been written about this, he said, totally amazed that anybody wouldn't know the difference between a hobo and a bum.

There isn't a town in the country that I can't go into cold and make twenty bucks in an afternoon, Hobo said. Money is as near as the nearest doorbell or a "No Experience Necessary" ad in the classifieds. Hobo's favorite is selling photograph studio coupons door-to-door; the seller gets to keep the money paid for the coupon because the studio makes its cabbage off the extra prints. "You just walk into any studio and say, 'I'm a coupon man' and you're all set." He pulled out a ten spot and ordered another round. "Hobos," he said, "pay their own way."

HOBO TOOK ME TO SEE HIS KINGDOM. It was a room on the sixth floor of a pensioner's hotel on Turk Street but it was as rich as an abbey. The four walls were a landscape of pictures of mountains and wildlife from the process color pages of *Arizona Highways* and maps from *National Geographic*. "That's so I can travel even when I'm sitting still," he said. His desk was an empty blond television casing with an old Underwood typewriter portable on top. A leather belt of a dozen or more harmonicas hung from the bureau like the bandoliers of Pancho Villa. Every available flat surface was stacked with galley proofs, tape cassettes, paperbacks, magazines, flashlights, fishing lines, framed and unframed snapshots, feathered hats, scarves, and brown shopping bags crammed with newspaper clippings. "Research," he said of the bags. Wooden and cardboard boxes stuffed with manuscripts in faded blue folders were stacked up the walls high as an elephant's eye. "This is my kingdom," Hobo said. "I wrote everything in those boxes. There's half a million words in this room."

Hobo's poetry and novels—four books have been published over the decades but he's lost them all in his travels—are of an era past of slow campfires and mulligan stews and lazy concertina Sundays. The now-world of fiberglass and bisexual beauty parlors and Cuisinart has no place in his life or his words. "I suppose I keep writing for the same reason I keep staying alive—to try and figure out why we're all here on this earth," he says. "I think it has something to do with recycling. There's so many molecules in your body and your brain. They'll eventually be recycled for use somewhere else in the universe. I think it's up to us to

improve those molecules as much as we can before we pass them on—
leave the world, at least its atoms, in better shape than we got them."
The philosophy of the Diogenes of the freight cars.

Hobo is going to the annual Hobo Convention in Britt, Iowa, in
August. He was there last year, but not many of the usual boys made it.
He still has some mulligan stew tickets left over; empty plates for dead
friends. "I guess I'll have to sell enough photo coupons for plane fare," he
said. "It's too dangerous to ride the rails to Iowa anymore." Hobo took
a swig of blackberry brandy from the half-pint in his pocket. He stared
out at the bay for a long while.

"Being a hobo," he said, "is getting to be a bummer."

[*San Francisco Chronicle,* April 11, 1978]

The Forgotten Lady of Chinatown

SOMETIMES SAN FRANCISCO can be pretty heartless to its near-greats. You screw up in this town and you're dead. And if you screw up and then die, you can end up without even an obituary.

This is a story about a woman who was one of San Francisco's leading characters for almost half a century. She was famous. Yet she died earlier this year in total obscurity. She was a chain-smoking, hard-drinking Chinese lady banker. She went to jail, but she was more saint than scoundrel. Her name was Dolly Gee.

Last week someone told me she had died. He had just heard it. He said she had died months ago. He couldn't believe that Dolly Gee could die and nobody would know about it. Neither could I. I went to the part of this newspaper that is called the library but in Jimmy Cagney newspaper movies on TV is called the morgue. I asked for the clips on Dolly Gee. I was handed a thick brown envelope crammed with articles that told the story of the triumphs and the tragedy in her colorful life. But it was a story without an ending. No obituary had been written. Her life just stopped in the crinkly newspaper clippings, abruptly, like an uncompleted freeway. I think we owe Dolly Gee an obit.

DOLLY GEE WAS THE MANAGER of the Chinatown branch of the Bank of America from 1929 to 1962. She was one of the best-known women in Chinatown. She was the first woman branch manager in the history of the world's largest bank. She was one of the B of A's most prized executives. Then she fell from grace with the suddenness of an angel whose wings had melted in flight. She was felled by a family secret and an oriental debt of honor.

Her story begins in the years before the 1906 earthquake and fire. Chinese were excluded then from every area of life in the city. Even their money was no good. A Chinese who walked into a bank to deposit cash or rent a vault would be shooed out the door.

Dolly Gee was born in China and came to San Francisco as an infant, in 1901. Her father, Charles Gee, went into the shoe business. He was an honorable man trusted by everyone. People in China who wanted to send money to America would send it to him to hold, since the banks would not take it. Charles Gee put their money in empty shoeboxes for safekeeping. During the 1906 fire, Charles Gee took a boat to Oakland with his shoeboxes. He went to the French-American Bank in Oakland and asked if they would please deposit this money for him that the San Francisco banks wouldn't take. The French-American bankers looked in the shoeboxes. There was almost a million dollars. They took the money.

Charles Gee went to work for the French bank. The bank would do business with him, but it did not want streams of Chinese coming in its doors. So people gave their money to Charles Gee and he put the money in the bank for them in his name. When Dolly was sixteen, she went to work for her father at the bank. Elders in Chinatown were shocked that a girl would work for a bank. Dolly ignored their disapproval. She was, at an early age, a modern woman. Chinese deposits grew to $2 million and the French-American Bank opened a branch in Chinatown. When the Bank of America took over the French-American Bank, Chinatown became one of the B of A's most profitable branches.

In 1929, the year of the stock market crash, Dolly Gee was named manager. That year her father told her a terrible secret. In 1919 Charles Gee had gone back to China and opened the China Specie Bank in Hong Kong. When he returned to San Francisco and his job with the French bank, many people in Chinatown gave him money to deposit in the Hong Kong bank. He was a trusted man. In 1923, the Hong Kong bank failed. There was no air mail in those days. Someone should have cabled, but no one did. It was two months before Charles Gee found out the bank was gone. During that time he had sent over $100,000 in Chinatown money to the busted bank. He couldn't recover it.

The Chinatown depositers never lost a dime. Dolly's father considered it a matter of honor to repay the money. He used all the money he had, and when that wasn't enough, he took money from dormant foreign accounts in the Chinatown branch bank. It was easy to do, since so many of the deposits from China were in his name. Soon, he was into the bank for $100,000. He juggled the books, which were kept in Chinese. The bankers never knew. This was the secret that banker father told banker daughter. Dolly had to decide whether to turn her father in or continue the deception. She, too, became a Robin Hood. The secret would last over thirty years.

Under Dolly Gee, the Chinatown branch grew to be the sixtieth largest of the B of A's approximately eight hundred branches. Deposits totaled $20 million. She ran the whole show. The B of A trusted her completely. Through these boom years, she kept juggling the books, to keep her father's secret. The Bank of America came to value Dolly Gee beyond her ability to bring in deposits. In 1936, when A. P. Giannini made some disparaging remarks about Chinese, Chinese Americans began a run on B of A branches that reached serious proportions. It was Dolly Gee who stopped the run. The gravel-voiced, chain-smoking lady banker became one of the most familiar figures in Chinatown. Everyone knew Dolly. At night, she would go to the gambling houses, hoping some day to win enough to repay her father's debt. She never did. A friend said that in her three decades as head of the Chinatown branch, Dolly never took a vacation. She couldn't afford to. Someone might discover the juggled books in her absence.

When her father died in 1956, all of Chinatown attended this honorable man's funeral. Dolly kept his secret another six years, until December of 1962. Testimonial dinners were being prepared for her. She decided she couldn't be honored with this on her conscience. She went to the president of the Bank of America and told him the secret. Over the years, interest had inflated the original $100,000 her father had repaid Chinatown depositors in the twenties to over $300,000. Dolly Gee took responsibility for the debt. She went to the FBI and told them everything. Even though she was cooperating in reconstructing the complexities of the debt, the FBI arrested her on Christmas Eve and took her to jail in her nightgown. She was sixty-four.

Chinatown was aghast. Rumors began to fly that she had lost the money gambling. When the story about her father came out, some people in Chinatown said Dolly should never have told; her father was an honorable man and his name should be left in peace. There was no peace for Dolly Gee. She pleaded guilty, even though she never took a dime for herself. She was sentenced to five years at Terminal Island. When her lawyer, William J. Gintjee, visited her in prison, she told him she didn't want to get paroled early. "I couldn't pay back the money—I'll pay the time," she said.

"Dolly seemed almost relieved about going to prison," Gintjee said. "Apparently this was a terrible burden on her conscience all those years."

She was released in 1965 after doing sixteen months. She returned to Chinatown and lived quietly on a pension. She walked with a cane. Everybody in Chinatown knew Dolly. Everybody said hello on the street. Dolly lived her last few years in a nursing home. She had few visitors. A friend who visited her shortly before her death found her surviving on hot dogs. She was very excited when he brought her a bottle of her favorite whiskey, Johnny Walker Black.

She died in the beginning of the year. Hardly anyone knew she was gone. No one had a memorial service for her. No one called the newspapers. No one she lent money sent flowers. Maybe she wanted it that way, a friend said. "Maybe she was ashamed. But she shouldn't have been. It's very sad."

Sometimes it's easy to forget what makes San Francisco what it is. It is not the cable cars or the flower stands or the fog. It's not Tony Bennett, or even Herb Caen. It's the people. Some of them, like the city itself, have not been perfect. That is no reason to forget them. In some cases, like Dolly Gee, it is all the more reason to remember them.

Happy obit, Dolly.

[*San Francisco Chronicle,* September 5, 1978]

Cookie Picetti:
A Slice of the Way Things Used to Be

"Y OU WANNA SEE ME?" Cookie said, as I walked in the door of the bar. His eyes were the black of the gibbet in Goldsmith's poem. This brought to mind the forty I owed him. "Where you was?" said Cookie.

These are words that fry men's souls. They are a red light in the traffic of existence. They are the words used by Mr. Lawrence (Cookie) Picetti when the Bank of Italy, of which he is president and sole proprietor, desires to retire a loan. At that moment, woe betide those who do not have the requisite cabbage in their pocket.

The Bank of Italy is located in his Blue Star Café at 708 Kearny Street. There are no branches. It has lent money to generations of Frisco drinkers—cops, lawyers, poultrymen, architects, sailors, mailmen. These are his customers. Borrowing money from Cookie has become such a part of their lives that there have been guys who give him their stash and then borrow it back as drink requires. "I haven't got my allowance yet," I heard a grown man say to Cookie the other day.

In the book of the city, Cookie rates at least a chapter. He is what San Francisco used to be about, when it was a great waterfront city instead of the picture-postcard corporation-headquarters town it has become. His bar is across from Portsmouth Square, sandwiched between the dreadful Chinatown Holiday Inn and the dirty bookstore on the corner of Clay. It is a wisp of the Old City, of steam beer on draft and almost-free lunches and concertina Sundays and vice sliced thin and rare.

In the thirties, when San Francisco was the open city of legend, Cookie was driving a cab and running errands for the McDonough brothers, the bail bond kings whose domain was the dark side of the city. Competition was fierce, and one of Cookie's duties was to wake up judges in the middle of the night and get them to sign orders setting bail so the McDonoughs could get the fee. Cookie once banged on a judge's door at 5 a.m. with a bail order for three Chinese gamblers arrested just an hour before. "But Cookie," pleaded the pajama-clad judge, "couldn't the Chinamen wait until eight o'clock to get out?" Cookie handed the judge a pen. "I'm sorry, Your Honor, but if I didn't get to you first some other bondsman would and they'd get the premium instead of the McDonoughs." "Oh, I see," the judge sighed, signing the paper.

Cookie gave me my baptism into the real world of beneficent San Francisco corruption. One day in the early sixties I walked into his bar with the sword of death visibly dangling over my head. "Whatsdamatter, kid?" he asked me from behind a cigar without benefit of moving his lips. I explained that I had only four hours to surrender myself at the Hall of Justice or an all-points bulletin was going out for my arrest on the charge of defrauding a merchant's lien.

This state of affairs had evolved innocently enough: I had heedlessly driven my new black Jaguar roadster over a highway dividing strip, ruining the automobile's stomach lining. I took it to a garage run by an Italian just off the boat, who apparently stuffed the engine with pasta and pronounced it cured. When I drove it away, after a dozen blocks the engine fell into the street. I had the machine towed to another car hospital and stopped payment on the Italian's check. When I got a letter requesting my appearance at the D. A.'s office, where the furious Italian had gone to complain, I righteously ripped it up. The D. A. routinely issued a warrant for my arrest, and the fraud detail had left a note on my door that if I didn't surrender within four hours the APB was going out on my person. My entreaties to the Italian mechanic to withdraw his unjust charge in return for my paying him his unearned money had only served to whet his appetite for revenge against this young punk with the fancy car.

"Whosdaguy tryna arrest ya?" Cookie asked. I told him the name of the arresting officer. "Him, HE ain't gonna arrest you, for chrissakes," Cookie said. "Why didn't ya tell him you was a friend of mine?" With that he dialed the phone, asked for the fraud detail, asked for the inspector—a chap who has long since retired—and proceeded to more or less explain the situation by swearing at the person on the other end of the phone for presuming to arrest one of his customers.

Cookie handed the phone to me. "Here—talk to him," he said. I ventured a frail hello. "Hey, I didn't know you were a friend of Cookie's," the inspector said. "Why didn't you tell me that? Look, here's what we'll do. I got the blue copy of the warrant here, and I'll go downstairs and lift the green copy out of the other file, and I'll rip them up. I can't get the white copy out of the other D. A.'s office, but they don't pay much attention to these type of things unless someone's screaming, and Cookie knows a guy who can talk Sicilian turkey to the Italian and you can get this patched up before he starts bugging the D. A. again, so you'll be okay. Okay?"

I gratefully hung up the phone. Cookie was chomping his cigar. He took it out of his mouth and said, "You should get that guy a few bottles of Old Crow. That's what he drinks." I said I'd get the cop a case. Cookie gave me a look like I had just eaten his pet goldfish. "Three bottles is what I said," he said. "You get him three. Any more and you'll spoil the guy."

The man talks tough, but he's as soft as an ice-cream cone in June. There was the time Big Chef died. Big Chef was a retired maritime cook, a huge black man with hands as big as baseball gloves. He would come in the bar and order a double shot of Jack Daniels, and the glass would disappear in his grip. He came in twice a day every day. Chef didn't have any relatives. When he died, Cookie went to the funeral parlor and discovered he was the only person there. He sat alone in the room with Chef, in the casket. After an hour he walked to the casket and leaned over and put his hand on Chef's dead black arm and said, "That's all right, Chef, I'm here."

The old Hall of Justice—the Dum De Dum Dum one where Chief Ironside had his office and where they filmed *Lineup,* perhaps the worst cop series TV ever made—was a few doors from Cookie's. Mr. Picetti consequently liquored the cops and bail bond brokers and courtroom hangers-on and the various Tarzan lawyers who swung from the scales of justice. Jake Ehrlich always took the entire jury to Cookie's for drinks after a verdict in one of his trials. He always had something to celebrate because he never pleaded guilty. Other San Francisco lawyers of legend—Jim MacInnis, Vince Hallinan (who drinks only soda water), John Brennan, Johnny Fahey—were no strangers to Cookie's.

Of the classic Frisco lawyers, Fahey is the least sung. He was an anti-establishment redneck conservative who always carried a thick notebook on his hip that made it look like he was packing a gun. When he was a San Mateo justice of the peace he pioneered night court because he was busy selling real estate during the day. Often he would say, in Cookie's, "If I had known I was going to live this long I'd have taken better care of my body." Fahey narrowly lost an election for judge when a newspaper suggested he had two families, one in the East Bay and one in the South Bay. This made for some complications when he died in 1978, at age seventy. Fahey ended up having three funeral services—one for each family and one at St. Ignatius for everybody else to go to. "He was the most buried guy in town," said Fahey's good friend, Superior Judge Ed Cragen.

Cookie's Blue Star Café has what you might call a healthy respect for things as they were. If ever God's helicopter were to lift an entire San Francisco bar and place it in the Smithsonian, this would be the joint. Cookie's is a Pantheon of traditional values. There is no swearing in front of women, no Portnoyish complaints, and talk is not encouraged about the usual neuroses or postpartum crises popular among the goony birds who dip their bills at Perry's. There is the customary swapping lies, but no swapping spit as in singles bars. The rhythm method is still tall in the saddle here. The graffiti in the john include "Bestiality is a sheep thrill" and "Look in the toilet bowl and you'll see a reporter." The pictures on the walls lock San Francisco's past in black dime-store frames: here a picture of the Santa Rosa lynchings of 1920, there a framed script page from *Dragnet* when Jack Webb said to Ben Alexander, "Let's go to Cookie's for a drink," everywhere pictures of cops in fifties haircuts. The place is bathed in an unworldly brown-yellow light the color of a tintype. There are no plastic plants; aside from the customers, the only thing living in the place is the yeast in the beer.

Cookie's is first and last a cop bar. "I knew every chief of police in San Francisco since 1920—the only one I never knew was that Gain. I'm glad he never came in here. I wouldn't want him," Cookie says. "The greatest of the chiefs was Charlie Dullea—he took no shit from nobody." The unpopularity of Charles Gain had in part to do with his Ayatollah-like decrees against cops drinking in bars. An inquiring reporter once asked Cookie about Gain's infamous anti-sipping Permanent Order No. 5, which encouraged cops to turn informer on other cops who lift a glass. This was in 1976. Cookie's answer remains a classic in the annals of San

Francisco ambiguity: "Cops drink in my bar? No, sir. No way. Never. Nope. Not in the thirty-four years I been here."

The proximity of so many cops and judges to his premises gave Cookie a good deal of what the indelicate would refer to as "juice," but he says those days are gone forever, along with a lot of other things that used to make sense in this town. "Nowadays, I couldn't get a dog out of the pound with a three-dollar bill," Cookie says.

The bar remains to many among the town's movers and shakers a temple to the way San Francisco Used-To-Be-When-It-Worked, but the great and small all leave the bar the same way. Cookie, who was seventy-six this month, and is his own sole employee, begins to weary of the day around eight-thirty in the evening. The end is always the same, as it is ritual. First Cookie puts on his Harry Lime black homburg. That is the signal for the beginning of the final-finals. Then he puts on his Sherlock Holmes overcoat, which knows no seasons. That is the signal for the final final-final. Then he puts out the garbage, and the customers follow. "I put the garbage out; then I put the live garbage out right after," says Cookie.

Lawrence Picetti and the former Margie Murray will be married fifty-five years this August. They have four children, fourteen grandchildren, and three great-grandchildren. On Cookie's wall is a life-size blowup of a picture of the young Cookie and Margie in their courting days. He looks like a Genovese Clark Gable and she is all Jeanette MacDonald. Margie was a dancer when Cookie met her. She was the type of woman Bing Crosby must have had in mind when he said, "San Francisco has a natural touch of class." Cookie frequently points to a drawing above the bar of a woman leading a donkey. The picture came with the place when Cookie took it over from the McDonough brothers back in 1942, through a transaction the exact nature of which has been lost in the mists of time. "See that woman? That's Margie. And the ass she's leading is me," Cookie says. "If it weren't for her, I'd've been a bum."

Cookie has not, himself, had a drink in sixteen years. He went on the water wagon one day in 1964, "just like that." He said he doesn't miss it; more to sell to the customers. When he drank, he drank plenty; his drink was V.O. and Coke. I once asked him why such a combination. "I didn't like the taste of whiskey," Cookie said.

Most pleasant mornings, you can find Cookie standing in his shirt sleeves and suspenders, hat on his head, shading a nose that sits on his face like a spare part, taking the sun in front of the chipped-blue-tile front of his empire, watching the River Kearny flow by. One gets a sense of a padrone surveying his domain, of God in his heaven. What with hacking cabs and the McDonough brothers and the bar, Cookie has been working at the same corner of Clay and Kearny, on the street where he was born, for almost half a century. That there is no statue of Cookie in Portsmouth Square across the street is proof that this town does not honor its great.

[*San Francisco Chronicle,* June 20, 1980]

The Franz Liszt of the Tenderloin

*L*AST WEEK, WHEN THE U.S. MAILS brought the record to the Tenderloin hotel, all the hands in the lobby grabbed for it because in the Tenderloin everything is up for grabs. But Ervin was waiting for it. He didn't have to raise his cane. It was hands off. The rat pack seemed to sense something was special.

Ervin Nyiregyhazi walked slowly across his hotel lobby and sat down in a frayed plump chair that was leaking stuffing like a Thanksgiving turkey. You had to look closely to notice the fine-tuning tremor in his hands as he opened the recording. It was sandwiched between slices of cardboard like the ones that come from the record clubs when you forget to send the record back, but inside was different. Stamped in gold were words that said it was a special promotion copy not to be sold for love or money. There across the cover in big letters was his name, Nyiregyhazi. "All Liszt Concert," it said. "A divine madness," a music critic said, on the cover, about the way Nyiregyhazi plays the piano. Ervin Nyiregyhazi, who is seventy-five years old and as anonymous as any poor soul in the Tenderloin, looked at his courtly Hungarian face staring out from the album cover and smiled the beatific smile of an angel who has been promoted from devil.

This is a town that strokes and curdles genius and sends it off to spoil elsewhere: Bret Harte to England, Ambrose Bierce to Mexico. Yet a genius came here unannounced in his seventh decade and in the cold comfort of our slums resurrected his art from the ashes of his troubled past. He had hardly touched a piano in thirty years when he recorded secretly here in January. When the music critic of the *New York Times*, Harold C. Schonberg, a man not given to hyperbole, heard Nyiregyhazi, he praised him as no less than the very reincarnation of Franz Liszt.

The *San Francisco Chronicle*'s Robert Commanday was less enthusiastic, however. He insisted Nyiregyhazi played a lot of wrong notes, and called him an instant cult figure. Well, to paraphrase Shaw, if all critics were laid end to end they would not reach a conclusion.

THE LISZT OF THE TENDERLOIN put down a double bourbon and expressed satisfaction. "Goudt," he said. "Viskey is goudt far you because it lessens inhibitions. All my life has been a struggle to git rid of damnable inhibitions." We had left the Tenderloin and crossed town to the oasis of Cookie Picetti's, on the Gaza Strip of Kearny between Chinatown and the Financial District. The pianist was dressed in a conservative blue suit and a tie that looked as though it had come from a Pacific Union Club garage sale. His large brown eyes had the vulnerability of a doe and, deep within them, the fire of an unbanked spirit.

If Nyiregyhazi is Liszt incarnate, the flip side of this complicated man is that of a straight Oscar Wilde. He's gone through nine wives ("some died," he said) and at seventy-five is scouting for a tenth. He said his life had to be totally free, sexually and creatively, so that his art could grow unrestrained in the hothouse. For this he has paid a high price, but he would be the first to say it was worth it. "In life Oscar Wilde was my Bible," he said, pronouncing it "Oscar Vilde." The bottom line of this artistic stubborness was that if Nyiregyhazi had to play the piano on anyone else's terms, he'd rather not play at all. It came damn close to that.

Nyiregyhazi was a Budapest child prodigy—of the cut of Mozart—who has been tormented by his genius all his life the way some saints have been taunted by Beelzebub. When he was eight he played for Queen Mary at Buckingham Palace. In 1920, when he was seventeen, he took Carnegie Hall by storm, then the Boston Symphony by acclaim. He was hailed as one of the all-time-great concert pianists in the history of the instrument. By 1925 he was sleeping on the subways. He got there by following Wilde's advice: "opposition to the rules of the world." That can be translated as bucking the system. The system he bucked was the professional concert managers. The young superstar pianist sued them for conduct unbecoming businessmen. He lost, and was blackballed. Every stage door slammed shut in his face. Like some musical Judge Crater, he simply disappeared from the concert world. "I ended up playing for the Mafia," said Nyiregyhazi, looking admiringly at the law-and-order rogue's gallery of cops' pictures lining Cookie's barroom wall.

He recalled one Prohibition night so vividly that I could see it like a movie: He was giving a private concert for upwardly mobile mafiosi on Central Park West. He was playing Brahms. Many of the mobsters had tears in their eyes; Nyiregyhazi's style of playing is to talk to the keys the way St. Francis talked to the birds, and the chirp in the lullaby reminded the mobsters of their mothers. This was how he made money to pay the lawyers to continue his losing battle against the concert managers who had turned on him when he asked for a second bowl of porridge. Afterward, outside a Little Italy restaurant in a light snow that bleached the night sky, as the mafiosi, their bellies full of culture, drove off in their black machines, he stood alone reading by streetlight of the wreck of his marriage in the early edition of the *Daily News*. The night before, his first wife, an older woman of means, had tried to emasculate him, literally, with a kitchen knife. But the newspaper told her version and she had sued for divorce, asking more money than the young pianist even could imagine existing. It was the first in a spectacular string of often embattled marriages that would make Nyiregyhazi the favorite classical pianist of the tabloid press. One of his wives was a stunt pilot. The papers loved that.

Nyiregyhazi took refuge in the home of Theodore Dreiser, the great novelist. The two were close friends. There were whiskey and Dreiser's theories of life's pockmarks. The two geniuses raged over a world being made safe for hypocrisy. The Hungarian began wearing a mob-type derby and proclaimed himself a "musical gangster." He would change a score as the spirit moved him, "if it gives me pleasure." His beloved Liszt would understand, although lesser musical purists would not; genius has its own path—it follows another composer's soul, not just his notes. This is a musical battle that Nyiregyhazi would have with conservative critics all his career, and one that is far from over. The pianist's other great friend and drinking buddy in those days was Bela Lugosi, the movie actor who often played in horror films. Through Lugosi he developed friendships with professional ghouls and vampires, whose company he preferred to that of music critics.

Nyiregyhazi gave up concert piano more than three decades ago, spurning "the grubby world of musical commerce." He plunged into an orgy of composing that resulted in more than seven hundred works. Most of these have been heard by no one but himself and his changing guard of wives as Nyiregyhazi became a one-man assault on the institution of marriage. Some of his compositions are whimsical—there is a numbered series of seven titled *Victory for Whiskey*. Others are political. Standing on the balcony of a fleabag El Paso hotel on the morning of November 22, 1963, he says now, Nyiregyhazi said he had a premonition that Kennedy would die that day. He immediately began composing a work on Kennedy's death and the evil he saw in Texas. Later, after he read the Warren Commission report, he wrote a second composition. It was titled "The Southern Conspiracy to Throttle Kennedy."

The pianist's last marriage, in 1972, was true love. The love of that woman brought him back to the piano. Her name was Elsie Swan. She was ten years older than he. She was a former lover. She was alone and bedridden and about to be institutionalized. He married her to take care of her. "I loved Elsie even more than I love Liszt," he said.

In 1973, to scrounge money for Elsie's medicine, Ervin Nyiregyhazi gave a concert at Old First Presbyterian Church in San Francisco. He had not been near a piano in years. He disdained practicing. He sat down and played Liszt the way no one has ever heard. People there could barely describe the sound coming from the Baldwin. It seemed less of man's making and more of the swell and roar of the ocean, and of dominions of angels ringing bells. A music buff who had chanced on the concert by the fellow with the strange name recorded it on a tape cassette. It was sent to the International Piano Archives in New York, where he created a bigger sensation than the day Jimmy Carter said he saw a flying saucer. The great nineteeth-century romantic school of piano playing, thought to be lost to time, was alive and well in San Francisco.

A Ford Foundation grant was arranged for Nyiregyhazi to record under studio conditions. He had never made a record before. The first record, released last year, turned even most sourpuss critics' heads 360 degrees. The second record was the one that arrived at Nyiregyhazi's Tenderloin hotel last week. Elsie died before she heard either of them.

Few people might have known Nyiregyhazi was in San Francisco had not Michael Walsh, enterprising music critic of the *Examiner,* written about the pianist at the beginning of the year. With a second wow

Nyiregyhazi recording about to be released, the Eastern music critics are beginning to look to the Tenderloin as to Mecca. So now we know who's here. Ervin Nyiregyhazi, the world's longest musical dropout, had dropped back in, in San Francisco. The town has an authentic genius in residence. The way things are going around here, it could use one.

I asked Nyiregyhazi a nonmusical question. What was the secret of having nine wives? He thought a moment.

"Marry women who own their own houses," said the genius.

[*San Francisco Chronicle,* August 10, 1978]

A Real Frisco Guy

"If you want to drink, you should do it. If you care more about drinking than you do for your work or your health, then by all means you should drink. But you never should make any apologies for your excesses, and no trips to the sanitariums. Just drink, and die, and leave the rest to the angels. Hah!"

—Sadakichi Hartmann

F RANKIE THE BOOK double-parked his truck on Union Street to run into the store to see if the proprietor wished anything at the track. A guy with shoulders like a wire coat hanger who had just come off a two-week screamer was standing stoop-shouldered in front. "Bad news," the guy said. "Morty died last night."

The Book took this like a howitzer in the head. He left his truck for the cops to tow away and fell across the street to Perry's, where he broke his beer-only promise to his sainted mother. He downed three straight shots, but reality kept flipping like a bum picture tube. It was a while later before the Book could put exactly what he felt into the short form of the English language. "When I heard Morty died, I felt like I was evicted from my heart," he said.

Morty Miller was the storekeeper most loved by what you might call the sporting set in town. Some of these people actually play sports. Some of them write about them. Most of them bet them. All of them drink. They drank at Morty's; more properly, they drank *with* Morty. The sporting crowd followed him from store to store—from the Templebar downtown, to the Stadium Club in the high arctic of Candlestick Park, to his last place on Union Street, the hetero's Castro Street, where Frankie the Book left his truck in the middle of the street when he heard the news. This was news that would make a printer jump out of the composing room window rather than set it in type.

Morty Miller was a man immortal in convivial annals; a guy as rare as an 1865 cognac; a guy who loved equally opera and horses; a first-nighter at both seasons who loved sweets the way dogs love petting; who would go to a tablecloth French restaurant and order eight desserts for dinner, a chocolate mousse for salad, and an eclair for an entree; a night person who loved crazy hats and put on ceremonial faces out of Modigliani and made everyone laugh; a great comic actor whose proscenium was his backbar; a Jewish saint who was over-generous and pretended he was stingy; who did everything his way and laughed like a barking seal in the face of death; a high roller who loved travel and good cigars and whose lady love painted nails at I. Magnin. This was a real Frisco guy.

Never in the star-studded history of degeneracy in this town have so many of the heavy-duties among the movers and shakers and players of the night people been so thrown for a loss as when Morty Miller went unexpectedly through the narrow door. "Morty's thrown the ace-deuce," Gene Basket said over the horn the morning he heard. Basket has by conservative medical estimate launched more livers on the course downstream than any other Frisco saloonkeeper. He has a smile as cheery as new ice cubes and talks the way a basset hound looks. Basket and several of Morty's good-time buddies were decorating the mahogany at the La Barca Room on Lombard last week, drinking in honor of their fallen friend. This was real mourning. The week before, after Morty died, there was a wake at his Union Street place. The store was jammed with electronic journalists and maybe half a million matchbook collectors who had barely been in Morty's to use the toilet when he was alive. Some among the heavy-duties took exception to this.

The La Barca, where Morty's people had tumbled downhill, has cool Mexican tiles and a big ugly goldfish that looks like J. Edgar Hoover. Its real attraction is room. The sporting set needs room to drink. Most of them started drinking together at the Buena Vista decades ago, but split the B.V. when it got too crowded. They are not big on the Union Street school of drinking, which includes body shopping and spit swapping; most of them have not successfully managed to rid themselves of the tree blight known as modesty. They drank on Union only because of Morty, and Morty ran their kind of place, if not excessively so. He once fired a cocktail waitress for the unwearing of underwear.

By his friends is a man known, said Yeats. Morty's friends included the sports poli from Chub Feeney to Bob Lurie to Franklin Mieuli to Bill Rigney, from Ron Fimrite to Ken Macker, and diverse powers that be from union honcho George Evankovich to Sheriff Mike Hennessey to state appeals court justice Bill Newsom to former secretary of state Dean Rusk. Gathered at the La Barca for the continuing wake were books like in your branch library. Morty liked to spread his action and shopped for points the way housewives shop for values in Crisco. Among the bibuli in mourning were the Four Horsemen who were Miller's running companions—mind this is not running as in jogging—Gene Basket and Frank Carrillo the jeweler and Frank Cadera the bartender and Jimmy Bernard, the little matador who owns the La Barca. There were longtime customers and friends such as Marty Hoag, the Cable Car clothing salesman, and Steve Stoll and Jimmy Igoe and the amazing Glenn Dorenbush, the flag admiral of serious saloons, who by his fond memory has had a drink with Morty Miller most every day for the past nineteen years.

All of these guys are refugees from an embalming parlor. Dorenbush's death has been predicted annually for at least the last ten years. The night Morty died he was out with Dorenbush to 3 a.m., lecturing his friend about taking better care of himself. He was always worrying about someone else. When Morty died he was busily planning with fellow restaurateurs Perry Butler and Ed Moose the party for Dorenbush's fiftieth birthday, which is today. Dorenbush is furious that Morty didn't live to see him beat the odds. Morty only made it to half past forty-nine. None among these experts in demolishing the human framework could seem to believe that Morty had thrown the shoe first. This was so sober-making it required drinks. By the other night the rolling wake was well into its second week. It was a wake out of Ripley. Frank Cadera looked around at the cast of characters at the bar. "This is taking on attributes of an excuse," he said.

One of the things about real Frisco guys—the late Howard Gossage comes to mind—is that they are generous to a fault, always spending energy doing something for somebody else, always grabbing the check. Morty Miller didn't like to buy people drinks when he was behind the plank—that wasn't his way of running a store—but he was forever buying his customers drinks and meals at other guys' stores. It went from his till to his pocket to other tills. Morty fancied himself an art collector, and if a friend admired a painting or something, he took it off the wall and gave it to him, as in the shirt off your back. People would give him presents and he'd give them away to other people. This generous guy tried to pretend he was cheap. He'd give you a rose and argue that it was a thorn. He loved to haggle the way he learned growing up in New York. "No tip on the tax," he'd say, paying a dinner tab.

Morty Miller was a study in rumples. He had fuzzy, rumply hair and a face like a folded-up canvas fire hose. He seemed to have no hips; his pants hung down and bunched up his rear end while his shirt bunched out in front over his stomach. "I'm a slave to fashion," he would say. He had the loveable shaggy look of an A. A. Milne drawing. There was a cigar forever sticking out of his mouth and his backfield was always in motion. He came from a generation that had worked its ass off—he'd paid his own way since he was ten—and he wasn't about to slow down even though he had a bad ticker, which eventually went out on him.

He worried about almost everything—"One of Morty's projects in life was to aggravate himself," said Bob Lurie, his friend and former employer at the Stadium Club. If he wasn't worrying about his business, or his friends Basket and Dorenbush dying, Morty was worrying about some other guy's saloon: "Some of the guys in this business use their stomachs for cash registers," he said more than once, shaking his head. But he always worried out loud and always played it for the laughs, the way he played everything. During the starkers streaking craze, he once streaked the Templebar. He wore a funny hat. "Morty was the clown of all clowns—that's really what he loved to do," said Jimmy Bernard, admiringly. "Morty's love song to me was 'Send in the Clowns,'" said his girlfriend, Claudia.

Morty loved the track. He waltzed around it like an ice skater cutting figure eights. He knew everybody—the waiters and the bartenders and the pari-mutuel men. At the track he always carried a portable radio held up to his ear, like when people listen to the baseball game, only he was listening to the opera. One day a guy came up to Morty at the Turf Club and tapped him on the shoulder. "What's the score?" the guy asked. "*Madame Butterfly*," Morty said.

Morty couldn't read a racing form. He bet by the numbers. He was often lucky enough to get even. Jim Igoe the lawyer tells of sitting with Morty at Golden Gate Fields. Morty was puffing his cigar and listening to opera and at peace with the world. He borrowed Igoe's glasses to look at the girls in the crowd. Morty asked Igoe what he thought about the next race. The lawyer peered at his form. "I think it's between the four and the six," he said. Igoe covered himself on both the four and the six horse. He asked Morty which one he had bet. "I put a twenty on the five," Morty said.

"But I told you it was between the four and the six," Igoe said.

"I thought you were talking code. I thought you didn't want to let the other guys know it was the five," Morty said.

The five horse went wire to wire and paid $13.20. Morty gave Igoe a funny look. "Don't you ever tell me it's between the four and the eleven," he said.

Morty wasn't lucky in everything. A deal he had made to sell his store went sideways after he died. The word among his friends was that the price dropped fifty grand. Claudia, his girlfriend, is keeping the place open while she decides what to do. It's hard to see how there can be a Morty's without a Morty.

In the golden days of San Francisco, when the bay came up to Montgomery and Pisco Punch was the preferred drink, it was said of one who had truly been on the town and had savored its many delights that he was "seeing the elephant." It can truthfully be said of Morty Miller that he saw the elephant, but that is a phrase of another century, and he was a child of his own. It was left for his book to say it right: "Anybody who never knew Morty Miller," said Frankie the Book, "that's a horse on them."

[*San Francisco Chronicle,* August 23, 1980]

Shooting Craps in Style

*M*ONTY THE DUCK WAS THERE IN SPATS, and Hydro Willy the Cucumber wore his best hat. Cactus Jack, who drove all the way from Moss Beach, buttoned up his cardigan when he saw the cut of the joint. The word had gone out in the heat of a dead Memorial Day Sunday: Jimmy the Glove was floating a game—a real crap game.

Words such as those have not been heard in San Francisco since the recent ice age of Vice Squad Captain Gerald Joseph Shaughnessy, when the city elders made bold to nail nuns to the cross of bingo. The Tenderloin voodoo drums put out the word all Sunday afternoon: only class players. Tuxes. Ties, too. Jimmy the Glove was always known for class.

You couldn't find the door right away. It was down an alley full of night sounds. The bell nested in a bed of splinters. The mailbox opened from inside. An eyeball stared out unblinking.

"Hello. Helll-ow."

The approved code was given.

"All right. Allll righhht." The eyeball beat the mailbox shut by a wink.

We were inside an auto body repair shop. The doorman wore a three-piece white linen suit and a four-in-hand. He skirted roped-off Cadillacs with their innards showing and led the way up a rough wooden ramp to a polished oak door. Inside was the Rue de la Pay. In a loft out of a Soho dream there were night people in a splendor recently unknown in these parts. The women had perfect Sea and Ski cleavages and cigarettes in holders and dresses as long as Oakland. The guys had cuff links that a hock would swap for Aladdin's lamp. Cigarette smoke covered everything like gauze over a burn victim. In the middle of the mob, at command central at the crap table, stood Jimmy the Glove, needles of concentration flashing in his eyes. "Action on every roll, folks, there's action on every roll. If you want my advice don't play the propositions. They're losers, just like in elections. Put your money on the line and play the odds against the house. You'll never get better odds than this anywhere. Nevada is a stacked deck."

Jimmy the Glove is in his fifties the way Jack Benny was in his thirties. He learned the game the hard way at Pearl Harbor, after the raid, when the boys were locked all night in blacked-out barracks behind tar-papered windows and the commandant let Jimmy convert the pool tables to gaming tables for the troops. Jimmy could set up a crap game anywhere, even on the battlefield, people said with genuine admiration. In the forties and fifties, Jimmy ran the most theatrical floating crap game in the local arena. When *Guys and Dolls* came out as a movie, Jimmy's customers laughed at Marlon Brando. Jimmy's game was known as "Fading the Main." No big-deal-schlemiel tables—Jimmy just lay down a carpet of green, got down on his knees like Al Jolson, and covered everybody's action. Gimmie five. Gimmie ten. Gimmie a piece of that come bet. In the Tenderloin, having a piece of Jimmy was like having a piece of the rock.

Jimmy's act has been dark for years. He brought it out again Memorial Day weekend to benefit the *Deep City Press,* the cab drivers' magazine. Even though the game was for charity, Jimmy preferred the maximum security precautions that were in effect Sunday night. He also asked that the players dress, like himself, in tails, in class to which they were unaccustomed. Jimmy kept track of the frantic action on the table with the cool of an air traffic controller. "Rake in the losers first—then pay the winners," he admonished the green cashiers who stood with him at the shallow pit. "Two bad boys from Illinois," Jimmy shook his head when a blonde threw two aces on her first roll. "All good hands start with craps. Shoot again."

Jimmy guided the amateurs through the night and put reins to the more experienced types who had materialized from the sewers upon hearing of Jimmy's action. He gave an evil eye to a player with a pinky ring bigger than his knuckle. "This is for a good cause," he said. Monty the Duck and Hydro Willy the Cucumber, who got that name because he used to grow them hydroponically, moved to post position on either side of the man with the ring to make certain Jimmy's wishes were heeded. Jimmy with his dice stick carries the weight of a bishop with his miter. The diamond crapped out. Jimmy raked in his money. He picked up the dice and turned them, then showed them to this person. "See, this is your point. You just threw them upside down."

It was a beautiful thing to see. There was a crowd but no shoving, drinking but no drunks, swearing but no foulness. Most of the players were young, and many had never played before, and Jimmy showed them the game the way they play it in the Hall of Fame. This is supposed to be something illegal. It was a time warp out of the San Francisco when Shanty Malone was king of the publicans and the Fly Trap had great food and "high-rise" meant elevator and all over town the clack of dice in cigar store back rooms was music in everyone's ears. That San Francisco is either gone or against the law, and so is Jimmy the Glove, and his game Sunday night had ritual aspects of Christians sneaking into the catacombs to celebrate Mass.

The game ended at 3 a.m. When the players cashed in their chips, it turned out the bank had lost thirty bucks. The bank belonged to the cabbie magazine for which the game had been held. Jimmy dug in his pocket and pulled out half a yard and threw it in the bank. That put the charity ahead twenty.

"Go home winners," said Jimmy the Glove.

[*San Francisco Chronicle,* May 31, 1978]

The Cops Who Laughed and Loved

Officer Jimmy Stevens was a cooing cop, a flatfoot overflowing with affection for the whole big beautiful wacko world he lived in. He loved his family. He loved his wives. He loved all women. He loved to have a gargle. The only thing he hated was to arrest people. If he had to arrest a bum, he'd tell the booking sergeant, "Hey, Sarge, this is a real good guy." He called everyone he ever met a real good guy. And he meant it. When Jimmy Stevens traveled the Mission District, he rode on a gold elephant. He had a wave and a smile for everybody he saw. He was the original laughing policeman. Some of the stories he used to tell on himself were pretty funny.

Jimmy used to watch *Mannix* every day before he went to work. The private detective was his idol: He always won and he got to drink on the job and the girls all fell for him. Jimmy admired the way Joe Mannix knocked guys out on the telly, with real style. One day two street kids were fighting on the sidewalk and Jimmy had to break up the beef. He remembered how Mannix had banged two guys' heads together and knocked them both out. He bent down and grabbed each kid by the hair and banged their heads together, only he forgot to take his head out of the middle. He woke up on the sidewalk with the kids kneeling beside him saying, "Hey, officer, you all right?" *West Side Story* would have been better with scenes like that.

Jimmy Stevens seemed to spend a good deal of time in the supine position. He once responded to a call in the Mission about a husband beating up his wife. The husband was a big hulk who was sitting at the kitchen table sipping a beer when Jimmy came in. The wife was in a bathrobe. She had a shiner as big as a full moon. Jimmy told the husband that he had to take him to the station. The husband said no way in hell, get out of my house. Jimmy was getting ready to do a Mannix number on him when the wife came up behind him and said, "Leave my man alone" and crowned him with a cast-iron frying pan. Jimmy woke up on the floor as the cops from the backup unit were hauling off the husband. "Hey, not him, HER!" he yelled at the cops.

A hundred or so cops were delighting in retelling tales of Jimmy Stevens at a dinner Friday night at the Police Athletic Club building inside the Hunters Point shipyard. The dinner was sponsored by the Mission District Publicans in memory of two dead cops—Stevens and his late partner, Charlie Anderson. Anderson and Stevens were two look-alikes who acted alike. They were always jacking one another up and telling stories on themselves and had people all over the Mission laughing with them.

Jimmy's tale: Charlie was afraid of dogs, and Jimmy loved to tell the story of the time Charlie made him ring the doorbell because a dog was barking inside. Jimmy told Charlie not to worry because the dog didn't sound big. "Oh no, you get in front; he might be a big dog with laryngitis," Charlie said.

Charlie's tale: One morning Jimmy dropped his then-wife off at her waitress job and said he had to go to the station to get into his uniform but would be back to have breakfast with her. He stopped by his girlfriend's on the way back to the coffee shop where his wife worked. The wife noticed lipstick on his collar and cooked him up a big plate of ham and eggs and dumped it over his head. "Here's your breakfast, dear," she said.

Friday night's gathering of the Mission clan was unusual in that both cops have been dead for some time—Anderson died last year and Jimmy went through the narrow door back in the seventies—but they were such good guys that a group of cops and bar owners decided to hold an annual golf tournament and dinner in their honor. They wanted to have the fun of retelling the stories about them. The Czar of the Police Athletic Club, Mark Hurley, pulled out all the stops for Friday night's dinner. A guy from the coroner's office did the cooking, and the off-duty boys in blue raved and ribbed about the food. One wise-guy cop kept yelling at the coroner-cook that the chicken livers in the sauce didn't taste like chicken.

"Jimmy Stevens would come into the bar in uniform and put down a twenty and buy everyone a drink. If you did something wrong, as long as you didn't do it in front of him, he didn't see nothing," said bartender Richie Mori, a veteran of the Mission District bar wars, raising a toast to the deceased. "Jimmy was what he said about everybody else—a real good guy," said Mori. "I never heard of Jimmy Stevens arresting anybody—never," said bar owner Paddy Nolan, to applause. This was some toast to an audience of cops.

In the world of friendly, fun-loving cops like Jimmy Stevens and Charlie Anderson, there were only good guys. Instead of arresting kids, they'd kick them in the butt and send them home and tell them they'd better not see them doing that again. They'd loan a bum ten bucks rather than bust him for vagrancy. They took chances on helping people, knowing they'd get stung now and then. As Ben Hecht once said of a special kind of man, they gladly played Galahad even though they knew the fight was fixed. There are so many stories like these about cops in this town. Unfortunately, you usually have to wait until they're dead before it's safe to put the fun stories about them in the newspaper, what with the bluenoses among the brass.

[*San Francisco Chronicle*, December 11, 1984]

When Funerals Were Fun

*J*ACK LOCKHART WAS THAT DEVILISHLY HANDSOME undertaker from Frisco with the baby blue wan lake eyes and the curly blond hair. Back in New York he'd be wearing his double-breasted herringbone as proud as a robin's breast while he sat with a couple of admiring cuties at the Stork Club. The year was 1948, and the kid from the Golden Gate could show Gotham a thing or three about having a good time. San Franciscans were big spenders in those days, and among the biggest and the best with a buck were the jolly morticians on Valencia Street's stiff row who waved you good-bye in style befitting the maharajah of Jaipur.

San Francisco not only knew how to live better back then, it knew how to die better. A good wake could last a week and, if it was good enough, the undertaker might carry on the party himself. Jack Lockhart was double the fun of the swinging, singing undertakers of the glorious Frisco forties and fifties. In addition to owning a funeral parlor, he owned a bar. Both were on Valencia Street, just a few blocks apart. The bar was on the corner of 14th and the other place was between 18th and 19th. Lockhart didn't see much difference between the two businesses. "In both places I'm taking care of stiffs," he said. He was proud of being the only "bartician-mortician" in captivity. A far as is known he was the first such animal to saloon in the Stork Club. The match girl asked for his autograph.

The other day I took a hike with Jack Lockhart down memory lane. We strolled along stiff row—which is what they called Valencia Street in the good old days when dying was in flower. In the first dozen blocks of Valencia and immediate environs there were more than a dozen funeral parlors. These catered to the Mission. Divisadero had a string of mortuaries that got the Fillmore trade. Post Street got the swells.

Even though people still seem to do it, dying is no longer a growth industry. All over town there are deceased mortuaries that have been recycled into the strangest things. At 16th and Guerrero there's a site that is now an AA bar. Most of the Mission's abandoned mortuaries have been turned into churches or restaurants. Some still have the Digger O'Dell look; others, like the Noe Valley Bar and Grill on 24th Street, have been so tricked up you'd never recognize the deceased. We stopped at a churchlike building painted a bilious electric blue; Valencia, between 15th and 16th. "That was J. C. O'Connor's place. He died," said Lockhart. "I think it was some sort of a yoga church for a while. Now it looks like nobody's in there. Just ghosts." The New College of California, between 18th and 19th, was once the splendid Wieboldt's mortuary. Across the street is a Spanish white stucco fortress with a Baby Ruth–brown tile roof. There, for fourteen years, Lockhart potted the Mission's finest with his fun-loving partner, Mike Driscoll. Now it's an antique store. "These used to be my slumber rooms," Lockhart said when we walked inside. "Oh," said the sales lady. All in all, the mortality rate in the funeral business defies the actuarial tables. "People are living. Mortuaries are dying," said the former bartician-mortician, philosophically.

"Jazus, there must be nobody dying in this town now. It must be the greatest town in the world. Like Shangri-La," said Paddy Nolan, in wonder at the litany of dead funeral parlors Lockhart had said on his fingers, like the Rosary. Nolan, behind the plank, was pouring a bourbon and ginger for Lockhart, who thirsted from the walk down stiff row. When Lockhart sold his bar on 14th Street, he gave his stuffed dog who had passed away on VE Day—but was petted by Lockhart's customers for decades thereafter—to Nolan, who interred the beast in the basement of his 18th Street bar. We were drinking on hallowed ground. Speaking of the dead put a smile as big as the first moon of the month on Lockhart's round face. "I met my wife over a corpse," Lockhart said. "She was an embalmer. She had a job at another place, but she'd come over after work and moonlight on my stiffs."

Back in the forties, when Lockhart got into the business, there were more than forty burial stores in town. Morticians used to chase corpses the way lawyers chase ambulances. Lockhart would tip someone in the coroner's office to push business his way. "The guy would get 10 percent of the case," Lockhart said. "He was supposed to recommend three funeral parlors to pick from. So he'd say, 'Now there's this one on Fillmore Street and this Chinese one if you want—and then there's Driscoll and Lockhart down the street, they're pretty good.'"

One time Lockhart cared for a horse player who had left instructions that he wanted to be buried in the plot in the cemetery that was closest to Tanforan. He also left a C-note in an envelope to buy the pallbearers drinks at Coattail Molloy's in Colma after they planted him near the horses. "Now, there was a guy who really knew how to die," said Lockhart.

The last gasp of daring mortuarial competition—"Godeau's folly"—was in the fifties. "Old man Godeau"—of the venerable and still extant undertaking establishment of that name—"had this idea to build a huge van that would carry the casket, the family, the pallbearers, the whole shebang. He designed it himself and had a prototype built back East. He thought it would revolutionize the industry. Well, the thing was shipped out here and its maiden voyage was to Holy Cross. It was like christening an ocean liner. The family got in with the casket and the pallbearers got in and everybody fit. Then they got to Holy Cross and they couldn't get in the gate. The damn thing was too wide. Everybody had to abandon ship. It was the talk of the town."

It isn't just the fun funeral parlors of Lockhart's Frisco that have gone the way of all flesh. "There used to be over thirty breweries here, more beers than Carter's got pills. But they were all run out of town. And bakeries—you need to have two or three in every neighborhood. But no more. And movie theaters—you used to be able to walk up Mission Street and see the best movies without going downtown. The Wigwam, the El Capitan, the Valencia, the Rialto, the Lyceum…all gone. I don't know what the ordinary Joe can do here nowadays. There's no more choices. There used to be four or five plunges and there were the rides at Playland and Fleishhacker Pool and steam trains and ice skating and roller skating and it wouldn't bust your pocket to do any of it. Now—the other day at Woolworth's it was $1.10 for a hot dog at the stand-up counter. No sit-down, no nothing."

Ah, what golden years, and how the locust has eaten them.

[*San Francisco Chronicle,* April 27, 1979]

Vespers for USF

*T*HE UNIVERSITY OF SAN FRANCISCO, the largest Catholic market-place of higher learning west of Chicago, is a cliff-dwelling institution squatting Irish-Aztec fashion high in the northwestern contour of San Francisco on a steep and once grassy knoll, a geographical stub some-where in between a serious slope and a proper hill, the former domin-ion of a vast Masonic cemetery, the Jesuits now occupying the crest; the lowlands on the east are the leaseholds of poor to lower-middle-class blacks, and, on the west, middle-to upper-middle-class whites of Rus-sian and Greek Orthodox and Dutch Protestant stock; to the north is the Catholic-Gothic Lone Mountain, a coeducational college for ladies located on another sharp rise which was also formerly a graveyard; to the south is the man-made Panhandle of Golden Gate Park, formerly a sand dune, which served as a verdant Gaza Strip during the sixties, separating the Jesuits from the love-crazed hippies of the adjacent Haight-Ashbury.

The most distinguished architectural artifact on the fifties campus was the last resting place of a family of beer czars named Wieland; their titanic monument, its enclosures guarded by gargoyles, was said to resemble in many details Grant's Tomb on the Hudson. But that was torn down, although reluctantly, by the Jesuits, to provide sorely needed separate toilet facilities for the nuns who began attending night theol-ogy courses at the university. Only a headless sundial remained of the former glory. However, students were kept mindful of the consecrated, if Masonic, ground on which they treaded by occasionally tripping over tombstones.

The campus was otherwise no beauty spot.

Dominating everything was a place of worship: St. Ignatius, a twin-spired, Gothic-cathedral-sized church, a poor man's St. Peter's with both a rotunda and a campanile tacked on the rear. From the church the rest of the campus went downhill physically and architecturally. A series of rocky outcroppings in the center of the vertical city block was known euphemistically as Loyola Pass, said to be the windswept domain of ghosts of Jesuits past and of Oscar Wilde, so beware. The rocks were topped with wooden and stucco shacks of *Grapes of Wrath* vintage. On the grounds were several new edifices of Pentagon-modern architecture painted in bilge pastels; several old buildings of parish hall styling colored the stubborn gray of concrete; miscellaneous frame structures, among them a ramshackled four-story firetrap which slept forty Jesuits at their peril and was plastered with "no smoking" signs; and dozens of corrugated-metal-roof army huts in sagging use as classrooms, left over from the Second World War, when the campus for almost all educational intents and purposes became a military training post. The remainder of the grounds were used as a parking lot, save a downtrodden field where gung-ho Catholic ROTC cadets marched daily; there was also a stark patch of grass that was ornamental and meant to be kept off. The asphalt was grease-stained; the buildings were fog-stained; the tin roofs of the huts were rose-stained. The overall appearance was of a strip-mining site, or a dust bowl army base under constant aerial bombardment by hordes of defecating pigeons; such swarms in fact overflew the campus on a saturation schedule. Once, writing bright copy for the school yearbook, I described the place as "a strange composite of the ludicrous and the sublime"; I was at least half-right.

[HOT TYPE AND COLD FEET]

What began as St. Ignatius College in the time of the vigilantes, due to Jesuit cunning in the thirties, became known by the more grandiose name of the University of San Francisco. This nomenclature has been accepted by the city with remarkably solid complacency, the school having produced several great basketball teams and graduated thousands of civil servants, lawyers, cops, and judges into the city bureaucracy. That, plus its close identification with the army, plus the Jesuits' military and patriotic posture, have made the university to the law-and-order establishment in San Francisco what Notre Dame is to football in the Midwest. In keeping with Irish Catholic and Jesuit tradition, the student body was still, in the early sixties, men only; the one crack in that dike was the admission of nursing students, tied by their bedpans to the St. Mary's hospital a block away, who came to classes wearing baggy white Supp-hose and green-striped training uniforms that vaguely resembled sanitary-napkin wrappers.

I had heard for years the Jesuits' fabled reputation as the best teachers and real intellects, the rich cream in the church's Irish coffee—my absinthine experiences with the high school Brothers of Mary having left me with a yearning for a sweet Catholic taste in my mouth. I climbed to the windswept, rock-bound campus a considerable time before classes were to begin, walked into the office of the campus newspaper, the *Foghorn,* signed on for the first issue, and argued with the news editor that he should use the preferable Vogue Bold for front-page headlines instead of that awful and twerpy Cario Condensed.

While coasting along on this new journalistic supermobile, I ran into a Jesuit. That first Jesuit whetted my appetite for more.

He was the head of the Theology Department. I met him over a martini. He was personable, considerate, amusing, suave, and he bought the drinks, which turned out to be a good thing as he drank like a Jesuit fish. He exuded intelligence and confidence the way lesser men impart bravado, but he was the real thing; there were no tin nickels, or tin angels, in his makeup. An Old Testament scholar, he was handsome as the devil, a comparison I hesitated to make. He didn't even look like a Jesuit, let alone just a priest; he looked like a Hollywood leading man playing a Jesuit. As it turned out there was some basis for that analogy, as he was the Reverend Willis Egan, the brother of Richard Egan, the movie star. I had never seen a Richard Egan movie, but after that I saw every one of Father Egan's brother's pictures, even *The View from Pompey's Head.*

Father Egan told me to call him Willis, a disarmingly intimate request that, I was to discover later, the more spidery Jesuits employed to put their human fly victims at a loss, but something I never held against him.

The editor of the *Foghorn* in that year of 1956 was a tall and friendly Protestant fellow of military bearing and an outstanding Roman nose shaped like the prototype of the French Concorde. His name was John Doty, his full name being John Alden Doty, which is about as Protestant as such matters can get, and for that or other reasons he was contemplating, in his senior year in college, converting to the Roman Catholic faith; Willis Egan, the theology dean who looked like Johnny Weissmuller hopped up on Vitamin E, was his instructor, mentor, and gentle prodder. Doty's instructions in the ancient faith usually took place over drinks, so to get me out of other people's hair, or because he was amused by the crazy red-hot freshman who stood around slobbering over the type charts, or because he was just a nice guy, he asked me to join them for a little rum and romanism.

I had this sudden unsinkable feeling that my ship had come in. Here I was, a freshman on his first day in a real Catholic college, drinking martinis with the chairman of the Theology Department.

We discussed the proper theology of the necessary distinction between *Animus* and *Anima*, between Eros and Agape, the struggle of opposites for existence, St. Augustine on the restless and inner famine of the soul (a concept wholly appropriated by the existentialist philosophers under the guttural "angst"), the concept of nature of the Jesuit poet-seer Gerald Manley Hopkins as being "million fuelled" of endless contradictions and energy and the rhythm of opposites, the question of who would be Job's comforter, the theories of Baron Von Hugel on the positive effects of grace that can turn homeliness into heroism, of Dr. Rougemont on the degeneration of romantic love into Gnosticism and the consequent collapse of the backbone of European civilization, of the Christian mysticism of Pete Cyprien de la Nativité, of man's fate of loving in the dark, of the pull on us all of the hopeless love of sun and moon.

We were driving back when Doty delivered me a breath of warning. "You shouldn't think," he said, making a right turn onto the campus at the nearest tombstone, "that Father Egan is your typical Jesuit."

[YOU PRAY FOR A 'C,' MISTER]

The next morning I went to my first theology class. Theology was a required course at USF; two units every semester for four years, passing grades necessary for graduation. The priest was a former army chaplain, a walking ashtray with a pipe in his mouth and a curious purple tattoo

the greatest trapdoor constructor of all times, bugging and rigging hundreds of the great manor houses of England to provide hiding places for Jesuit spies in the time of Queen Elizabeth. Jesuits were the first Henry Kissingers, thousands of them in green-black robes scurrying all over Europe, attempting to control royal courts via the intricate mechanism of the confessional box, putting a *dauphin* in their back pocket here, pushing a false *tsarevich* for the throne there. Sex was the only exception to the general principle of plasticity so characteristic of the Jesuit approach to moral and religious absolutes, their hard line on carnality leading them to extreme doings such as removing the stairs to Madame de Pompadour's apartment so as to render more difficult the access of Louis XV to her bedchamber. The entire order was almost captured rosary beads and all by Czar Alexander I, but they remained the super-loyal Blue Meanies of the pope, doing his bidding no matter what, even to the extent of rushing to recall in 1945, in the manner of General Motors recalling defective Chevrolets, the Jesuit ethics textbooks then in use in Catholic colleges, to revise the section on "just warfare" so as to make morally permissible the recent use of the atomic bomb by the United States at Hiroshima.

Every USF noon, the cracked bell tolled and everyone had to stop dead in their tracks, like a freeze-frame in a movie, and be still while a whiskey-voiced Jesuit boomed out the Angelus over a loudspeaker. Students were encouraged to tie scapulars around their necks (scapulars are Catholic talismans, little pieces of brown ribbon or felt with holy pictures dangling from the center, resembling a fig leaf for a midget). The bookstore hustled St. Christopher medals, and half the automobiles parked on the campus carried extra insurance in the form of tiny white plastic statues of the Blessed Virgin glued atop the dashboard.

USF has since changed, for the better, but I don't think that's necessarily for the best. As ridiculous as the institution was, it is always preferable, as James Joyce has mumbled, to have something to rebel against than to be bored. In the end this may be the most positive attribute of San Francisco Catholicism.

[*City of San Francisco,* October 21, 1975]

On
the
Ramparts

The Battles of Selma*

*T*HE LEGAL-SIZE MIMEOGRAPHED FORMS were deadly complete—name, address, next-of-kin, authorization for representation by counsel. Everyone who marched had to fill one out in case of arrest, injury, or death. But there weren't enough forms to go around Sunday morning when the marchers came in from Boykin and Jones and Marion, from Atlanta and Chicago and New York. They came to Brown's Chapel—the red-brick church towering over the red-brick apartment buildings of the George Washington Carver Homes housing project in the Negro section of Selma.

Brown's Chapel was the assembly point for the planned march over U.S. Highway 80 through the swamps and hills and white racist strongholds of rural Black Belt Alabama to the ornate colonial capitol at Montgomery, where the dual flags of the Confederate States of America and the Sovereign State of Alabama hung together limply in the still air around the capitol dome.

The girl handing out the forms said she needed more. A Negro boy ran down unpaved Sylvan Street, which intersects the federal housing project, and turned right on Alabama Street toward the Student Nonviolent Coordinating Committee (SNCC) headquarters located three blocks uptown. He went to the top floor of a rickety, three-story Negro office building with unlighted hallways and atrophied doors set in warped doorjambs. From the Selma City Jail directly across the street, police watched the young Negro go into the dreary building and come out a few minutes later carrying a freshly printed pile of registration

Coauthored with David Welsh, with reporting from John Beecher, Matthew Clarke, James Forest, Thomas P. McDonnell, Desmond O'Grady, Terence Prittie, Bob Robertson, Robert Scheer, David St. Clair, Arthur Waskow, and William Worthy

forms. They knew he was going back to Brown's Chapel, as they knew most everything else about the movements of Negroes in Selma. Dallas County sheriff Jim Clark, the tough front man of the Selma racists, lives with his wife in a jail building apartment. He amuses himself in the morning by spying, with high-powered binoculars, into the SNCC offices. Sheriff Clark is an early riser.

This kind of police-state activity is accepted as routine by Negroes. Selma is a tough town. It was a slave trade center in the antebellum years. Lynchings are an ingrained part of local custom. It is a dangerous town for "uppity" Negroes and civil rights "agitators." Sheriff Clark commands a handpicked band of over two hundred "volunteer" possemen who ride horseback about the state, curing with bullwhips, clubs, and guns any social disturbances involving labor union organizers or civil rights activists. The birthplace of the Alabama White Citizens' Council, Selma proudly numbers among its native sons such eminent modern Southerners as Birmingham police commissioner Eugene "Bull" Connor. Only 1 percent of Selma's fifteen thousand Negro citizens have dared to register to vote.

This historic Confederate city on the banks of the muddy Alabama River is a citadel of Southern resistance to integration. Only in the Trailways bus station do Negroes and whites mix. This is why SNCC, in 1963, selected Selma as a prime target for its organizing activities. The Confederate establishment immediately began to skirmish with the civil rights invaders, and when Dr. Martin Luther King and his Southern Christian Leadership Conference (SCLC) joined forces with SNCC in Selma early this year, the Confederate "police action" escalated into a conflict of military proportions not seen in the South since the Battle of Selma nominally ended the Civil War in April of 1865.

Like all wars, this one became deadly serious after the first casualty. Jimmie Lee Jackson, a twenty-six-year-old Negro woodcutter, was gunned down by an Alabama state trooper during a racial demonstration in nearby Marion. When he died eight days later in Selma's Negro Good Samaritan Hospital, he was a war hero. The Montgomery march of Sunday, March 7, was called more to honor Jimmie Jackson than to seriously petition Governor George Wallace (the titular president of the Confederacy) for the redress of racial inequities he has sworn to preserve.

Wallace had ordered the march squashed. On that quiet Sunday morning all the loyal military forces of the white police state of Alabama were organizing for an overkill.

As the young Negro left the SNCC offices with a fresh supply of registration forms, his progress was reported to the Confederate Command Post operating in Sheriff Clark's Dallas County Courthouse offices in downtown Selma. "The nigger's leaving there now...He's goin' back down Alabama Street...carryin' papers...back to the church..." The intelligence came over the two-way radio in thick, surly Southern tones. A middle-aged woman wearing rimless glasses, a Confederate flag pinned to her white blouse, sat on a stool, her legs crossed, writing everything down. A large sign near the doorway of the first floor suite read "Quiet Please, We Are Trying to Monitor Three Radios." The woman leaned over and handed the message to the sheriff's deputy, an attractive brunette, who sat with perfect posture behind a gray metal desk. She was constantly occupied with telephone and two-way radio, relaying information to the Confederate forces massing outside the Selma city limits. Excellently groomed and cooly efficient, she wore her brown sweater and brown skirt like she knew the uniform concealed a faintly plump but nonetheless classic Southern figure. A gold deputy's badge was pinned above her bosom. (Selma wags say that Sheriff Clark demands the best in horseflesh for his posse—and the best in woman-flesh on his office staff.)

This demure deputy was important to the morale of the sheriff's office. She represented the "other side" of Selma: the life of good manners and traditional Southern gentility; the life of the exclusive "country club" set. The Selma country club rests on gracefully sloping hills just outside the main business district, as far removed as possible from the weather-torn, decaying shacks lining the unpaved streets of the Negro residential section and the high-roofed, wooden-front stores operated by Jewish merchants in the Negro shopping district. Also far removed from the slopes of the country club are the factories which manufacture locks and bricks and lumber and cotton oil and produce the profits which enable the substantial citizens of the "other Selma" to live comfortably, often luxuriously, in fine homes of classical architecture and to order the right things from the Neiman-Marcus catalogue.

These elder families of Selma are at the apex of a pyramided racial and socioeconomic structure based on the suppression of the Negro—

but the "good citizens" never engage in violence to maintain it. Instead they leave the beatings and the whippings and the terrorizing to lower-middle-class whites. But they condone and applaud these activities, and without this approval from the top, the systematic repression of the Negro would collapse into directionless violence. The twenty-two-year-old deputy, daughter of one of Selma's better families, well understood this delicate relationship. Because she was privy to the secret Confederate battle plans for Sunday, she had driven the fifty miles into Montgomery the day before to have her hair specially done. She knew this was going to be a memorable, victorious day for the South. She wanted to look her representative best.

ONE OF THE COMMAND POST RADIOS CRACKLED: "There's three more cars of niggers crossing the bridge. Some white bastards riding with them. Heading for Brown's Chapel." The bridge was the Edmund Pettus Bridge, a stumpy concrete edifice stretching between the debris-lined bluffs of the sluggish Alabama River and linking Selma with Highway 80 (the Jefferson Davis Highway), the road to Montgomery. This was the bridge the marchers would have to cross. At the other end the Confederate forces were massing for the kill.

It was early afternoon. The state troopers were preparing to block off traffic on the heavily traveled thoroughfare. They moved their patrol cars into position on both sides of the divided highway, facing the north. It was from the north that the Union forces would come.

Sheriff Clark's good friend, Colonel Al Lingo, head of the Alabama State Troopers, sat in an unmarked car at the side of the highway, watching his men prepare for battle. The generalship of the Confederate forces was Lingo's responsibility; Sheriff Clark's deputies and his possemen took orders from him this day. It was not the first time that Lingo and Clark had combined forces to defeat insurgent Union troops. They had worked together to quell demonstrations at Birmingham and Tuskegee, Gadsden and at the University of Alabama. But today was something special. Clark and Lingo, at the request of the Confederate commander-in-chief, Wallace, had worked out battle plans that would not only scatter the Union forces but make their defeat an object lesson. Blood was in the air. The white citizens of Alabama had grown weary of "moderate" handling of the Selma voter registration demonstrations led by Dr. Martin Luther King. Selma's public safety director, Wilson Baker, had insisted on mass arrests to control the demonstrators. Now the Confederate leadership wanted something more effective. Selma city police were told to stay out of the march break-up. The state troopers and Sheriff Clark's deputies would handle things in their own fashion. "If the Negroes refuse to disperse, we shall not make mass arrests," Colonel Lingo said. He said it the way a general says his side will take no prisoners.

Lingo and Clark had gone to ingenious extremes to make sure their troops were adequately supplied with the proper weapons to fight the unarmed marchers. They issued two-foot-long cattle prods (battery-charged, devilish instruments about the thickness of a half-dollar and with a point at the end which sears human skin when it touches). Lingo also laid in a complete supply of tear gas with wide-nozzle guns capable of spraying gas over a broad area, circular tear gas bombs, and tear gas shells shot from special guns. Each man had a gas mask and long billy club (some of the more dedicated had weighted their clubs by drilling holes and inserting metal rods). In case the Union forces fought back, both sheriff's deputies and troopers had carbines and shotguns in their cars. Many of Sheriff Clark's possemen carried long bullwhips. These were personal property, not state issue. The men wore riot helmets emblazoned with Confederate flags. Colonel Lingo is partial to the red, white, and blue flag of the Confederacy. When he assumed command of the Alabama Highway Patrol, after Wallace was elected governor, he changed the name of the patrol to "State Troopers" and ordered Confederate flags affixed to the front license plates of trooper patrol cars.

Colonel Lingo was satisfied with the military preparations. He leaned back and waited, looking toward the bridge and the north.

FILLING OUT A MARCHING FORM at Brown's Chapel was sixteen-year-old Viola Jackson of Selma (no relation to the late Jimmie Lee Jackson). *Have you ever been arrested?* NO. *Have you ever been beaten?* YES. *Do you have any ailments that should be checked before the march?* NO. She handed in the paper and went outside where the marchers were forming.

The detailed form was typical of the style of military organization that the SNCC people and Dr. King's lieutenants adopted for the Selma campaign. The march itself was planned in military style: participants were to line up two abreast, grouped into squads of twenty-five people, and then into companies of four squads each. The leaders of the march—John Lewis of SNCC and Hosea Williams of SCLC—had originally planned to organize the squads on paper. But the last-minute influx of marchers made that impractical, so everyone was ordered outside to the playground behind Brown's Chapel and told to line up in pairs. Forty-five minutes later, six companies were ready to march.

The Union leadership had, in its own way, prepared for the expected confrontation with the Confederate forces: four ambulances were parked on Sylvan Street; ten doctors and nurses, mostly from New York, had flown to Montgomery and driven to Selma the night before. They were volunteers of the Medical Committee for Human Rights. When the march started, they followed in the file of ambulances at the end of the line.

Viola Jackson found herself in the second company, first squad. Standing in front of her was a young Negro wearing a sweatshirt. His marching companion was a tall white youth wearing a blue windbreaker jacket and a blue cap and carrying a round knapsack on his back. They introduced themselves. The Negro was Charles Mauldin, an eighteen-year-old junior at R. B. Hudson High School, Selma's Negro high, and president of the fifteen-hundred-member Selma Youth Movement. Slight of build and articulate of expression, he was polite and friendly. The white was Jim Benston, an unsalaried member of the SCLC Selma staff. Benston is twenty and blond and has a scraggly yellow beard. He is from Arkansas and is hated by the cops because they consider him a double traitor: to the South and to his Caucasian race. He became a prime target for clubbing.

The march began without heraldry. Viola Jackson and Charles Mauldin and Jim Benston walked close together as the three-block-long line moved slowly down Sylvan Street and up Water Avenue, through the Negro business district, to the bridge. Groups of Selma citizens stood in sullen, compressed groups on street corners and watched. The marchers passed the Selma Radiator Shop. A white man taunted Viola: "Black bitch. Got a white boy to play with, huh?" As they reached Broad Street—the main street of Selma that leads onto the bridge—a white woman driving a green pick-up truck tried to run down Benston. He leaped out of the way. Police had refused to direct traffic for the marchers, except to halt cars as the long line turned onto the bridge at Broad Street. So the marchers had to be wary of white citizens with cars. The last thing Viola and the two boys saw as they walked onto the bridge was the troopers and possemen stationed by the *Selma Times-Journal* building, waiting patiently. They knew the marchers would be coming back.

THE VIEW FROM THE OTHER SIDE of the Pettus Bridge—looking toward Selma—was less than inspiring. The old brick buildings that line the bluffs above the slow-flowing river were gradually falling away. The sloping bluffs were spotted with bricks, discarded building materials, and decaying underbrush. Viola Jackson and Charles Mauldin and Jim Benston could look back at the river bluffs and the long line of marchers behind them on the bridge, but they couldn't tell what was happening ahead of them on the highway. All they could see were police cars, state trooper cars, sheriff's cars—a silent, stationary armada filling all four lanes of the Jefferson Davis Highway. Viola whispered that she had never seen so many police cars in one place in her life. A large, surly crowd of Selma white citizens—hooting, snorting, like spectators at a bull fight—stood on the trunks of parked cars or jammed the frontage area of roadside businesses, seeking ringside seats. Newsmen were herded together in front of the Lehman Pontiac building some distance from the marchers and assigned several troopers for "protection."

State troopers, headed by Major John Cloud, lined the highway three deep. Colonel Lingo watched from his automobile parked near Lehman's Grocery. As the marchers approached, Major Cloud hailed them: "This is an unlawful assembly," he said. "You have two minutes to turn around and go back to your church." The leaders of the march were now within several feet of the phalanx of troopers who held their clubs at the ready. Major Cloud took out his watch and started counting. The silence was total. Exactly one minute and five seconds later Major Cloud ordered, "Troopers forward." The blue-clad troopers leaped ahead, clubs swinging, moving with a sudden force that bowled over line after line of marchers. The first groups of Negroes went to the ground screaming, their knapsacks and bags spilling onto the highway.

The white spectators cheered.

The marchers, pushed back by the billy club attack, grouped together on the grassy, gasoline-soiled dividing strip in the center of the highway. They knelt and began to pray. The troopers rushed in again, hanging heads, and then retreated. Viola and the two boys knelt together. For two minutes, a tense silence was broken only by the sound of the Confederate forces strapping on their gas masks and the buzz-buzz-buzz of the cattle prods. Sheriff Clark ordered his possemen to mount up. "Get those goddamn niggers—and get those goddamn white niggers," he said.

As the troopers heaved the first tear gas bombs into the praying Negroes, the crowd of several hundred white onlookers broke into prolonged cheering. "Give it to the damn Yankees. Give it to the niggers." The first were feeler bombs; the marchers coughed and gagged but didn't move. Then the troopers let loose with a heavy barrage of gas shells. Several bombs landed near Viola and the two boys, and then they couldn't see each other anymore.

For Charles Mauldin, it was like a quick visit to hell. "The gas was so thick that you could almost reach up and grab it. It seemed to lift me up and fill my lungs and I went down." Some of the marchers panicked and ran. They couldn't see where they were going and they ran into cars and buildings. A young girl collapsed inside the treads of a tractor. Mauldin pulled her out. Marchers scrambled over a barbed-wire fence, tearing their clothes and scratching their stomachs, and ran down blindly toward the muddy river. The troopers, protected by gas masks, moved through the gasping, fainting Negroes and beat them with clubs. When Mauldin finally staggered in retreat back onto the bridge, a posseman on horseback rode by and hit him across the neck with an eight-foot bullwhip. "What do you want, nigger? Jump off the bridge? Well, go on, jump." The troopers and the possemen herded the fleeing Negroes across the bridge with cattle prods, clubs, and whips. Those who were too young or too old to move fast enough got hit the most. When they got to the Selma end of the bridge, the possemen and deputies who had been patiently waiting there attacked them anew with clubs and whips and chased them through the streets down toward the Negro quarter.

For Jim Benston, it was worse. After the first tear gas attack, he lay on the ground trying to breathe. He looked up and a trooper was standing in front of him, staring down through the big goggle-eyes of his gas mask. The trooper slowly lifted his tear gas gun and shot it off directly into Benston's face. "I was knocked out for maybe five minutes. When I woke up I was in a cloud. I couldn't breathe and I couldn't see. I was coughing and I was sick. It was like the world had gone away. I laid there on the grass for a few minutes and then I felt around me, trying to see if anybody else was still there. I couldn't feel anybody. They were all gone. I was the only one left." Benston staggered off to his right, through a used car lot, and collapsed in a small field. A dozen or so other marchers lay there, bleeding, coughing, trying to catch their breath. Then Benston heard horses, and shrill rebel battle yells. The possemen were charging the band of prone marchers. All the posse had clubs and some of them had whips and they struck out at anything they could see. "They tried to get the horses to run over us," Benston said. "They came charging through where we were laying on the grass and tried to hit us with the horses, but the horses had more sense. One posseman tried to get his horse to rear up and land on top of a man near me, but the horse wouldn't do it. Horses have more sense."

The marchers got up and ran toward the bridge. The possemen rode in front of them and set off tear gas bombs in their path, forcing them through the new pockets of gas. On the bridge, Benston was clubbed at least twenty-five times. As he ran down the narrow pedestrian sidewalk, possemen would take turns, galloping by, clubbing him, laughing. He pulled his knapsack up to cover his head and neck. "That knapsack saved my life," he said. Some of the possemen, crazy with excitement, tried to force their horses up onto the narrow walkway to run down the fleeing marchers. As the possemen galloped up and down the concrete bridge, swinging clubs and whips, one sheriff's volunteer leaned forward and screamed in his horse's ear, "Bite them, bite them, bite the niggers." The possemen chased Benston's group for two blocks into Selma, until the streets became crowded. Possemen don't generally whip people in public.

For Viola Jackson, it didn't last long. She was knocked down on the dividing strip and dug her fingernails into the ground. The thick tear gas hung like heavy cigarette smoke between the blades of grass and curled around her fingers. She managed to get up and tried to run, but she couldn't go on. Her breath came shorter. Then she couldn't see, and she fell down onto the ground and didn't get up. More shells fell nearby, and the gas covered her fallen body like a blanket.

The police at first wouldn't let the waiting Union ambulances onto the bridge to pick up the wounded. When they did, finally, the volunteer drivers and doctors and nurses worked frantically, loading the injured and racing them to the Good Samaritan Hospital.

Sheriff Clark's possemen chased the Negroes down to the housing project but were stopped by Selma safety director Baker. Baker said he had his city police surrounding the project area and saw no need for further force. The *Selma Times-Journal* quoted Clark as replying to Baker: "I've already waited a month too damn long about moving in."

In the ensuing thirty minutes before the possemen and the troopers cleared out of the housing project, the First Baptist Church on Sylvan Street was raided by Confederates. They fired tear gas into the church, then went inside and threw a Negro teenager through a devotional window. They also tear-gassed one of the Negro homes along Sylvan Street and chased children through the project with their horses. Some of the younger Negroes began to throw bricks at the troopers, and, in a few moments of extraordinary juvenile passion, the troopers picked up the bricks and threw them back. The angry, shattered marchers crowded into Brown's Chapel, where John Lewis of SNCC told them (before he went to the hospital for treatment of a head injury), "I don't see how President Johnson can send troops to Vietnam. I don't see how he can send troops to the Congo. I don't see how he can send troops to Africa and can't send troops to Selma, Alabama."

At the Good Samaritan Hospital, a modernistic building dedicated in 1964 and operated for Selma's Negroes by the Edmundite fathers, the emergency rooms looked like a scene out of *Birth of a Nation*. The wounded marchers were propped on carts and tables and on the floor— bleeding and sobbing. The sickening odor of tear gas filled the emergency rooms. Tables were removed from the employees' dining room and the injured were laid on the floor. The tear gas victims, coughing and gasping violently, overflowed into the hospital corridors. Several hours later, most of the eighty-four people taken to the hospital were deposited in a makeshift recovery area—the lounge of the hospital's nursing home—to await friends or relatives. Seventeen were injured seriously enough to be admitted for treatment—fractured ribs, fractured wrists, head wounds, broken teeth. Among those admitted was Viola Jackson, sixteen, "for extended treatment of tear gas effect and hysteria."

After the Negroes in the project were forced indoors, Sheriff Clark's posse rode uptown, looking for more Negroes. They yelled at Negroes walking on the streets and beat with their nightsticks on the hoods of cars with Negro drivers. "Get the hell out of town. Go on. We mean it. We want all the niggers off the street."

By dusk, not one Negro could be found on the streets of Selma.

[SHOW OF FORCE]

Although the contest is unlikely ever to be held, Jim Clark could win, hands down, the title of best-dressed sheriff in the Black Belt. He owns seventy-four shirts and twelve pairs of boots, and Wednesday afternoon, as the Confederate forces were lining up before the national television cameras for a massive show of force on Sylvan Street, the dapper, segregationist sheriff was at his resplendent best. His boots were spit-polished ("white spit," Clark told an inquiring reporter), the crease on the pants of his dark business suit cutting-edge sharp, the alabaster purity of his crash helmet broken only by a painted Confederate flag. In his lapel was the symbol of Clark's philosophy of law enforcement in Dallas County, Alabama: a round white button bearing the single word "NEVER." This is Clark's rejoinder to "We Shall Overcome," and it appeared "NEVER" would be the order of the day as the armed forces of the State of Alabama assumed battle formation a half block down from Brown's Chapel on dusty Sylvan Street. State troopers, sheriff's deputies, city policemen, Alabama Soil Conservation officers, even Alabama Alcoholic Beverage Control officers, lined up in two- and three-squad-car rows on Sylvan Street, flanking in reserve to the right and left down Selma Avenue and filling yet another block of Sylvan Street beyond the boundaries of the Negro housing project. The mayor of Selma had said the Union could not march today and the troops were here to see that they would not.

This huge assemblage of police cars and troopers was good tonic for Sheriff Clark. He moved in between his deputies' cars, playfully snapping the rawhide hanging from his billy club at the khaki-clad buttocks of his possemen. He didn't act at all like a soldier who had just been dressed down by his commander-in-chief.

Governor Wallace had summoned Clark to his capital offices the day before and told him to call off his posse and their whips and horses. Jim Clark has been sheriff of Dallas County since 1955 and has used his posse to handle labor organizers and to crack the heads of Negroes with complete impunity, and this was the first time he was ever called on the carpet. He stood on the coffee-colored rug in the governor's office and stared at the pale yellow walls of the executive suite as Wallace, who seemed concerned about Alabama's image, upbraided Clark for the posse's Attila the Hun tactics on Sunday, before the lenses of television cameras. The governor wasn't really mad about the whips, but he was mad as hell about the television cameras. When Clark left, red-faced and angry, he had instructions to keep his men out of the omniscient television eye. The sheriff was also told that Wilson Baker would call the shots in Selma, and he didn't like that, either.

But Clark's possemen were out today, armed only with clubs and guns (no horses or whips), to join the massing of the Confederate forces, and the sheriff felt good. The Union forces planned a forbidden march to the green-stone-front Dallas County Courthouse this Wednesday afternoon. The march was an open secret. There were few strategic secrets on either side because these days of racial crisis in Selma were covered by some two hundred members of the press as if it all were a national political convention. Newscasters had broadcast reports of the planned courthouse march early that morning.

Clark has a special feeling for the courthouse. It is his duty as sheriff to protect it. The sheriff is a man of descriptions. He calls the courthouse the "temple of justice." He does not like Negroes defiling the temple. Clark looked down Sylvan Street toward Brown's Chapel, where the Union forces were holding a meeting inside. He calls Brown's Chapel the "church of thieves." He glanced toward Wilson Baker, whose city police were holding the front line of the Confederate forces. There is no public record of how Sheriff Clark describes Baker, and that is just as well because it wouldn't be a nice description. Clark hates Baker's guts.

Wilson Baker, a big man with mild mannerisms, leaned against a squad car and puffed on a cigar through a brown plastic holder. He is the director of public safety of Selma. For "public safety director," read "police chief." "Public Safety" is a strange phrase, but it is a big thing in the Confederate State of Alabama. Across from the gold-domed capitol at Montgomery there is a large foreboding building that houses the state's Department of Public Safety. This is Alabama's Pentagon. It is the headquarters of the state troopers and is undoubtedly the most elaborate highway patrol office in America. Another of Colonel Lingo's titles is state director of public safety. Mr. Baker, however, is one of the few police officials in Alabama who does not make the title ludicrous by his actions. He thinks like a dedicated cop and not like a storm trooper. In Alabama law enforcement, when it comes to dealing with Negroes, this is an unusual sort of thinking. He would rather cajole or, at worst, arrest civil rights demonstrators than beat them. This moderate approach has alienated him from Sheriff Clark. "Those two have been at it all month long like two dogs in a pit," a Justice Department observer in Selma said. In the last two months of racial demonstrations, Baker's tactics have kept the lid on this troubled and tense town. Massive violence came only once—Sunday at the bridge, when the Clark/Lingo coalition took over.

Baker has been criticized recently by Selma white townspeople—both racists and "moderates." They feel the demonstrations have gone too long and too far. But Baker is the kind of tough cop who does his job without regard to public opinion. This is not to say that Baker isn't a segregationist. He is. But he is a segregationist who seems to have some feeling for the Negro's struggle for human dignity. "If I was a nigger, I'd be doing just what they're doing," he once said.

THE UNION DEMONSTRATORS BOILED out of Brown's Chapel. They stood in the street, chatting casually, as if they had just come out of a regular Sunday service, then began to form ranks under a worn chinaberry tree. There were some five hundred of them, a good 60 percent of them white, and most of that number ministers and nuns. Baker strode forward to the front echelon of Selma police officers who were lined up across Sylvan Street. Beyond them, the Confederate forces stretched in a flow of color worthy of a *Camelot* set: first, more city policemen in white helmets and dark blue uniforms; then, several hundred feet back, stretched in a solid mass from the end of Sylvan Street, the sheriff's deputies, in dark-brown uniforms; then the sheriff's posse, distinguished by their obesity and irregular dress of khakis and blue denims; behind the posse, the ranks of Alabama Soil Conservation officers, nominally game wardens, with green cars and green uniforms and green helmets; then several battalions of state troopers wearing blue helmets with Confederate flags painted on them, light-blue breeches and boots, dark-blue blouses. The troopers' unmarked cars, the metal Confederate flags affixed to the front bumpers, filled adjoining streets in an impressive display of Alabama's military might. Jets from nearby Craig Air Force Base streaked overhead, but nobody looked up.

The marchers formed up four abreast and started down Sylvan Street toward the line of police a half block away. When they got within twelve feet, Baker stepped forward and raised his big left hand in a lazy arc, the cigar still between his fingers: "Reverend Anderson, you cannot march today." Standing beside Baker was Joseph T. Smitherman, Selma's young and nervous mayor. The Reverend L. L. Anderson, a Selma Negro leader who was heading the marchers, made his reply directly to the mayor:

"We are asking Your Honor to permit us to march to the courthouse. We are not registered voters but we want to be; it is our God-given constitutional right. We shall move like the children of Israel, moving toward the promised land."

The mayor blinked. The streets were jammed with spectators. People stood on nearby rooftops. The omnipresent television cameras were trained directly on him. Newsmen shoved microphones under his nose. He was the mayor: thirty-five years old, a former appliance dealer, a close political ally of Governor Wallace. It was his decision to ban any further demonstrations or marches outside of the Brown's Chapel area. And he had the heritage of the mayor's office to uphold. (One of his predecessors, ex-mayor Chris Heinz, was the founder and head of the Alabama White Citizen's Council.) He cleared his throat, twice, and folded his slender arms in front of the dark business suit which looked like it belonged on someone a size larger. "You have had opportunity after opportunity to register your people to vote," he said. (The Dallas County Courthouse is open two days a month to register new voters.) "We have enforced the laws impartially...We expect to see our orders obeyed." The mayor said this like a man who knows his rhetoric doesn't have to be convincing when he has several hundred troopers with clubs in their hands waiting just up the street.

The mayor stepped back to the sanctuary of the squad cars. The newsmen crowded in around Baker and the Reverend Anderson. "I would like to introduce some people of good will, who have some statements to make," said Anderson. "You can make all the statements you want, but you are not going to march," replied Baker. A Negro nun from St. Louis, Sister Mary Antona, was called toward the waiting microphones by the Reverend Anderson. "I feel privileged to come to Selma. I feel that every citizen has the right to vote," she said. When Anderson called a second speaker, an Episcopalian priest from Greenwich, wearing a brass-buttoned black cashmere blazer, Baker turned and walked away from the police line. "Wait, I have a statement to make to you," a minister said. "Make statements to the press. I'm not accepting any," Baker snapped back.

They did just that. The nuns, ministers, priests, rabbis, lay church leaders, and the Negro leaders who made up the majority of the marchers, spoke to the press for the next ninety minutes while the youngsters in the housing project played and giggled on the sidewalks. The tremendous contingent of Confederate forces sat in their cars or stood on the road and scratched themselves, smoked cigars, drank coffee, and ate sandwiches delivered in a small green pick-up truck from the sheriff's office. There were thirty-three speakers, all chosen by nomination and voice vote during the meeting at Brown's Chapel, as representatives of groups from thirty states who had come to bear witness in Selma. "The symbols I see here are foreign symbols. I see a foreign flag painted on those helmets. I thought we were Americans together," said one Negro minister, the Methodist chaplain at Howard University. "One can't help thinking that there are better ways to spend the money it costs to keep all those hundreds of troopers between our humble group and the courthouse," said Rabbi Everett Gendler of the Jewish Center at Princeton University. "We are here to share the suffering of the Negro people of Selma," said a representative of the Freedom Democratic Party of Mississippi. "The question is," he yelled over the broadcasting-company microphones, covered like golf clubs with a sock of black felt to cut wind noise, and directing his words at the rows of police standing with clubs in their hands, "The question in my mind is, am I in Selma or am I in hell?"

As the speakers talked on, damning Selma with all the moral fervor at their command, it became evident that only their fellow marchers and the newsmen were listening. The spectators walked idly about on the sidewalk; children chased each other in between the rows of brick apartment buildings; the troops broke ranks, stood in small groups chatting, sipping Cokes, slipping their riot helmets back to let the sun on their foreheads. Mayor Smitherman picked up one of the sandwiches and fiddled with the wax paper wrapping for a moment before he opened it. A gold wedding ring hung loosely on his finger. He looked unhappily at the crowd of demonstrators. "I don't understand it," he said. "Martin Luther King can walk into the White House any time he wants for conferences with the president, but the mayor of Selma can't even get an appointment. I sent the president a telegram asking for a meeting, but some sort of fifth assistant answered it."

"King? Where is King?" a man asked. "He's in town," said the mayor. "I don't know why he isn't here."

MARTIN LUTHER KING wasn't there because he was in trouble in his own movement. His absence explained the absence, also, of the usual throngs of Selma teenagers who gave life and spirit and rhythm to every mass Negro meeting in Selma, and of the tough, militant SNCC workers who had been in Selma for two years now. King wasn't there because he was afraid he would be publicly booed by his own people. The teenagers of Selma and the SNCC people weren't there because they were disgusted with King—and were tired of praying and speechmaking. They wanted to march.

Dr. King was at the home of a Selma Negro dentist, Dr. Sullivan Jackson. It was there, early Tuesday morning, that the pajama-clad Nobel Prize winner met with former Florida governor LeRoy Collins, now head of the federal Community Relations Service and President Johnson's unofficial ambassador to the Union forces. Collins had been sent by special jet from Washington to work out a compromise that would avoid repetition of Sunday's bloodshed on Tuesday afternoon, when another attempt at the march to Montgomery (this one led by Dr. King) was scheduled to cross the Edmund Pettus Bridge. A federal judge had issued a temporary restraining order against the march, and Dr. King was in a quandry. His organization prided itself on never violating the law—or a court order; yet, he had pledged to lead this march (King was absent Sunday), and civil rights workers and ministers from all over the South were gathering at Brown's Chapel. They all wanted to march. Collins offered a typically Johnson compromise: He had conferred with Colonel Lingo and obtained a pledge that the marchers would be unharmed if they turned back a small distance down Highway 80. Lingo had even drawn a rough map, showing where the Union forces must halt. Collins handed the Confederate map to King: this way, he said, both sides would save face—and King would have a dramatic moment. King hesitated, then took the map. He sent a message to the crowd at Brown's Chapel: "I have decided it is better to die on the highway than to make a butchery of my conscience."

There was, of course, no danger of butchery. The plan worked. The marchers were halted, knelt, said a prayer, and turned back. The deal became obvious to SNCC people when Colonel Lingo, in a mild Southern doublecross, pulled his troopers back, leaving the highway to Montgomery open as King rose to lead his followers in retreat to Selma. The move was meant to embarrass King, and it did. King later called the second march "the greatest confrontation for freedom" in the South. The youth and the SNCC people called it a sellout. King was accused of "betraying" the movement and collaborating with the enemy.

King's fall from favor was only momentary. The diverse elements in the Union expeditionary force were united later that week by the death of the Reverend James J. Reeb, a white Unitarian minister from Boston, who died of wounds from a nighttime beating at the hands of some Selma white citizens as he left a restaurant in the Negro district. But though momentary, King's disgrace was significant because it illustrated in dramatic fashion a longstanding split in the Union leadership.

It was the same split that divided the abolitionists in the 1850s and the 1860s over whether to support Lincoln and work within the Republican Party for their goals or to continue to take outside, radical social action. It is the old polarity between action and negotiation, between politics and revolution. It is the struggle between those who would work within the establishment and those who reject the establishment policies of compromise and consensus, and agitate for more direct solutions. This division is evident in the methodology of the civil rights movement, from the NAACP on the right to SNCC and then the black nationalist groups on the left.

In Selma, the SNCC people, who were there first, and Dr. King's SCLC, which became active in Selma early this year, are divided on certain broad goals—primary among them SNCC's support for a third, independent political party in Alabama, modeled after Mississippi's Freedom Democratic Party. SCLC would rather the Negroes register in the existing political parties. SNCC wants Selma's people to develop their own leaders; SCLC is inclined to have them follow the leadership of Dr. King, his assistant the Reverend Ralph Abernathy, and other SCLC officials. Despite these differences, the two abolitionist organizations have developed an effective working organization in Selma. They realize they need each other in the jungles of the Black Belt.

The coalition dissolved—for a while—that Wednesday afternoon. Many SNCC people stayed away from the march. The Selma youth, the black *jeunesse,* took things a little more seriously. They revolted.

THE REVOLT WAS FORMING while the demonstrators in the street finished their speeches and were told by Baker, again, that they could not march. So the ministers and the nuns and the priests and the disparate volunteers knelt on the ground and said the Lord's Prayer—the Protestant version—and then turned and walked back to Brown's Chapel, their arms locked, singing "We Shall Overcome."

Meanwhile, in the First Baptist Church a half block away at the corner of Sylvan Street and Jefferson Davis Avenue, the black *jeunesse* were meeting. They decided to go to the courthouse. Despite the leadership compliance with the city ban, in the elemental impetuosity of youth, they went. These teenagers are the marrow in the backbone of the Selma movement. They had the staying power and the vitality that kept the demonstrations going. In all-night vigils which began Wednesday, they kept the rhythm, singing and chanting at a level of constant vivacity that amazed veteran observers of civil rights demonstrations. These kids are a contradictory mixture of hipster and idealist; they are rebels with a cause.

The clerics, in a mildly self-congratulatory mood after their long session of denouncing the evils of Selma, settled back in the battered pews of Brown's Chapel. Suddenly, the absence of the teenagers became obvious. It was like being at a Wagnerian opera and soon realizing that the drums were gone from the orchestra. A man rushed to the front of the church with a frantic message. The ministers and priests ran outside and down Sylvan Street to where the teenagers and the police were massing ranks. They just about got there too late.

The kids made it two blocks—almost halfway to the courthouse—before an advance guard of state troopers pulled in front of them. The Union-blue-uniformed Confederates got out of their Southern-gray cars and began to push the kids back down Jefferson Davis Avenue with their clubs. A few teenagers got bloody heads, and one or two got their teeth cracked. They were taken into the first-aid station in the First Baptist Church. Baker drove up in his white Chrysler. As he got out of the car, the *jeunesse,* some three hundred of them, equally mixed boys and girls, were massing in the intersection, ready to charge the Confederates and run through and over their cars if need be to get to the courthouse. More and more cars of city police and state troopers pulled up on Jefferson Davis Avenue. The troops got out and made a solid phalanx across the intersection. Baker waved the press off to one side, pulled out a bullhorn, and told the kids to disperse. But more of them came running down the street. The youthful brigade was surging at the corner, chanting, undulating, ready for action.

The ministers, breathless, ran between the cops and the kids. With hands linked they formed a human chain in an attempt to edge the *jeunesse* backward, but the kids would have none of it and pushed against the ministers. More Confederate cars sirened up. The clerics looked worried, scared. The teenagers' eyes were shining as they pushed the cordon of ministers, inch by inch, toward the Confederate lines, and sang: "Ain't gonna' let nobody turn me round, turn me round..."

Jimmy Webb, a short, vivacious Bible student, with green collegiate cardigan and the speaking style of a cheerleader, stood in front of the chanting youths and yelled: "You want to go to the courthouse. I want to go to the courthouse. We all want to go to the courthouse. But this is not the way. Let's wait till Bevel gets here [James Bevel, the overall-clad minister with shaved head and Iranian skullcap, who heads SCLC's Alabama project] and we'll plan what to do."

One boy spit on the ground. "Plan! We were halfway to the courthouse and some pseudo-leader stopped us and said we should regroup and plan our approach. Then the cops came. If we hadn't've planned we'd be at the courthouse right now."

The ministers kept pushing the youths backward, their arms still locked in a solid row. The police were also in a row formation, holding their clubs out horizontally. The clerics managed to begin moving the *jeunesse* back up Sylvan Street, toward Brown's Chapel. Stragglers were shoved along by the police. "We'll go inside the chapel and talk this over," one minister said. A young Negro boy was leaning, defeatedly, against a battered tree near the corner and in one quiet remark to a companion he expressed all the complexity and the shattered idealism of the division in the Union forces. "I don't know," he said softly. "I just don't want to go back to that church and pray some more."

[CHARGE OF THE BIBLE BRIGADE]

In one of those extraordinary coincidences that can move men to memorable deeds, millions of East Coast television viewers on the evening of Sunday, March 7, saw the movie *Judgment at Nuremberg* immediately following the spectacle of troopers and possemen gassing, beating, and whipping the Selma Negroes at prayer. The hideous parallel between Auschwitz and Selma was obvious, even to the insensitive. Were it not for this accident of programming, Selma, Alabama, might just have been news, but never history. The pictures from Selma were unpleasant; the juxtaposition of the Nazi stormtroopers and the Alabama state troopers made them unbearable. A high tide of revulsion crossed the nation that evening, and by morning exceptional things were happening.

People literally rushed into the streets to express their outrage in cities from Washington, D.C., to Toronto. In Chicago, sympathetic Selma demonstrators clogged rush-hour Loop traffic; Detroit's Democratic mayor and Michigan's Republican governor marched together to demand federal intervention. In Atlanta, Dr. Martin Luther King announced that he would personally lead another march on Tuesday and called for help from people of all faiths. The response from Jewish, Protestant, and Catholic clerics was rapid and astonishing. Never, in the history of the United States, has organized religion collaborated to such an extent on an issue of social justice. The clergymen did not merely exhort—they led the way.

California Episcopal bishop James Pike flew from New Orleans;

Methodist bishop John Wesley Lord from Washington; the Reverend Dr. David H. Hunter, deputy director of the National Council of Churches, from New York. The United Church of Christ, the Union of American Hebrew Congregations, the American Baptist Convention, the Lutheran Church in America, the Rabbinical Assembly, the Disciples of Christ, the Roman Catholic Church—all had representative delegations en route to Selma, from St. Louis and Chicago, from Cleveland and Tampa, from Los Angeles and New York.

Even more significant was the participation of hundreds of Catholic priests and nuns. Their arrival in large numbers in Selma shocked both white racists and Negroes; it also shocked some of the priests' and nuns' superiors who, when it was all over, were still wondering how it happened. Although the Catholic bishops of America have made two strong statements condemning racial prejudice, they have been slow to involve themselves or their priests in the civil rights movement. The Catholic hierarchy has tended to caution priests against getting "too involved"; in some dioceses, Los Angeles for instance, Catholic priests and nuns are forbidden to take part in civil rights demonstrations. The list of clergymen jailed and beaten in the South is long, but almost devoid of Catholic priests. Before Selma, a nun marching and singing "We Shall Overcome" was unthinkable.

The shock of Selma hit the Catholic hierarchy in two ways. In St. Louis, liberal cardinal Joseph Ritter gave his blessing to priests and nuns headed for Selma. St. Louis "landed" the first contingent of demonstrating nuns in the Deep South. In Baltimore, Sister Cecilia Marie was teaching her sixth-graders geography when the bell in the classroom loudspeaker tinkled. "Sister Cecilia, do you want to go to Selma?" Sister Cecilia wanted to go. She dismissed the class, walked to the convent, "took fifty dollars of novitiate money and went." The story was different, however, in other dioceses, where a combination of accidents, confusion, and outside pressures operated to unleash priests who had been frustrated in their desire to demonstrate as early as Birmingham in 1963. The situation in the diocese of Washington, D.C., was typical.

ARCHBISHOP PATRICK O'BOYLE, of Washington, D.C., a conservative but realistic man, spent Monday morning weighing the problems of prudence and public relations. Many priests had telephoned his office, requesting permission to go to Selma. Nuns were calling up who wanted to picket the White House. Archbishop O'Boyle had previously forbidden nuns to participate in any demonstrations, including the March on Washington in 1963. The archbishop himself, after some hesitation, joined that march. There he encountered John Lewis of SNCC and afterward let it be known that he had no use for Lewis' brand of militancy. He disliked the idea of his priests being exposed to the Lewis philosophy in Selma.

On the other hand, if he denied permission to the priests, the bad publicity could be disastrous. The Council of Churches of the Greater Washington Area had chartered a plane to take Washington clerics to Selma. The *Washington Star* and the wire services had called early that morning to ask if any Catholics were going on the flight. Prudence, the archbishop felt, might well forbid his priests going; but prudence also would allow it. He made his decision: the priests could go, providing they stay away from reporters and from SNCC; the nuns could picket, "just this once," if their superiors approved.

Many Catholic priests were happily amazed. They rushed to the airport hoping to take off before something happened to change the situation. Some priests didn't even stop to pack a bag. Their concern was prescient. The subtle pressures of church politics quickly built up resistance to the Selma adventure. Conservative prelates objected. It was pointed out to Bishop O'Boyle's aide, Auxiliary Bishop John S. Spence, that Bishop Thomas J. Toolen of Mobile (whose diocesean area includes Selma), was in Washington and nobody had even *asked* him his opinion. (Bishop Toolen's opinion would not be difficult to predict. He is a Southern bishop. Priests in his diocese do not take part in racial demonstrations.) The auxiliary bishop frantically told a secretary to call the airport and stop the Washington priests. But the secretary deliberately scrambled the phone call and the plane left—the Catholics aboard. No attempt was made to bring them back. When word of rescinding the permission leaked out, priests who had not yet left didn't answer their telephones. They all made it to Selma. (When the priests returned, Archbishop O'Boyle congratulated them; if he were younger, he said, he would have considered going himself. At the same time, the nuns who had been picketing in Washington were "strongly urged" by Auxiliary Bishop Spence not to participate in a Sunday memorial service for the murdered Reverend James Reeb. This was a reversion to form, in a diocese where Auxiliary Bishop Philip M. Hannan wrote a congratulatory note to Dr. Klaus Herrmann of American University for his insights into SNCC. Dr. Herrmann had told students that SNCC was communist-infiltrated and "substantially under control of the Communist Party." Bishop Hannan wrote Dr. Herrmann: "I regret the delay in heartily congratulating you upon your wise action in counseling the students concerning the SNCC. Your action was wise and courageous. God bless you." Such are the vagaries of hierarchical politics.)

The clergymen who got to Selma early Monday night got their first exposure to what they considered radicalism. Many of them didn't like it. Mario Savio, the rebel leader at the University of California at Berkeley, his bushy head popping in and out of the pews in Brown's Chapel, talked to demonstrators, agitating for more forceful action the next day. Some of the clerics—Protestants, Catholics, and Jews—became concerned. They had come to Selma to help Martin Luther King, but wanted nothing to do with Mario Savio. They sent a spokesman to one of King's lieutenants, who assured them that King would be calling the shots. They seemed greatly relieved. Yet these same men, by Saturday, after five frustrating days of facing the Confederate forces, were to develop an elemental radicalism of their own.

THE RAINS CAME TO SELMA on Thursday. It was the second day of the vigil—a vigil maintained day and night in Sylvan Street for the dying minister from Boston who had come to Selma, like all the others, to give witness to the justice of the Negro cause. Confederate troops blocked off both ends of Sylvan Street on Wednesday afternoon. The Union forces were entrapped in the ghetto and they elected to camp on Sylvan Street, day and night, playing a waiting game with the Confederate leadership.

As the sky darkened into dusk the downfall became heavy and cold. The umbrellas, cardboard boxes, and newspapers that protected the demonstrators came down, replaced by a makeshift tent of canvas and watertight tarpaulins. The supporting poles protruded from the mass of black and white humanity huddled together for warmth in the muddy street. As the final strains of light played out, the Alabama sky appeared a deep, heavy purple that moved down to smother the wet red-brick buildings of the project. Selma police had strung an ordinary household clothesline across Sylvan Street several hundred yards up from Brown's Chapel. This was the point, dubbed the "Selma Wall" by the *jeunesse,* beyond which the demonstrators could not move. The *jeunesse* troubadours sang impromptu songs to the thin strip of cotton hemp. Among them, to the tune of Jericho:

A clothesline is a Berlin Wall,
Berlin Wall, Berlin Wall,
A clothesline is a Berlin Wall,
In Selma, Alabam'.

Reverend Reeb died that night of massive head injuries. When news of his death came to Sylvan Street, a low moan went through the crowd. It could be heard outside the tent, through the heavy rains, by the Confederate forces sitting in their cars on the other side of the rope. Killed in Action: the Reverend James J. Reeb, second fatality of the Battle of Selma. If some of the clergymen had begun to wonder why they were there, on a wet, unpaved street in Alabama, standing under an absurd-looking shelter, facing the steady headlights of a solid wall of police cars extending for blocks, they had their answer in the anguished cry of pain and fellowship coming from the Negroes. A man of God, a white man, had died trying to help them. There, in a moan, was the Gospel; and this—the reality of wet shoes and cold feet, black and white hands clasped together, bodies clinging to each other for warmth—this was giving witness.

The encampment continued through the night and round the clock through Friday and Saturday and Sunday. Finally, on Monday, by a federal judge's order, the Confederate cars pulled back and the Union forces marched to the courthouse. The rains stopped Saturday, and the clergymen who had spent two days staring down the Confederate forces decided to end the waiting game. At a mass meeting in the First Baptist Church, they voted to advance to the courthouse. The Bible Brigade was ready to charge.

A Negro in a green army parka shouted instructions to the Union force of three hundred assembled at the Selma Wall: "Only marchers in this line; everybody else get off the street." The demonstrators tensed up.

The advance line of Confederate forces moved in closer. Baker picked up the radiophone in his white Chrysler and called for more troops. Mayor Smitherman, looking nervous, blinked at the organizing Union forces. He chewed gum and fumbled with a cigarette. The city, in a sudden burst of public-relations consciousness, had distributed to newsmen a copy of a sympathetic telegram sent to Mrs. Reeb from the Selma City Council. It was a nice telegram and the mayor was worried that the press would ignore it if the Union forces charged over the Selma Wall.

The Confederate forces were lining up several men deep across Sylvan Street, ready for a frontal attack, unprepared for the flanking movement the crafty clergymen were about to attempt. Some eighty Catholic priests, twelve nuns, and thirty ministers and rabbis, walking three deep, came marching down the housing project sidewalk. Baker saw the Bible Brigade approaching and rushed to block the charge. Five policemen ran with him.

AT THE HEAD OF THE BLACK-GARBED BRIGADE was one of King's generals, the Reverend C. T. Vivian, and Father John Cavanaugh, former Notre Dame University president. Vivian, a short man with a small mustache and a long brown overcoat, took the offensive. He called a halt to the long line of clerics and nuns and hailed Baker. "We wish to go to the courthouse and pay homage to our fallen brethren. Do you recant of the opportunity of letting ministers go to pray?"

Baker planted his 250-pound frame firmly on the sidewalk. "You do not have a permit to parade."

"Mr. Baker," Vivian said, "you have three choices: you can let us pass or you can beat us or you can arrest us, but we are going to go on."

Baker didn't get a chance to answer. Vivian swerved on one foot and abruptly the brigade did a column right and jogged doubletime between the brick apartment houses. Confederates leaped out of their cars. Baker and his men dashed down a back street and came abreast of the charging clergymen in a small clearing between the rectangular apartment buildings.

Baker and Vivian found themselves face-to-face. Vivian tried to push forward; the priests around him pushed against policemen; the policemen pushed back. There were yells and oaths and the sounds of scuffling feet. Baker was outraged. "Stop pushing me," he yelled at Vivian, his strong voice loud so the crowd could hear. "A man of God pushing me. I can't believe it. A minister defying the law. A man of God committing violence." Vivian ran to the right, attempting to duck between another row of buildings, the clerics moving en masse behind him. Again police cut them off. There was more scuffling. "Put on record that the violence here was by the ministers," Baker snapped at the throng of newsmen who crowded into the small housing project garden area. A nun reached up and tapped a burly trooper on the shoulder. "The flowers," she said. "You're standing all over these poor people's flowers."

A Soil Conservation company moved into position on Lawrence Street, directly behind the project. State troopers stood rows deep on each side of the clearing. City police moved in from the rear. The Bible Brigade was surrounded. The clergymen stopped moving forward. They lined up and held an impromptu prayer service for Reverend Reeb. The second-story windows of the project buildings were jammed with women and children looking out at the strange confrontation in their yard. Cameramen scrambled to rooftop vantage points.

Vivian told the clergymen to face down the Confederates blocking the path. Baker ordered newsmen out of the area. "I declare this to be an unlawful assembly," he said. "If it is not disbanded in sixty seconds, I will arrest Vivian." Vivian exploded into Baker's face: "You would arrest a Negro, but not a white. This is an example of your racism. Why else would you arrest a Negro? If one of us is wrong, all of us are wrong. This is the injustice of Alabama."

Baker looked bemusedly at Vivian. The clergymen began to chant, "All of us, all go, all go, arrest us all." They locked arms and stood their ground. Baker laughed. "Oh no," he said. "Not all of you. I'm not going to arrest all these priests." Again Vivian berated him. "You're putting on a good show, Vivian, but you're not faking me," Baker said. He ordered his policemen to turn their backs on the Bible Brigade. The confrontation settled into a standoff. The nuns and the ministers sang "We Shall Overcome" and "Glory, Glory Hallelujah." A band of *jeunesse* joined the clerics and sang "Ain't gonna let Captain Baker turn me round, turn me round." Baker winked at Vivian; the minister smiled back. Thirty minutes later, the Bible Brigade disbanded, retreating to Brown's Chapel. It was not, however, a moment of goodwill. As the Confederate forces pulled back, one of the green-clad Soil Conservation officers said to a comrade: "Boy, would I like to beat the head in of one of those agitating nuns."

A week later, a lone picket paraded in front of St. Patrick's Cathedral in Manhattan. He carried a sign that said: "How can Catholic priests defy a police line? How can they disobey the law?" In the unreal world of Selma, Alabama, it seemed very reasonable for men of God to break the law of man.

[THE INFILTRATION]

We are on the one-yard line...Do we let the Negroes go over for a touchdown...or do we raise the Confederate flag as did our forefathers and tell them, "You shall not pass"?

—Eugene "Bull" Connor, to the Selma White Citizen's Council

THE GOON WITH THE PAINT CAN laughed a lot as he sprayed green paint on the white girl's hair. He was aiming toward her neck, trying to get the paint to run down inside her blouse, when the spray faltered and then stopped. He shook the can and pressed hard on the button, but it was out of air. The container made an empty clatter as it hit the sidewalk.

Negroes were there—many of them—but they made dull targets. You could get a nigger anytime. But here was a white girl, cowering with the small group of Negroes against the plate-glass window of the Selma Chevrolet Agency. She was irresistible. Her green-spattered hair now matched the face of a little Negro girl, the goon's second victim. Now he was opening a can of black motor oil, to darken the white girl's legs. That was what she deserved, coming uptown on a Saturday afternoon with all those niggers.

The Chevrolet Agency is on Lauderdale Street, next to the Dallas County Courthouse. It was a very bad place to be for the seventeen Negroes and the white SNCC girl. They had infiltrated uptown from Sylvan Street in twos and threes, regrouped several blocks from the courthouse, marching triumphantly the rest of the way. But possemen moved in and prodded them with clubs toward the auto agency. Over one hundred white citizens of Selma stood on the sidewalk opposite them, silent, staring, abrasive. After months of demonstrations, and the long, frustrating week of rebellion on Sylvan Street, the hourglass measure of patience of these people had played out. It was the talk of the town: the police were getting soft. They weren't doing their job. They weren't cracking Negroes' heads. It was a mob reaction. The goon was joined by several compatriots on the perimeter of the small band of infiltrators, now kneeling in prayer on the grease-stained concrete. The gathering mob across Lauderdale Street looked on, morbid.

Brown-shirted sheriff's deputies, led by Chief Deputy L. C. Crocker, stalked up. A deputy shoved his club under the throat of a young Negro girl and the group stopped praying. The warring command posts of Wilson Baker and Jim Clark have a status of forces agreement in Selma: the courthouse was in the sheriff's domain. That was why it was a very bad place for the Negroes and the white girl. The goon and his friends listened intently to the dialogue between Crocker and King's assistant, eighteen-year-old Jimmy Webb. They liked what they heard. Webb asked the chief deputy to escort the small group through the hostile streets of downtown Selma, back to Sylvan Street.

"I'm not going to give you any protection," Crocker answered. It was late afternoon. Soon it would be dark. The whites smiled.

Webb pressed the chief deputy on the issue of equal justice under the law—and prayer. "I don't have to pray for anybody I don't wanta'," Crocker said.

"You've got to learn to love before you can pray," the white girl with the green hair said to Crocker.

His head snapped up. "You just pray for your little niggers—and you leave me alone."

One white, giant slug of a man stood almost in the center of the little group. His head craned slowly back and forth between Crocker and Webb. As he made a studious effort to follow the conversation, he whistled mean and low.

"I can't do anything for you," Crocker said. "I don't have enough men to provide protection. If anything happens to you, fill out a form and file a complaint and then we'll look into it. And I'm not going to block you off or arrest you. I'm just going to leave you here and let you fend for yourself." The chief deputy and his assistants turned their backs and walked away, leaving the infiltrators to the townspeople of Selma. More whites moved in to reinforce the goon and his friends. At the intersection, a patrol of Selma's white *jeunesse*—tough kids from the white high school, complete with sideburns and razor cuts—pulled up in an open convertible. The sidewalk line of whites stretched from corner to corner. "I'm going to take that little nigger over there to the barber's and give him a haircut—right down to his neck," said one of the whites. "What do you want, freedom? You black pig asses got more freedom than you deserve," said the goon. It was a very tense moment.

SUDDENLY, A WHITE CHRYSLER stopped in the middle of the street. Wilson Baker got out. He pushed his way into the center of the quiet band of infiltrators. He looked very worried. Webb asked Baker for protection. The public safety director looked at the line of whites across the street. Then he looked at the loose circle of toughs forming around the Negroes. "I don't know how I'm going to give you protection," he said. "I will try to get you back to the rest of your group and you'll have protection there." Baker told them to walk to the corner, quickly, and turn right onto the street that led through town, back to the housing project.

The infiltrators held a conference. They were young and indecisive. They had come this far, got all the way uptown. Now they didn't know what to do. "Maybe we should stay here and pray," one boy suggested. *"Come on,"* Baker said. "For Christ's sake get *out* of here." His urgent tones startled the patrol. Then, for the first time, they realized the dimensions of the white crowd across the street; they understood the meaning of the goon with the spray can. They were scared. They moved awkwardly down the sidewalk and began to sing, weakly, hesitantly, "We Shall Overcome."

Baker ignored the whites. He didn't say one word to them. But his presence silenced them. The goon and his friends followed on the heels of the retreating infiltrators. The mob across the street moved also. People who had been watching from parked cars started their engines. The white punks in the open convertible double-parked where the infiltrators would have to pass. *"Come on,"* said the patrol's one-man escort, "move faster." The Negroes and the white girl, still indecisive, slowed down. They took short, casual steps, like they were window-shopping.

Baker urged them: "I don't have all day. You know what's going to happen to you if I leave you here alone." Still, the infiltrators moved devilishly slow, back toward Sylvan Street. The group of whites walking behind them was larger now. A long line of cars, led by the white *jeunesse,* kept apace on the street. The unreal procession passed a Selma billiard parlor. The whites inside pressed angrily against the window—their faces gargoyles of hatred. They were shocked and furious to see Negroes uptown in a group. Some of the players put on their coats and rushed outside to join the white mob. Beads of perspiration came to Baker's forehead. "Please, move on…You know these cars behind you are unsafe."

SATURDAY SHOPPERS WERE EN ROUTE HOME. Their cars slowed down as they passed the Negroes. A woman cursed. Hate stares abounded—from the passing cars, from people in parked cars. Still, the infiltrators moved sluggishly, taunting the whites, testing them, teasing Baker. Finally, the even-tempered public safety director lost his composure. He threw up his hands. "All right, I've done all I can. If you want this trouble, I just can't keep you from it." He stepped into the street and hailed the white Chrysler that had been driven alongside by an aide. He got in and the car sped away. The white *jeunesse* in the convertible raced up, parallel to the Negroes. The punks who were walking behind closed in, menacing, insulting. "Marchin' the cows back home." "Bunch of brown-nosed niggers, makes me sick." One white teenager ran up behind a frightened Negro and hit him, hard, on the head. Another sent a fast kick toward the groin of a small Negro boy. The goon with the motor oil threw a rock at the white girl's neck. A block behind, a mob about fifty strong closed in.

But Baker came back. He had changed his mind. He knew that only he could save the infiltrators. "Knock it off," he yelled at the whites. He was angry with the white punks, even angrier with the snail-paced Negroes. Jimmy Webb, who was setting the provocative pace, sneered at Baker's exhortations to hurry. "We can take a leisurely walk if we want to," he needled. More brawny teenagers joined the young whites in the open car. They sat on the trunk, grinning, watching. A white punk on a motorcycle joined the caravan. Webb halted the infiltrators at a corner. "Let's take our time crossing." This was too much for Baker. "Are you trying to get these kids killed?" he asked. Then he grabbed Webb's green cardigan and motioned the Chrysler over to the curb. Webb was shoved inside. "You're under arrest, Jimmy. You can take your time going to jail." The project was still two blocks away.

The infiltrators balked at the corner. "We won't move until Jimmy is released," the girl with the green hair said. Baker grabbed her arm firmly and took her across the street. Then he hustled the next Negro across the intersection. A detective began to grab the Negroes and rush them across the street. He started roughing them up. Baker touched his arm, motioned for him to take it easy. The back entrance to the project was now a half block away, and the mob, fearful of losing its prey, moved almost on top of the young Negroes. Baker begged them to keep moving. They faltered, disorganized, drifting aimlessly toward the project. One of the whites kicked a Negro girl in the back.

Baker's face was taut. He was thoroughly exasperated with the Negroes. "You can't do anything when you're dealing with fools." The retreating group hesitated to cross over to Lawrence Street, which runs in back of the project. The white punks raced by in their open convertible, making obscene gestures at the Negroes. Another mob—about fifteen hard-faced, rough white men—were grouped in front of a grocery store near the Lawrence Street corner. They shouted threats as the infiltrators walked by; some of them shook their fists and ran up to the Negroes. "So you want to mix with the white folks."

"Don't you know enough to stay where you belong?"

"You'll get your freedom at the bottom of a river." This was the first time that week a mob of whites had gathered outside the project; it was a bad sign. The town was in an ugly mood.

Confederate forces encircled the entire housing project. A solid line of state troopers and Soil Conservation agents parted, allowing the infiltrators to enter the sanctuary of Sylvan Street. Once inside the project, the Negroes broke into a run, rushing to tell their friends about their exciting patrol. Baker's relief was visible. His shoulders dropped an inch. He looked very tired. Norris McNamara, a *Time* photographer who had been covering the Selma demonstrations for many weeks, went up to him. "Mr. Baker, that was a very decent thing you just did." Baker looked at the photographer. He was surprised and a little embarrassed at the compliment. "The niggers don't appreciate it," he said.

[SHADOW BRIGADE]

From the window of the U.S. Attorney's office in Selma, on the third floor of the gray-stone Federal Building, observers representing the United States of America have an excellent view of the Dallas County Courthouse across the street. It was from these windows that FBI agents, as long ago as October 1963, watched as Sheriff Clark's deputies beat and arrested two Negroes for taking food and water to friends who had been standing all day in line in the vain hope of registering to vote. And from these windows, beginning January 18, 1965, observers from the United States Department of Justice witnessed the blatant, triumphant, and brutal violation of the constitutional rights of some three thousand Selma Negroes who were cursed, beaten, spit upon, kicked, and arrested by officials of Dallas County, Alabama. Their "crime" was their pitiful attempt to gain the franchise to vote.

The laws of the United States of America give power to federal officers to make immediate arrests when, in their presence, a person's right to vote is abridged or a person seeking to fulfill that right is intimidated. Yet, despite the bloody view from the Federal Building in Selma, no arrests were made. Instead, the federal representatives remained in the strict role of observers—watching, taking notes, transmitting horror stories to Washington—remaining in the background just like the observers of a "friendly foreign power" should in a country that is experiencing serious internal strife. In terms of direct intervention by Washington, Selma might just as well have been Switzerland. The Negroes who were being beaten and kicked for trying to vote asked only that Washington act in Selma as it had acted in Saigon. After all, they said, Selma was closer to home.

But Washington remained distant. A few more observers were sent to Selma, work was begun on a new civil rights bill, and Attorney General Nicholas deB. Katzenbach explained to a *New York Times* reporter why the government could not send a platoon of federal marshals to Selma: This would be possible, Katzenbach said, only if Washington had "three or four days notice" of what was going to happen and assurance that the marshals would be needed for "not longer than seven or eight days." It is not recorded whether Mr. Katzenbach subsequently requested Sheriff Clark and Colonel Lingo, as Southern gentlemen, to do the honorable thing and inform Washington four days in advance the next time they planned to gas and beat Negroes. Katzenbach also said that he "hoped and prayed" the Washington government would not have to grant the urgent requests from the Union forces to send federal troops into Selma. Sending troops, Katzenbach said, was a "very serious step." He said the primary job of law enforcement "rests and should rest with the local authorities." Local authorities like Sheriff Jim Clark and Colonel Al Lingo.

When the Union cause was abandoned in the South toward the end of Reconstruction, the Confederacy was left free to have "local authorities" regulate Negroes as they saw fit, regardless of the law of the rest of the land. That law, administered by Southern officials, becomes something entirely different in Albany, Georgia, than it is in Albany, New York. But the attorney general, unlike his predecessor Robert Kennedy, did not deny that the federal government had sufficient powers to intervene to protect the life and limb and American citizenship rights of Negroes in Confederate states. Katzenbach came right out and said the government had the powers, all right. But he said it didn't want to use them. Meanwhile, President Johnson was busy running the war ten thousand miles away and didn't hear the battle cries at home. Only after Bloody Sunday, March 7, did the fact that the South was at war again assume a measure of reality for him. The fifth—and, in many ways, the most significant of the Battles of Selma—was the campaign that was waged to align the "Shadow Brigade"—the might of the "friendly foreign power" in Washington—on the Union side. It was a battle that was fought on many fronts.

[THE BATTLE OF SELMA]

The main front, of course, was Selma. The Union forces there knew exactly what they were doing: they were creating a crisis; they were capturing the imagination of the country; they were reviving the sagging momentum of the civil rights movement. But most of all, they were asking Washington to act.

The plaintive requests for action—for legislation, for troops to break up the conspiracy against freedom maintained in the Confederacy

—came out of Selma in many ways: from the diminutive nun, her habit crowned with a makeshift cellophane rain bonnet, who kicked up her sensible black walking shoes in a demure gesture of defiance as she chanted, "We want freedom, we want freedom"; from the enthusiastic Negro *jeunesse,* who stood in the rain for three days and two nights serenading the Confederate forces; from the elderly rabbi who stared in disbelief at the block upon block of Alabama police cars massed at Sylvan Street, saying over and over to himself, like a cantor in the synagogue, "Insane, insane..."; from Cager Lee, the eighty-two-year-old grandfather of the murdered Jimmie Lee Jackson, who walked in the front line with Dr. Martin Luther King Jr. on the Great March to Montgomery, and said, "Yes, it was worth the boy's dyin'"; from Mrs. James Reeb, who stood bravely in front of a battery of microphones in the Birmingham hospital where her husband had died and told the Southern reporters that the cause of equality was so important that if her husband had to die for it, she accepted his death.

[THE ALTAR FRONT]

The fifth battle of Selma was fought also from the pews and pulpits of the nation. Not all clergymen came to Selma, but there were few in those black days of shock and crisis after Bloody Sunday who did not talk about it. Many of the ministers and priests and rabbis who went to Alabama found themselves surprised at their own militancy. Even more surprising, perhaps, was the very tough talk in the sermons and statements of clerics across the country. They thought Selma was inexcusable. They thought the federal government should be doing something about it. They said so. The prayers and the petitions, for the most part, weren't directed against Governor Wallace. They were directed to Lyndon Johnson. They demanded action.

One of the gentlest of the Negro leaders in Washington, a holy man, gave a measure of the new militance when he said grimly, upon hearing that the Reverend Reeb had died: "If the president and the attorney general had done what we asked them to and sent marshals to Selma on Monday, Jim Reeb would have been walking safe on the highway to Montgomery. I can't help saying it: they're partly responsible for his death. Not just Wallace."

Two ministerial delegations arrived at President Johnson's oval office to demand that troops be sent to Alabama. They were blunt in their questioning and scornful of many of the president's answers. Johnson, shocked by their militance, took to reading them passages from his old civil rights speeches to show he really was on the Negroes' side. The clergymen went away openly dissatisfied.

Young ministers and priests were outspokenly skeptical of Johnson's new voting bill. They questioned the willingness of the administration to face down, with force if necessary, the "wicked exercise of fascist power" in Alabama, in enforcing the bill. One minister made the analogy to last year's civil rights bill: "The new civil rights law lets a black man get a room in a motel—so he can lie awake all night and wonder when the bomb is going off."

Clergymen who had been to Selma returned to their pulpits to tell their fascinated congregations bleak stories of brutality—and inspiring tales of human dedication. Through all the sermons and the prayers ran one constant theme: brave people are bearing witness; why isn't the government doing what is necessary to protect them? Administration officials, visited by irate clerics, found themselves on the defensive. And President Johnson, for the first time, found himself under attack from the pulpits. Typical was the comment of Dr. Duncan Howlett of All Souls Unitarian Church in Washington, D.C., a church where the Reverend Reeb was once assigned. Dr. Howlett blasted Johnson for meeting with Confederate president Wallace. Johnson might just as well spend his time receiving "a delegation from the Communist Party," the minister said.

[THE STREET FRONT]

In his third-floor office in the Brotherhood of Sleeping Car Porters' headquarters in Harlem, Bayard Rustin turned thumbs down on the idea of a second March on Washington, in protest over Selma. "If I've learned anything," the organizer of the historic Washington march said, "I've learned that you don't repeat yourself." He said this with the particular poignancy of a man who had staged an enormously successful school boycott in New York City one year, then followed it with a complete flop the next.

The place for a Selma protest march, Rustin said, was Harlem. The Negro leaders in the room agreed and proceeded to plan a Sunday afternoon demonstration that brought fifteen thousand people out into the Harlem streets.

They picked wordings for signs: "We Demand Federal Registrars"; "We Demand Federal Marshals"; "Let Black Men March in Selma." (The word "Negro," Rustin said, can get you into trouble in Harlem; you've got to say "black man.") Someone suggested a sign that said: "Back King in Selma." Rustin anticipated protests over that: "Now, I know that some of you are going to point out that SNCC was in Selma long before King was, but we ought to realize the situation and realize the importance of keeping Martin's name up on top." Nobody said anything. The sign stayed.

Rustin's secretary came into the room. She reported, in icy tones, that President Johnson had sent yellow roses to the Birmingham hospital bedside of the dying Reverend Reeb. "Flowers instead of marshals, that's what they give us. That's really big of him," she said.

A Negro leader nodded. "It couldn't have been worse with Goldwater. At least, not much worse," he said.

Rustin himself, speaking on Sunday during the mass march in Harlem, expressed the impatience and criticism that was being directed toward the White House from similar rallies all over the country. "Oh, President Johnson, don't make us black folks any more angry, please," he said, in measured tones.

And across the nation, from Casper, Wyoming, the birthplace of the Reverend James Reeb, to Philadelphia's Independence Hall, the birthplace of the nation, vigils and protests, marches and mass meetings were being held, day and night—an unprecedented national burst of empathy with the beleaguered Union forces in Selma. Demonstrators walked in fountains in San Francisco, fasted for thirty hours in Albuquerque and marched fifty miles in subfreezing weather in Wisconsin.

In San Mateo, California, the nineteen-year-old son of a Jewish couple who had escaped the ovens of Germany during the Second World War left a note for his parents explaining why he had to go to Selma:

Dear Mom and Dad:

Why must I go? I feel it necessary to explain—to you—to you who must bear the burden.

If I were to dedicate my life to anything—it would be that *no* man would ever have to suffer these tortures of lesser ones. *No,* they aren't killing 6,000,000 in Selma—but if they kill six is it any less of an indictment? Is it more excusable?

If Joe Brown is told he is inferior and his rights denied him, are we any less guilty for closing *our* eyes? I think not.

I cannot allow the world to forget your parents—it is this I dedicate myself to. Let each man stand with his head high and then let us talk of a "Great Society."

Why Selma? It is time the President moves. We've had enough stalls—enough evasion.

The time has come for man to stand and be proud.

Now! 1965. Not 1990!

Now! Selma is the start of making 1965 that year. If it does not start successfully—it will fail. If we fail—then we will all bear the shame.

Whatever I can do to help—I will. Make an attempt not to worry. Remember I am doing what I must do.

Please, try to *understand.*

With all of my love,

Your son—David Landsberg.

[THE INTERNATIONAL FRONT]

The battery of war correspondents who sat in Selma's majestic Albert Hotel and dispatched millions of words about the South at War opened a front that the Confederates hadn't counted upon. Their reports angered the conscience of the nation—and of the world. There was sympathy abroad for the Confederate cause during the Civil War one hundred years ago. But the war waged by the South in 1965—the war against the Negro—provoked different reactions, reactions that Washington took note of:

From Rome—"The plague of intolerance toward Negroes continues to be the central most difficult problem in democratic America, something which is a bad example…for other countries. Intolerance infects most sectors of white America and makes ex-colonial peoples mistrust Washington's policies, with the result that they turn to Communist powers whose oppressive methods are protected by silence. America will only be the moral as well as political leader of the free world when its twenty million Negro citizens have the same rights as whites…rights now being fought for in Selma, Alabama."

From Rio—Everyone agrees that the United States is giving itself a terrible reputation with underdeveloped countries. Johnson is showing, by his recent statements concerning sit-ins at the White House, that he is more interested in the Negro vote than in the Negro problem. Rio's daily *Journal do Brasil*, usually pro-American, was exasperated with the events in Selma. They published a front-page picture of a Negro being beaten and dragged across a Selma street by the jacket. The newspaper commented: "It always ends the same way."

From Cambodia—*Ramparts'* correspondent Robert Scheer found an ironic reaction: This country is so worried and preoccupied with events in Vietnam, it has no time for expressions of concern over the war in Selma. United States forces in Alabama cannot divert our attention from the United States military adventure in Southeast Asia.

From London—First reaction in Britain toward the news of violence in Alabama was one of anger. This was expressed in a *Manchester Guardian* editorial drawing attention to the supreme brutality of club and truncheon and asking whether the ability of the Negro to refrain from violence can last much longer. The *Guardian* criticized America's use of "tools of the jungle" against peaceful marchers.

[THE WASHINGTON FRONT]

One of the young SNCC workers who saw the president on the Saturday following Bloody Sunday had the audacity to rebuke Johnson for worrying over the sleep that Luci and Lynda had lost during the unprecedented civil rights demonstrations at the White House. "A lot of people in Selma didn't sleep last night, either," the SNCC worker said, "and your daughters can just stay awake until the troopers stop beating us up in Selma." This shocked Lyndon Johnson. But it was just one in a series of shocks in a week when the president learned that he is going to have an extremely difficult time arriving at a government by consensus if some of the people contributing to that consensus are racists and white supremacists.

Lyndon Johnson, the master manipulator, had made perhaps the greatest political miscalculation of his political life: he underestimated the speed and intensity of the nation's reaction to Selma. People were horrified. They were grieved. They were angry. They sought a catharsis. They looked to the White House—but they found nothing. No call for a day of contrition and mourning, no statement of outrage, no personal presence in Selma, no symbolic arrest of Sheriff Clark or Colonel Lingo. Nothing but an announcement that there would be a new voting rights act as soon as the lawyers could finish drafting it. Wait calmly, please. This cold reaction, mixed with the hot feelings about Selma, caused a storm over the capital. The White House had its first sit-ins. Pickets marched up and down Pennsylvania Avenue. The capital was in a ferment.

Slowly, cautiously, the "friendly foreign power" in Washington began to exercise the powers of its omnipresent Shadow Brigade. Alabama was, after all, within its sphere of influence. At the Justice Department, where demonstrators were sitting-in in the hallways, Attorney General Katzenbach borrowed an enlarged map of Alabama from the Agriculture Department and spread it out on his red carpet. John Doar, who has the civil rights desk at the Justice Department, was in Selma and kept his boss posted on developments by two "hot" lines that fed into an office squawk box. LeRoy Collins, a man the administration can trust to slow things down when it is desirable, was dispatched to Selma as Johnson's ambassador to the Union forces. (The Civil Rights Commission, which conceivably could become spokesman for the civil rights movement, as the Commerce Department is for business, is not trusted by the administration.) Justice Department attorneys were dispatched to plead the Union case for the right to march the fifty miles to Montgomery, in federal court.

The Washington government responded, in a halfway fashion, to the

impassioned request for troops. Johnson put some seven hundred soldiers on alert in the early morning shortly after the Reverend Reeb was
fatally clubbed in Selma—but it was too late to save the minister. The
troops were never sent. And Johnson, after a summit meeting with the
petulant Confederate president George Wallace, nationalized the 1,863
Alabama National Guardsmen and sent them—along with 1,000 U.S.
Army troops, 100 FBI men, and 100 federal marshals (the marshals had
four-days' notice, this time)—to guard the Great March to Montgomery, finally made by the Union forces.

This United States intervention followed a pattern of clumsy moves
by the "friendly foreign power," which only served to aggravate conditions. On Tuesday, when Collins bargained with the Confederates for
the standoff at the bridge, presumably to help Union president Martin
Luther King, King ended up with a damaged reputation and split forces.
On Wednesday, Collins worked late into the evening at Brown's Chapel
parsonage and effected an agreement with Selma officials, that would
have allowed Union forces to march to the courthouse. But Mayor
Smitherman balked—then tore up the script.

President Johnson, the great legislator, sees a law—his voting bill—
as the answer to the pickets and the demonstrators who have been disturbing the domestic tranquility of the "Great Society." The voting law
is strong, and if enforced could be effective, but it is only offering the
Negroes what they were tendered one hundred years ago but never
really received. The lesson of the Battle of Selma is that laws alone will
not "get the Negroes out of the streets." In 1963 Negroes went into the
streets over public accommodations and President Kennedy thought
a public-accommodations law would get them out. Instead, Negroes
in Selma went back into the streets over voting rights. Now President
Johnson thinks a voting rights law will get them out. But next the
Negroes will go into the streets over jobs. And housing. And getting
the schools *really* integrated. That is the strategic lesson of the Battle of
Selma. The Union forces don't want limited victories; they want uncon-
ditional surrender: they want *all* their rights. Until the federal government understands this, and assumes the leadership to give Negroes their
full rights of citizenship, there will be more Selmas.

[*Ramparts*, June 1965]

The "Vietnam Lobby"*

AMONG THE STACKS OF WOOD-BASED ENGRAVINGS filed in dusty pyramids in the *New Leader*'s editorial offices is a generously-sized, full-faced reproduction of the late Ngo Dinh Diem. The typed label on the back that used to identify Diem as "Vietnam's Democratic Alternative" has been torn off. The steel plate is worn from rubbing, face down, against the shellacked surface of the public school surplus-type furniture in the magazine's quarters in the old social democratic Rand School Building on New York's still-cobblestoned 15th Street.

The *New Leader*'s cut file is a strange place to begin the story of the "Vietnam Lobby," but then it is a strange story. It is the history of a small and enthusiastic group of people—including a cardinal, an ex-Austrian socialist leader, and a CIA agent—who maneuvered the Eisenhower administration and the American press into supporting the rootless, unpopular, and hopeless regime of a despot and believed it actually was all an exercise in democracy. That this group was able to accomplish this against the better thoughts of Eisenhower and over the traditional wariness of the press is testimony to its power and its persuasiveness. Another chapter of the history of the "Vietnam Lobby" is how its thesis came to be accepted by a broad consensus of liberals and intellectuals in America—a consensus that only recently has begun to splinter and is still largely intact.

The thesis is based on an overriding belief in the beauty of the American way of life—and in the nefarious nature of communism. It is the belief that the only reason a nation might vote communistic is because it hasn't been properly exposed to the democratic way of life: If a people know democracy, they will vote democratic. And if it becomes necessary on occasion to tolerate undemocratic means to achieve the ulti-

Coauthored with Robert Scheer

mate democratic goal—well, it is all for the people's own good. For the *New Leader,* a liberal, militantly anticommunist biweekly with a strong belief in social reform, this theory was naturally applicable to the case of Diem, a firm anticommunist. The *New Leader* in 1959 hailed Diem's "Democratic One-Man Rule." To the school of liberalism where anti-communism is the *sine qua non,* the idea of a "Democratic One-Man Rule" is not an anomaly.

The story of the "Vietnam Lobby" is a case study in American politics from the mid-fifties to the early sixties, and the role of the *New Leader* in that period is worth singling out for special attention because the magazine played a smaller but similar role in spreading the thesis of the nation's most famous pressure group—the China Lobby. The dis-illusioned idealists and ex-radicals that C. Wright Mills once dubbed "the NATO intellectuals" were prominent in both lobbies. Like the *New Leader,* they were willing to believe the best about anything or anyone anticommunist.

THE HISTORY OF THE "VIETNAM LOBBY" dates from a meeting in a Tokyo tea room in 1950. There Wesley Fishel, a young Michigan State University political scientist, had a serious conversation with Ngo Dinh Diem. Diem was in the seventeenth year of a self-imposed exile. A sort of Catholic mandarin, he was by family background, personal inclina-tion, and training, a member of Vietnam's feudal aristocracy. The man-darin sense of survival called for cooperation with the French, and Diem had risen to the rank of governor of Phat Diem Province in the French colonial civil service. A militant anticommunist, in 1933 he helped the French fight the Communists who were then leading the Vietnamese anticolonial revolt. But Diem decided that France and Vietnam were incompatible, and went into exile. It is illustrative of his character that he chose voluntary exile rather than remain in his country and fight with the "masses" (which included the Communists) against the French. Diem was a firm believer in the ways of God dictating the acts of men. He would wait for some Hegelian force to sweep him back onto the center-stage of his country's history. Providence, in 1950, took the form of Wesley Fishel.

The young professor was impressed by Diem's long wait to rule his country and his views on independent nationalism, anticommunism, and social reform. Fishel urged Diem to come to the United States to seek this government's support. When Diem agreed, Fishel arranged for Michigan State to sponsor the trip. On the Michigan State campus, Diem found kinship and support among both faculty and administration—a relationship which later developed into the university's extensive aid project to Diem's government, where a team of some twenty professors did everything from drafting his budgets to training his secret police. Outside the academic world, Diem found support in the hierarchy of the Catholic Church. Diem's brother, Bishop Can, arranged for the Vietnamese exile to stay in Maryknoll seminaries in New Jersey and New York. This was Cardinal Spellman's territory, and the cardinal and the Vietnamese mandarin soon developed a close relationship. And no wonder. Diem was an anticommunist *and* he was a Catholic. His brother was even a bishop. One could not approach the cardinal with better credentials.

In addition to the academicians and the clerics, Diem found to his surprise that he had a strong appeal with American liberals and intellectuals. When Diem was in the United States, from 1950 to 1953, Senator Joseph McCarthy was on the loose and liberals felt it mandatory to show their anticommunism. The liberal-intellectual world was still quaking from the shocks of the loss of China, the Korean War, and the conviction of Alger Hiss. To suggest dealing with Communists—*any* Communists—on any terms was unthinkable in this climate. Yet Communist forces in Asia had monopolized the undeniably popular twin battle cries: nationalism and social reform. The liberals searched for a "third way." They thought they found it in the anticommunist Diem as the leader of a "free" Vietnam. To think that the Vietnamese people would suddenly give to an absentee aristocrat the credit and gratitude for the fruits of the twenty-year anticolonial war the communists had been leading against the French was, to say the least, naively optimistic. It also ignored Vietnamese history. It proved disastrous. The same tragic results were to occur a decade later when, again ignoring recent history, the Kennedy-Johnson administrations followed the same fruitless military path of the French before them.

One of the first liberals to openly champion Diem was inveterate traveler and Supreme Court justice William O. Douglas. Justice Douglas had just returned, discouraged, from a visit to Vietnam. An influx of American military aid hadn't helped the French in their losing war against Ho Chi Minh's Viet Minh forces. The Viet Minh clearly had the support of the people; but the Viet Minh were communist-led, and thus clearly unacceptable as leaders of Vietnam. Then Douglas met Diem in Washington and became enthusiastic. The justice arranged a breakfast with senators Mike Mansfield and John F. Kennedy and introduced them to Diem. Both men were taken with him. And during the next few years, before Dien Bien Phu, both Mansfield and Kennedy were extremely critical of the French presence in Vietnam and of the Eisenhower administration's support of them.

They called for an "independent nationalist alternative," a phrase which later was to become a cliché. Kennedy, in a major speech immediately before the Geneva Conference in April of 1954, warned against any negotiated solution that would allow participation in the Vietnamese government by Ho Chi Minh. The communists, he said, would then eventually take over because they were so popular. Instead, he called for an independent—i.e., a democratic and anticommunist—Vietnam, supported by the United States. This Vietnam Diem was to lead.

The Geneva Conference, of course, called for no such thing. It affirmed the independence of the colonial government of Vietnam and called for an end to hostilities. A sort of interim trustee arrangement was agreed upon whereby the French would preside in the south and the Viet Minh in the north for two years, ending in national elections in 1956 when the Vietnamese people would choose their own government. Those elections were never held because the "Vietnam Lobby" didn't want them. Clearly, Ho Chi Minh would have won a popular vote—and that would have been the end of the "independent nationalistic alternative." Thus men as diverse in their backgrounds as Spellman, Douglas, and Kennedy—not to mention John Foster Dulles—came to support an aggressive policy against a popular adversary in the name of freedom, and to believe in it.

THE TELEPHONE OPERATOR IN THE CHANCERY was used to such things, but even she blinked a little when Cardinal Spellman picked up the telephone and said: "Get me Joe Kennedy." When these two powerful

men got on the line together, one winter afternoon in 1955, they settled quickly, as men of decision do, the steps that had to be taken to
swing the wavering Eisenhower administration solidly behind the young
regime of Premier Ngo Dinh Diem. The report of this extraordinary
conversation comes from Joseph Buttinger, an official of the International Rescue Committee, who was sitting in Spellman's office. Buttinger had just returned from Saigon, and he brought bad news. Diem's
administration was in trouble. Buttinger thought Diem was the only
hope of Vietnam, but needed to consolidate his power. There was
opposition from the Vietnamese, from the French, and from some key
Americans. Diem could not survive without increased United States
support, yet the present United States commitment appeared in danger of waning. Eisenhower's special ambassador to Vietnam, General J.
Lawton Collins, was openly sceptical of Diem's ability to establish a
viable regime. The journalist Joseph Alsop felt Diem's base of support
was too narrow to effectively rival the popular Viet Minh. Eisenhower
himself was not particularly sympathetic to Diem. The general recognized Ho Chi Minh's popularity, and was opposed to the effort to install
an "alternative" as both undemocratic and of dubious success, as he later
remarked in his book *Mandate for Change.*

But the Eisenhower administration, not noted for its rigidity of purpose, was vulnerable to the political pressures marshaled by Cardinal
Spellman and the elder Kennedy. Kennedy arranged for Buttinger to
meet with Senator Mansfield and some key State Department personnel in Washington. His son, Senator John F. Kennedy, was in California,
but Buttinger had a long conversation with the senator's assistant, Ted
Sorensen. Spellman took care of the press. He set up meetings for Buttinger with editors of the *New York Times,* the editorial board of the *New
York Herald Tribune,* and key editors of both *Time* and *Life.* Two days later
the *Times* printed an editorial containing the Buttinger thesis. Buttinger
himself took pen in hand and wrote an article for the *Reporter* praising
Diem as democracy's "alternative" in Southeast Asia.

To fully appreciate Buttinger's role in the "Vietnam Lobby" it is necessary to go back to Diem's ascendance to the premiership in July 1954.
The new premier from his first day in office began to crush all opposition and concentrate power within a small, nepotistic group. Diem's
targets included the private armies of the religious sects, anticommunist

Vietnamese leaders who made the mistake of also being anti-Diem, and the identifiable Viet Minh partisans remaining in South Vietnam. This did not make for popular acclaim, but Diem wasn't looking for popularity. He knew that his base of support was minuscule, that he would have trouble with the majority of the population who had been supporting the Viet Minh in the long war against the French. So force was the only way he could effectively ready his people for the "democratic alternative." His authoritarian tactics were not widely reported in the American press until eight years later, when he fell from favor. Diem's strong-man rule in South Vietnam gave the United States two policy choices. It could keep the Viet Minh from power, block the scheduled 1956 national elections, prevent unification of the country, hang on, and trust for the best. Or it could follow the new French policy of flexibility in a hopeless situation, allow the elections, learn to live with an unquestionably greater Communist influence in Vietnam, and accept the necessary parallel of a lessening of Western power there.

There were arguments for both positions within the Eisenhower administration. Helpful in pushing the United States into a "hard line" of support for the authoritarian Diem was an unusual array of visitors to Saigon in the early days of the new premier's rule.

Cardinal Spellman, who told an American Legion Convention that the Geneva agreements meant "taps" for freedom in Southeast Asia, flew to Vietnam to hand-deliver the first check of Catholic Relief Agency aid. Wesley Fishel, the Michigan State University professor, took up residence in the Presidential Palace and became one of Diem's chief advisors. Also bedding down in the palace was Wolf Ladejinsky, a New Dealer who had stayed on in the Agriculture Department only to be plowed under in the McCarthy period. Diem hired Ladejinsky to study land reform, which convinced many American liberals that Diem was serious about social reforms. (These reforms proved later to be not only inefficient but laughable. Diem tried to restore the colonial property balance by returning to absentee landlords land that the bewildered peasants thought they owned—land the Communists had given them during the revolutionary period.)

Another important visitor to Diem was Leo Cherne, the president of the International Rescue Committee. Founded to help refugees from Germany in the Hitler period, the committee turned during the Cold

War to aiding refugees from Communist countries. Cherne spent two and a half weeks in Vietnam and came away convinced that Diem had great potential as an anticommunist leader. He then sent his assistant, Joseph Buttinger, to set up a Vietnam operation for the committee. There Buttinger met Colonel (now General) Edward Lansdale, the CIA's man in Saigon, hero of Eugene Burdick's *The Ugly American* and villain of Grahame Greene's *The Quiet American.* Lansdale, a gregarious former San Francisco advertising man who believes in "selling" the American way abroad, is given sole credit in David Wise's recent book on the CIA, *The Invisible Government,* for the United States support of Diem. That is not quite fair. It ignores the hard work of Cardinal Spellman and Buttinger. It was the unlikely triumvirate of the CIA man, the cardinal, and Buttinger, an ex-Austrian socialist leader, that was responsible for forming United States policy behind Diem.

Lansdale went through channels. He convinced CIA director Allen Dulles of Diem's worth. Dulles talked to his brother, the secretary of state. And John Foster Dulles brought the word to Eisenhower. Spellman's influence was important in certifying Diem as a solid anticommunist, no small thing in the McCarthy era. Buttinger made the contacts in the ex-radical and the liberal circles which were to eventually support the consensus of the "Vietnam Lobby" for the next six years.

Buttinger's background is important in understanding the eagerness with which he accepted Diem as the "alternative." A disillusioned socialist, Buttinger saw in the stocky, five-foot-five premier the nationalist answer to communism that he had himself attempted to provide as an Austrian socialist leader in the thirties. Buttinger was then one Gustav Richter, the provincial youth leader of the Social-Democratic party, which had been forced underground by the waves of victorious fascism. Buttinger fought back, but it was an embittering experience. His one accomplishment, he relates in his memoirs, *In the Twilight of Socialism,* was to halt the spread of the Communists. But just when Buttinger had reorganized his party, the Nazis goose-stepped in. He fled to Paris and then to New York, and in flight the certainty of his world of socialist politics vanished, and so did his ideology. Buttinger did not join the Socialist Party in America, though in a continuing search for new ideas to replace his fallen Marxist certainty he dabbled in socialist politics as an editor of *Dissent* magazine.

He took to Diem with the enthusiasm that can only be mustered by an ex-radical who, once again, has something to believe in. He had been in Vietnam only four days when, at Lansdale's request, he met Diem. He was to meet with him frequently during the ensuing three months. Lansdale took Buttinger under his wing and introduced him to the top security people in Diem's government and the Vietnamese army. This convinced Buttinger that Diem had the strength to remain in power, if only the United States would give him complete support. Before Buttinger left for the United States in December 1954, he had several five- and six-hour conversations with Diem. He returned a man with a mission: to settle for nothing less than a total commitment to Diem by the United States. With the aid of Lansdale and Cardinal Spellman, he succeeded, and the "Vietnam Lobby" was born.

THE "VIETNAM LOBBY" was an unusual alliance of ex-left intellectuals, conservative generals, and liberal politicians. Its primary goal was to convince the public that "free Vietnam" was accomplishing miracles and could withstand the Red onslaught if the United States would continue its support. One year after Buttinger's return from Vietnam, in the fall of 1955, the "lobby" achieved a measure of formal organization with the establishment of the American Friends of Vietnam. The Friends, for the next six years, were in the forefront of the fight to maintain Diem's regime as a "showcase of democracy."

Like all such organizations, the American Friends of Vietnam had a letterhead with a string of impressive names running in small print down the side. But the Friends' list was unusual because it was virtually a roll call of the liberal center: senators John F. Kennedy and Richard Neuberger, intellectuals Max Lerner and Arthur Schlesinger Jr., representatives Emmanuel Celler and Edna Kelly, diplomat Angier Biddle Duke. For balance, there was socialist Norman Thomas (who has since changed his position radically) and ultraconservative J. Bracken Lee. Two famous generals, "Wild Bill" Donovan and "Iron Mike" O'Daniel, were cochairmen.

The Friends was run by its fourteen-member executive committee. An analysis of the committee reveals a curious relationship between the Friends, the International Rescue Committee, and a New York fundraiser and public relations man named Harold Oram. The relationship is extraordinary because the executive committee of the International Rescue Committee, the executive committee of the American Friends of Vietnam, and Harold Oram's executive personnel were all pretty much the same people.

It was Oram, then public relations man for the International Rescue Committee and a former promoter of thirties' leftist causes, who later became associated with anticommunist and liberal center groups, and whom Buttinger first approached for help when he returned from Vietnam in late 1954. Oram arranged through a friend at the Catholic Relief Agency in Washington for Buttinger to meet with Cardinal Spellman.

Two months before the organization of the American Friends of Vietnam was announced, Oram's public relations firm signed a contract to represent the Vietnamese government for $3,000 a month plus expenses. They stayed on the job until 1961. Oram was a member of the executive committee of the American Friends of Vietnam. So was Elliot Newcomb, his partner at the time the contract was signed with the Diem regime. Newcomb left the firm a year later, but remained on the executive committee and was subsequently treasurer. The executive secretary, and later corporation secretary and assistant treasurer of the American Friends of Vietnam, was a young man named Gilbert Jonas— Oram's account executive and "campaign director" on the Vietnam account. Oram and Jonas were registered as foreign agents acting for the Republic of Vietnam during the same period they held key executive positions on the Friends, a seemingly independent committee dedicated to the blameless purpose of working "to extend more broadly a mutual understanding of Vietnamese and American history, cultural customs, and democratic institutions."

The interlocking directorates of the International Rescue Committee and the Friends was more to be expected than the strange connection between the Republic of Vietnam and the Friends of Vietnam. Nine of the fourteen directors of the Friends were also members of the board of directors of the International Rescue Committee, or were its employees. Both Leo Cherne and Joseph Buttinger were on the Friends' board. Cardinal Spellman was represented by Monsignor Hartnett, a key official of the Catholic Relief Agency. Two writers for the *New Leader,* Norbert Muhlen and Sol Sanders, were also on the executive committee of the

Friends. The anticommunism and quest for social reform that characterized the *New Leader* was typical of the philosophies of men on these two
groups: New Deal liberals like Leo Cherne and ex-radicals like Buttinger, Oram, and Jonas. Jonas later became public affairs director of the
International Rescue Committee and served on Kennedy's presidential
campaign staff in 1960 as an advisor on minority-group problems.

Oram earned his $3,000 a month. Diem was not always an easy man
to keep popular. His consolidation of power in Vietnam had authoritarian
overtones, and his off-the-cuff remarks were often blatantly undemocratic. The first task of the "Vietnam Lobby" was to package Diem as
a commodity palatable to the American public. The packaging operation assumed grand-scale proportions during Diem's triumphal "official
visit" to the United States in 1957. Diem landed aboard President Eisenhower's personal plane, addressed a joint session of Congress, then took
off for New York and breakfast with Cardinal Spellman. Mayor Robert
Wagner hailed him as the man "to whom freedom is the very breath of
life itself." At a dinner jointly sponsored by the International Rescue
Committee and the American Friends of Vietnam, Angier Biddle Duke
presented Diem with the Admiral Richard F. Byrd Award for "inspired
leadership in the cause of the free world."

Diem's American advisors took care that his speeches were liberally
salted with democratic clichés. Many of Diem's speeches were written
by Buttinger, others by Sol Sanders. Sanders, a Friends' director who
was writing articles on Southeast Asia for the *New Leader,* had been close
to Diem when the Vietnamese leader was in exile in America during
the early fifties. They enjoyed a poignant reunion, recalling those more
difficult times when both were low on funds and Diem would come into
New York by train from the Maryknoll seminary in Ossining and have
tea with Sanders in a Greenwich Village café. (Sanders, now an Asia correspondent for *U.S. News and World Report,* was one of Diem's few friends
who remained loyal to the end—even when he fell from U.S. favor.
To Sanders's credit, he resigned from the American Friends of Vietnam when the executive committee fired off a congratulatory telegram
to the generals who had deposed and murdered Diem. The telegram
arrived while Diem's body was still, literally, warm.) But in 1957 Diem
was the certified president of South Vietnam, and during three years
in office had managed to crush rival religious sects and independent

politicians and surround himself with a court of American advisors—Michigan State University professors, military advisors, A.I.D. officials, Catholic Welfare aides.

Diem, however, had achieved little else in three years in office. But during his visit to America the "lobby" promoted the "miracle" myth. Everything that Diem did, or attempted, was described as a miracle. Articles appeared in magazines, from the *Reporter* to *Look*, hailing the "miracles" of political stability, land reform, refugee settlement, and economic development allegedly achieved by the Diem regime. But the "miracle" was actually only a miracle of public relations.

The "Vietnam Lobby" also perpetuated a second myth—that free elections for all Vietnam, which would include the communists, and which were called for in the Geneva agreements, were simply a means of enslaving the free people of Vietnam. Since the Communist-backed Viet Minh would almost certainly win, because they had "duped" the populace, the United States was actually striking a blow for freedom by keeping the people of Vietnam from holding a national election. We were "saving" them from themselves, and at the same time teaching them the golden way of American democracy through Diem's "show-case" government. This type of rationale Kipling used to write poems about.

In many ways the most important of the myths promoted by the "Vietnam Lobby" was the refugee myth. The dramatic story of one million refugees fleeing to the south from the communist north supported the theory of the North Vietnam leaders as "devils" and Diem's regime as the sanctuary of freedom. Naive, well-meaning publicists like Dr. Tom Dooley projected this view with extraordinary success in the United States. What Americans were not told was that the refugees were almost all Catholics, many of whom had fought with the French against the Communist Viet Minh, and who realized they could get better treatment under the Catholic Diem. These refugees were settled and well cared for through extensive American aid, becoming a privileged minority in South Vietnam. But Diem had to use repressive police measures to keep in line the remainder of the population (thirteen million) which did not share the Catholics' visceral hatred of communism, and in fact were sympathetic toward the Viet Minh. It took an equally dramatic event—the protest of self-immolation by a Buddhist monk—to center attention on Diem's preferential treatment of the Catholic minority.

The "lobby" had a myth for almost every occasion. When things began to go badly for Diem in 1961, the Kennedy administration rationalized the radical increase in this nation's military involvement in Vietnam by adhering to the myth that aggression by the communists had wrecked Diem's progressive programs, and even forced him to adopt some totalitarian means—temporarily, because of the crisis, of course. So persuasive and pervasive were the myths postulated by the "Vietnam Lobby" that few people were willing to believe that the source of the trouble might lie with Diem himself.

THE CROWD IN MADISON SQUARE GARDEN was dressed like it was a coming-out party instead of a political rally. But the tweeds and swept-back coiffures were proper because the Young Americans for Freedom's big "Tshombe Freedom Rally" in October of 1962 was something of a coronation ceremony: the right-wing college group was presenting awards to its heroes. John Wayne got an award. So did John Dos Passos and Strom Thurmond. And so did Marvin Liebman.

Marvin Liebman is a forty-one-year-old ex-communist-turned-publicist for right-wing causes—apparently a good publicist, judging from the way the YAF chose to honor him. Liebman provides an interesting link between the activities of the two great Cold War pressure groups: the China Lobby and the "Vietnam Lobby." A late-blooming member of the China Lobby, Liebman quit the Communist Party in 1945, but it was not until 1957, while working with the International Rescue Committee, that his politics took a sharp curve to the right. Liebman, working for Harold Oram's public relations firm (his name appeared on Oram's stationery alongside that of Gilbert Jonas during the middle fifties), was instrumental in setting up the Committee of One Million Against the Admission of Communist China to the U.N.

Liebman became a sort of right-wing establishment man. He was secretary of the Committee of One Million, an advisor to the Young Americans for Freedom, and a collaborator with *National Review* editor William F. Buckley Jr. in setting up the Committee for Freedom of All Peoples—which was outdone in its protest over Krushchev's visit to the United States only by the *National Review*'s black-bordered cover.

The China Lobby, like the "Vietnam Lobby," fused liberal and right-wing elements in the impassioned promotion of an anticommunist leader (for Diem, read Chiang Kai-shek), whose prime and perhaps sole qualification for leadership was his anticommunism. Ross Y. Koen, in his book *The China Lobby in American Politics* (remarkably unavailable since shortly after its 1960 publication), names among the prime outlets for pro-Chiang propaganda *Life,* the *Reader's Digest*—and the *New Leader.*

The *New Leader*'s role in the China Lobby became a cause célèbre in 1963 when Senator William Fulbright's Foreign Relations Committee released testimony stating that Chiang Kai-shek's New York publicity firm had paid the *New Leader* $3,000, in 1958, to publish a pro-Chiang article. There are two conflicting accounts. One was given to Senator Fulbright's committee by Mr. Hamilton Wright Jr., a principal in the publicity firm then working for Chiang. "As I recall, they [*New Leader* editors] approached me and said, 'Look, you are representing the Republic of China. We have this wonderful article that has been written, and we are going to put this out as a special supplement. Now, it is going to go; you know our circulation is to the intellectual group and, gee, we just don't have enough money to get this into print all the way. We can certainly use a contribution.'"

The other version is the *New Leader*'s. It is even more interesting because it blames the whole thing on Marvin Liebman. S. M. Levitas, the *New Leader*'s longtime editor and a bitter anticommunist out of the East European socialist tradition, died in 1961. The magazine's new editor, Myron Kolatch, wrote Fulbright and said that a check of the files revealed no such payoff. Kolatch said that the $3,000 came to the *New Leader* from the American-Asia Education Exchange in connection with an article, "Communist China: Power and Prospects," by Dr. Richard L. Walker. The article was to appear in a special issue of the magazine and Levitas asked the Exchange to purchase ten thousand reprints for $3,000 to help finance the issue. Levitas was a member of the Exchange. The author, Dr. Walker, was on its board of directors, and Marvin Liebman, whom the *New York Times* described as "a publicist connected with Nationalist Chinese causes," was the secretary-treasurer. The Exchange, in fact, operated out of Liebman's publicity office. Kolatch said that he subsequently learned that the Exchange got the $3,000 from Liebman, who got it, in turn, from Chiang's publicity firm. The *New Leader,*

Kolatch said, had not been aware that the funds originated in the Nationalist China camp.

The China Lobby/"Vietnam Lobby" syndrome came full circle in the spring of 1964 when Liebman was revealed as the promoter of an advertisement in the *Washington Star*, signed by the parents of American soldiers killed in Vietnam, that called for an extension of the war.

The *New Leader,* in recent years, has lost much of the blind anticommunism which allowed it to accept too readily the positions of the China Lobby and the "Vietnam Lobby," according to author Paul Jacobs: "The *New Leader* today is much different than it was under Levitas. For Levitas, the primary role of the magazine was fighting the communists and very often he subordinated all else to it. Considering the bitter experience the non-communist left had with the communists, Levitas' position was understandable. But the tragedy was that it led not only to an obsession but to an inability to accept the fact that changes were taking place inside the communist world. Today the *New Leader* does have a better understanding of the problems the world faces and an article is no longer measured only by how anticommunist it may be."

But the *New Leader* school of anticommunism—shared in the fifties by the *Reporter* and other liberal publications and such groups as the International Rescue Committee and the Congress for Cultural Freedom—is important because it helped to shape the Cold War as we live it today. When World War II ended, the State Department and the Pentagon had to formulate policies for a world where the communists were now the enemy—but where splinter socialist movements, both "democratic" and "undemocratic," were emerging all over Europe and Asia. It was obvious that we couldn't be against *everybody*. Instrumental in helping decide where to draw the line was the circle of ex-radicals and disillusioned intellectuals, and social democrats such as Levitas, whose principled anticommunism dated from the creation of the Third International. Where a State Department career man might be insensitive to the crimes of the Third International against the intellectuals, old Bolsheviks, and the Jews, a former East European socialist like Levitas could speak with passion about who were the good guys and who were the bad guys—and which side the United States should support in the name of anticommunism.

The same liberals who backed Diem fought Senator Joseph Mc-Carthy, but they fought McCarthy on his own battleground of anticommunism. This was the only ground acceptable in the hate climate of the fifties and the anticommunism of the ex-radical turned "liberal" had paramount influence in the hard line of America's postwar politics. The "Vietnam Lobby" was the ultimate product of this school of liberal Cold War anticommunism. Unlike the businessmen, missionaries, and military politicians that joined the China Lobby for self-seeking reasons, the members of the "Vietnam Lobby" were True Believers. They were on a Crusade for Democracy. Looking at the world through anti-Red glasses, they convinced themselves that a Diem could be a democrat. They had trouble convincing Eisenhower, so they pressured his administration into line. Then they set out to convince the country. They succeeded, and the myths that they created—that we were "asked" to step in by the Vietnamese people, that we are protecting "democracy" by blocking elections—remain long after Diem to haunt the State Department white paper, and President Johnson's speeches.

Senator Fulbright, in a recent speech on ideology and foreign policy, cited a thought of William Makepeace Thackeray that applies with extraordinary precision to the "Vietnam Lobby": "The wicked are wicked, no doubt," wrote Thackeray, "and they go astray and they fall, and they come by their deserts; but who can tell the mischief which the very virtuous do?"

[*Ramparts,* July 1965]

The University on the Make:
Madame Nhu & MSU*

*T*HE VIETNAMESE SOLDIER IN THE SENTRY BOX stood at attention as the chauffeured limousine bearing license plate No. 1 from the government motor pool roared down the long driveway of the French villa, picked up speed, and screeched off along the road toward the palace where the president was waiting breakfast. The year was 1957, the city was Saigon, and the man who lived in the huge villa with its own sentry box was no Batman of the diplomatic corps. He was only Wesley Fishel of East Lansing, Michigan, assistant professor of political science at Michigan State University.

Peasants who scrambled off the road to make way for the speeding professor might have wondered what was happening, but Fishel's academic compatriots could have no doubt: he was "making it." To make it, in the new world of Big University politics, was no longer as elemental as publishing or perishing. You needed "contact" with the outside world. You had to get a government contract. You had to be an operator. And some people viewed Professor Fishel in South Vietnam in the mid-1950s as the Biggest Operator of them all.

Some professors on the make have had a bigger press, but none deserves notoriety more than Wesley Fishel. Eugene Burdick, for instance, got a lot of publicity out of his quickie novels and underwater beer commercials on television. But no academician has ever achieved Fishel's distinction in getting his school to come through with enough professors, police experts, and guns to secure his friend's dictatorship. That was what Wesley Fishel was about on that humid Saigon morning, burning rubber to visit Ngo Dinh Diem. The presidential palace was known informally and with some degree of jealousy by the United States Mission in Saigon as the "breakfast club," because that was where

Coauthored with Robert Scheer and Sol Stern

Diem and Fishel and Wolf Ladejinsky, the agricultural expert left over from the New Deal, ate morning melons several times a week and discussed the state of the nation.

Leland Barrows, the United States Mission chief, was disturbed because he couldn't get to see Diem anywhere near that often. And Fishel was particularly closed-mouthed about his regular morning conferences. Saigon in the early days of the Diem regime was a status-minded city, and Fishel had a bigger villa than Barrows, bigger, even, than the American ambassador's. This residential ranking attests to Fishel's importance as head of the Michigan State University Group in Vietnam, an official university project under contract to Saigon and Washington, with responsibility for the proper functioning of Diem's civil service and his police network, the shaping up of the fifty-thousand-man "ragamuffin" militia, and the supplying of guns and ammunition for the city police, the civil guard, the palace police, and the dreaded Sûreté—South Vietnam's version of the FBI. No small task for a group of professors, but one which Michigan State took to as if it were fielding another national championship football team.

One lesser-known and perhaps more unpleasant task of the MSU professors was to provide a front for a unit of the United States Central Intelligence Agency. This is a role that both Professor Fishel and Michigan State University have now chosen to forget. It is described here as a specific, if shocking, documentation of the degree of corruption and abject immorality attending a university which puts its academic respectability on lend-lease to American foreign policy.

[JOHN A. HANNAH, THE PRESIDENT AS COACH]

The decay of traditional academic principles found in the modern university on the make may well be traced to Harold Stassen and Clark Kerr, but it is best exemplified by President John A. Hannah of Michigan State University. Stassen, in the International Cooperation Administration, was responsible for the concept that American universities should be tapped as "manpower reservoirs" for the extension of Americanism abroad, and Clark Kerr, the embattled Berkeley savant, first came up with the vision of the large university as a "service station" to society.

Hannah, an Eisenhower liberal with a penchant for public service, has made these concepts the *raison d'être* of MSU.

Hannah, in a blustery way, represents the best traditions of the American Success Story. The son of an Iowa chicken farmer, he took a degree in poultry husbandry from Michigan Agricultural College in 1922. Then, like the football hero who works for thirty years in the college bookstore because he can't bear to leave the campus, Hannah stayed on in East Lansing. He taught chicken farming, married the president's daughter, got his first taste of public service during a stint with the Department of Agriculture as an NRA administrator, came back to campus, and in 1941 succeeded his father-in-law as president.

MSU, under President Hannah's tutelage, is more service oriented than the average Standard Oil retail outlet. MSU's School of Agriculture aids farmers, its School of Hotel Management turns out educated room clerks, its School of Police Administration graduates cops sophisticated in the social sciences. MSU once offered a Bachelor of Science degree with a major in Mobile Homes under a program financed by the trailer industry. But it is in the field of international service that Michigan State has really made it. A shiny new building on campus houses MSU's Center for International Programs—an edifice built, incidentally, with funds from the administrative allowance on the seven-year Vietnam contract. The university has over two hundred faculty members out every year in the boondocks of the world running "educational projects" in thirteen countries including Colombia, Taiwan, Turkey, Brazil, and Okinawa. *Time* magazine recently acknowledged the MSU president's extensive influence on the role of American universities overseas by recording Hannah's boast that he can "tap his campus specialists, get an answer to most any question for government or research groups within thirty minutes." Now *that* is service.

The list of countries MSU is presently "helping" is lopsided with military dictatorships, but it is not President Hannah's style to question the assignment his country gives him. A former assistant secretary of defense under General Motors' Charles Wilson, Hannah sees the military, like football, as an important character-building element in life. His view of the modern university is tied to the liberal concept of America as the defender of the free world. That the university must prepare young citizens to assume this proud task, and to be a leader abroad in areas chosen for it by the federal government, is Hannah's educational credo.

Despite Hannah's obvious pride in the work his university is doing overseas, he is particularly reticent in discussing its most extensive foreign operation. In a colorful brochure about MSU's international programs, given away free to visitors, there is only one sentence about the Vietnam Project—despite the fact that this was the largest single project ever undertaken by an American university abroad, a project that spent the incredible amount of twenty-five million in American taxpayers' dollars in giving "technical assistance" to the Republic of South Vietnam under Ngo Dinh Diem. This one-sentence treatment of MSU's Vietnam operation is like reducing to a photo caption in the school yearbook the story of the prize-winning basketball team—because the coach was caught taking bribes.

A key to MSU's apparent official desire to forget about the Vietnam experience, dubbed the "Vietnam Adventure" by some professors who worked on the project, might be found in the unexpressed fear that the details of the university's "cover" for the CIA may become public knowledge. If pressed for an answer, Fishel denies any such role and so does President Hannah. "CIA agents were not knowingly on our staff—if that were true we didn't know about it," Hannah said recently in his office, sitting beneath the portrait of Lincoln that hangs above his desk. But this assertion of innocence is flatly contradicted by the disclosures of other professors who held administrative positions in the project. Indeed, the weight of evidence is that MSU finally had to ask the CIA unit to go elsewhere because its presence had become such embarrassing general knowledge in Saigon and East Lansing. Economist Stanley K. Sheinbaum, the campus coordinator of MSU's Vietnam operation for three years, was flabbergasted by Hannah's denial: "If John Hannah can make up something like that, he calls into question his competence as a university president," he said.

[WESLEY FISHEL, THE PROFESSOR AS PROCONSUL]

One indication of Wesley Fishel's power in Saigon in the heyday of the Diem era was provided by a veteran of that period who recently paid a return visit to Saigon. "I heard people talking about what 'Westy' would think," he said, "and for a minute I thought that Wesley was back." "Westy," in the Saigon vernacular, is General William Westmoreland, but those in the know used to talk about "Wesley" in the same awe-struck fashion. There is one public reminder of the transfer of power. "Westy" is now running the war out of the same office building, a recon-verted apartment house at 137 Pasteur Street, that used to be "Wesley's" headquarters.

Like most fateful alliances, the Diem-Fishel axis had humble begin-nings. The pair met in Tokyo in July of 1950 when each was going nowhere in his chosen field. Diem was an exiled Vietnamese politi-cian with a mandarin personality and a strong sense of predestination but few tangible hopes of assuming power in his war-ravaged country. Fishel was just a run-of-the-mill academician, a young political scientist from UCLA who had written a nondescript thesis on Chinese extra-territoriality and was about to accept a position at Michigan State.

Both were ambitious, looking for an angle, and Napoleon-sized. Diem was 5' 4"; Fishel, a well-built, curly-haired man with the stance of a bantam rooster, appears to be about the same size. The men became friends and a relationship developed by extensive correspondence over the ensuing year. They exchanged favors early. Fishel had his friend appointed consultant to Michigan State's Governmental Research Bureau and helped arrange a long stay in the United States during which Diem picked up substantial backing among prominent Americans from Cardinal Spellman to Senator Mike Mansfield. In return Diem in 1952 asked the French to let Michigan State furnish technical aid to Vietnam at United States expense, but the French refused.

Fishel, however, had ultimate faith. An East Lansing colleague recalls that one day Fishel cornered him in the faculty lounge and, with the exu-berance of one who could no longer restrain himself, whispered excitedly, "My friend Diem is going to be premier of Vietnam one of these days!" The prediction was taken lightly; Fishel had neither the swagger nor the stripes of a kingmaker. But when Diem was named premier in July 1954, almost his first official act was to request Washington to send Wesley to Saigon to advise him. Fishel arrived within weeks, and just weeks later Diem asked for the second time that MSU set up a technical assistance program in Vietnam. The request, this time, had smooth sailing.

With Fishel already in Saigon, there was virtually no one on the

East Lansing campus with any knowledge about Vietnam when Diem's assistance request was relayed through official Washington channels. President Hannah, not one to let the possibility of a substantial contract go by, tapped four faculty members for an "inspection team" and put them on a plane to Saigon in almost whirlwind fashion. The four were Arthur Brandstatter, an ex-MSU football hero who now heads the Police Administration School; James Dennison, the university's public relations man; Edward Weidener, then chairman of the Political Science Department; and Economics Department chairman Charles Killingsworth. None of these men had any experience in academic or technical assistance roles overseas, nor did they have any expertise in Far Eastern affairs, a deficiency they attempted to repair by reading newspaper clippings on Vietnam during the plane ride. The first time they met as a group was when they fastened their seat belts.

Saigon was a city in ferment in September 1954, when MSU's "inspection team" arrived. Diem was nominally in power, but he had no real support except among a small number of middle-class Catholics and Saigon merchants. The French were preparing to pull out, the Saigon police were controlled by the Binh Xuyen pirate sect, the private armies of the religious sects were in substantial control of the Vietnamese lowlands, the Vietnamese army was in fledgling revolt against Diem, and the civil service machinery was in a state of stagnation.

The professors found their colleague Fishel and General Edward Lansdale of the CIA maneuvering furiously to consolidate Diem's support, an effort that culminated with the endorsement of Diem by the United States Security Council in the spring of 1955. The professors also learned that Diem was suspicious of the members of the United States Mission in Saigon, many of whom he felt held pro-French sentiments. The one American Diem really trusted was Wesley Fishel, and this trust was reflected two weeks later when the MSU inspection team returned to East Lansing and recommended a massive technical assistance contract, unprecedented in the history of university operations overseas. This contract committed Michigan State to do everything for Diem, from training his police to writing his constitution.

Contract negotiations bogged down over technical matters, but the jam was broken in the early spring of 1955 by a telephone call from Washington to Hannah requesting that the red tape be cut and MSU involve itself in Vietnam—in a hurry. Fishel once indicated in an interview that the request came from former vice president Nixon, but he now denies this, and so does President Hannah. The phone call, Hannah told the *Detroit News*, came from an authority "even higher than Nixon." This leaves a choice of John Foster Dulles; his brother, CIA chief Allen Dulles; or Eisenhower himself. At any rate, President Hannah did his duty as he saw it. The first MSU professors joined Wesley Fishel in Saigon in late May of 1955.

In 1956 Fishel abandoned his role as "advisor" to Diem and assumed the title of Chief of Mission of the MSU Group. For the next four years, he was the most important American in Vietnam. "Wesley was the closest thing to a proconsul that Saigon had," said one of the MSU professors. The assistant professor of political science entertained frequently and lavishly in his opulent villa, and if his parties got a little out of hand the Saigon police obliged by cordoning off the street. No professor has ever made it so big; in the academic world, Fishel was sovereign.

But if the proconsul lived well, so did his lieutenants. East Lansing is hardly a Midwestern Paris, and for most of the professors the more exotic and freewheeling life in Saigon was the closest thing to the high life they had known. Academicians and their families, at first a little uncomfortable, assumed the easy ways of the former French colonial masters. They moved into spacious, air-conditioned villas, rent-free, in the old French section of Saigon, bought the better scotches at the American commissary at $2 a bottle, hired servants at $30 a month, were invited to all the better cocktail parties because they knew "Wesley," went tiger hunting for laughs, and, with various "hardship" and "incentive" salary hikes, made close to double their normal salaries. (A professor earning $9,000 for teaching class at East Lansing got $16,500 a year for "advising" in Vietnam—tax-free.)

The "Vietnam Adventure" also did wonders for the professors' tenure. Despite the activist nature of their work in Vietnam and the lack of any substantial scholarly research during the project, two-thirds of the MSU faculty who went to Saigon got promotions either during their tour of duty or within a year of their return. Professor Fishel, in particular, scored points. His published work was virtually nonexistent and he was absent from his classes for years at a time. But, in 1957, MSU promoted him to the rank of full professor.

[HEAR-NO-CIA, SEE-NO-CIA]

Central Intelligence Agency men were hidden within the ranks of the Michigan State University professors. They were all listed as members of the MSU Project staff and were formally appointed by the University Board of Trustees. Several of the CIA men were given academic rank and were paid by the university project. The CIA agents' instructions were to engage in counterespionage and counterintelligence. Their "cover" was within the police administration division of the Michigan State Group. The CIA unit was self-contained, and appeared on an official organization chart of the MSU Project as "VBI Internal Security Section." This five-man team was the largest section within the police administration division of the MSU Vietnam operation. The police administration division in turn was by far the largest of the three divisions of the MSU Group.

"VBI" was Michigan State shorthand for "Vietnamese Bureau of Investigation," the new name the professors had given the old Sûreté, the Vietnamese special police. The head of the "Internal Security Section" of the VBI under the Michigan State operation was Raymond Babineau, who was in Saigon from the outset of the MSU Project. The other men were hired later by the university and listed on its staff chart as "Police Administration Specialists." All four—Douglas Beed, William Jones, Daniel Smith, and Arthur Stein—gave their previous employment as either "investigator" or "records specialist" in the Department of the Army. The CIA contingent, despite the continued denials of Fishel and Hannah, was identified by two former project officials—Stanley Sheinbaum and Professor Robert Scigliano, an MSU political scientist who was assistant project chief of the MSU Vietnam group from 1957 to 1959. It is also confirmed, in writing, by Scigliano and Professor Guy H. Fox, a former MSU project chief, in a book titled *Technical Assistance in Vietnam: The Michigan State University Experience,* published by Praeger in 1965.

Sheinbaum, as part of his duties as campus coordinator, hired Stein, Smith, and Jones. At the time all he knew about the men was that they came from the "Department of the Army." Sheinbaum recalls that he was proceeding to investigate the background of the three applicants before accepting them when he was told that "it wouldn't be necessary to check out these guys." The message came from Professor Ralph Smuckler, a former Vietnam Project head. Sheinbaum said he was on the job for eighteen months before he was taken into the administration's confidence and told about the CIA men. "Smuckler pulled me aside one day and told me that I should know that these CIA guys were there, but that we didn't talk about them," he said.

Professor Scigliano's first brush with the CIA came during his first meeting with the police advisory group in Saigon. He said that Babineau, whom he knew from the organizational chart as head of the VBI Internal Security, was introduced as a CIA man. The other CIA agents were also introduced, and Babineau made a short speech in which he expressed hope that the professors and his people would get along well. Scigliano recalls Babineau saying, "We hope we don't get in your way." A professor and his wife became friends with one of the CIA men and his wife, and the couples often dined together. "We talked about books and music," he said, but there was an unspoken rule that they would never mention the CIA. The entire unit operated on an identical hear-no-CIA, see-no-CIA basis. They worked out of offices in one corner of the police administration floor of the beige converted apartment building that housed the MSU Project. The CIA men came in early in the morning, stayed for about an hour, and then locked their offices and left for the day. They all drove their own cars and their French was the most fluent on the project. If the CIA men got nothing else from their fraternization with Michigan State University, they became the first persons in the spy business to gain academic recognition. "Some of the CIA guys attained faculty status at MSU—some as lecturers, some as assistant professors, depending on their salaries. I know, because I remember signing the papers that gave them faculty rank," Sheinbaum said.

The CIA unit operated within its Michigan State "cover" until 1959. Scigliano and Fox state in their book, in what must rank as one of the more terse statements of the decade: "USOM [United States Operations Mission] also absorbed at this time [1959] the CIA unit that had been operating within MSUG [Michigan State University Group]." In plain language, Michigan State threw the CIA men out. One of the principal factors leading to the MSU decision was that by 1959 just about everybody in the know was cognizant of the CIA operation. This was not only embarrassing to the legitimate professors but it served to taint the reputation of the limited amount of solid academic work that was done during the project. For instance, an anthropologist working far out in the Vietnamese flatlands was flabbergasted to find a local police chief interrupt his work on the grounds that he was digging up bones on behalf of the United States Central Intelligence Agency. The decision to terminate the CIA unit was brought to Professor Scigliano by Smuckler. Babineau was not in Saigon at the time, so Professor Scigliano gave Jones the bad news. He recalls that Jones was "quite upset," as was the United States Mission, which wanted the CIA unit to stay right where it was— sheltered by the groves of academe.

Within weeks, the entire "VBI Internal Security Section" had moved over to the offices of the United States Mission to operate, presumably, more in the open. By 1959, the United States was making little pretense of following the Geneva Accords anyway.

[ACADEMICS IN ARMORED CARS]

In the spring of 1955 Diem gained control of the army. The United States, which was (and still is) providing the entire South Vietnam army payroll, said it wouldn't give out any more checks unless the army played ball with our boy. Diem then used the army to crush the sect that had controlled the Saigon police and elements of the far-flung Sûreté. The gargantuan task of rebuilding the entire Vietnam police apparatus, from traffic cop to "interrogation expert," as a loyal agency of the Diem government then fell to Michigan State University.

Diem, lacking popular support, could only retain power through an effective police and security network. The American embassy urgently signaled the MSU contingent to concentrate on this problem, and, like good team players from a school with a proud football tradition, the professors went along. The professors not only trained Diem's security forces but, in the early years of the project, actually supplied them with guns and ammunition. In doing so, the East Lansing contingent helped to secure Diem's dictatorship and to provide the base and the arms for the "secret police" which were to make Madame Nhu and her brother infamous at a later date.

If not academic, the professors were at least professional. Many supplies—revolvers, riot guns, ammunition, tear gas, jeeps, hand-cuffs, radios—were requisitioned by the East Lansing School of Police Administration from stocks left over from America's aid to the French Expeditionary Corps. These supplies were then turned over to the Viet-namese who would strive to achieve Diem's own form of "consensus" government—a consensus gained largely by hauling the dissenters off to jail. Despite the largesse left by the French, the professors found it necessary to order some $15 million in additional "equipment" from the United States Mission. Listen to some of the official progress reports sent home to East Lansing by the professors:

> November 8, 1955: "During the month of October we received notice of Washington's approval of the recom-mended expanded police program...Conferences were held at USOM on October 10 and the Embassy on October 23 and 24, trying to coordinate Internal Security Operations in Vietnam in which our government has an interest."
> April 17, 1956: "The training of the commando squads of Saigon-Cholon police in riot control formations has con-tinued during the month...A report on riots and unlawful assembly is nearing completion."
> June 5, 1957: "Training of the Presidential Security Guard in revolver shooting began during the month. Thirty-four VBI agents completed the revolver course."
> September 11, 1957: "Eight hundred pairs of Peerless handcuffs arrived in Saigon, but distribution is being delayed pending arrival of 400 additional cuffs."
> February 17, 1958: "The training of 125 military and Civil Guard fingerprint technicians at the VBI proceeds satisfacto-rily. The Palace Guard is being put through another class in revolver training, with 58 men receiving instruction. Forty members of the VBI completed firearm training."

AS BEFITS A UNIVERSITY PROJECT, many of the professors indulged in their academic specialties. Ralph Turner, a professor of police administration, feels that one of the project's most singular achievements was the program whereby every Vietnamese citizen would be given an identification card—with a special American touch. The cards were laminated so the poor, plasticless Viet Cong would have difficulty forging them.

Dean Brandstatter did not move lock, stock, and pistol to Saigon, but he managed frequent "inspection trips"—as did some eleven of the university officials, including President Hannah, all of course at government expense. Brandstatter, a former military policeman, utilized his expertise to immediate effect during one of his first trips. Rumors of a coup against Diem were escalating, and the East Lansing official personally inspected the Palace Guard to see that they had enough guns to meet the threat. Brandstatter, a large, jovial man in his early fifties, and devoted follower of MSU's football fortunes, played talent scout for the police operation. The services that the MSU team was called upon to perform for Diem's security apparatus were so esoteric that even its heralded School of Police Administration wasn't up to the job. Brandstatter had to recruit specially trained cops from all over the country. Fingerprint experts, small-arms experts, and intelligence experts came from the Detroit police force, the New York police force, the FBI, and even the Department of Defense. Other professors, doing civil service work, felt a little left out and labeled the onslaught of police experts "mercenaries." This might seem a little unkind, but the term seems somewhat applicable since, at one point in the project, only four of the thirty-three police advisors had roots at the Michigan campus; the others were nomads. The project, of course, still bore the name—or the "cover"—of the MSUG, since these "mercenaries" were all put on the MSU payroll and provided with faculty status. In the action-filled world of the service-station university, not only do the professors become activists but the cops aspire to professorships.

[DECLINE AND FALL]

Ngo Dinh Diem was a nice man to buy guns for, but in other areas of human endeavor the professors discovered that he could be a tough man to do business with. Even Wolf Ladejinsky, who broke bread regularly with Diem, was subject to occasional indignities. When an issue of the *New Republic* appeared in Saigon containing an article mildly critical of the Diem regime, the president sent Ladejinsky packing off from the palace to buy up all the copies from the dozen English-language kiosks in Saigon. The game in Saigon was to cater to Diem's pettiness and paranoia, and for the most part the men from Michigan State played it. There appeared to be a conscious effort within the project administration to prepare reports pleasing, or at least palatable, to the president. Milton Taylor, an MSU economics professor who went to Vietnam as a tax advisor, said that his reports were often rewritten by the project head. When he questioned this practice he was told that there were "higher considerations" at stake; other universities were in hot pursuit of the juicy Vietnam contract.

It became necessary to forsake principles for the good of the project. At times, in the Saigon of the late 1950s, that must have been difficult. Professor Adrian Jaffe of the MSU English Department, one of the most persistent critics of his university's "Vietnam Adventure," recalls some vivid street scenes. Each morning, men, and more often than not women and children, were hauled out of the jail directly across from his office at the Faculty of Letters of the University of Saigon, handcuffed, thrown into a van, and driven away to an island concentration camp known as a sort of Devil's Island à la Diem. Professors in the project, because of their intimacy with the Vietnamese security apparatus, knew this was happening, Jaffe said, but his colleagues said and did nothing.

The moral question raised by Jaffe is dismissed by many veterans of the project as "unprofessional." Perhaps more professional was the work of Wesley Fishel, who, as late as November 1959, wrote an article in the *New Leader* with the obfuscating title "Vietnam's One-Man Democratic Rule." The text requires no recounting, except to observe that Fishel uses adjectives for Diem that only Jack Valenti might dare use for Johnson.

The failure of the MSU professors to bear witness against what are now known to be Diem's outrageous violations of civil liberties raises serious questions about them as men. But their failure as professionals in exercising the traditional role of the independent scholar as critic accounted in large part for the general ignorance of the United States public about the true nature of Diem's regime. Professors, presumed to be men of principle, were on the scene in Vietnam and had to be accepted as the best unprejudiced source of information. David Halberstam, after all, simply could have been mad at Madame Nhu. The same disastrous vacuum of information occurred in this country only a decade before when the China experts, almost to a man, were purged as Reds and com-symps, and yahoos were all the public had left to hear. In Vietnam, at least, there was a Buddhist monk with the fortitude to burn himself—and the public suddenly wondered how what they had been reading about Diem for six years could have been so wrong. But the professors, by this time, were long back in East Lansing. The MSU Vietnam Project ended rather abruptly in 1962. The university claims that it terminated the arrangement in the name of academic freedom— but the truth is, unfortunately, more complex.

Diem, painfully aware of the slightest criticism, was infuriated by the modicum of critical material published in the United States in the early sixties by veterans of the MSU "experience." Professor Jaffe and economist Milton Taylor wrote an essay for the *New Republic* in 1961 that set Diem's paranoia percolating. The author dared to suggest that the president rid himself of the Nhus. The contract between Diem and Michigan State stipulated that members of the project could not use materials gathered on the job "against the security or the interests of Vietnam." In other words, they were to keep quiet. Taylor recalls that many of his colleagues in Vietnam felt he was being "disloyal" in publicly criticizing Diem.

The president was also miffed that in 1959 MSU had drastically curtailed its police work after being urged both by Diem and the United States Mission to plunge more deeply into paramilitary work than it already had. MSU's reluctance was understandable, since a greater degree of involvement would just about require its professors to shoot off howitzers and drill troops in the jungle. Nevertheless, the university genuinely believed that its contract would be renewed in 1962. President Hannah even sent a special envoy, Alfred Seelye, dean of the Business College, to Saigon to smooth things out by telling Diem that the university was prepared to weed out any future troublemakers in the project by selecting personnel more likely to "write scholarly scientific studies and not sensational journalistic articles." Diem, however, surprised everybody. He was adamant: no more MSU.

With no deal in sight, the business dean proceeded to make a strong declaration in defense of the academic freedom of MSU professors and beat Diem in announcing that the contract would not be renewed.

[THE RUINS]

Like a factory that has contracted for a job and then completed it, there is little evidence on the MSU campus that it was ever involved in Vietnam. Thousands of pages of mimeographed reports and documents sent from Saigon have been piled haphazardly in out-of-the-way files in the university library, uncatalogued and unused. MSU has not a single course, not even a study program, to show for its six years in Vietnam. Professor Wesley Fishel still flies in and out of East Lansing, but now he goes to Washington and advises the administration on Vietnam, a role which allows him to visit Saigon occasionally—where he has the look of a man who would like another try. But there is nothing for him to do. Fishel has been careful to exclude the infamous *New Leader* article from the otherwise thorough sixty-four-page bibliography on Vietnam and Southeast Asia which he distributes to his students.

MSU is still big on police. There are, literally, policemen all over the campus, almost beyond the wildest expansion of the human retina. There is the campus police—a complement of roughly thirty-five men in blue uniforms. Then there are the professors and visiting firemen at the School of Police Administration. Finally, it is hard to find a parking spot on campus since so many police cars are occupying the stalls; state police headquarters adjoins MSU.

With all this protection the university officials should feel safe. But they do not. President Hannah has lately been publicly worried about the possibilities of what he terms a "Berkeley-style" revolt. The vice president of student affairs bluntly stated that MSU had been "selected" as the "next Berkeley." Hannah, fearful of "outside agitators," has suggested that there is an "apparatus" at work on campus that is a "tool for international communism." The university police have a special detail charged with keeping tabs on student political activities, especially anything "radical." Several years ago a member of this "Red squad" endeared himself to the student daily by trapping homosexuals in a state-built bathroom. These conditions would be sufficient enough for the light hearted to suggest that MSU is a Lilliputian police state, but that is silly. Professor Alfred Meyer of the Political Science Department, during his course on the Soviet political system, always gets a good laugh by telling the students to take a good look around campus if they want to know what the Soviet system is like.

Hannah's concern over Berkeley is more than apocryphal. If the Berkeley experience meant any one thing, it meant that the university wasn't doing its job. It had lost its sense of purpose; it no longer had meaning to the students. In that sense East Lansing is, assuredly, another Berkeley. The university on the make has little time for nonconforming students and rarely enough for conforming students. Its service function is the first priority. The students are, in Clark Kerr's idiom, only the "raw material" that has to be processed. That was the making of the Berkeley revolt, and the ingredients are available in excess portions at Michigan State.

Acting dean of international programs Ralph T. Smuckler is perhaps the one person at MSU who got something lasting out of the "Vietnam Adventure." He derived an ideology, and it is an ideology that goes Clark Kerr one better. Smuckler sees the future of the social sciences in the worldwide scope of the "action" projects he is now directing in Formosa—as he did in Vietnam. "Classroom teaching is a tame business," said Smuckler, "and anybody who doesn't see how his discipline fits into the overseas operations of the university is already obsolete." To question the assumption that the academician of tomorrow must be an operator is to ask but part of the essential question about MSU's "Vietnam Adventure." And to ask whether the university officials are liars, or whether the MSU Project broke the spirit of the Geneva Accords, is also neglecting the primary question.

The essential query, which *must* be asked before the discussion of Michigan State's behavior can be put into any rational perspective, is this: What the hell is a university doing buying guns, anyway?

[*Ramparts,* April 1966]

J. William Fulbright:
A Profile in Courage*

"Let us ever discriminate between fable and truth, and keep
our minds in the same subjection with respect to whatever
surprises and astonishes us, as to whatever appears perfectly
conformable to their circumscribed and narrow views."

—Voltaire

*A*MERICA HAD ENTERED THE THIRD DECADE of the era of the Cold
War. In response to the challenges, real or imagined, of the past twenty
years, America had created the most powerful military-industrial system the world had ever known. It flexed its muscles and the rest of the
world looked with awe upon the enormous power and versatility of the
young colossus. It was not just that the American military had planted
its impressive installations in every corner of the world. Americans had
also demonstrated their finesse in the arts of international persuasion
and influence. Americans spread out all over the world. Whether it was
a CIA agent subverting an established government in Latin America or
a Peace Corps volunteer showing a peasant in Afghanistan how to purify
his drinking water, Americans were leaving their imprint everywhere.

But power does not always have its way. It atrophies from misuse and
from insensitivity to the surroundings in which it is applied. It was to
have been the "American Century," but something went wrong. Somehow at the beginning of the third decade of Cold War, with American
power at its pinnacle, the gears no longer meshed. The machine began
to break down. The crisis for American power stemmed from the desire
of other peoples to make their own histories and revolutions. Because
America itself had begun to lose hope in new beginnings, it defined the
world in such a way as to preclude the possibility of a popular revolution for others. But the crisis was due also to the domestic habits and
attitudes developed during twenty years of Cold War. A myth became
dogma: that communism, the unchangeable, aggressive enemy, must

*Coauthored with Milton Viorst and Sol Stern

be fought everywhere if American well-being and security were to be ensured.

War requires a rigid system of political priorities, and the Cold War imposed such a system on America. The name of the system was the bipartisan consensus. The minimum condition for inclusion in the system was the acceptance of America's Cold War mission, a posture that for twenty years had gone virtually unchallenged. American liberalism might have stimulated debate and consideration of alternative policies, but from the beginning the liberals chose to move with the consensus. The liberals, who might have challenged the consensus, who might have refused to serve power, were instead excited by the lure of power and the chance to be party to big, history-making decisions.

During those years of Cold War there were sufficient warnings. Even President Eisenhower, sounding like C. Wright Mills, warned Americans of the danger of allowing the Cold War to become institutionalized and the danger of the military-industrial complex that these institutions had spawned. But the drift continued. In 1960 a young man came to the White House with a sense of history and style, and liberals flocked to the seat of power hoping that their pragmatism had paid off. It was a pleasant interlude, with intimations of possible change. But fate soon put a Texan in the White House to resolve all doubts in favor of the Cold War verities. And one day America woke up to find itself bogged down in a senseless and brutal war in a small Asian country.

Many persisted in seeing that war as an unfortunate aberration, as an accident that America had stumbled into and was now perpetuating only because of the special obtuseness of the Texan in the White House. But it was not an aberration. The Texan was the very embodiment of the consensus. His almost religious compulsiveness in pursuing the elusive victory in Asia was, like Captain Ahab's pursuit of the white whale, consistent with the dominant American political character. He and his mates, Dean Rusk and Hubert Humphrey, could tell their critics with some justification that they were merely acting on the basis of assumptions that had guided the American ship of state for the past twenty years. Style, too, had helped to define the consensus. The dominant political style still stressed the importance of working from within, of not rocking the boat, of muted debate that scarcely questioned basic assumptions. Congress, having long ago acquiesced in the new style, had been transformed into a transmission belt instead of a center of debate. What was desperately needed was someone of importance and influence to break with the system and propose alternatives that challenged the Cold War assumptions.

That was what J. William Fulbright did at a time when events were spiraling almost out of control. At a time when most people were still playing the consensus game according to the rules, Fulbright stepped dramatically forward and went into political opposition to voice unspeakable thoughts about American foreign policy. It was a crucial moment in American history. The country was being stampeded into a war with China. American values were being distorted. Someone had to step forward. This is his story.

FOR ELEVEN EXTRAORDINARY AFTERNOONS this winter, out of the same little box that fouls American living rooms with *Peyton Place* and old Tom Mix movies, flickered the grim visage of the high priest of intellectuality of the Senate of the United States. Taciturn yet righteous, affable yet obviously frustrated, fidgeting under the kleig lights, J. William Fulbright of Arkansas had taken to television, and daytime television at that, to lecture the president of the United States, the secretary of state, the secretary of defense, the joint chiefs of staff, the Congress, the Washington press corps, and some twenty-three million housewives in various stages of undress and comeliness, on the consummate madness of American foreign policy in Asia. It was a difficult and no doubt disagreeable experience for the senator. A Southerner who maintains his gentle native mountain mannerisms, Fulbright is a conservative modern-day patrician, who shuns the limelight and would no more grab for newspaper space than a fork at dinner. A serious scholar learned in history and law, he was prepared, by training, to be rather the sage of the Establishment than its gadfly.

But there he was, the afternoon soap operas and middle-brow quiz shows suspended, his shell-rim glasses riding down his nose, peering with a winsome gaze into the cameras hastily installed in the hearing room of the Senate Foreign Relations Committee. The red eye on the cameras went on and the Arkansas senator began a historic series of hearings in which he questioned the legitimacy of United States interests in Asia, the logic and indeed the rationality of a fellow Southerner and Rhodes scholar, Secretary of State Dean Rusk, and impugned the honesty and at times seemed quizzical about the sanity of the Asian policies of his old friend and political colleague Lyndon Baines Johnson.

It was not a mark of his personality but rather a quirk of American history at midcentury, that cast Senator Fulbright in the role of dissenter. Fulbright, the conservative, the Southern Democrat who knew well the traditions and the prerogatives of consensus politics, had broken with his reserved style of operating and had taken the lead in a bitchy, quixotical, and perhaps hopeless fight to limit America's Empire abroad. In what must have seemed an unsettling historical irony to the conservative Fulbright, his foils were those populists, Lyndon Johnson and Hubert Humphrey, the men of the people turned Empire builders. They used the satisfying and inspiring prosody of American populism to justify the slaughter, in the name of democracy, of a yellow people removed from America and its democratic traditions, not only by thousands of miles and a great ocean but by centuries of an alien culture. In the unsettling politics of the Cold War consensus, the liberal democrats of his party and the conservatives of the opposition party had formed an alliance whose unquestioned assumptions seemed to be moving America inexorably and without any significant debate toward the military occupation of Asia and impending war with China. Not only did Senator Fulbright decide to break with this consensus but he chose to use his great public presence to legitimize criticism of the war, and in so doing the man from Arkansas found himself, unexpectedly, in the mainstream of native American radicalism.

SENATOR FULBRIGHT'S ACT MUST BE COUCHED within the twin cycles of penance and redemption. For it was Fulbright, more than any other man, who was responsible for the Senate's perfunctory passage of the Tonkin Gulf Resolution—a legislative blank check upon which the president has drawn as if there were a run on the bank. International incidents, taken as a category of events, often possess ludicrous qualities. But the Gulf of Tonkin incident went beyond the ludicrous to the phantasmagorial. Fulbright's later anguish at having given Johnson sanction to "take all necessary steps" in what proved to be a full-scale

WARREN HINCKLE

undeclared war is most understandable in view of what now appears to be the unreal nature of the events of Tonkin Gulf in August of 1964.

In late July of 1964, a brash, mustachioed South Vietnamese Air Force commander, Nguyen Cao Ky, boasted to a *New York Times* correspondent that the Air Force, led by himself, had dropped "combat teams" inside North Vietnam three years before, well before the heralded "infiltration" of North Vietnamese combat units into South Vietnam. Ky's American advisor, Air Force general Joseph H. Moore, tried to shut him up. Moore, according to the same correspondent, suggested that Commander Ky "did not have a complete command of English and might be misinterpreting questions." But Ky unabashedly admitted that he had flown a combat mission in North Vietnam recently, and that the United States was training South Vietnamese pilots for "large-scale" attacks. This was in absolute contradiction to American policy at the time, and remains an embarrassing disclosure in view of the State Department's insistence that it was the *North* which extended the war.

Then the strange chronology that was later to hound Fulbright unfolded: On July 31 and August 1, South Vietnamese commandos, under cover of a naval barrage, attacked the North Vietnamese islands of Hon Me and Hon Ngu in the Gulf of Tonkin. The destroyer USS *Maddox* was either thirty miles away from North Vietnamese territory at the time (according to the State Department) or ten miles away (according to Admiral Robert B. Moore) or three miles away laying the barrage (other sources). At any rate, the next morning the *Maddox*, in official navy language, "became aware" that three PT boats were trailing it. After several hours, according to *Time* magazine, the *Maddox* fired "three warning shots across their bows," a difficult feat of gunmanship since the PT boats were due astern. "Warning shots" haven't meant anything but a serious shoot-out since the days of Hornblower, and after a futile exchange of torpedoes and shells, the ships went their own ways.

The next incident, two days later, had Hornblowerian qualities bordering on the epic. The Pentagon account of the "attack" at high sea on August 4 had even William F. Buckley Jr. shaking his head in incredulity: a group of North Vietnamese PT boats sought out destroyers of the United States Seventh Fleet at the outrageous distance of sixty-five miles at sea, and, after cruising near the U.S. warships for three hours, launched a three-hour major sea battle in rough seas and bad weather during which no damage or evidence of the attack was recorded by U.S. vessels. Two PT boats were reported sunk. But there were no survivors and no debris collected from the torpedo boats, and sailors aboard the U.S. destroyers, to this day, are under strict orders not to talk about the incident. The North Vietnamese government said the incident simply never occurred, and as Washington pundit James Reston mused why North Vietnam would dispatch hit-and-run torpedo boats to prompt a three-hour sea engagement that could only give an enormous propaganda advantage to the United States, American planes began bombing North Vietnam in a "retaliatory action" that has been continuing, in mounting intensity, to this very day.

The ghostly action at Tonkin Gulf proved of extreme utility. Americans always unite when attacked, even in miniature, and Johnson rushed into Congress a resolution that made a national cause of a distant war of heretofore uncertain motivation. The bizarre detail and doubtful legitimacy of the alleged events in Tonkin Bay are important. They evoked in Senator Fulbright a skepticism about the accuracy of government pronouncements. He was to conclude, later, that the administration was lying not only to the public but also to him, and probably even to itself.

But in August of 1964 the senator from Arkansas had other considerations on his mind. He was consumed with the fear of a strong Goldwater showing in the coming presidential election. Goldwater, to Fulbright, represented the very antithesis of rationality. And reason, to Fulbright, is everything—the golden rule, the means, the end. The Arkansas scholar recoils from missionaries and visionaries—his style is facts first; from the facts he will reason, usually slowly, to a conclusion, even if the conclusion proves opposite to a position he previously held.

When he dwelled, sometime later, on the facts of the Tonkin Gulf incidents, he was mortified. He retracted his earlier stance and made his public *mea culpa* on a national television show: "I have to say to myself," he said in the dull, almost toneless drawl that can empty the Senate galleries, "that I have played a part in that that I am not at all proud of, that at the time of the Bay of Tonkin I should have had greater foresight in the consideration of the resolution. That would have been a good time to have precipitated a debate and a reexamination, a reevaluation of our involvement...I went along with the urging, I must say, of the administration...I made the mistake..."

Fulbright's failure to recognize the significance of the Tonkin resolution bothers him all the more because it was not just a case of mistaken fact; it embodied a fundamental error of judgment. The Arkansas senator had set up an arbitrary polarity—Goldwater was the madman, Johnson the man of reason. Anything he might do to split the party—asserting his prerogatives as the Senate watchdog of foreign policy, picking apart the Tonkin resolution—might aid Goldwater. Besides, and this is where Fulbright now realizes he made his greatest miscalculation, the senator from Arkansas put his trust in the former senator from Texas. The two men were long-time friends, their wives even closer. Fulbright had supported Johnson against Kennedy for the Democratic nomination in 1960, and Johnson had let it be known that he felt Fulbright would have been the best choice for Kennedy's secretary of state. Fulbright viewed Johnson as a humane, intelligent, and dynamic man and believed the president when he said he had no desire to widen the war and would use his mandate moderately.

What Fulbright did not foresee—indeed, could not foresee—was what the frustrations and the temptations of the Vietnam War would do to Mr. Johnson. Where Johnson's attributes served him admirably in domestic politics, they became monstrous in foreign affairs, outside his native milieu. His humaneness turned easily to self-righteousness, his intelligence to scheming, his dynamism to impulsiveness. Johnson as a congressman and senator was always an active proponent of a massive and growing military establishment, a firm advocate of quick and effective retaliation against any "enemy" who might dare to cross America's path. When the sticky Vietnam situation proved infinitely more complex than getting a housing bill through Congress, Johnson became increasingly frustrated, acting out of instinct to punish those who thwarted him. The punishment went, necessarily, to the Vietnamese people.

Johnson assumed a public posture of moderation and patience, but his quiet, deliberate words clashed with his deeds. His pledge to Fulbright to not act rashly proved empty. And Fulbright could only reluctantly conclude that the frustrations of Vietnam were depriving Lyndon Johnson of his rationality.

THE TELEPHONE RANG at 10:45 a.m. in Senator Fulbright's private office in the sterile new Senate Office Building. He was reading a book taken from the low bookcases that line his walls. He picked up the receiver with a gesture indicating distaste. Telephones are for activists, for operators; Fulbright prefers quiet, leisurely conversations over dinner with intellectual equals. The call was from the White House. The familiar voice with the soft flow of the Pedernales River was coming over the wire: "Ah'm sho glad to have got yo' advaas, Bill."

The president of the United States talked on at the other end of the wire, but the chairman of the Senate Foreign Relations Committee was barely listening. It was a conversation he had heard too often. The senator listened politely until the president was through, then said good-bye and hung up. The call was put through to thank Fulbright for sending over a memorandum prepared by his staff. Fulbright had substituted memos for frequent calls at the White House. The president had dominated their conversations, scarcely allowing Fulbright the chance to say hello, and Fulbright had simply tired of listening to him. Now another long mimeographed memo, Fulbright knew, had already been filed in key wastebaskets at State. He was certain the president had paid no attention to the ideas contained in the memo—fresh, challenging, dissenting ideas. Fulbright had, over the years, carefully built up his staff as a grove of academe in the briar patches of Washington officialdom. But the people at State and the new breed in the White House paid only polite, perfunctory notice to their work. The yahoos were riding high in the saddle: Dean Rusk, who gave Fulbright shivers, had out-hawked Secretary of Defense Robert McNamara and roosted behind the president's ear. Rusk's hard line for Asia was backed by Walt Rostow, then chairman of the Policy Planning Council, recently moved into the White House; and for South America by Thomas Mann, a tough-minded Texan who as Johnson's assistant secretary of state for Latin America had scrapped the official Kennedy policy of support for constitutional democratic regimes and initiated a junta hunt; and by George Ball, the undersecretary of state and guardian of the status quo in European affairs.

As chairman of the Foreign Relations Committee, Fulbright did not seek to impose his predilections on the administration's foreign policy priesthood, but only to see that this priesthood was not unduly burdened with dogma. Unquestioned dogma, Fulbright knew, can lead to fanaticism. But his patient efforts to dispel dogma met with growing frustration. It was apparent in his remarkable 1964 speech, "Old

Myths and New Realities," when he expressed publicly for the first time some of the apprehensions he felt about the conduct of U.S. diplomacy. He said, "There has always—and inevitably—been some divergence between the realities of foreign policy and our ideas about it. This divergence has in certain respects been growing, rather than narrowing; and we are handicapped, accordingly, by policies based on old myths, rather than current realities. This divergence is, in my opinion, dangerous and unnecessary—dangerous because it can reduce foreign policy to a fraudulent game of imagery and appearances; unnecessary because it can be overcome by the determination of men in high office to dispel prevailing misconceptions by the candid dissemination of unpleasant but inescapable facts."

"I HAVE A FEW DOUBTS, GENTLEMEN." Seth Tillman, Fulbright's speech writer and intellectual confidant, looked up. When the senator said he had a "few doubts" it could mean a major policy decision was forthcoming. Fulbright had asked Tillman and other members of the inner circle of his Foreign Relations Committee staff to gather in a Washington restaurant for a late lunch. It was a Saturday afternoon in August of 1965. The men did not realize it at the time, but they were to participate in a fundamental decision that would, in the field of foreign policy, make their staff the closest thing to a shadow cabinet the United States has known.

The issue was the Dominican Republic. The Foreign Relations Committee had been holding hearings behind closed doors for weeks, and the testimony was both disturbing and dismaying—so dismaying that the senators on the committee had become divided over what should be said to the public, and it was apparent that no report would be issued. So Fulbright had to decide if he should speak out; this was a most serious and anguished decision, for in order to speak at all candidly about the administration's action in the Dominican Republic it was necessary to infer that the president of the United States was lying.

It was the lying, the reckless fabrications uncovered in the Dominican hearings, that so stunned and horrified Fulbright. When pro–Bosch Army officers began the revolt, the administration said it was sympathetic to the democratic aims of the revolution, but in reality acted from the outset to prevent a rebel victory. When the Marines landed in Santo

Domingo, Johnson said they were there to protect endangered American citizens, yet the Marines' real mission was to aid the right-wing anti-rebel forces. When this became apparent, the administration justified its action by releasing fantastic stories about rebel atrocities—Johnson stated there were "one thousand to fifteen hundred bodies that are dead in the streets," a body count that later shrunk to six. Then it was announced that the rebel forces were dominated by communists—and listed, in an accounting reminiscent of the late junior senator from Wisconsin, exactly fifty-three communists. And when even this number was discredited, Secretary of State Rusk solemnly reminded the nation that there was a time when only "seven people" sat in a beer hall with Hitler, and Secretary Mann volunteered, "Look at Cuba. There were only twelve people in the beginning, and yet they took it over."

Fulbright, though outraged by the deceptions he uncovered, did not act impetuously. This Saturday-afternoon meeting had been preceded by many other lengthy consultations with his staff—all directed at one question: Should Fulbright publicly expose the hypocrisy of the administration? To do so would not only embarrass his party and his old friend the president but would effectively cut the senator off from the White House. That meant a break with the Senate traditions that Fulbright so cherished. It meant taking the case for rationality to the people in a struggle that was certain to be argumentative, confusing, and costly to the careers of those involved.

Seth Tillman looked across the table at Fulbright and realized that the senator had made up his mind. He had stretched out in his chair; the annoying potbelly that had lately provoked the former University of Arkansas star halfback into regular sessions at the Senate gym bulged slightly under his well-cut vest. Tillman, formerly a brilliant political scientist at the Massachusetts Institute of Technology, shared the senator's fervid regard for the intellectual process. He knew where the balance scales would tip: to speak out now was to advocate rationality, to dispel misinformation, to bolster truth. There was, really, little choice.

A few hours before he stood on the Senate floor to blast Johnson's Dominican adventure, a text of the speech and a letter of explanation were delivered by messenger to the White House. The letter has never been answered. And Fulbright has never received another phone call from the president. He became persona non grata at the White House.

And he was now free to broaden his criticism of Johnson's foreign policy: there was Vietnam and, behind Vietnam, China.

LIKE MR. PICKWICK'S SHORT BLACK GAITERS, J. William Fulbright's glasses are an indistinguishable part of his personality. He uses them to see through, but that is a preliminary function that has become almost atavistic. The tilt of Senator Fulbright's glasses can express interest, boredom, chagrin, or disillusion. When held at arm's length off his face, they may be the first thrust of a Fulbrightian inquisition. And on the days that Secretary of State Dean Rusk testified in the crowded, overheated Senate hearing room, the spectacles were continually poised for combat. In the televised drama of the first open debate on United States Asian policy the American public was his audience. But Dean Rusk was his foil.

The contrast between Rusk and Fulbright is symbolic, almost archetypal. Rusk is a missionary with a grievously misplaced sense of the inevitable, purveying the American gospel with a global hard-sell. Fulbright is the cool man of reason, making decisions on the basis of practicality, more concerned with what America can do than what perhaps it should do. Their differing positions reflect what American foreign policy is, and what Fulbright wants it to be.

The conflict between these two men is all the more bitter because of the similarity of their backgrounds. Both are Southerners. Rusk was originally a poor white and Fulbright a patrician, but both were raised in the backcountry of the old Confederacy when memories of the Battle of Shiloh and the craft of carpetbaggery were still raw. Both became Rhodes scholars; both began their career as college teachers. Both have extremely reserved, rather dull personalities, and prefer a seminar room to a public platform. But there the resemblance ends. Dean Rusk is an unfrocked John Foster Dulles, Fulbright an Ozark-bred Voltaire. Rusk shares Dulles' evangelistic sense of America's responsibility for the destiny of nations. He is convinced that there is good and evil in the world, and that America is good. Communism is evil. Like any apostle worth his salt, he sees no gray area in between. Nor is he particularly troubled by any end-means dilemma. The very apex of morality to Rusk is the effort to advance a nation's capacity to repulse evil and render its people freedom, democracy, Coca-Cola, and all the other benefits that

America can provide. It was Dean Rusk the apostle who responded to the senator's questions on daytime television. Rusk began and ended the hearings with the rote view that the sole cause of the Vietnamese war was the aggression of Hanoi and Peking, and stubbornly restated the thesis that America, by bombing the hell out of an Asian country, is effectively resisting the evil of communism.

There were times during Secretary Rusk's recitation when Senator Fulbright didn't seem to be listening. The glasses slid even further than usual down his nose and his eyes drifted up above the gray horizon created by cigarette smoke swirling in the artificial light of the television lamps. This history cannot record what the senator thought during those moments of introspection, but it is likely that once, at least once, he ruminated on the irony of the selection of Dean Rusk as secretary of state, which was one of the great accidents (Fulbright would call it a catastrophe) of our times.

Exhaustive investigation by future historians may prove otherwise, but there is now no evidence to prove that John F. Kennedy chose Dean Rusk as his secretary of state on other than a transitory, eleventh-hour whim. Despite the pain he had taken to assure a spectacular beginning to his administration, he came virtually to the eve of taking the presidential oath without a secretary of state. He had almost tired of the search when the name of Rusk, a former assistant secretary of state for the Far East, appeared at the top of the list. Kennedy recalled reading an essay by Rusk in *Foreign Affairs* in which he celebrated U.S. power to get things done in the world. That fit in with Kennedy's concern at the time for an aggressive diplomacy. Rusk had both Establishment ties and was noncontroversial; nobody could find anything bad, or even interesting, about him, so Kennedy apparently said why not?

IT IS ONE OF THE MYSTERIES OF WASHINGTON, where even the cleaning ladies have evil memories, why no one remembered how Dean Rusk had resigned from the State Department in 1951: He walked out in a snit because we weren't going to bomb China. As head of Asian affairs, Rusk was the most outspoken advocate of the MacArthur position on the Korean War, which, in the nice phraseology of today, would be called pro-escalation. Then it was just called bombing. Rusk, obviously influenced by his eight years in the military, agreed with MacArthur that there was "no substitute for victory." Those who know the secretary insist that he is bitter to this day over the treatment of MacArthur, that he believes it was American diplomatic mistakes, if not duplicity, that "lost" China, and actually feels a personal sense of guilt about it.

The bitterest irony of Kennedy's choice of Rusk as secretary of state dedicated to "our capacity to act" was that the young president found himself, in the last months of his life, coming to recognize and accept the basic limitations of American power. But if Rusk was uncomfortable in the atmosphere of détente in the last period of the Kennedy administration, he positively luxuriated in the tougher temper of the Johnson administration. The secretary of state is now head hawk in a large and growing aviary at the White House. Johnson is a man of action and Rusk counsels action. In the face of failure, Rusk counsels more action, more bombs. It was what he counseled in 1951, but nobody listened to him then.

They were listening to him now, with a terrifying unanimity, at State, at Defense, at the White House. Fulbright can only probe and challenge both the assumptions and logic of Rusk's brand of fast-freight diplomacy. He hoped, through the unlikely medium of daytime television, to show that reasonable men could fashion another definition of our national interest than committing a quarter of a million men to the suppression of a small Asian country. He had brought his case to the people.

"I'M NO SAINT," FULBRIGHT OFTEN SAYS, usually with a slight note of exasperation. He says it to liberals who cluck-cluck in formalized horror over how Fulbright can be *so* right about foreign policy and *so* wrong about things like civil rights. This is a dichotomy that doesn't bother Fulbright as it apparently did not disturb the great Southerners who at the same time held slaves and were the dominant voices of reason and democratic theory in the nineteenth century U.S. Senate. Fulbright, as a Southern man, has great sympathy for the situation of Negroes—but also retains great indignation over what to him were the atrocities of Reconstruction. He makes no attempt to compromise these conflicting tendencies, and feels no need to do so. His voting record is illiberal on both civil rights and Israel, but Fulbright doesn't care. This often totally exasperates liberals—but if Fulbright were less of a gentleman he could point out that the civil rights leaders cater to the administration by not speaking out against an immoral and racist foreign policy and are vulnerable to the same holier-than-thou criticism they extend to him. But it is not the style of J. William Fulbright to whine.

Fulbright is no pacifist. He predicted disaster for the Bay of Pigs operation, but supported a possible American invasion of Cuba during the missile crisis of 1962. In spite of qualms about the Vietnam involvement, as late as in late June he delivered a Senate speech supporting administration strategy. Fulbright has been disturbed not by questions of morality about the Vietnam War, but by the spiritualistic sense of the inevitable—-the gradual occupation of Asia, the drifting toward nuclear war with China—that made the administration seem to him a band of one-eyed colossi, gazing into a crystal ball tuned to only one channel.

When he couldn't educate the president, he sought to educate the public. And it may be the final irony of the act of J. William Fulbright that Johnson's impetuous reaction to the televised questioning of his policy—in rushing to Honolulu to a hasty summit meeting with puppet premier Ky against the wishes of his more sensitive advisors—has led to a chain of events that may bring about a new South Vietnamese government inclined to ask the United States out of their country. In such an eventuality, it may be difficult for even Rusk, even Johnson, to say no.

Fulbright has changed since he assumed the leadership of the disloyal opposition. His recent speeches present more than a conservative sense of the necessity of limiting the use of U.S. power. He presents an understanding of the inevitability of popular revolutions in Asia, South America, and Africa, and the impracticality of the United States in attempting to control them. In a recent speech, the senator formally assumed the patronage of the traditional brand of American radicalism that has lost acceptability in recent years: "In a democracy dissent is an act of faith. Like medicine, the test of its value is not its taste but its effects, not how it makes people feel at the moment but how it inspires them to act thereafter. Criticism may embarrass the country's leaders in the short run but strengthen their hand in the long run; it may destroy a consensus on policy while expressing a consensus of values. Woodrow Wilson once said that there was 'such a thing as being too proud to fight'; there is also, or ought to be, such a thing as being too confident to conform, too strong to be silent in the face of apparent error. Criticism, in short, is more than a right; it is an act of patriotism, a higher form of patrio-tism, I believe, than the familiar rituals of national adulation."

The end product of these thoughts is destructive of the Cold War consensus that has sapped America of much of its vitality and reduced the rhetoric of democracy to a series of clichés. Perhaps this is what Senator Fulbright the historian has decided he must be about.

[*Ramparts,* June 1966]

The Social History of the Hippies

*A*N ELDERLY SCHOOL BUS, painted like a fluorescent Easter egg in orange, chartreuse, cerise, white, green, blue, and, yes, black, was parked outside the solitary mountain cabin, which made it an easy guess that Ken Kesey, the novelist turned psychedelic Hotspur, was inside. So, of course, was Neal Cassady, the Tristram Shandy of the beat generation, prototype hero of Jack Kerouac's *On the Road,* who had sworn off allegiance to Kerouac when the beat scene became menopausal and signed up as the driver of Kesey's fun-and-games bus, which is rumored to run on LSD. Except for these notorious luminaries, the summit meeting of the leaders of the new hippie subculture, convened in the lowlands of California's High Sierra during an early spring weekend last month, seemed a little like an Appalachian Mafia gathering without Joe Bananas.

Where was Allen Ginsberg, father goddam to two generations of the underground? In New York, reading his poetry to freshmen. And where was Timothy Leary, self-styled guru to tens or is it hundreds of thousands of turned-on people? Off to some nowhere place like Stockton, to preach the gospel of Lysergic Acid Diethylamide to nice ladies in drip-dry dresses. The absence of the elder statesmen of America's synthetic gypsy movement meant something. It meant that the leaders of the booming psychedelic bohemia in the seminal city of San Francisco were their own men—and strangely serious men, indeed, for hippies. Ginsberg and Leary may be Pied Pipers, but they are largely playing old tunes. The young men who make the new scene accept Ginsberg as a revered observer from the elder generation; Leary they abide as an Elmer Gantry on their side, to be used for proselytizing squares only.

The mountain symposium had been called for the extraordinary purpose of discussing the political future of the hippies. Hippies are many things, but most prominently the bearded and beaded inhabitants of the Haight-Ashbury, a little psychedelic city-state edging Golden Gate Park. There, in a daily street-fair atmosphere, upward of fifteen thousand unbonded girls and boys interact in a tribal, love-seeking, free-swinging, acid-based type of society where, if you are a hippie and you have a dime, you can put it in a parking meter and lie down in the street for an hour's suntan (thirty minutes for a nickel) and most drivers will be careful not to run you over. Speaking, sometimes all at once, inside the Sierra cabin were many voices of conscience and vision of the Haight-Ashbury—belonging to men who, except for their Raggedy Andy hair, paisley shirts, and pre-mod western Levi jackets, sounded for all the world like Young Republicans. They talked about reducing governmental controls, the sanctity of the individual, the need for equality among men. They talked, very seriously, about the kind of society they wanted to live in, and the fact that if they wanted an ideal world they would have to go out and make it for themselves, because nobody, least of all the government, was going to do it for them.

The utopian sentiments of these hippies were not to be put down lightly. Hippies have a clear vision of the ideal community—a psychedelic community, to be sure—where everyone is turned on and beautiful and loving and happy and floating free. But it is a vision that, despite the Alice in Wonderland phraseology hippies usually breathlessly employ to describe it, necessarily embodies a radical political philosophy: communal life, drastic restriction of private property, rejection of violence, creativity before consumption, freedom before authority, and de-emphasis of government and traditional forms of leadership. Despite a disturbing tendency to quietism, all hippies *ipso facto* have a political posture—one of unremitting opposition to the Establishment which insists on branding them criminals because they take LSD and marijuana, and hating them, anyway, because they enjoy sleeping nine in a room and three to a bed, seem to have free sex and guiltless minds, and can raise healthy children in dirty clothes.

The hippie choice of weapons is to love the Establishment to death rather than protest it or blow it up (hippies possess a confounding disconcern about traditional political methods or issues). But they are decidedly and forever outside the Consensus on which this society places such a premium, and since the hippie scene is so much the scene of those people under twenty-five that *Time* magazine warns will soon constitute half our population, this is a significant political fact. This is all very solemn talk about people who like to skip rope and wear bright colors, but after spending some time with these fun and fey individuals you realize that, in a very unexpected way, they are as serious about what they're doing as the John Birch Society or the Junior League. It is not improbable, after a few more mountain seminars by those purposeful young men wearing beads, that the Haight-Ashbury may spawn the first utopian collectivist community since Brook Farm. That this society finds it so difficult to take such rascally-looking types seriously is no doubt the indication of a deep-rooted hang-up. But to comprehend the psychosis of America in the computer age, you have to know what's with the hippies.

[GAMES PEOPLE PLAY, MERRY PRANKSTER DIVISION]

Let us go, then, on a trip. You can't miss the Tripmaster: the thick-necked lad in the blue-and-white-striped pants with the red belt and the golden eagle buckle, a watershed of wasted promise in his pale blue eyes, one front tooth capped in patriotic red, white, and blue, his hair downy, flaxen, straddling the incredibly wide divide of his high forehead like two small toupees pasted on sideways. Ken Kesey, Heir Apparent Number One to the grand American tradition of blowing one's artistic talent to do some other thing, was sitting in a surprisingly comfortable chair inside the bus with the psychedelic crust, puffing absentmindedly on a harmonica. The bus itself was ambulatory at about fifty miles an hour, jogging along a back road in sylvan Marin County, four loudspeakers turned all the way up, broadcasting both inside and outside Carl Orff's *Carmina Burana* and filled with two dozen people simultaneously smoking marijuana and looking for an open ice-cream store. It was the Thursday night before the summit meeting weekend and Kesey, along with some fifteen members of the turned-on yes men and women who call him "Chief" and whom he calls the "Merry Pranksters" in return, was demonstrating a "game" to a delegation of visiting hippie firemen.

Crossing north over the Golden Gate Bridge from San Francisco to Marin County to pay Kesey a state visit were seven members of the

Diggers, a radical organization even by Haight-Ashbury standards, which exists to give things away, free. The Diggers started out giving out free food, free clothes, free lodging, and free legal advice, and hope eventually to create a totally free cooperative community. They had come to ask Kesey to get serious and attend the weekend meeting on the state of the nation of the hippies. The dialogue had hardly begun, however, before Kesey loaded all comers into the bus and pushed off into the dark to search for a nocturnal ice-cream store. The bus, which may be the closest modern man has yet come to aping the self-sufficiency of Captain Nemo's submarine, has its own power supply and is equipped with instruments for a full rock band: microphones, loudspeakers, spotlights, and comfortable seats all around. The Pranksters are presently installing microphones every three feet on the bus walls so everybody can broadcast to everybody else all at once.

At the helm was the Intrepid Traveler, Ken Babbs, who is auxiliary chief of the Merry Pranksters when Kesey is out of town or incommunicado or in jail, all three of which he has recently been. Babbs, who is said to be the model for the heroes of both Kesey novels, *One Flew Over the Cuckoo's Nest* and *Sometimes a Great Notion,* picked up a microphone to address the guests in the rear of the bus, like the driver of a Grayline tour: "We are being followed by a police car. Will someone watch and tell me when he turns on his red light?" The law was not unexpected, of course, because any cop who sees Kesey's bus just about *has* to follow it—would probably end up with some form of professional D.T.s if he didn't. It is part of the game: the cop was now playing on their terms, and Kesey and his Pranksters were delighted. In fact, a discernible wave of disappointment swept across the bus when the cop finally gave up chasing this particular U.F.O. and turned onto another road.

The games he plays are very important to Kesey. In many ways his intellectual rebellion has come full circle; he has long ago rejected the structured nature of society—the foolscap rings of success, conformity, and acceptance "normal" people must regularly jump through. To the liberated intellect, no doubt, these requirements constitute the most sordid type of game. But, once rejecting all the norms of society, the artist is free to create his own structures—and along with any new set of rules, however personal, there is necessarily, the shell to the tortoise, a new set of games. In Kesey's case, at least, the games are usually fun.

Running around the outside of an insane society, the healthiest thing you can do is laugh. It helps to look at this sort of complicated if not confused intellectual proposition in bas-relief, as if you were looking at the simple pictures on Wedgewood china. Stand Successful Author Ken Kesey off against, say, Successful Author Truman Capote. Capote, as long as his game is accepted by the system, is free to be as mad as he can. So he tosses the biggest, most vulgar ball in a long history of vulgar balls, and achieves the perfect idiot synthesis of the upper-middle and lower-royal classes. Kesey, who cares as much about the system as he does about the Eddie Cantor Memorial Forest, invents his own game. He purchases a pre-forties International Harvester school bus, paints it psychedelic, fills it with undistinguished though lovable individuals in varying stages of eccentricity, and drives brazenly down the nation's highways, high on LSD, watching and waiting for the cops to blow their minds.

At the least, Kesey's posture has the advantage of being intellectually consistent with the point of view of his novels. In *One Flew Over the Cuckoo's Nest,* he uses the setting of an insane asylum as a metaphor for what he considers to be the basic insanity, or at least the fundamentally bizarre illogic, of American society. Since the world forces you into a game that is both mad and unfair, you are better off inventing your own game. Then, at least, you have a chance of winning. At least that's what Kesey thinks.

[THE CURRY IS VERY HOT; MERRY PRANKSTERS ARE HAVING POT]

There wasn't much doing on late afternoon television, and the Merry Pranksters were a little restless. A few were turning on; one Prankster amused himself squirting his friends with a yellow plastic water-gun; another staggered into the living room, exhausted from peddling a bicycle in ever-diminishing circles in the middle of the street. They were all waiting, quite patiently, for dinner, which the chief was whipping up himself. It was a curry, the recipe of no doubt cabalistic origin. Kesey evidently took his cooking seriously, because he stood guard by the pot for an hour and a half, stirring, concentrating on the little clock on the stove that didn't work. There you have a slice of domestic life, February 1967, from the swish Marin County home of attorney Brian Rohan. As might be surmised, Rohan is Kesey's attorney, and the novelist and his aides-de-camp had parked their bus outside for the duration. The duration might last a long time, because Kesey has dropped out of the hippie scene. Some might say that he was pushed, because he fell, very hard, from favor among the hippies last year when he announced that he, Kesey, personally, was going to help reform the psychedelic scene. This sudden social conscience may have had something to do with beating a jail sentence on a compounded marijuana charge, but when Kesey obtained his freedom with instructions from the judge "to preach an anti-LSD warning to teenagers" it was a little too much for the Haight-Ashbury set. Kesey, after all, was the man who had turned on the Hells Angels.

That was when the novelist was living in La Honda, a small community in the Skyline mountain range overgrown with trees and, after Kesey invited the Hells Angels to several house parties, overgrown with sheriff's deputies. It was in this Sherwood Forest setting, after he had finished his second novel with LSD as his copilot, that Kesey inaugurated his band of Merry Pranksters (they have an official seal from the State of California incorporating them as "Intrepid Trips, Inc."), painted the school bus in glow sock colors, announced he would write no more ("Rather than write, I will ride buses, study the insides of jails, and see what goes on"), and set up fun-time housekeeping on a full-time basis with the Pranksters, his wife, and their three small children (one confounding thing about Kesey is the amorphous quality of the personal relationships in his entourage—the several attractive women don't seem, from the outside, to belong to any particular man; children are loved enough, but seem to be held in common).

When the Hells Angels rumbled by, Kesey welcomed them with LSD. "We're in the same business. You break people's bones, I break people's heads," he told them. The Angels seem to like the whole acid thing, because today they are a fairly constant act in the Haight-Ashbury show, while Kesey has abdicated his role as scoutmaster to fledgling acid heads and exiled himself across the bay. This self-imposed Elba came about when Kesey sensed that the hippie community had soured on him. He had committed the one mortal sin in the hippie ethic: telling people what to do. "Get into a responsibility bag," he urged some four hundred friends attending a private Halloween party. Kesey hasn't been seen much in the Haight-Ashbury since that night, and though the Diggers did succeed in getting him to attend the weekend discussion, it is doubtful they will succeed in getting the novelist involved in any serious effort to shape the Haight-Ashbury future. At thirty-one, Ken Kesey is a hippie has-been.

[THE ACID TESTS—FROM UNITARIANS TO WATTS]

Kesey is now a self-sufficient but lonely figure—if you can be lonely with dozens of Merry Pranksters running around your house all day. If he ever gets maudlin, which is doubtful, he can look back fondly on his hippie memories, which are definitely in the wow! category, because Ken Kesey did for acid roughly what Johnny Appleseed did for trees, and probably more. He did it through a unique and short-lived American institution called the Acid Test. A lot of things happened at an Acid Test, but the main thing was that, in the Haight-Ashbury vernacular, everyone in the audience got zonked out of their minds on LSD. LSD in Pepsi. LSD in coffee. LSD in cake. LSD in the community punch. Most people were generally surprised, because they didn't know they were getting any LSD until it was too late. Later, when word got around that this sort of mad thing was happening at Acid Tests, Kesey sometimes didn't give out LSD on purpose, just so people wouldn't know whether they did or did not have LSD. Another game.

The Acid Tests began calmly enough. In the early versions Kesey merely gave a heart-to-heart psychedelic talk and handed LSD around like the Eucharist, which first happened at a Unitarian conference in Big Sur in August of 1965. He repeated this ritual several times, at private gatherings in his home in La Honda, on college campuses, and once at a Vietnam Day Committee rally at Berkeley. Then Kesey added the Grateful Dead, a pioneer San Francisco rock group, to his Acid Tests and, the cherry on the matzos, the light-show atmospheric technique of projecting slides and wild colors on the walls during rock dances. This combination he called "trips." Trip is the word for an LSD experience, but in Kesey's lexicon it also meant kicks, which were achieved by rapidly changing the audience's sensory environment what seemed like approximately ten million times during an evening by manipulating bright colored lights, tape recorders, slide projectors, weird sound machines, and whatever else may be found in the electronic sink, while the participants danced under stroboscopic lights to a wild rock band or just played around on the floor.

It was a fulgurous, electronically orgiastic thing (the most advanced Tests had closed-circuit television sets on the dance floor so you could see what you were doing), which made psychedelics very "fun" indeed, and the hippies came in droves. Almost every hippie in the Bay Area went to at least one Acid Test, and it is not exceeding the bounds of reasonable speculation to say that Kesey may have turned on at least ten thousand people to LSD during the twenty-four presentations of the Acid Test. (During these Tests the Merry Pranksters painted everything including themselves in fluorescent tones, and bright colors became the permanent in-thing in psychedelic dress.) Turning so many unsuspecting people on to LSD at once could be dangerous, as the Pranksters discovered on a 1965 psychedelic road show when they staged the ill-fated Watts Acid Test. Many of the leading citizens of Watts came to the show, which was all very fine except that whoever put the LSD in the free punch that was passed around put in too much by a factor of about four. This served to make for a very wild Acid Test, and one or two participants "freaked out" and had a very hard time of it for the next few days.

After the California legislature played Prohibition and outlawed LSD on October 6, 1966, Kesey wound up the Acid Test syndrome with what was billed as a huge "Trips Festival" in San Francisco. People who regularly turn on say the Trips Festival was a bore: it embodied all the Acid Test elements except acid and, happily for the coffers of Intrepid Trips, Inc., attracted a huge crowd of newspapermen, narcotics agents, and other squares, but very few hippies. The Merry Pranksters slyly passed out plain sugar cubes for the benefit of the undercover agents. Suddenly San Francisco, which for a grown-up city gets excited very easily, was talking about almost nothing but "trips" and LSD. Hippies, like overnight, had become fashionable. If you are inclined to give thanks for this sort of thing, they go to the bad boy wonder of Psychedelphia, disappearing there over the horizon in his wayward bus.

[THE GHOSTS OF SCENES PAST,
OR HOW WE GOT HERE FROM THERE]

Like Frederick J. Turner and Arnold Toynbee, Chester Anderson has a theory of history. His theory is psychedelic, but that is perfectly natural since he is a veteran acid head. Anderson, a thirty-five-year-old professional bohemian who looks forty-five, considers himself the unofficial historian of the psychedelic movement and has amassed enough footnotes to argue somewhat convincingly that the past fifteen years of social change in the United States—all the underground movements, and a significant part of the cultural changes—have been intimately connected with drugs.

If he is going to press his argument all the way, he may have to punch it out with Marshall McLuhan, who no doubt would assert that such phenomena as hippie colonies are nothing but a return to "tribal" culture, an inevitable reaction to our electronic age. And any social historian worth his salt will put it that every society has found some way to allow the sons and daughters of its middle class to drop out and cut up. (Most hippies, by the way, are from middle-class stock, so what's the difference from, say, the Teddy Boys? Maybe lots, maybe none.) But there is no disputing the cultural and artistic flip-flops this country has gone through in the last decade. The jazz musicians' vogue meant something. So did the beat generation. So, we suppose, did pop art, and rock and roll, and so, of course, the hippies. If, in briefly tracing the derivation of the hippies from their seminal reasons in the intellectual uneasiness of the early fifties, we chance to favor the testimony of Chester Anderson, it is only because he was there.

That was some bad year, 1953. There was a war on in Korea, a confusing, undefined war, the first big American war that wasn't the one to end all wars, because the aftermath of World War II had blown that phobia. And now the Bomb was with us, and with it the staccato series of disturbing headline events that stood for the Cold War; college was the only escape from the draft, but eggheads were becoming unpopular, Stevenson had lost the election, and the Rosenbergs had been executed. It was all gloom, gloom, and dullsville, and if you were young and intellectual you were hard-pressed to find a hero or even a beautiful person. The only really alive, free thing, it seemed, was jazz—and the arrival of the long-playing record had sparked a jazz renaissance, and with it the first drug heroes: most kids sympathized with Gene Krupa's marijuana busts, the agony of Lady Day's junk hangup was universal, and Charlie Parker had his own drugstore.

Lady Day's way wasn't the way of the new generation, Chester Anderson will be quick to tell you, because she was on "body" drugs. Whatever else body drugs—heroin, opium, barbiturates, alcohol, tranquilizers—may do, they eventually turn you off, and contemporary heads like to be turned on—i.e., senses intensified, stimulated rather than depressed. "Head" drugs, which do the latter, are both cheaper and easier to get than body drugs, and come in approximately eighteen varieties in three different classifications—natural drugs like marijuana, hashish, peyote, morning glory seeds, Hawaiian wood rose seeds, and certain types of Mexican mushrooms; artificial psychedelics like mescaline, LSD, psilocybin and psilocin, and whatever the ingredient is that makes Romilar cough syrup so popular with young heads; and synthetic stimulants which, used in large doses by heads, are known as "speed"—dexedrine, benzedrine, and methedrine.

But in the early fifties there wasn't such a complete psychedelic medicine shelf to choose from, and the culturally disenchanted pioneers who began to settle new colonies in New York's Greenwich Village and San Francisco's North Beach had to make do with pot. In a climate dominated by Dwight Eisenhower in the newspapers and Ed Sullivan on television, they also began to turn on to the pacifist, humanist philosophies of Asia—particularly Buddhism, most especially Zen—while Christianity as a workable concept became more meaningless, despite the exemplary efforts of such men as Brother Antoninus and Thomas Merton. American churchmen seemed to have neither the patience nor the fortitude to deal with people who were, well, unsettled. Folk music, which had been slowly dying, perked up a little, and there was a new interest in fresh, tuned-in poetry. As the fifties approached middle age and McCarthy went on the rampage, the few signs of life in a stagnant society centered around the disoriented peace movement, the fledgling civil rights movement, the young political left, jazz and folk music, poetry, and Zen. Most of these followers were, of course, taking pot, while the rest of the country remained on booze and sleeping pills.

(If, in memory of the eighty-fifth anniversary of Anthony Trollope's death, we may be permitted an aside to the reader, it would be to say that one of the things that is considered original, but is in fact not, about the hippies is the concept of "dropping out" of society. Without adopting the histrionics of Hogarth crusading against the masses drinking gin, it is true that alcohol is an opiate which serves to help tens of millions of busy businessmen and lethargic housewives to "drop out" of any essential involvement in life and remain political and artistic boors. But alcohol is legal so nobody cares. If pot and LSD were ever legalized, it would be a mortal blow to this bohemia. Hippies have a political posture essentially because of the enforced criminality of their daily dose, and if taking LSD meant no more in society than the commuter slugging down his seventh martini, the conspiratorial magic would go out of the movement.)

MEANWHILE, IN SAN FRANCISCO, Allen Ginsberg remembers an evening in 1955 which could stand as well as any for the starting point of what was to become the most thorough repudiation of America's middlebrow culture since the expatriates walked out on the country in the thirties. The vanguard of what was to be the beat generation had gathered at the Six Gallery on Fillmore Street for a poetry reading moderated by Kenneth Rexroth, a respectable leftish intellectual who was later to become the public defender of the beats. Lawrence Ferlinghetti was in the audience, and so were Kerouac and his then sidekick Neal Cassady, listening to Michael McClure, Phil Lamantia, Gary Snyder, and Philip Whalen read their poetry. Ginsberg was there too, and delighted everyone with a section of the still unfinished "Howl," better known to beats as the Declaration of Independence.

Two distinct strains in the underground movement of the fifties were represented at this salient gathering. One was a distinctly fascist trend, embodied in Kerouac, which can be recognized by a totalitarian insistence on action and nihilism, and usually accompanied by a Superman concept. This strain runs, deeper and less silent, through the hippie scene today. It is into this fascist bag that you can put Kesey and his friends, the Hells Angels, and, in a more subtle way, Dr. Timothy Leary. The other, majority, side of the beats was a cultural reaction to the existential brinkmanship forced on them by the Cold War, and a lively attack on the concurrent rhetoric of complacency and self-satisfaction that pervaded the literary establishment all the way from the *Atlantic Monthly* to Lionel Trilling. Led by men like Ginsberg and Ferlinghetti, the early beats weighed America by its words and deeds, and found it pennyweight. They took upon themselves the role of conscience for the machine. They rejected all values and when, in attempting to carve a new creative force, they told America to "go fuck itself," America reacted, predictably, with an obscenity trial.

The early distant warnings of the drug-based culture that would dominate the Haight-Ashbury a decade later were there in the early days of North Beach. Marijuana was as popular as Coke at a Baptist wedding, and the available hallucinogens—peyote and mescaline—were part of the beat rebellion. Gary Snyder, poet, mountain climber, formal Yama-bushi Buddhist, and a highly respected leader of the hippie scene today, first experimented with peyote while living with the Indian tribe of the same name in 1948; Ginsberg first took it in New York in 1951; Lamantia, Kerouac, and Cassady were turned on by beat impresario Jaime de Angulo at his Big Sur retreat in 1952. And beat parties, whether they served peyote, marijuana, or near beer, were rituals, community sacraments, setting the format for contemporary hippie rituals. But the psychedelic community didn't really begin to flourish until late 1957 and 1958 in New York, and for that story we take you to Chester Anderson in the Village.

[WAS THE KINGSTON TRIO REALLY RED GUARDS?]

On Thanksgiving Day 1957, Chester Anderson was turned on to grass by a bongo-playing superhippie who went by the code name of Mr. Sulks. Grass, if you don't know and don't have an underground glossary handy, is translated marijuana, and from that day forward, Anderson, who once studied music at the University of Miami so he could write string quartets like Brahms, became a professional Turn-On and migrated with bohemia, east to west to east to west, from the Village to North Beach back to the Village to the Haight-Ashbury, where he can be found today—a prototype of the older psychedelic type who mixes with the drifting, turning on kids to form the central nervous system of any body of hippies.

The first psychedelic drug to reach the Village in any quantity was peyote, an obscure hallucinatory cactus bud used by Indians in religious ceremonies. Peyote was cheap and plentiful (it can still be ordered by mail from Laredo at ten dollars for one hundred "buttons") and became highly touted—Havelock Ellis and Aldous Huxley recommended it. The only problem with peyote was that it tasted absolutely terrible, and, as peyote cults sprang up, peyote cookbooks came out with recipes for preparing the awful stuff in ways that would kill the taste. "Man," Chester recalls a head telling him at the time, "if I thought it'd get me high, I'd eat shit." As with most new head drugs, the taking of peyote was treated as a quasi-religious event. The first time Chester took it, he did so with great ritual before a statue of the Buddha. Peyote was the thing in late 1957, and by the summer of 1958 mescaline, the first synthetic psychedelic, was widely distributed. The heads reacted like unwed mothers being handed birth control pills—they were no longer dependent on nature. Turn-ons could be *manufactured*!

According to Chester's files, LSD didn't arrive in any large, consumer-intended supply in the Village until the winter of 1961–62, and not in the Bay Area until the summer of 1964, but by that time something unusual had happened to America's psychedelic gypsies: they had become formal enemies of the State. Massive harassment by the cops in San Francisco, and by the coffeehouse license inspectors in New York, had led the heads and the young middle-class types who came in caravan proportions, to test the no-more-teachers, no-more-books way of bohemian life, to view the Establishment as the bad guy who would crush their individuality and spirituality in any way he could. This is the derivation of whatever political posture the hippies have today. It will be significant, of course, only if the Haight-Ashbury scene doesn't go the way of the beat generation—assimilated by a kick-hungry society. For the serious, literary beats, it was all over but the shouting when the Co-existence Bagel Shop became a stop on sightseeing tours.

In 1962, the Village was pulsating with psychedelic evangelism. LSD was so cheap and so plentiful that it became a big thing among heads to turn on new people as fast as they could give LSD away. Pot, also, was being used more widely than ever by middle-class adults, and spread from the urban bohemias to the hinterlands by small folk music circles that were to be found everywhere from Jacksonville, Florida, to Wausau,

Wisconsin. At the same time, almost the entire Village was treating LSD like it was a selection on a free lunch counter, and a scruffy folknik called Bobby Dylan was beginning to play charitable guest sets in the Washington Square coffeehouses. "Things," Chester said, "were happening more rapidly than we knew." What was happening, Mr. Jones, was that folk music, under the influence of early acid culture, was giving way to rock and roll. Rock spread the hippie way of life like a psychedelic plague, and it metamorphosed in such rapid fashion from the popularity of folk music that a very suspicious person might ask if seemingly safe groups like the Kingston Trio were not, in fact, the Red Guards of the hippie cultural revolution.

There was a rock and roll before, of course, but it was all bad seed. The likes of Frankie Avalon, Fabian, and Elvis Presley sent good rock-and-roll musicians running to folk music. Then absolutely the world's greatest musical blitz fell and the Beatles landed, everywhere, all at once. The impact of their popular music was analogous to the Industrial Revolution on the nineteenth century. They brought music out of the jukebox and into the street. The Beatles' ecstatic, alive, electric sound had a total sensory impact, and was inescapably participational. It was "psychedelic music." "The Beatles are a trip," Chester said. Whether the Beatles or Dylan or the Rolling Stones actually came to their style through psychedelic involvement (Kenneth Tynan says the recent Beatles song "Tomorrow Never Knows" is "the best musical evocation of LSD I've ever heard") is not as important as the fact that their songs reflect LSD values—love, life, getting along with other people—and that this type of involving, turn-on music galvanized the entire hippie underground into overt, brassy existence—particularly in San Francisco.

Drug-song lyrics may, in fact, be the entire literary output of the hippie generation. The hippies' general disregard for anything as static as a book is a fact over which Chester Anderson and Marshall McLuhan can shake hands. For acid heads are, in McLuhan's phrase, "postliterate." Hippies do not share our written, linear society—they like textures better than surfaces, prefer the electronic to the mechanical, like group, tribal activities. Theirs is an ecstatic, do-it-now culture, and rock and roll is their art form.

[DR. LEARY—PRETENDER TO THE HIPPIE THRONE]

The suit was Brooks Brothers '59, and the paisley tie J.Press contemporary, but the bone-carved Egyptian mandala hanging around his neck, unless it was made in occupied Japan, had to be at least two thousand years old. Dr. Timothy Leary, B.A. University of Alabama, Ph.D. University of California, LSD Cuernavaca, and 86'd Harvard College, was dressed up for a night on the town, but as his devotees say of this tireless proselytizer of the psychedelic cause, it was work, work, work. Tonight Leary was scouting somebody else's act, a swami's at that, who was turning on the hippies at the Avalon Ballroom by leading them in an hour-long Hindu chant without stopping much for breath. The Avalon is one of the two great, drafty ballrooms where San Francisco hippies, hippie-hangers-on and young hippies-to-be congregate each weekend to participate in the psychedelic rock and light shows that are now as much a part of San Francisco as cable cars, and a lot noisier. This dance was a benefit for the new swami, recently installed in a Haight-Ashbury storefront, with a fair-passage sign from Allen Ginsberg, whom he had bumped into in India. The hippies were turning out to see just what the swami's schtick was, but Dr. Leary had a different purpose. He has a vested, professional interest in turning people on, and here was this swami, trying to do it with just a chant, like it was natural childbirth or something.

The word professional is not used lightly. There is a large group of professionals making it by servicing and stimulating the hippie world—in the spirit of the Haight-Ashbury we should refer to these men as merchant princes—and Timothy Leary is the pretender to the throne. Dr. Leary claims to have launched the first indigenous religion in America. That may very well be, though as a religious leader he is Aimee Semple McPherson in drag. Dr. Leary, who identifies himself as a "prophet," recently played the Bay Area in his LSD road show, where he sold four-dollar seats to lots of squares but few hippies (Dr. Leary's pitch is to the straight world), showed a technicolor movie billed as simulating an LSD experience (it was big on close-ups of enlarged blood vessels), burned incense, dressed like a holy man in white cotton pajamas, and told everybody to "turn on, tune in, and drop out."

In case you are inclined to make light of this philosophic advice you should not laugh out loud. Because Dr. Leary is serious about his work, he cannot be dismissed as a cross between a white Father Divine and Nietzsche, no matter how tempting the analogy. He has made a substantial historical contribution to the psychedelic scene, although his arrest records may figure more prominently than his philosophy in future hippie histories. Since, something like Eve, he first bit into the sacred psychedelic mushroom while lounging beside a swimming pool in Cuernavaca, he has been hounded by the consequences of his act. Since Dr. Leary discovered LSD, he has been booted out of Harvard for experimenting a little too widely with it among the undergraduate population, was asked to leave several foreign countries for roughly the same reasons, and is now comfortably if temporarily ensconced in a turned-on billionaire friend's estate near Poughkeepsie, New York, while awaiting judicial determination of a thirty-year prison sentence for transporting a half ounce of marijuana across the Rio Grande without paying the Texas marijuana tax, which has not been enforced since the time of the Lone Ranger.

If he were asked to contribute to the "L" volume of the World Book Encyclopedia, Dr. Leary would no doubt sum up his work as "having turned on American culture," though his actual accomplishments are somewhat more prosaic. Together with Richard Alpert, who was to Dr. Leary what Bill Moyers was to President Johnson, Leary wrote an article in May 1962 in, surprise, the *Bulletin of the Atomic Scientists*. The article warned that, in event of war, the Russians were likely to douse all our reservoirs with LSD in order to make people so complacent that they wouldn't particularly care about being invaded, and as a civil defense precaution we ought to do it ourselves first—you know, douse our own reservoirs—so that when the Reds got their chance the country would know just what was coming off. It was back to the old drawing board after that article, but Alpert and Dr. Leary made their main contribution to the incredibly swift spread of LSD through the nation in 1964 by the simple act of publishing a formula for LSD, all that was needed by any enterprising housewife with a B-plus in high school chemistry and an inclination for black-market activity. Dr. Leary's religious crusade has been a bust, convert-wise, and not so salutary financially, either, so he announced recently that he was dropping out, himself, to contemplate his navel under the influence. It would be easier to take Dr. Leary seriously if he could overcome his penchant for treating LSD as a patent snake-bite medicine.

An enlightening example of this panacea philosophy is found back among the truss ads in the September 1966 issue of *Playboy*. In the midst of a lengthy interview when, as happens in *Playboy*, the subject got around to sex, Dr. Leary was all answers. "An LSD session that does not involve an ultimate merging with a person of the opposite sex isn't really complete," he said, a facet of the drug he neglected to mention to the Methodist ladies he was attempting to turn on in Stockton, California. But this time, Dr. Leary was out to turn on the *Playboy* audience. The following selection from the interview is reprinted in its entirety. Italics are *Playboy*'s.

> PLAYBOY: We've heard that some women who ordinarily have difficulty achieving orgasm find themselves capable of multiple orgasms under LSD. Is that true?
>
> LEARY: In a carefully prepared, loving LSD session, a woman will inevitably have several hundred orgasms.
>
> PLAYBOY: Several *hundred*?
>
> LEARY: Yes. Several hundred.

After recovering from that intelligence, the *Playboy* interviewer, phrasing the question as diplomatically as possible, asked Dr. Leary if he got much, being such a handsome LSD turn-on figure. Dr. Leary allowed that women were always falling over him, but responded with the decorum of Pope Paul being translated from the Latin: "Any charis matic person who is conscious of his own mythic potency awakens this basic hunger in women and pays reverence to it at the level that is harmonious and appropriate at the time." Dr. Leary also said that LSD is a "specific cure for homosexuality."

The final measurement of the tilt of Dr. Leary's windmill, his no doubt earnest claim to be the prophet of this generation, must be made by weighing such recorded conversations against his frequent and urgent pleas to young people to "drop out of politics, protest, petitions, and pickets" and join his "new religion," where, as he said recently: "You have to be out of your mind to pray." Perhaps, and quite probably so.

[WHERE DUN & BRADSTREET FEARS TO TREAD]

Allen Ginsberg asked ten thousand people to turn toward the sea and chant with him. They all did just that, and then picked up the papers and miscellaneous droppings on the turf of Golden Gate Park's polo field and went contentedly home. This was the end of the first Human Be-In, a gargantuan hippie happening held only for the joy of it in mid-January. The hippie tribes gathered under clear skies with rock bands, incense, chimes, flutes, feathers, candles, banners, and drums. Even the Hells Angels were on their good behavior—announcing that they would guard the sound truck against unspecified evil forces. It was all so successful that the organizers are talking about another be-in this summer to be held at the bottom of the Grand Canyon with maybe two hundred thousand hippies being-in.

The local papers didn't quite know how to treat this one, except for the *San Francisco Chronicle*'s ace society editor, Frances Moffat, who ran through the crowd picking out local socialites and taking notes on the fashions. Mrs. Moffat's intense interest reflects the very in, very marketable character of San Francisco Hippiedom. Relatively high-priced mod clothing and trinket stores are as common in the Haight-Ashbury as pissoirs used to be in Paris. They are run by hippie merchants mostly for square customers, but that doesn't mean that the hippies themselves aren't brand-name conscious. Professing a distaste for competitive society, hippies are, contradictorily, frantic consumers. Unlike the beats, they do not disdain money. Indeed, when they have it, which with many is often, they use it to buy something pretty or pleasureful. You will find only the best hi-fi sets in hippie flats.

In this commercial sense, the hippies have not only accepted assimilation (the beats fought it, and lost), they have swallowed it whole. The hippie culture is in many ways a prototype of the most ephemeral aspects of the larger American society; if the people looking in from the suburbs want change, clothes, fun, and some lightheadedness from the new gypsies, the hippies are delivering—and some of them are becoming rich hippies because of it. The biggest Robber Baron is dance promoter Bill Graham, a Jewish boy from New York who made it big in San Francisco by cornering the hippie bread-and-circuses concession. His weekend combination rock-and-roll dances and light shows at the cavernous, creaky old Fillmore Auditorium on the main street of San Francisco's Negro ghetto are jammed every night. Even Andy Warhol played the Fillmore. Although Graham is happy providing these week-end spiritual experiences, he's not trying to be a leader. "I don't want to make cadres, just money," he said. Graham's crosstown competitor is Chet Helms, a rimless-glasses-variety hippie from Texas who has turned the pioneer, nonprofit San Francisco rock group called the Family Dog into a very profit-making enterprise at the Avalon Ballroom.

A side-product of the light-show dances, and probably the only other permanent manifestation of hippie culture to date, is the revival in a gangbusters way of Art Nouveau poster art. Wes Wilson, who letters his posters in 18-, 24-, and 36-point Illegible, originated the basic style in posters for the Fillmore dances. Graham found he could make as much money selling posters as dance tickets, so he is now in the poster business, too. The posters, at one dollar apiece, as common as window shades in the Haight-Ashbury, demand total involvement from the reader, and are thus considered psychedelic manifestations of the existential, non-verbal character of hippie culture. What's it all about? A shy, bush-bearded, and very nice little postermaker named Mouse!, when asked his definition of hippie art, replied:

Haight Street, the Fifth Avenue of Hippiedom, is geographically parallel to Golden Gate Park but several blocks uphill, where rows of half-vacant storefronts once indicated the gradual decline of a middle-class neighborhood. But all that changed, dramatically, during the past eighteen months. Haight Street now looks like the Metropolitan Opera Company backstage on the opening night of *Aida*. The stores are all occupied, but with mercantile ventures that might give Dun & Bradstreet cause to wonder. Threaded among the older meat markets, discount furniture stores, laundromats, and proletarian bars are a variety of leather goods shops, art galleries, mod clothing stores, and boutiques specializing in psychedelic paraphernalia like beads, prisms, and marijuana pipes, and of course there is the Psychedelic Shop itself. The Psychedelic Shop is treated as a hippie landmark of sorts, but the Haight-Ashbury scene was percolating long before the Thelin brothers, Ron and Jay, stuffed a disconcertingly modern glass and steel storefront full of amulets, psychedelic books, a large stock of the underground press, and some effete gadgetry for acid heads. The hippie phenomena began to metamorphose from a personal to a social happening around the fall of 1965 after the kids at Berkeley turned on to LSD, Ken Kesey started holding Acid Tests, and the Family Dog staged its first dance.

Instrumental in spreading the word was the *Chronicle*'s highly regarded jazz critic, Ralph J. Gleason. Gleason is read religiously by hippies. Besides explaining to his square readers what is happening, he is also the unofficial arbiter of good taste in the Haight-Ashbury community. Gleason was quick to tell Ken Kesey, in print, when he was out of line, and did the same for Dr. Leary. Gleason's writings tuned in other members of the *Chronicle* staff, and the extensive, often headline publicity the newspaper gave to the hippie scene (Kesey's return from a self-imposed Mexican exile was treated with the seriousness of a reasonably large earthquake) helped escalate the Haight-Ashbury population explosion.

So there is plenty of business for the hippie merchants, but some of them, like the Thelin brothers, are beginning to wonder where it will all lead. At the prodding of the Diggers, the Thelins are considering making the store a nonprofit cooperative that will help "the kids get high and stay high" at low cost. They may also take the same steps with the *Oracle*, the Haight-Ashbury monthly tabloid. The majority of the hip merchants, however, are very comfortable with the ascending publicity and sales, and have as little vision of what they are helping create than did Alexander Bell when he spilled acid on himself. If you have any doubts left about the thoroughly successful commercialization of the entire hippie scene, you should look at the comic pages between *Dick Tracy* and *L'il Abner*, where a few weeks back there was this, well, episode, in the comic strip called *Rex Morgan, M.D.*:

Unless most parents sent their children to bed before they got to the comics that week, everybody now knows all about trips. This just goes to prove that somewhere in the wild, psychedelic world there's a buck to be made.

[WILL THE REAL FRODO BAGGINS PLEASE STAND UP?]

Except for the obvious fact that he wasn't covered with fur, you would have said to yourself that for sure there was old Frodo Baggins, crossing Haight Street. Frodo Baggins is the hero of the English antiquarian J. R. R. Tolkien's classic trilogy *Lord of the Rings,* absolutely the favorite book of every hippie, about a race of little people called Hobbits, who live somewhere in prehistory in a place called Middle Earth. Hobbits are hedonistic, happy little fellows who love beauty and pretty colors. Hobbits have their own scene and resent intrusion, pass the time eating three or four meals a day, and smoke burning leaves of herb in pipes of clay. You can see why hippies would like Hobbits.

The hustling, heroic-looking fellow with the mistaken identity was Emmett Grogan, kingpin of the Diggers and the closest thing the hippies in the Haight-Ashbury have to a real live hero. Grogan, twenty-three, with blond, unruly hair and a fair, freckled Irish face, has the aquiline nose of a leader, but he would prefer to say that he "just presents alternatives." He is in and out of jail seventeen times a week, sometimes busted for smashing a cop in the nose (Grogan has a very intolerant attitude toward policemen), sometimes bailing out a friend, and sometimes, like Monopoly, just visiting. The alternatives he presents are rather disturbing to the hippie bourgeoisie, since he thinks they have no business charging hippies money for their daily needs and should have the decency to give things away free, like the Diggers do, or at least charge the squares and help out the hippies.

Grogan has a very clear view of what freedom means in society ("Why can't I stand on the corner and wait for nobody? Why can't everyone?") and an even clearer view of the social position of the hippie merchants ("They just want to expand their sales; they don't care what happens to people here; they're nothing but goddamn shopkeepers with beards.") Everyone is a little afraid of Grogan in the Haight-Ashbury, including the cops. A one-man crusade for purity of purpose, he is the conscience of the hippie community. He is also a bit of a daredevil and a madman, and could easily pass for McMurphy, the roguish hero in Kesey's novel set in an insane asylum. There is a bit of J. P. Donleavy's *Ginger Man* in him, too.

A few weeks ago, out collecting supplies for the Diggers' daily free feed, Grogan went into a San Francisco wholesale butcher and asked for soup bones and meat scraps. "No free food here; we work for what we eat," said the head butcher, a tattooed Bulgar named Louie, who was in the icebox flanked by his seven assistant butchers. "You're a fascist pig and a coward," replied Grogan, whom Louie immediately smashed in the skull with the blunt side of a carving knife. That turned out to be a mistake, because the seven assistant butchers didn't like Louie much, and all jumped him. While all those white coats were grunting and rolling in the sawdust, a bleeding Grogan crawled out with four cardboard boxes full of meat.

This was a typical day in Dogpatch for Grogan, who has had his share of knocks. A Brooklyn boy, he ran away from home at fifteen and spent the next six years in Europe, working as a busboy in the Alps, and, later, studying filmmaking in Italy under Antonioni. Grogan had naturally forgotten to register for the draft, so when he returned to the United States he was in the army four days later. That didn't last long, however, because the first thing Grogan had to do was clean the barracks. His idea of cleaning barracks was to throw all the guns out the window, plus a few of the rusty beds and artistically displeasing foot lockers. Then he began painting the remaining bed frames yellow. "I threw out everything that was not esthetically pleasing," he told the sergeant.

Two days later Grogan was in the psychiatric ward of Letterman Hospital in San Francisco, where he stayed for six months before the authorities decided they couldn't quite afford to keep him. That was shortly after an army doctor, learning of his film training, ordered Grogan to the photo lab for "work therapy." It was a "beautiful, tremendously equipped lab," Grogan recalls, and since it wasn't used very much, he took a picture of his own big blond face and proceded to make 5,000 prints. When the doctors caught up with him, he had some 4,700 nine-by-twelve glossies of Emmett Grogan neatly stacked on the floor, and all lab machines—driers, enlargers, developers—were going like mad, and the water was running over on the floor. "What did you do that for?" a doctor screamed. Grogan shrugged. "I'm crazy," he said.

He was released a little later, and acted for a while with the San Francisco Mime Troupe, the city's original and brilliant radical theatre ensemble. Then last fall, when the Negro riots broke out in San Francisco and the National Guard put a curfew on the Haight-Ashbury, the Diggers happened. "Everybody was trying to figure how to react to the curfew. The SDS came down and said ignore it, go to jail. The merchants put up chicken posters saying 'for your own safety, get off the street.' Somehow, none of those ideas seemed right. If you had something to do on the streets, you should do it and tell the cops to go screw off. If you didn't, you might as well be inside." Something to do, to Grogan, was to eat if you were hungry, so at 8 p.m., at the curfew witching hour, he and an actor friend named Billy Landau set up a delicious free dinner in the park, right under the cops' noses, and the hippies came and ate and have been chowing down, free, every night since. The Haight-Ashbury has never been quite the same.

[A PSYCHEDELIC "GRAPES OF WRATH"]

Every bohemian community has its inevitable coterie of visionaries who claim to know what it is all about. But the Diggers are, somehow, different. They are bent on creating a wholly cooperative subculture and, so far, they are not just hallucinating, they are doing it. Free clothes (used) are there for whomever wants them. Free meals are served every day. Next, Grogan plans to open a smart mod clothing store on Haight Street and give the clothes away free, too (the hippie merchants accused him of "trying to undercut our prices"). He wants to start Digger farms where participants will raise their own produce. He wants to give away free acid, to eliminate junky stuff and end profiteering. He wants cooperative living to forestall inevitable rent exploitation when the Haight-Ashbury becomes chic. Not since Brook Farm, not since the Catholic Workers, has any group in this dreadfully co-optive consumer society been so serious about a utopian community.

If Grogan succeeds or fails in the Haight-Ashbury it will not be as important as the fact that he has tried. For he is, at least, providing the real possibility of what he calls "alternatives" in the down-the-rabbit-hole-culture of the hippies. Grogan is very hung up on freedom. "Do your thing, be what you are, and nothing will ever bother you," he says. His heroes are the Mad Bomber of New York, who blissfully blew up all kinds of things around Manhattan over thirty years because he just liked to blow things up, and poet Gary Snyder, whom he considers the "most important person in the Haight-Ashbury" because instead of sitting around sniffing incense and talking about it, he went off to Japan and became a Zen master. "He did it, man."

This is an interesting activist ethic, but it remains doubtful just what the hippies will do. Not that many, certainly, will join Grogan's utopia, because utopias, after all, have a size limit. The New Left has been flirting with the hippies lately, even to the extent of singing "Yellow Submarine" at a Berkeley protest rally, but it looks from here like a largely unrequited love. The hip merchants will, of course, go on making money. And the youngsters will continue to come to the Haight-Ashbury and do—what? That was the question put to the hippie leaders at their summit meeting. They resolved their goals, but not the means, and the loud noise you heard from outside was probably Emmett Grogan pounding the table with his shoe.

The crisis of the happy hippie ethic is precisely this: it is all right to turn on, but it is not enough to drop out. Grogan sees the issue in the gap "between the radical political philosophy of Jerry Rubin and Mario Savio and psychedelic love philosophy." He, himself, is not interested in the war in Vietnam, but on the other hand he does not want to spend his days like Ferdinand sniffing pretty flowers. This is why he is so furious at the hip merchants. "They created the myth of this utopia; now they aren't going to do anything about it." Grogan takes the evils of society very personally, and he gets very angry, almost physically sick, when a pregnant fifteen-year-old hippie's baby starves in her stomach, a disaster which is not untypical in the Haight-Ashbury, and which Grogan sees being repeated tenfold this summer when upward of two hundred thousand migrant teenagers and college kids come, as a psychedelic *Grapes of Wrath*, to utopia in search of the heralded turn-on.

The danger in the hippie movement is more than overcrowded streets and possible hunger riots this summer. If more and more youngsters begin to share the hippie political posture of unrelenting quietism, the future of activist, serious politics is bound to be affected. The hippies have shown that it can be pleasant to drop out of the arduous task of attempting to steer a difficult, unrewarding society. But when that is done, you leave the driving to the Hells Angels.

[*Ramparts*, March 1967]

Humanae Vitae

I HAVE BEEN SUBJECT TO THE ROMAN CATHOLIC CHURCH'S teaching on birth control twice during my formal schooling, originating with my high school religion teacher, a florid-faced Brother of Mary whom I always presumed was a homosexual because, when proximity allowed, he habitually stroked the pants legs of the boys. When the chapter on sex came due in the course of the semester he appeared disinterested in it, and simply told the class to read the religion textbook and be prepared to explain, in an examination, the basic workings of the rhythm system and the circumstances under which married couples were allowed to use it. I dutifully memorized everything, but never quite understood the functioning of the thermometers and other gadgetry, though I retained a vivid picture of St. Paul's warning about spilling one's seed.

However, in my junior year in college I received a most thorough indoctrination in the church's position, which came in a manner that for excess of detail and religious ferocity may have rivaled Stephen Dedalus' retreat. For the purpose, a guest lecturer was brought into our religion class, a tough, balding Jesuit who had been an army chaplain and had, as he put it, "seen the world." He began by dispelling the notion that a chaste priest was unqualified to teach the rules of sex—after all, did a doctor have to endure cancer in order to cure it?

The special lectures lasted three weeks, during which the most remarkable illustrations were chalked on the blackboard. We learned the mathematics of menstrual cycles better than our multiplication tables; we were instructed in the art of interpreting the most minute gradations in the readings on our future wives' rectal thermometers; we discovered that Freud had taught that artificial contraception was psychologically harmful; and we became schooled in the disposition of unwanted or untimely erections. We were assured that medical science was on the threshold of advances which would make the rhythm system "foolproof" (needless to say, such advances never came to fruition and rhythm remains the most frustrating and untrustworthy system of regulating one's issue), which would mean that Catholic couples need refrain from the full exercise of marital privilege for only a few days each month. But we were warned, most sternly, that the immutable and obvious dictates of natural law said that one could never begin an act and not carry it to its natural end. Therefore any activity or thought that might lead one to become excited, our instructor said, was also forbidden during certain periods of the menstrual month. Perhaps somewhat carried away by the anatomical frankness of previous discussions, I was booted out of class for asking if that meant we had to look at a calendar before getting a hard-on.

Either by way of such ritualistic expositions, or via the Sen-Sened breath of the priest wafting through the mesh screen of the confessional booth, most Catholics have had such insensate and barbarous conditions laid upon their personal lives. But even in America the church, for all its Irish Catholic Stalinism, could not enforce guilt when its faithful didn't feel guilty. Gradually, individually, American Catholics increasingly practiced forbidden methods of birth control, and with the advent of the pill—invented by a nice old Catholic doctor who, incidentally, *looked* like a pope—the battle for rhythm was, statistically, just about all over. A sardonic monsignor of my acquaintance remarked last year that almost the only large segment of the Catholic population still using the rhythm method were nuns and priests engaged in extracurricular affairs.

But it is difficult to be a Catholic and not feel a little bit guilty, and most of us felt a great sense of relief with the advent of Pope John and the liberalizing decrees of the Ecumenical Council—it was taken for granted that the church's outmoded teachings on birth control would soon go. As with the end of Prohibition, everybody had a drink to celebrate. So it was slightly disturbing when Pope John in effect took the decision on birth control away from the bishops by setting up a secretive six-man commission to investigate the subject and report directly back to him. (It is not generally known that John's commission was quite conservative in makeup—in contrast to the variegated fifty-seven-member commission named by Pope Paul.) But the council debated the issue anyway, with the sentiment being for some form of modification in the church's position. Cardinal Suenens of Belgium warned in 1963, prophetically, that the church would have "a new Galileo case" on its hands if it failed to modernize its teaching on contraception.

There were precedents for change. The church had long ago abandoned the papal teaching that made charging interest a sin. The Vatican Council, in its decree on religious liberty, summarily dismissed Pope Gregory XVI's 1832 contention that man did not have a right to freedom of conscience. Also—and most importantly—Pope John's remarkable encyclical, *Pacem in Terris,* laid the theological groundwork for a reversal of the old natural-law arguments against contraception by reordering the priorities of Catholic theology. Traditional scholastic philosophers—the men who staff the rationalization desk of Catholic theology—looked first at the nature of things, and only secondarily at the thing itself. This generic approach, whereby inflexible laws were deduced by inexorable logic from abstract principles, had the natural effect of asserting the primacy of wholes before parts, and of duties before rights, along with a host of other anti-personal and elitist philosophical implications.

As opposed to his church's customary preoccupation with "essence," Pope John's concerns were clearly existential. Individuals' rights were to him more primary and evident than their abstract nature. By this reshuffling of Catholic priorities, Pope John threw his lot in with the progressive and avant-garde theologians in America and Europe, who had been busy redefining what they called the "personhood" of man not as a figment of Aristotelian calculus but rather as a concrete, unique person who is preeminently free and thus continually giving shape and form to his own existence. Shades of Protestantism perhaps, but that was where the church was going, and where Pope John was taking it. Or more remarkably, in view of the retrograde usage of papal power historically, that was where he was allowing it to develop.

The Roman Catholic Church has been hung up on sex longer than on any other single subject, a heritage no doubt of the successful Manichean split of matter and spirit, or body and mind, into bad guys and good guys. The early fathers of the church had no easy time of it. Origen, in an excess of Stoic purity, castrated himself in order to end the temptations of the flesh; much later Abélard experienced a similar fate after the shame of shacking up with Héloïse. As early as 595 A.D., Pope St. Gregory the Great decided that sex, even for the singular purpose of procreation, had to be at least a venial sin. This sexual hysteria had not appreciably subsided when in 1854, over twelve hundred years later, Pius IX proclaimed the Immaculate Conception, for no discernible reason other than that a group of probably dirty-minded celibates around the Vatican couldn't stand looking at all those statues of Mary and imagining the Mother of God doing it.

The church's teaching on sex—most particularly its ban on birth control—was most rigidly formulated by St. Augustine, although his views on Eros were heavily influenced by an early obsessive preoccupation with the Manicheans, and perhaps with his mistress. But it is more enlightening to look at St. Augustine's teaching on lying than at his morose and predictable views on intercourse. The very principle he raises to define the proper use of the tongue is, somewhat incredibly, the one just espoused by Pope Paul VI in *Humanae Vitae* to state the contemporary Catholic position on the proper use of the sexual organs.

Lying, the Bishop of Hippo held, is wrong because man was given his tongue only for the communication of truth. Like George Washington, St. Augustine found it impossible to tell a lie; there were no redeeming circumstances whatsoever. He offered the extremist example of a man seeking refuge from robbers in someone's home. The master of the house, if questioned by the thugs, must be willing for the pursued man—and perhaps himself—to die, rather than lie about who was hiding in the broom closet.

This was the rule in Catholic moral theology for many centuries, and the obviously agonizing absolutism of the principle led to a mammoth theological controversy—greater, by far, if one counts in centuries as the church does, than the argument over birth control. Finally, after bending every which way, the scholastic philosophers came up with the casuistic and Jesuitical principle of a "mental reservation," which was clearly artificial and stupid but at least had the virtue of allowing Catholics to lie in the state of grace. Surely, if the church could find a way to make life easier for man's tongue, one would hope it could do as much for his penis.

Surely. But, surely not. "Sexual intercourse even with a lawful wife is unlawful and shameful, if the offspring of children is prevented," wrote St. Augustine in the fourth century. And that, with some scholastic refinements by St. Thomas Aquinas in the thirteenth century, has remained the basic Catholic doctrine. St. Thomas set the church teaching on masturbation by insisting that any seminal emission without coitus was unnatural—a theory still taught in most Catholic high schools today when warning the boys to keep hands off. (One could argue that since the female suffers no seminal loss when masturbating, her masturbatory activity is natural and therefore moral. Over such fine points of sexual ethics, castles-full of moral theologians have occupied themselves for centuries.)

Of course, Christians as a class have always been rather weird about sex, with attitudes ranging from the hostile to, at best, the ambiguous. The idea that sexual pleasure for its own sake is sinful and intercourse is only justified in the procreation of children has hardly been an exclusive of the Church of Rome. John Calvin was a hard man; even Luther's marriage to a nun did not serve to bias Protestantism in favor of free love; and then there was Hester Prynne. Indeed, it wasn't until this century that the consensus of Christendom against deliberate family limitation even began to break up. Protestant do-gooders like Anthony Comstock led the crusade in the United States against the public sale of contraceptives, and the Church of England, as recently as the First World War, was reaffirming its opposition to "preventives" and offering sexual abstinence as the only alternative to a large family.

The bishops attending the famous Lambeth Conference of 1930, where the Anglican Church gave its reluctant approval to "artificial" means of birth control, were deeply divided on the subject, and for decades thereafter there was much guilt-assuaging in the ranks of Protestantism. Indeed, it was not until the Lambeth Conference of 1958 that the Anglican bishops dared to use the forthright language that liberal Catholic bishops were to use just a few years later in the Vatican Council, when they stated that the method of controlling the number and frequency of children was totally the concern of the individual conscience.

Pope Pius XI, who otherwise distinguished his pontificate by giving his blessing to Hitler and signing a concordat with Mussolini, wasted no time in reacting to the 1930 Protestant declaration of independence from St. Augustine. The encyclical *Casti Conubii* restated in overkill rhetoric the church's traditional teaching on sex in marriage and condemned artificial contraception as "shameful and intrinsically immoral" and "an unspeakable crime," among other things.

Casti Conubii, aside from putting hellfire in the minds of Catholic couples who were dabbling in condoms, is significant because the pope mentioned, almost in passing, medical research into the ovulation cycle of women that was exploring "safe" periods when conception could not occur. He left the obvious interpretation that, for proper reason, intercourse limited to infertile periods would not violate church doctrine. This was not giving away much, since the biology of this phenomenon was at the time rather uncertain. "The ordinary working-class healthy woman has no safe period at all," Dr. Marie Stopes said in 1924. However, two independent studies published in 1930, one by a Japanese gynecologist, Dr. K. Ogino, the other by a Czech, Professor H. Knaus, reported rather definitely that ovulation took place either twelve to sixteen days (in Japan) or fourteen to sixteen days (in Prague) before menstruation. They concluded that since the male sperm could only survive for two or three days after coitus, any sexual intercourse from, say, three days after menstruation to the outside calendar limit for the beginning of ovulation would, by the God-given laws of nature, be sterile.

That puts a big dent in the typical screwing month, but to the celibate, prudish, and frequently octogenarian moral theologians of the thirties, periodic abstinence from such an animalistic activity as copulation was good for body and soul alike. Thus Catholic theologians hailed the Ogino-Knaus report as if it were a new scientific proof for the existence of God, since it gave the church a middle road between Pius XI's rigid condemnation of contraception and the brutal psychological and economic realities which dictated that Catholic couples should not produce offspring like bunny rabbits.

Although Rome had no formal comment, books on the "rhythm method" began to be published with the semiofficial approbation of American and European ecclesiastics. Thus the church's acceptance of the method came through a gradual *fait accompli*, and it was not until 1951 that Pope Pius XII put the church down in writing as approving the "regulation of offspring" by the "licit method" of rhythm. Pius XII's calm pronouncement was actually revolutionary, for it broke with the standing Catholic position that God alone had the "right" to decide the size of a family and man could not limit his issue on his own initiative.

The church's traditional teaching is summed up in this sentence from a 1927 ethics book: "If God sends another mouth to feed, he will find means to fill it."

Except for the two encyclicals in this century, the church has very little doctrine on contraception, probably because modern science appears to have been slow in developing efficient birth control devices for the masses. Until well into the nineteenth century, the primary method of avoiding births—what Augustine and Aquinas were referring to when they wrote against "contraception"—was a practice called "coitus interruptus," a process which is self-defining and which the church lumps into the sin of "onanism," after Onan, the son of Judah, who is accused by St. Augustine of pulling a fast one, for which account he is said to have been put to death by God.

Considering the rather awful single-mindedness Rome has exhibited over the centuries in insisting that man has no business being master of his reproductive facilities, the "rhythm" decision, allowing Catholics to control their family's growth by selectively plotting periods of intercourse, appears on the one hand too arbitrary and on the other too open-ended. The church had usually rejected or ignored advances in science, yet in the case of birth control it had changed some of its most rigid doctrines in an almost casual manner on the basis of a developing scientific study. Therefore, it could hardly argue, as Paul attempts to do in *Humanae Vitae,* that subsequent advances in biology might not also effectively modify its doctrine. By suddenly allowing family planning through rhythm, the church also compromised the standard Christian belief that the primary or sole purpose of marriage was the begetting of children. To then continue to justify the rhythm method while condemning other means of contraception is, in the end, an impossible philosophical task. The rhythm decision punched a hole in the dike of Catholic absolutism on birth control, and Pope Paul's attempt to plug the leak with *Humanae Vitae* is theologically inconsequential. Paul will eventually die, and another pope will eventually issue another encyclical updating his retrogression. That is the way things go in the Catholic Church.

The church's liberals, of course, are outraged, mostly because they were beginning really to believe in the efficacy of prayer. Euphoric over

Pope John, wishful thinkers about Paul, the laymen and priests who are now doing all the screaming about the encyclical have forgotten the authoritarian nature of the structure that serves their church. They also forgot, until Paul reminded them, who was pope. Liberals don't like such factual unpleasantries intruding upon their projections of reality, and as a result they have become publicly outraged at the pope, which makes for good copy—like *Newsweek*'s anonymous Detroit Catholic mother who snorted, "Who is the pope to come into my bedroom?" But the reaction of Georgetown University's conservative philosopher Germain Grisez had more bearing on the motivation for the pope's encyclical: "If one is a Catholic, one is a Papist. And if one is a Papist, then one cannot say, 'Rome has spoken and the cause goes on.' One has to say, 'Rome has spoken, the cause is finished.'"

In many ways, here is the classical political struggle: the liberals have logic, science, psychology, and theology on their side; the pope has power.

Paul knew exactly what he was doing. He fully understood the arguments of the liberals but chose to reject them. For all the horror it has caused Planned Parenthood, *Humanae Vitae* is not primarily an encyclical about Catholic ethics. It is, very crudely, an effort by a man who is a conservative but not a reactionary to regain pontifical control of the church from the top, after Pope John got the bishops all excited about "collegiality," which is the church's version of participatory democracy. The essence of the encyclical is an appeal to authority, not to reason: "This is what the church has always taught." Ironically, what the church has always taught is that birth control is a question of natural law which can be resolved through the use of reason. England's caustic Archbishop Thomas Roberts pointed out that contradiction: "One does wonder about a rational faculty that seems to have been ordained for the exclusive use of theological thinkers of a certain persuasion."

The key to the reading—and dismissing—of *Humanae Vitae* can be found in the minority report of Paul's fifty-seven-member Birth Control Commission, the text of which was happily stolen by the *National Catholic Reporter*. The majority, of course, came out for basic changes in the church's line on contraception. The minority report was signed by four theologians, three of them Jesuits. It almost ignored theological considerations, asserting that the Vatican must remain immobile on the issue of contraception because "if the Church should now admit that the teaching passed on is no longer of value, teaching which has been preached and stated with ever more insistent solemnity until very recent years, it must be feared greatly that its authority in almost all moral and dogmatic matters will be seriously harmed."

A careful textual exegesis will find a similarity of motivation in Pope Pius XI's 1930 encyclical blasting the Protestants. In their winning argument, the authors of the minority report reminded Pope Paul that Pius XII's *Casti Conubii* was written in direct response to the 1930 Lambeth Conference. "Is it now to be admitted," the four horsemen of the minority report asked in 1968, "that the Church erred in this her work and that the Holy Spirit rather assists the Anglican Church?"

[*Ramparts,* September 7, 1968]

Guerrilla War in the USA

*I*T IS NOT UNUSUAL FOR A GOVERNMENT TO DENY any success, much less any reality, to a guerrilla movement opposing it. Batista, for instance, let out continual rumors that Castro was smashed to smithereens when he wasn't, and the reports of Che Guevara's death in Bolivia were greatly exaggerated at least a dozen times before the CIA could deliver a corpse to match the story.

The pattern of obfuscation in the United States is different. It allows for screaming and hollering about the terrible violence that is coming down on this country, and then degenerates into a blubbery debate about whether violence, in general, is cherry, lemon, or lime, or even American at all. Since the administration raising the issue of violence is itself the largest practitioner of that trade both at home and abroad, that would seem to give the boot to the question. But there is a talented vice president on the prowl whose opprobrious rhetoric keeps the confusion alive by speeches to Rotarians and other Bedouins and know-nothings across the Gaza Strips of the Midwest and Southwest.

Despite all the official and unofficial outrage at H. Rap Brown's assertion that violence was as American as cherry pie, the National Commission on the Causes and Prevention of Violence took some 350,000 words last year to say that, in fact, was the case, and that nonviolence was not exactly in the mainstream of how Americans got things done. The only thing new is guerrilla violence, which has never occurred in the United States before, but that revelation is apparently being saved for another commission. Thus the central reality of violence in society has become the new American cliché. But most people don't bother to differentiate among the kinds of violence—right-wing, left-wing, government, criminal, and just plain demented—instead they lump all violence into one burdensome rock for this age where Armageddon takes place in primetime.

This tendency, promoted by the government, has delayed any declamatory awareness of the massive development in the United States of the specifically calculated violence of modern guerrilla warfare. But if the bombings continue this fall at the current hurricane pace, it is only going to take someone to say it is so and guerrilla warfare will become a catchword of the seventies along with women's liberation and the miniskirt. Whether it will be as easily popularized and assimilated is entirely another question. While the government's semantic holding action against guerrilla war is already slipping, it does remain true that certain realities, especially unpleasant ones, take a long time to penetrate the American consciousness—a phenomenon social critic John Jay Chapman referred to as the "habitual mental distraction" of Americans. It is now getting to the point, however, where it won't require the services of a computer to project a war out of the rapidly multiplying attacks of guerrilla terrorism and sabotage. March of 1970, for example, was a typical month without any major civil unrest or campus or ghetto riots. During March there were sixty-two left-wing guerrilla actions against targets in seventeen states, among them:

Selective Service Headquarters in Urbana, Illinois, Colorado Springs and Boulder, Colorado, were firebombed.

The Minnesota Selective Service Headquarters in St. Paul was heavily damaged when sprayed with black paint in a freak sneak attack.

Time bombs were discovered at army installations in Oakland, Brooklyn, and Portland.

A post office was dynamited in Seattle, the Federal Building was firebombed in Champaign, Illinois, and a courthouse blown up in Cambridge, Maryland.

Firebombings and arson attacks caused light-to-extensive damage at eight colleges, and physical attacks on buildings and security guards took place at the University of Puerto Rico and Loop City College in Chicago. During the same period, six high schools were bombed and two damaged by arson.

Guerrilla attacks against police took place in Richmond, California; Chicago; Billings, Montana; Detroit; Boulder, Colorado; and Cleveland. Dynamite, firebombs, and sniper fire were employed in the actions.

In Manhattan, the IBM, General Telephone, and Mobil Oil buildings were bombed, and incendiary devices were set off in Bloomingdale's and Alexander's department stores. During the month there were seventeen bombing attacks against corporations and banks in eight states.

The geometric progression of such actions tells the story: the sixty-two guerrilla actions in March 1970 were roughly double those of March of the previous year, when thirty-nine attacks took place against schools, federal installations, police, and corporations. In March of 1968 there were only fourteen attacks; in 1967 there were four; and two such instances occurred in March of 1966 and 1965.

It is surmisable that the administration does not require this magazine [Scanlan's] to tell it that guerrilla warfare is going on in the country. It should not strain even the competency of the FBI to uncover such shocking statistics. But just who is going to tell the people is something else. The government doubtless has its own reasons for maintaining radio silence about the guerrilla war, but its semantics at times become strained. President Nixon, deploring violence in September in a major address at landlocked, conservative Kansas State University, went to awkward extremes to avoid the use of even the adjective "guerrilla" (except to refer to the "Palestinian guerrillas," which was all right, apparently, because that was out of town). In describing American bombers and snipers, the president instead variously employed the descriptive labels "disrupters," "a small minority," "destructive activists," "small bands of destructionists," "acts of viciousness," "blackmail and terror," and "assaults which terrorize." One reason for the administration's compulsive evasion of the term is that it just sounds so bad. Guerrilla war psychologically is in the "It-can't-happen-here" category for America. And the admission of the existence of guerrilla warfare would prompt a host of embarrassing questions, not the least of which is why can't the government stop it?

The fact is that every branch of the federal government with as much as a pinky in law enforcement is actively but furtively attempting to catch itself some guerrillas. The FBI, the Secret Service, the Treasury Department, the Pentagon, the CIA, and even the Bureau of Mines are all in on the chase. With all the resources at their disposal to monitor and supervise reputed revolutionaries, it must be a matter of considerable professional and political embarrassment that the combined law enforcement, military, security, and spy establishment of the United States has been unable to catch even a literal handful of the thousands of underground revolutionaries who, now as a matter of daily benediction, harass the government with sniper fire or bombs.

Guerrillas interviewed in the course of preparing this report found it a matter of exultant amusement that the government's intelligence system has turned out to be such a basket case. The Pentagon's Counter Intelligence Analysis Division has a subversive data bank with 1.5 million names and even circulates a little red book entitled "Organizations and Cities of Interest and Individuals of Interest." The Secret Service has indices of one hundred thousand radical names and extensive dossiers on fifty thousand revolutionaries presumed to be dangerous. If those figures have any rational or scientific base, that is quite some draft pool for guerrilla soldiers. The FBI has 194 million fingerprints in its files and quick access to 264 million police records, 323 million medical histories, and 279 million psychiatric dossiers. It also claims to have an infiltrator in a top position in every revolutionary group in America. Yet the nearest the FBI has gotten to the Weathermen is to hang their pictures in post office galleries.

To be fair to the FBI, authorities in other countries faced with indigenous guerrilla war of the type we are experiencing in the United States have fared little better in capturing insurgents. In Brazil, even the extensive repression of a relatively upfront police state has failed to derail measurably the half dozen guerrilla groups following the teachings of Brazilian guerrilla theorist Carlos Marighella. Uruguay's military is also at a loss to stop the operations of the notorious Tupamaros, whose bank robbing and kidnapping tactics may represent the next stage of emulation by American guerrillas.

["ARMED PROPAGANDA"]

The patron saint of constant flux and change is Heraclitus, a grouchy pre-Socratic philosopher who pointed out to the surprise of practically everyone in the fifth century before Christ that you can't step into the same river twice. His didactic analogy is quite contemporary with the Marxist-Leninist heresies of modern guerrilla theorists. They hold that each country's revolution is necessarily different from previous ones—successful or unsuccessful—and that the means a guerrilla movement adopts will eventually define its ends, if the guerrilla minds his Mao and keeps his politics close to the inclinations and concerns of the people.

The revolutionary ideology that Mao defined in his treatises on guerrilla war is regarded in most instances as absolute, major exceptions being his political structure and the encrusted bureaucracy of vertical communism. Contemporary guerrilla war is an ever-changing revolutionary dialectic with common tactics which must of necessity develop differently in differing national circumstances. Now that may sound unassuming and even reasonable, but the freewheeling political and tactical positions that American guerrillas espouse along this line are sufficient to give heartburn and heart attacks to the traditional Marxists for whom the history of orthodox communism is perhaps half the struggle to establish the dictatorship of the proletariat and the other half the ensuing struggle over who is going to dictate to the dictatorship. It was a game in which just about anyone was eligible to play except the proletariat. The hit-and-run tactics of guerrilla war have changed little since the days when the Maccabees were hotfooting the Syrians. But that formerly pure tactical set of military assumptions has developed into a distinct revolutionary ideology in the twentieth century, particularly under Mao. More recently, in Latin America it has undergone another metamorphosis into a burgeoning revolutionary theory all its own that threatens to disinter established Marxist-Leninism.

The primary theoretician of the "new guerrilla" is Régis Debray, a young French philosopher-journalist and close friend of Fidel Castro. Debray has been under house arrest or worse in Bolivia since 1967, when he was accused by the right-wing government of having traveled to the hills to break bread with Che Guevara. His imprisonment has been an international intellectual cause célèbre, even prompting a group of French journalists to petition the Bolivian authorities for his release on the unique grounds that "one must admit the legal existence of *guerrilla correspondents* [their italics], who must obviously be granted the same status as war correspondents." A left-wing government came to power in Bolivia several months ago, but as of this writing it has not sprung Debray, a fact which may attest to his controversial status within the communist world.

Debray's slim volume *Revolution in the Revolution?* fulfills the quip that the road to war is paved with good books. His revisionist analysis of the Cuban revolution leads Debray to argue that the classic Marxist patterns of revolution and guerrilla warfare must be scrapped for more up-to-date and egalitarian methods. The old Chinese and Soviet models will not do; indeed no models are necessary. The successful guerrilla war will be entirely homegrown, without the interference of what could only be termed "outside agitators," otherwise known as orthodox Communists. In his scorn for the ossification of Communist Party machinery and the conservative and dictatorial methods of Marxist-Leninist institutions, Debray led the field in anticipating two of the most consequential political sensibilities of the 1970s: the New Left affection for "participatory democracy," and the worldwide radical student movement's struggle to free men equally from the institutional controls of Western capitalism and Eastern bureaucracy. Accepting Mao's concept of the guerrillas being one with the people as the *sine qua non* of a successful guerrilla movement, Debray rejected Mao's principle that "politics directs the gun." Rather, it is the gun, in the form of successful guerrilla actions against definable manifestations of imperialism and oppression of the people, which defines and develops successful revolutionary politics. This shattering revision of traditional Marxism offs the Communist Party from its traditional and cherished role as the political vanguard which sets the correct "line" for the people. The guerrillas, through terrorist and military actions geared to gain propaganda successes, gradually politicize and assemble the exploited classes on their side. Communist bureaucrats are left out in the cold.

What drives most professional observers of the new American revolutionaries to such fits of distraction and disgust is their lack of discernible "goals," of "something to replace what they want to tear down," their emphasis on the primacy of revolutionary tactics over political structure. Yet this reality, so defiant of traditional politics, is the carefully thought out ideological cornerstone of contemporary guerrilla theory as it is being practiced in Latin America and experimented with under the unique conditions that the United States has to offer any pioneers. The traditional left, and particularly the older left—from social democrats on the right to leftover descendants of the Luddites on the left—takes about as much joy in guerrilla politics as Spiro Agnew.

Like Heraclitus' river, guerrilla theory is ever-changing. The Cuban "model" rejected the traditional communist theory of creating a mass party and then proceeding to win allies for a united front for which guerrilla forces would act only as an "iron fist" when so instructed by the party. Instead, Castro's small band of eighty-one dedicated men themselves became the vanguard by instituting guerrilla actions that were not initially aimed at military victories but as an ideological organizing tool to recruit more guerrillas. Other guerrilla struggles that followed this pattern also began with small numbers—the Irish Republican Army had around two hundred men, the Stern Gang and Irgun in Israel began with even fewer, the Algerians with around five hundred.

American guerrilla groups passed through this initial period several years ago and now are in a second stage of "armed propaganda" which involves attacks geared to both undermining governmental authority and inspiring a revolutionary state of mind in others in the populace who share the guerrillas' developing political line. Even the most braggadocio of the guerrillas interviewed for this report did not predict the attainment of the next level of guerrilla war—larger and more regular forces carrying out more traditional military operations—in the near future unless their patient timetable was changed through large-scale repression by the government.

Castro's revolution was primarily rural-based—he once called the large city "a cemetery for revolutionaries"—but the IRA, the Irgun, and the Algerians successfully carried on urban guerrilla terrorist tactics. The current guerrilla struggles in Canada, Brazil, Argentina, and Uruguay are largely urban-centered. While holding to Debray's theory of the vanguard in the people, not a party, American guerrillas have largely adapted the methods of urban guerrilla war, which are uniquely suited to the high-strung, interlocking gears of a mammoth industrial society.

Future scriptwriters for Efrem Zimbalist Jr. may note that at this point in history the FBI was up against alien and unconventional tactics of sabotage, terrorism, and hit-as-hit-can military and psychological warfare to which the modern industrial society is acutely vulnerable. Tactics successfully employed by insurgent forces in Ireland, China, Israel, Algeria, Cuba, and currently in Latin American and African nations are being experimentally adapted to American surroundings by black urban guerrillas and the burgeoning middle- and upper-middle-class white revolutionaries who operate with relative impunity from college-oriented communities which have become cultural and political "enclaves" in America.

Not that the tactic of blowing up things for principle is foreign to America, nor even politically parochial. The McNamara brothers and others did it from the left when they gave a dynamiter's what ho to the *Los Angeles Times* building in 1910, and many of today's generation of bombers were old enough to go to the movies in 1949 and watch Gary Cooper as Howard Roark, the architect-as-man-of-steel in Ayn Rand's *The Fountainhead,* blow up buildings from the right. But the indicia of the contemporary guerrilla is not so much the use of infernal machines but the political and cultural acceptance of that violent tactic in the community to which he belongs. Thus large sections of this land—its new youth communities, its older black, brown, and Chinese communities—have developed a new importance as bases of support for domestic insurgency. It is in these communities that the traditional authority of the state has deteriorated most, and where the old system of values—capitalism, organized religion, the necessity of wedlock and the social unit of the family—is least appreciated by the young blood. Berkeley; Seattle; Madison, Wisconsin; and New York City are the largest of such political enclaves. They provide both the sources of guns and butter and the shared quality of life which has always been a necessary condition for the maintenance of a guerrilla struggle.

The golden rule of guerrilla war is to do unto the enemy no more than the people will support you in doing. This moral imperative hinges not so much on Mao's homey analogy about guerrillas being fish in the sea but on its practical corollary: no sea, no fish. The big flops in guerrilla war this century came about when the guerrillas lost their common touch with the masses, as in post-1945 Greece and the guerrilla wars in the Philippines; or when they never had a base within the population to begin with, as in Che Guevara's disastrous attempt to organize a whistle-stop guerrilla war in Bolivia. American revolutionaries take their world guerrilla history seriously and thus there is constant discussion among guerrillas as to just what "action" is tactically best at the moment for the political effect of the act to outweigh its violent means. There is always the problem of a "guerrilla backlash" which could alienate or scare off their active base of support among their less revolutionary peers.

At this early stage of an urban guerrilla movement, the tactics are largely geared to what Marighella calls "armed propaganda"—bombings which serve a political and psychological purpose in singling out "enemies" and at the same time embarrassing the government by its inability to catch the mad bombers. This is a delicate balancing act, and guerrillas occasionally blow it. But an integral part of guerrilla strategy is that civilians aren't supposed to get hurt, just scared. This doesn't necessarily make a Mr. Nice Guy out of a bomber; but true is true, and it simply is contrary to all guerrilla theory to go around blowing up people whom they expect, inevitably, some year, to side with the movement against the government. All guerrilla tactics are adaptable to the situation: in Brazil, guerrilla forces don't usually engage in bombings because they fear the government could turn it around by planting a bomb in a crowded marketplace and use the atrocity to turn the people against the guerrillas.

At any rate, this political safety-first among American guerrilla terrorists is why so few casualties have been sustained—despite the horrendous noise of all those bombs going off in the United States the last few years. Most bombing attacks are on buildings or other inanimate objects and usually take place at night when the premises are safer on both sides to blast. A warning is routinely delivered before the blast in case of a night watchman or unknown laggards. The graduate student at the University of Wisconsin got it because somebody fouled up the warning call. Most deaths in bombing attempts have been those of careless guerrillas who blew themselves up. Insurgents know that increased police repression helps to keep the community-opinion scales weighted on their side. So as long as the enclaves don't sustain a guerrilla backlash, the current flabbergasting pace of "armed propaganda" could continue far over the horizon.

All American guerrilla groups have revolutionary tactics in common, but few share any common ideology. Few, indeed, have a definable ideology or postrevolutionary program. Most are feeling their way along the bombing trail, letting the tactics, as it were, quarterback the action in the manner suggested by Régis Debray.

[THE EXPLOSIONIST RASPBERRY]

American guerrilla tactics are as different from violence past in this nation as Scrooge was from Tiny Tim. The staccato of terrorism punctuating American history has always been associated with a single issue, or, more exactly, a single hatred: that of the sheeted white Southerner for uppity blacks, or the exploited worker for his corporate overlord. The only group with a track record in bombing that could be said to have an overall political program were the high-profile anarchists of the 1880s and 1890s, and they made a point of principle out of having no program at all. The working-class arsonists in the north and northwest, as well as the arsonists of the sheet in the South, shared a naive frontier optimism that evil as they perceived it could be corrected, or destroyed, or at least sufficiently scared to death to make the existing society a better place for workers or racists, as their case might be. With the few exceptions of groups like the Wobblies, violence was practiced in America without benefit of any real political philosophy. Terrorists were moved to action by their own galling view of an outrageous flaw in the fabric of society— not from any rejection of the overall crazy quilt of society itself.

Not so today's guerrillas. They wish to trash the American dream, not sleep with it. Their tactics are embodied in an internationalist political perspective that sees their own country as the empress-torturer of oppressed people both next door and overseas, and they have in common a political analysis of the problem which is so severe that they have elected to engage in some form of armed struggle against their country, right or wrong.

The indigenous guerrillas who share this nightmare version of the American dream are of two broadly traceable ethnic, economic, and social groups. To classify them as black and white would be an oversimplification, although not a heinous one. Their rise to guerrilla status, indeed their very choice of targets, grows partially out of their economic and social condition, which in America is more a question of skin than class. Black and other nonwhite American guerrillas have their origins in that condition which sociologists and understanding liberals distantly and majestically refer to as culturally deprived, or oppressed, depending on the politics of the listening audience. They understand their own actions as guerrillas in the moral imperative of exploited third-world peoples attacking their colonial master, and see the ghetto geography of America as a territorial map to the unique condition of a people living in colonies located within the mother country instead of over Kipling's waves. The other catholic class of American guerrillas is the white and middle-to-upper-class citizens of college or dropout age who largely operate from those "enclave" communities fanning college campuses. They are generally distrustful of any Marxist eschatology, but generally accept a sophisticated and updated Marxist analysis of the American corporate state as an imperial presence in the underdeveloped world and cultural totalitarian presence in the overdeveloped world. They see America as a colossal computer running amuck in a postindustrial society which must be reprogrammed, if not destroyed.

Such tactical differences as exist between these two varieties of guerrilla are manifest in their choice of primary targets. The majority of sniper and bombing attacks on police are carried out by black guerrillas who view them (in the vernacular) as pigs who are the immediate and aggressive representatives of their colonial oppressor. (This view of police is shared, in theory and practice, by white revolutionaries who see police as the shock troops of the enemy.) Similarly, the judiciary and the entire machinery of justice are also targets for bombs which are aimed to clear the malfunctions in the machinery.

The first target for white guerrillas is the college and, increasingly, the high school. Next is the military, including and especially ROTC buildings on campus and Selective Service offices off campus. These two American institutions are the arch-offenders both in disrupting the lives of white guerrillas and in the exploitation of the lives of others. "First America steals a country's leather to make shoes, then we sell the shoes to the people, then we wipe our feet on them," one guerrilla told me. This is neither a logical analogy nor sophisticated Marxism, but in its crudity it represents the feelings of many revolutionaries of middle-class parentage. The schools are seen as the containers and suppliers of the human raw material of the corporate state, and the army is viewed as its private police to protect resources abroad from those with proper prior claims. Another favored target of white guerrillas is partial to the same reasoning: the corporations which have their straw in the pineapple of underdeveloped nations' economies, and the banking houses attendant to those corporations.

If the guerrillas can be said to uniformly agree on any goals of American guerrilla warfare in addition to fighting the hated war in Southeast Asia, it would be to support national liberation movements throughout the world and, of course, the black liberation struggle in the United States. A more limited if intriguing goal of the incendiary is to bring the war trashing home by bombing, looting, and burning the country to perfect distraction, thereby undermining the faith of the populace in the order and stability so essential to the workaday conduct of commerce. The highest profile among the practitioners of this art of the explosionist raspberry are the Weathermen, who make it a point of principle each time they blow up something to drive the FBI quite crazy by popping up somewhere in the country and telling how they got away with it. It is all a little in the manner of a terrorist's April Fool, but the joke appears always to be on the FBI.

[DAMAGE REPORTS]

The Bureau linked the Weathermen to the Chicago bomb factory it mothballed in March. And it required no ace policework to associate Weathermen with the accidental explosion that crumbled the Greenwich Village townhouse next to the loft of Dustin Hoffman, leaving three Weathermen members dead. Federal authorities have occasioned the indictments of just about as many of the Weathermen as they have names for. Twelve were indicted shortly after the Greenwich Village blowup, and this summer another thirteen alleged members of Weathermen were indicted in a bill of particulars which read like a Magna Carta for American revolution. It charged the guerrilla organization with "agreeing to organize a central committee to direct bombing operations with members assigned to Chicago, New York, Detroit, and Berkeley" and also establishing "clandestine and underground locals consisting of three or four persons who would be under the command of the 'Central Committee' and would carry out the actual bombing of police stations and other buildings."

So far, the only effect of the indictment has been for Weathermen to do just about what they were charged with planning, but without being caught. The FBI to date has been able to lock up only three accused

Weathermen, one of whom turned herself in, and this slim catch required kamakazi missions on the part of the police underground that crashed the Bureau's painfully planted infiltrators. All this while Weathermen was taunting and humiliating the pursuers, sending them fingerprints of the Weathermen leaders, openly forecasting major attacks and then pulling them off, as hasty journalists write, under the cops' noses. (In the case of the bombing of Manhattan police headquarters it was literally under their feet.)

Unlike organized crime, which by definition has to be at least organized, or even J. Edgar Hoover's ideal communist cell, which by now should have acquired Smithsonian rank, modern guerrillas require no layered structures of authority or communication. They would be betraying the studied exemplars of successful guerrilla experimentation if they did. Successful guerrilla actions minimally require a revolutionary consciousness and a can of gasoline, a weapon that is about as traceable as the common bobby pin. There are, however, guerrilla lend-lease arsenals stockpiled throughout the country, and occasionally law enforcement finds one. In March, for instance, police and FBI agents in a joint discovery found a bomb factory in a Chicago North Side apartment stocked with enough explosives to level a city block: bombs, blasting caps, explosive liquids, plastics, hydrochloric and sulphuric acid, and a variety of guns and ammunition. That haul was not even a firecracker in the tonnage of dynamite and other explosives regularly stolen from private sources in this country and lifted in truckload quantities from the military.

More indicative of the everyday manner of sabotage by guerrillas was an arrest in March in Rochester, New York—police found three young men carrying eighteen readymade firebombs onto the campus of New York State University. The majority of guerrilla attacks are more products of Yankee ingenuity than private arsenals. There is no storehouse needed for the arsonists' gasoline-soaked rag, the simple petrol bomb, or the pipe bomb stuffed with gun powder. The ingredients are all available for the going price plus sales tax at local hardware or sporting goods stores. As far as that goes, dynamite may still be purchased without a permit in many states, or it can just as easily be stolen.

Citizens are now alarmed because the care and exploding of homemade bombs is becoming a discipline too widely studied, but the alarm should have gone off about three years ago. Blueprints and pamphlets on guerrilla weapons are so readily available that one need only sift through the rubbish after a large demonstration on almost any campus to find throwaway instruction sheets in the art of guerrilla weaponry and tactics. Much of this formerly-difficult-to-get material was available to all takers, postpaid, through a right-wing publishing house in Colorado which used to be called Panther Publications but now has changed its name to something a little less political: Paladin Press.

The laissez-faire publishing of the military right, and some left-wing imports, combined with the ready availability of inexpensive photographic duplicating equipment, has made the literature of destruction as available as first-aid pamphlets. One reality of guerrilla war that can be taken as an absolute is that the guerrillas (and all potential guerrillas) have the bombs if they want to use them. Then there is the matter of the Library of Congress, which has available in excess of 1,000 reported books and pamphlets on the tricky art of destruction. The fledgling guerrilla can find in its card catalogue some 300 titles on blasting or incendiary bombs, and 850 titles on "explosives." Xerox copies cost a dime a throw. For that matter, the army only recently began thinking about applying some restrictions on the warfare manuals it hands out for the asking, and some unusual people have asked. Father Daniel Berrigan, the guerrilla priest, said that he and others of the Baltimore "Catonsville Nine" made the napalm they used to burn draft files. The instructions were found in the *Green Beret Handbook*, which was read to them over the long-distance telephone by a housewife in Southern California who kept the handbook up on the kitchen shelf with her other recipe books.

People in this country seem to think that you can quiet the drum beat of left-wing bombings by somehow curtailing the knowledge of explosives. This is a dangerous and foolish opinion. It is dangerous because it regards bombings as an aberration or temptation, completely misunderstanding the overall political nature of guerrilla war and the manifest abrasions in society that its successful waging implies. And it is foolish, not just because diagrams don't make people make bombs but because the widest possible dissemination of the strategical and technical literature of modern guerrilla warfare has already been accomplished in the United States. It would be as fruitful to worry about kids having guns if

Weathermen had turned Peter Pan and handed out automatic rifles to every American under voting age. The question is not whether guerrillas should have such weapons. They have them. And they can manufacture more. The question is what more they intend to do with them, and why.

Given the government's reluctance to let the cat out of the bag, some picture of the real extent of the damage being wrought in the nation from guerrilla actions must be put together piecemeal. The *Los Angeles Times* reported in 1969 that damages to Los Angeles schools totaled over $1 million from arson attributed to terrorist students, few of whom had been caught or charged. California's chief deputy attorney general Charles O'Brien put that statistic in more colorful if menacing language: "There have been more fires in Los Angeles than there were in Saigon during the Tet Offensive." The General Services Administration reported a $2.2 million taxpayer's loss in man-hours during the first six months of 1970 due to 130 evacuations of personnel from government buildings because of bomb threats. Such threats had increased ninefold—from 46 during 1969 to 383 in just the first half of this year. The GSA did not estimate real property damage from the actual bombings of government buildings and installations. However, *Scanlan's* researchers found newspaper reports of 59 left-wing attacks on government installations during the same period of the first six months of 1970. Actual damage reported to federal buildings and property, state buildings housing federal services, and armed services recruiting offices and bases from dynamiting, time bombs, arson, firebombs, pipe bombs, and sabotage totaled $2,061,305. However, damage figures in dollars were reported in only 18 of the 59 incidents; in many cases where an estimate was not given, the damage was described as "heavy," "extensive," or simply "destroyed." During the same six-month period, eight bombs were discovered on government property and disarmed before they could explode, and five time bombs were sent through the mail to the Selective Service offices in Washington and to the White House. These figures do not include attacks on more "neutral" property—for example, on April 24 and 27 bridges were dynamited in Maryland and Arizona.

Property damages sustained by colleges and government installations on campuses during the wave of arson and bombing attacks in American schools following the Cambodian invasion and the Kent State and Jackson State killings in May have yet to be estimated in any accurate fashion, but were of course massive. But there are solid figures indicating the quite staggering extent of merely routing guerrilla actions on American campuses. The American Insurance Association reported that property damage directly resulting from campus actions during the eight months from January 1 to August 31 of 1969 totaled $8,946,972. The insurance industry's figures were taken from holy sources—the Riot Reinsurance Data Bank, Fraud and Arson Bureau memoranda, and insurance adjusters' confidential loss reports. The nearly $9 million damage figure represented property damage by students in elementary schools, high schools, and colleges in seventy-nine cities. Most of the destruction took place on campus; off-campus actions done by students were included only when action was directly related to a campus incident.

That $9 million report card for students takes on added significance as an indicator of the magnitude of what has been happening on campuses since the halcyon days of panty raids. The insurance people pointed out that their total damage bill for *all* riots, civil disorders, and guerrilla acts in the United States during the same eight-month period amounted to some $15 million, which means that campus violence accounted for approximately 60 percent of the wreck and ruin in the insured regions of this nation. (The insurance carriers do not believe in guerrilla war as an act of God. Beginning in 1967, when arson and firebombing became common in high schools and colleges, the insurance companies who had to pay off began raising their deductible amounts. The first move in Los Angeles, where school fires increased 130 percent in one year, was to raise the deductible for school fire insurance to $25,000 from $1,000. Similar raises, some higher, went into effect for schools in most urban areas, and certain high schools which have become favored targets of youth guerrillas are rapidly becoming uninsurable.)

The campus is one of the two bases of operations for American guerrillas. The other is the urban ghetto, where small bands of black urban guerrillas are carrying on a running war with the police. The *New York Times* reported in September that 16 policemen had been assassinated this year and some 750 others injured in guerrilla sniper attacks and bombings. These casualties did not occur during riots or other disorders but represented individual sneak attacks on policemen by guerrillas. "There is more sniping and shooting in the streets of large American cities than in the streets of Saigon," Adlai Stevenson III said. At the time, Stevenson was locked in a battle for a U.S. Senate seat with a more-repressive-than-thou-Republican. Stevenson, who scampered to the right in order to emerge a winner in Illinois, may therefore be surprised to read that he has given comfort to the guerrillas by declaring one of their chief aims, that of bringing the war home to America, as achieved. Anyway, he said it, we didn't.

In addition to the war on police, urban centers have been rocked by the spate of bombings and other terrorist attacks against corporate headquarters, banks, and large department stores. Guerrilla actions against such institutions appear likely to double this year from last. *Scanlan's* researchers documented 86 attacks on corporations in 1969, but by the late summer of this year 110 such incidents had already been reported. Defensive measures are metamorphosing many company headquarters into virtual corporate fortresses. Locked lavatories are an increasingly common sign of the times. The J.C. Penney Company is installing specially coded door openers on its fourteen administrative floors in Manhattan. Dun & Bradstreet now requires employees to carry and show identity cards.

The federal government is fashioning its own Maginot Line against the guerrilla hailstorm. It is now as troublesome to enter many federal buildings during office hours as it is to get on an airliner during hijack season: guards open parcels, inspect briefcases, and require identification from those with a patina of the disenfranchised. The paranoia level in the Pentagon has risen with the decibel purr of special Pentagon police patrolmen steering electric-powered golf carts along the labyrinthian hallways in search of interlopers. When President Nixon signed the vaunted anticrime bill, FBI and Secret Service agents equipped with walkie-talkies guarded the Justice Department as if the ceremony were taking place at the plenary session of an SDS convention. The president has asked for one thousand new FBI agents, and the Secret Service is getting several hundred more men to beef up a new Home Guard to protect foreign diplomats from what they assume will be kidnap attempts by U.S. guerrillas in emulation of the recent happenings in Canada and Latin America. Such belt-tightening came on the rebound from Weathermen's self-proclaimed "fall offensive" in early October, during which many bombs went off from Santa Barbara to Rochester.

The fall onslaught of sabotage occasioned the first break in the government's radio silence about guerrilla warfare. The right wing, which knows a good conspiracy when it sees one, came right on with the word. In early October, John McClellan of Arkansas, the Senate's chief crime buster, described a "war against the police" as part and parcel of "a wave of guerrilla warfare" sloshing the nation. William C. Sullivan, an assistant to J. Edgar Hoover, repeated the word a few days later in a speech to a gathering of newspaper publishers in Virginia in which he talked about "commando-type units" in the Weathermen underground organized to carry out "urban guerrilla warfare." It should be noted that although this constituted the first official use of the forbidden word, it was employed in most contexts as an adjective, a synonym for terrorism. It was not given the stature of a noun, nor did anyone allow that "guerrilla" activities were anything but a very new thing in the United States.

Then those handmaidens of the leaked largesse of federal information, the newsweeklies, came up with their own versions of the new trouble. Noting that "it was hardly the administration's official line," *Newsweek* quoted an anonymous but "veteran Justice Department official" as making this "stark" but suitably melodramatic admission: "Face it, we're in what amounts to a guerrilla war with the kids. And so far, the kids are winning." *Time* found urban guerrilla warfare to be a problem suitable for framing on a global scale, and found guerrilla activities to be "relatively tame" in the United States compared with the situations in other countries. While allowing that guerrilla attacks had become "daily" occurrences in the USA, *Time* adopted the developing administration line by blaming much of the trouble here on secret guerrilla training camps in Cuba. Its stringers also scrounged up several psychiatrists to attest to the fact that the guerrilla phenomenon was based on people suffering from childhood damage to the psyche due to overly strict or overly weak fathers, or an "Icarus complex" that leads to sensational derring-do. After five quite incredible years of unreported guerrilla warfare, the American reading public is being eased upward in its political sophistication by reportorial analysis of this distinction.

[*Scanlan's Monthly*, January 1971]

Peculiar
and
Dangerous

Across the Street from a Tragedy

WEDNESDAY AT NOON I WATCHED a young woman dive head first through a plate-glass view window thirty feet above Castro Street and glide half-naked, spread-eagled to her death. The window erupted into a glass cauliflower as her body cannoned out. She must have been running ten miles an hour when she hit the window and was going forty when she hit the sidewalk. The glass seemed to rain over her body for a minute afterward. I watched this happen from my house across the street.

I telephoned for an ambulance and walked across Castro Street to where she lay crushed into the pavement. A crowd had gathered of the strolling gays and straight freaks who boulevard Castro in daytime. No one had thought to cover the unclothed lower half of her body. An old lady in a long red coat who was pulling a shopping cart stopped and made her modest with her shawl and went on about her business. The ambulance cried in the distance and the unseemly baby-blue police cars of the city began to screech up like there was a bank robbery in progress. An intern in whites appeared from somewhere and knelt to check her eyes with a pencil flashlight. He got up with a hopeless shrug.

The window where she took her dive was on the top left corner of a three-story apartment box at Castro and Beaver Streets. It had a view of the bay. She had taken most of the glass down into the street with her. Rubberneckers looking up through the hole could see two cops inside the apartment with a man with a beard. The crowd began to make noises like a lynch mob that the guy must have thrown her out the window. The man the cops brought downstairs had long blond hair and a scraggly Jesus beard. He wore a long purple dress and carried a knit purse. Somebody said he was her husband.

The ambulance came and went with the speed of an Iwo Jima landing.

The cops dragged the man in the purple dress back when he tried to climb into the ambulance with the bleeding woman. They stuffed him in the back seat of a squad car and took his purse away and put it in the front seat. The cops said they were taking him to Mission Emergency. They said his name was Peterson. The woman was his wife.

The cops and the ambulance were one, but the crowd hung around making the usual helpless comments. "She was naked, but I didn't wanna look," a passing mailman said. A gay man walked out of the building and stared at the carpet of glass. "Weird," he said. He was told that the jumper was a woman. "That's even weirder," he said, "because most of the people in this building are gay."

"This will never get into the papers," predicted Lee Meyers, a reporter for KPOO, the community underground radio station. Meyers was right. Neither paper ran it the next day; it was, after all, only a routine suicide. Unless you jump from the pretty bridge, or live in Pacific Heights, or do handsprings on your way out of this life, you can kill yourself in this town and have no one notice. I thought that it was not right that this woman, a neighbor I had never known, should die in this way without trying to find out why.

At Mission Emergency, the cops had finished with the husband wearing the dress. They didn't hold much to the murder theory; the guy was too frail to throw his cat through the window, let alone his wife. "She just took a good run from one end of the apartment to the other and went right out," said Officer Frank Palma. The husband was sitting in one of those plastic emergency room bucket seats staring into space. Then he looked up. "I'm sorry you had to see that," he said. He had looked out through the hole where his wife had jumped and saw me standing in the window of the room across the street where I write. I have lived on Castro Street for ten years and this was the first time I had ever communicated with one of the less-than-straight people in the neighborhood. I said I was sorry, too. We got a tepid root beer from the hospital vending machine and went upstairs to the small surgical waiting room to talk. Inside the double doors across the hallway, the doctors were straining to save the young woman. Her name was Claudia, and she was twenty-five. His was Steve, Steve Peterson. He was twenty-eight.

They had been married three years. She was a lesbian and he was gay. They loved each other. "We had sex with each other for a while but didn't like it—so that was quit pretty easy," he said. Instead they devoted their domestic life to the separate but mutual fulfillment of sexual preferences. That was why they came to San Francisco. They were married in Bloomington, Indiana, hometown to both. The ceremony was performed by a female justice of the peace who was the mother of one of Claudia's lesbian lovers. "We were always very open about everything with each other," he said.

Steve is a sculptor with a degree in fine arts and drawing. His parents are college professors, and he grew up next door to a retired Russian ballerina. In his youth he was the skateboard champion of Bloomington. He has worn dresses since he was in the seventh grade and tried on his mother's wedding dress on the sly. Now he wears Claudia's dresses. "She has very good taste," he said.

Claudia was in bad shape when he met her. Her tongue was hanging out from poisonous overdoses of Prolixin, which mindless shrinks had given her in an Indianapolis mental hospital. Her mother and brother and sister had, at various times, also been institutionalized. Steve on Claudia is testimony to the assault against the mind and soul that is the typical mental hospital: "They gave her shock treatments and separated her from her lesbian lover in the ward when they found them kissing in a bathroom. Then the doctors made her take birth control pills and tried to recondition her homosexuality by encouraging her to go to bed with men in the ward." Steve took her away from all that by marrying her. "We wanted to do something that was out of it. We thought we could solve the problems of society's discrimination against being gay this way. It added up to whatever hope was possible for us."

Together they set out on a westward odyssey. Their dream was to find the perfect homosexual lover for each of them and live together happily thereafter. The search took them to Boulder; Hilo, Hawaii; Carmel; and—six months ago—to San Francisco, which they approached as to Mecca. They paid for their $280-a-month view apartment on Castro Street from federal and state checks for psychiatric disability. He got social security and supplemental aid for schizophrenia. She got disability for depression. Together they got $600 a month. Steve saw a shrink once a week, "someone who was recommended to me by a male nurse that I had gone to bed with." But Claudia got no professional help the entire time she was here. The keepers of the dole paid her money for her acute depression and then let her sit around without help until she killed herself.

IN SIX MONTHS IN SAN FRANCISCO, Claudia, by Steve's count, had four lesbian lovers; Steve had five or six gay lovers. They all stayed in the tiny one-bedroom Castro Street apartment. Claudia's love life here was a series of bummers that finally led her to commit the ultimate felony on herself. "Claudia was looking for an intellectual relationship, but the dykes she met here were all into rape games. These women were always trying to make themselves look radical by acting macho—emulating in my opinion the most horrible characteristics of men—fights and unfair seductions and cruel personal putdowns. Claudia's lovers—who were mostly Duboce Avenue dykes—acted like dirty old men. During the seduction it was 'shut up and bend over' and after it was 'start talking and be put down.'"

In the last week, Claudia became withdrawn and uncommunicative. She kept to her room, reading a book that Steve had given her on how to write like Gertrude Stein and making voluminous entries in a scrapbook-sized personal journal. Once, in Boulder, when Claudia had slashed her wrists, Steve slashed his in sympathy. Last week, he kept asking her what he could do. She said she just wanted to be left alone.

Claudia stopped eating two days before her death. "I thought she was trying to see a vision, like they tell you in the legend of Don Juan that the Indians go into the desert and starve themselves until they see a vision of the new world." Tuesday night, Claudia came home with a vision. "She told me that everybody was pink or purple. I was pink. The Mafia was chasing her and burning her. She was in bandages like her mother was when her mother died in a fire. Claudia said that she had died. She said that I helped the Mafia burn her. She went into her room and wouldn't talk. I didn't know what to do. I went out and got some food but she wouldn't eat." He could hear her lighting cigarettes all night.

Wednesday morning, Claudia was in her room, exercising rocking. That was why she had no pants on, Steve explained. He went in and asked her if she should go get some help, but she said no. "What I said last night was the answer," she said. She kept rocking and writing in her journal. Steve was in his room off the kitchen, talking on the phone, when he saw Claudia sprint across the living room past the kitchen door. She kind of waved and yelled something that he couldn't hear. He heard the crash. He put down the phone and called an ambulance. Then he called his psychiatrist to ask for help. Then he walked over to the hole that had been the window and stared at me across the street. He wouldn't look down.

STEVE'S PARENTS ARRIVED IN THE EMERGENCY ROOM. They had driven up from Stanford, where they are on sabbatical. They are cultured, intelligent people, psychologists, writers of books. They were kind and gentle with their bearded son in the purple dress. Mrs. Peterson, a professor who is also first a mother, asked her son if he had had anything to eat. I left Steve with his parents and went to get a drink of something stronger than root beer. I stopped at the surgical nursing desk and asked how Claudia Peterson was doing. The nurse had never heard of her. The surgeon came over. I described the victim. "Oh, we didn't know her name," he said. "She came up here as a Jane Doe. She died forty-five minutes ago." I asked the doctor if he knew that her husband was waiting outside. "Oh Christ, nobody told me," he said. He went through the double doors in his green smock and his green cap to do his duty.

I drove back to the Castro Street apartment with the Petersons, parents and son, because before he called the coroner Steve wanted to see if Claudia had written any instructions in her journal about how she wished to be buried. Inside the apartment, Claudia and Steve's four cats were cowering in the farthest corner from the blown-out window. Steve picked up a fat gray alley cat and cuddled it. He spoke to the cat. "Weasel, Claudia won't be coming home anymore." Claudia's room had a rug and a sleeping bag. A radio tuned to KSAN was still playing. The floor was dotted with cigarette butts piled like Indian burial mounds. Beads, a five-dollar bill, and some change and discarded jeans were the landscape. Steve opened Claudia's journal. The last entry read: "12 PM— time! Hold me tight, ma ma. Vulcan volcano." She had written that and then raced across the room to the No Exit sign.

The doorbell rang; it was the landlord, Alfred Munson, a Department of Public Works employee who owns apartment buildings in his spare time. He had seen the glass. "I'm sorry, Mr. Munson, but my wife committed suicide today. She jumped through the window," Steve said. Al Munson is a tall, noncommital man with slicked-back gray hair and a ruddy face. He was wearing Big Bens and a striped work shirt. "Hmmmmm," he said. He said it about six times. Then, while the landlord and his men boarded up the broken window, Steve Peterson sat on the floor talking on the red telephone to his gay shrink and asking him how to cope. "It's funny," he was saying as we left. "Maybe that's what Claudia wanted to do all along."

"What's that?"

"Jump through the window. That's what she did."

STEVE REMEMBERED SOMETHING. Just after he saw Claudia run past the door toward the window, immediately after he had called the ambulance and his shrink, he had drawn a picture of her running by. He took a battered black notebook from his purse and opened it to the drawing of the last second he had seen his wife on earth. He ripped it out and gave it to me, and I gave it to the *Chronicle*.

[*San Francisco Chronicle,* November 19, 1977]

A First-Hand Look
at the Napa State Kids

O
N FRIDAY, THE FIFTH DAY OF HANUKKAH, in downtown Napa, a bell ringer the size of a fullback was making Christian noises on the stops of the main post office. He was crewcut, short, and stocky, the stuff of farmers. He wore a canvas apron that read "I Am a Bell Ringer." People hurrying by threw coins furtively into his pot. Across the road out to Napa State Hospital tinsel Christmas stalactites hung coldly in the air. The Greyhound will get you to Napa and back for $6.65. If you drive a car it takes seventy minutes from San Francisco without a pit stop. Either way it's a bad trip if you're going where I was.

The Napa Valley had a puffy dark roof on it; the night would bring tule fog; the weekend, rain. A blizzard of winter leaves swirled like brown snowflakes across the wide streets of the mental hospital, a fenced-in small town of concrete bungalows and turn-of-the-century frame buildings. The gate was open and the guardhouse empty. The grounds had the feel of a partially decommissioned army post. Inside a cinder-block building painted the pastel colors of a nursery, a girl of no more than eight looked up from her coloring book. Her eyes were as wide as dollhouse saucers. "Mister, are you gonna stay and see me?" The little girl was from San Francisco. She is one of twenty disturbed young children the city currently is paying to keep in Napa, out of sight and out of mind. The girl was used to hearing no for an answer. Before I would make excuses, she was back at her coloring book.

"They don't get many visitors—especially the kids from San Francisco," said a social worker in blue jeans who has been through the Napa mill. "Poor families—they're the ones who seem to want to come see their kids the most—can't often afford the bus fare; they have other kids at home that they have to take care of on almost no money. And people with money"—here she shrugged—"a lot of them put their kids in here because they just didn't want to deal with them. Some of them never show up, not even at Christmas."

San Francisco sends more kids to Napa than any other county in the state. The city has no facility for the residential care of its disturbed adolescents and has routinely sent them off to a psychiatric warehouse such as Napa. This deportation policy is of questionable civility and dubious effectiveness, and is hardly consistent with San Francisco's over-polished image as a city of tolerance and brotherly love. But not all San Franciscans in this season of the heart embrace the idea of no longer separating our sick children from their families and their friends. A well-planned proposal to do just that has met with opposition which can most charitably be characterized as hysterical from some supervisors and some citizens. Supervisor Terry Francois last week even raised the spectre of teenage murderers in our midst. I went to Napa to find out who these monsters are that Francois and others think we would be coddling.

CALIFORNIA'S MENTAL HOSPITALS were orphaned by Ronald Reagan and have yet to be adopted by Jerry Brown, who was fiddling with the future need of Californians in outer space while Napa slid further down the rathole of neglect. In many respects Napa resembles a pastoral Tenderloin where patients panhandle in the streets. Napa is where San Francisco sends almost half its disturbed adolescents—twenty out of forty-five kids from all sections of the city, the remainder of whom are sent to smaller facilities in other areas as far away as Trinity County. To the credit of the staffs of the childrens' and adolescents' programs at Napa, the kids are insulated from the Hogarthian psychodrama of the adult sections of the hospital. There are no Nurse Ratcheds on the children's staff and the young patients receive—even allowing for the legendary budgetary and staff deficiencies of Napa—a high level of care on the psychiatric level. As with everything at Napa, there is a but.

The but is that on the secondary support levels—nurses and sort of psychiatric paramedics called "psych-techs"—the people who give disturbed kids the day-and-night companionship and counseling vital to bringing them back from withdrawl land—Napa just doesn't have the troops to do the job. "Normal kids sit around and say, 'I just don't know what to do'—so you can imagine how disturbed kids are," said a social worker. "Without enough support staff, kids tend to sit by themselves in corners until somebody can get to them; sometimes, that's a long time." At the proposed Youth Campus at the Convent of the Good Shepherd in San Francisco's Portola Valley—where girls often more disturbed than the adolescents who will be assigned to the new program were quietly treated without incident for over forty years—the youngsters will receive such intimate care on almost a one-to-one basis.

The little girl with the coloring book looked up at me again, and then she looked down, quickly, as if afraid of being rejected. Around her in the sparsely furnished, sterile recreation room other kids—pre-teenagers mostly—played around and watched TV like any other kids, but you could see in their eyes a kind of hurt wonderment; they were asking without saying it what was there about them that made their parents leave them so alone in a place so far from home. These are nice kids, these ones we've cast into the psychiatric hedgerows. Almost all of them from San Francisco have the same background—a broken or disintegrating home, where one or both parents abandoned or rejected or brutalized or in some sick way psychologically shat upon a child that withdrew into fantasy seeking a less horrible world or began harmless antisocial acts seeking attention or punishment as a substitute for affection. All of them need help, and few want anything more complicated than simple love and understanding. Despite the low weekend Bell rates, love is a little hard to send over the long-distance telephone.

The irony and the sadness and the essential stupidness of the controversy in San Francisco is that the children to be treated at the Convent of the Good Shepherd are almost the opposite of the aggressive creatures that supervisors Francois and Dianne Feinstein, among others, have suggested in one way or another would be too dangerous or unsettling for the community to treat at home. In most cases, treatment in the community, and coordinated social work to counsel their families as proposed in the Youth Campus plan, is the very thing they need to get better. At Jack's, the nearest bar to the Napa State Hospital, I asked if they ever had any trouble with the inmates. "Naaah," said the bartender. "Every year or so one of them wanders in here, but we just give him a drink and send him back home. They're harmless."

Supervisor Pete Tamaras, hardly known for his radlib leanings, made the same point during the emotional debate last week when the Board of Supervisors voted 6 to 5 to reject the Youth Campus before a packed house of fired-up Portola Valley residents cheered on by the sandlot agitation tactics of District Eight supervisor-elect Dan White. Neighbors of the Youth Guidance Center, which houses real delinquents, have never complained of trouble with the children, Tamaras said, so on what did the Portola residents base their fears? Imagination, of course, with a dose of misinformation about what would be going on behind the high convent walls. Supervisor-elect White has become so vociferous in uniting his district in fear of these children that it is reminiscent of the "The Chinese Must Go" rabble-rousing tactics of Denis Kearney of the Workingman's Party in the late 1870s. By any standards of history or contemporary manners, it is a cheap shot to build a constituency on fear.

The facility that the Sisters of the Good Shepherd are making available to the city on financial terms that could only be considered charitable was made in heaven to take care of troubled kids—secure cottages, fully equipped classrooms, swimming pool, movie theater, gym, and other amenities of campus life on a twelve-acre wooded site near McLaren Park. It has been used for just such purposes for decades without any security problems, and the Youth Campus staff is anxious to meet the neighborhood's concerns by further beefing up existing security. The alternatives suggested by opponents, such as the Log Cabin or Hidden Valley youth facilities, would cost millions more to convert to lesser facilities and would be even more remote from San Francisco families than Napa. Mayor George Moscone is taking the high road on this one, vetoing the supervisor's rejection of the program. The Sisters, who see the Youth Campus program as a continuation of their own vocation, and plan to stay on the grounds and help with the good work if the Youth Campus is approved, are praying for him. "Pray for my daughter instead," the mayor, whose daughter is in the hospital, told Sister Columba, the convent superior. "I'll go to work on the supervisors if you go to work on the Good Lord."

Dr. William L. Spicer, the director of the Children's Program at Napa, thinks I owe the children there an apology. In an article two weeks ago I described Napa with some hyperbole as a place where zombies walked around and kids in football helmets sat in corners. "They read the things you write in the paper about them," said Dr. Spicer. Kids do sit in corners and some do wear football helmets at Napa, but after visiting them I agree with Dr. Spicer. They are anything but zombies; they are troubled, beautiful kids who deserve every chance to get well, and I do apologize. Sometimes when you are writing about victims you forget they can read.

These are San Francisco's children of Napa:

Linda, now sixteen, who suffered an emotional breakdown after her family immigrated from Southeast Asia a few years ago. The family couldn't deal with her problems at home. She was admitted to Napa, where she had continual cultural problems relating to the staff. She needed proximity to her family and the support system of the Asian community to get stronger, which Napa could not provide.

Roger, a black kid of fourteen, who had been in trouble since he was five. His mother took a hike and his father, while trying, couldn't handle the other children and Roger, who continually cut school and wandered. Roger was never violent but felt increasingly confused, alone, and unwanted. His father wanted to try to reintegrate his troubled family but had enough trouble getting to work every day, let alone getting to Napa.

Arthur, now twelve and attending a San Francisco private school, spent three years in Napa after his father and mother split. His father told him he had his own single life to live and there was little room in it for a son. His mother said he was interfering with her landing another husband, and put him up in Napa as "incorrigible" on a Wednesday afternoon. On Thursday she took off on a Caribbean cruise.

Roger would eat crayons and climb on the roof to get attention. The Napa psychiatrists were reluctant to discharge him to the care of a relative in San Francisco because of "destructive tendencies." The report said that Roger "needs glasses, refused to wear them, and has destroyed three pairs." The relative took the boy to a San Francisco eye doctor, who found his vision 20-20. The state doctors had insisted he wear strong glasses, which he took off to play since he couldn't see with them on. He played on the floor because there were no tables in the ward. Other kids stepped on his glasses on the ground.

Cathy is ten, the daughter of a white middle-class San Francisco couple. The father left home, and Cathy couldn't understand why. Then her mother asked her lesbian lover, who had two children of her own, to move in. The other kids beat up on Cathy and took her toys. When her mother insisted that Cathy call the other woman "Father," Cathy became severely depressed and withdrawn and was hospitalized.

If these kids are menaces to the community, I'm the Big Bad Wolf.

[*San Francisco Chronicle*, December 13, 1977]

Everyone's Out to Get Him

*"Just because you don't think they're out to
get you doesn't mean they're not."*
                                    —A. J. Weberman

*I*T WAS A PERFECT PLACE FOR A HIT, just like on the road back East where they tried to get him before, and Robert Lee Lewis gulped back the paranoia when the white van came at him across the dividing line on a lonely, spiral stretch of Highway 84 in the hills below La Honda one misty morning. There was a skid and a thud as the cars met in the mountain stillness. Lewis fought the fear rising in him. He told himself that he hadn't been living in his car for seven years while investigating organized crime and the CIA to have it end like this on a country road. Cool your roll, man, he said. This isn't a hit. It's just an accident. Lewis got out of his car and walked over to the van. It had a flat tire. Lewis told the driver he'd get out his tools and help him change the flat.

On his way back to his car, Lewis saw it: "All five lug nuts on my left rear wheel were loosened to the end. I'd just put on a new tire and tightened the lugs the night before. I hadn't driven but two miles. There was no way they could have come loose by themselves." Paranoia embraced Lewis like a wet grizzly bear. He looked up and down the isolated road. He looked at the van. He flashed that a white van had been somehow involved in the Orlando Letelier assassination in D.C. He dove into his car and started off like Mannix with his head below the window. He tore out down Highway 84 leaving the guy with the busted van staring after him in the drizzle. Lewis didn't stop to fix his wheel; he was sure they'd be right behind him. The topsy wheel got him down 84 and partway to Palo Alto on 288 before it spun off and the station wagon—stuffed like a Christmas goose with documents—sparked and sagged to a lop-sided halt on the freeway. Lewis filled a briefcase to the breaking point with FBI and CIA documents and Interpol reports and some stuff from SDECE, the French CIA, and a newspaper clipping showing that Richard Nixon was in Dallas on November 22, 1963, a day he says he was not.

He ran across wet fields until he found a side road where he felt safe hitching. His thumb got him to Palo Alto, and from there an underground railway of assassinationologists got him to Berkeley, and then to Sacramento, where he took sanctuary for two days in Controller Ken Cory's office, where he called me up on the state's nickel. That was how it all began. Bob Lewis has been hiding in my basement for weeks.

This story is about what it's like to have an honest-to-God megaparanoid person living in your basement. It's also about some of the things that have made him paranoid. As Thomas Pynchon, the novelist, once said, "Just because you're paranoid doesn't mean you aren't being followed."

"Write this down. It's important. Captain Wayne Bishop. Connecticut State Police. He was on leave to investigate JFK's assassination. They killed Captain Bishop and covered up his death, too. He knew about the connection between Jimmy Hoffa and Jack Ruby and he was getting too close to the truth. The same documentation was taken from me at gunpoint on a lonely road back East the day Hoffa was kidnapped. It's important you have this information in case I don't make it." It was Bob Lewis, on the telephone, from Ken Cory's office in Sacramento. He said the controller's people were helping him find out if the mob had tried to bump him off. I asked Lewis how he was in so tight with Sacramento. "I helped them out with their investigation of Howard Hughes," he said.

I'd first heard about Robert Lee Lewis a week before. Allan Francovich, a filmmaker friend who was making a movie about the CIA, had called. He'd run across this guy who'd been living out of his car for eight years investigating organized crime and political assassinations. People in Berkeley knew him. He'd worked for the McGovern campaign. His research supposedly connected everything: the French Connection, the CIA, the SLA, the Mafia, the Kennedy murders... "He might make a good story," Francovich said. A short time later I was plotting to send Lewis to live in Francovich's basement. He might make a good movie, I was going to tell him.

Lewis rang my doorbell at ten o'clock on a cold Tuesday evening, two days before Thanksgiving. He came in and sat down and chain-talked and chain-smoked nonstop for four hours. He is short and thin and intense and so enthusiastic he burns energy like a portable power pack. He wore a ski jacket zippered to the neck and a lumberjack cap jammed down to his eyebrows. His tiny face with its stream-of-consciousness mouth and wide brown eyes was all that showed out of the bunched-up clothing. He reminded me of a kimono doll on speed.

"They've tried to kill me before," Lewis was saying. "After I testified before the Watergate committee about Nixon wrecking Muskie's 1972 campaign by letting Hoffa out of jail, the Mafia tailed my car across country. They wanted to make it look like an accident. They sabotaged my brakes outside of Gallup when I was in a diner. A few miles later my brakes failed and I went over a cliff. I ended up in the hospital with a concussion. The FBI reports in my car were scattered all over the road where I crashed. While I was in the hospital the sheriff stole my dog. That's heavy, man."

Even though New Mexico is a danger zone for him, he says he snuck back into the state in 1976 to investigate the murder of reporter Don Bolles. "I lost two fingers the day Bolles died," said Lewis, who tends to integrate personal experiences with epochal events. "I was choppin' wood in Santa Cruz to get gas money for my research. The saw slipped and cut the tips off my fingers. I went right to the insurance company and settled for $7,000. I spent the money on the Bolles case." The jury is still out on that one according to Lewis: "Both Barry Goldwater and Joe Bananas were involved. They're covering it up. Tom Sanford, assistant managing editor of the *Arizona Republic*, told me a lot of things he couldn't print. Right after he told me, he was murdered. They said it was suicide. The last thing he said to me was, 'They're monitoring you.' And you wonder why I'm paranoid."

Lewis is a Bible-toting ex-con. He says he used to play chess every day with the Birdman of Alcatraz at the Federal Medical Center in Springfield, Missouri. Lewis said he began chasing conspiracies because he "promised the Lord" he would do something positive with his life when he kicked the heroin habit ten years ago.

Lewis talked on high speed into the night. He was an encyclopedia of conspiratorial detail. He knew the names of nine hundred organized crime figures he said ex-president Nixon had pardoned. He could connect the French Connection to Nixon, and that ball of wax to the Kennedy assassinations. He kept pulling FBI or CIA documents out of his briefcase to buttress his theories. "You gotta have documents, else nobody believes your trip," he said. Lewis said he had spent "thousands of hours" researching in the National Archives and the Library of Congress and working as an "unpaid volunteer" with the staffs of Senate and House investigating committees. He was worried about the stash of documents in the station wagon he had abandoned when paranoia took the wheel on Interstate 280. "When the cops see what's in those papers," he said, "they'll call the CIA for sure." Whenever his conspiracy rap slowed down, Lewis seemed lonely and a little lost. I asked him if he'd like to come for Thanksgiving dinner.

The next day I telephoned Controller Ken Cory's office. What were they doing with Bob Lewis, and had he helped the state investigate Howard Hughes? "Oh yes, we know him," said Cory aide Keith Seigmuller. "He brought us a lot of documents pertaining to Howard Hughes' estate. I don't know what use was made of them. He seemed very upset about his car and we were trying to calm him and help him on his way."

Lewis showed up for Thanksgiving. He sat between Quentin Kopp and Paul Krassner. He did most of the talking.

I WOKE WITH A HANGOVER TO A TERRIBLE CLATTER and stumbled downstairs to see what was the matter. It was Lewis. He was playing the victrola. "Mrs. Robinson," that infernal noise from the sixties, was haunting the house. I thought I had given the record to St. Vincent de Paul years ago. Lewis was sitting in front of the Christmas tree. He was darning his shirt. His hat was pulled so far down his forehead that he looked at you from the bottom of his eyes. "Morning, brother," he said. "I get so depressed from reading the paper about Guyana that I put on Simon and Garfunkel and it cheers me up."

Lewis followed me into the kitchen, drowning out Simon and Garfunkel with an a cappella conspiracy symphony about Jonestown. "It's a government m.o., man. Freedom of Information documents show that every left group in the country has had an FBI or CIA infiltrator manipulating it. You mean to tell me Jim Jones was the only exception?" I gave Lewis a stiff drink—he doesn't drink much, but seems to smoke three cigarettes at one time—and suggested that the paranoid blues were getting him to take everything personally. He jumped up like he'd sat on a hot rock. "Paranoid! Of course I'm paranoid! I've had five lug nuts unscrewed on my wheel and I've been living out of my car for seven years investigating the Mafia and I've got reason to be paranoid! Man, I'm running on high-octane paranoia. I'm Mr. Paranoia."

MR. PARANOIA DID NOT SURFACE AT NIGHTS. He went out investigating or stayed in his room in the basement reading the Bible and cross-fertilizing his Mafia-CIA notes. That was after my wife found him sitting on the hallway floor taking the cuckoo clock apart. Lewis would often be sitting around listening to Simon and Garfunkel when my kids came home from school. "That's a paranoid guy who's hiding in our basement," they would explain to their friends. Kids can handle anything.

Every day Lewis had a new conspiracy for breakfast. What was the significance of the Rockefeller part-ownership in the motel where the Secret Service hid Marina Oswald right after John Kennedy's assassination? Did Dorothy Kilgallen, the journalist and What's My Liner, die of an overdose of booze and pills or was it because she was the last person to interview Jack Ruby alone? The details were all mindboggling and Lewis could recite them all by rote. "I can explain this in thirty seconds," he would say. Hours later I'd be screaming for mercy. A pause for breath would remind him of another story: "CIA Cubans broke into Hoover's house and put poison on his toilet articles. That's how he died..."

Peter Dale Scott, a Berkeley English professor who is a respected writer on assassination topics, made this assessment of Lewis, whom he knows: "He does have a terribly byzantine kind of mind, which I think feeds his paranoia. But most of all of the documents he's brought me have seemed authentic; he performs a valuable service to those interested in solving the assassinations by traveling around sharing research documents and prodding congressional investigators to look into areas they might tend to neglect." Calls to several other professors around the country brought a picture of Mr. Paranoia as a dedicated if over-intense individual who travels the country like a conspiratorial Johnny Appleseed, planting documents where he goes. All agreed that his car—piled with years of collected documents—was the containing principle in his life, and without it he might tend to fall apart. Lewis pined for his car with the hopeless love of the sun for the moon. He feared that either the Mafia was watching it, or if paranoia had won out and it was an innocent accident last month, the cops would arrest him for leaving the scene of an accident, and a man in his position isn't safe in jail.

I prevailed on an attorney friend, Brennan Newsom, to contact the San Mateo sheriff, who had impounded Lewis' abandoned car, and explain about Mr. Paranoia. "They say the other driver has made a complaint, but if Lewis comes in and explains things they'll get the drivers together to work it out and he can get his car back," Newsom said. Lewis sat in the basement for a week wrestling with the decision. It was a paranoid's Gethsemane. "How do I know it won't be a trap?" he kept saying. He took to his Bible. I called Detective Katsumis of the San Mateo Sheriff's Department. He was getting a little impatient. "I understand the situation," he said. "If he comes in, we'll work it out. But if he doesn't I'm going to file hit-run charges against him."

Yesterday Lewis bit the bullet of his own paranoia. In the company of a friend, Ted Rubinstein, an assassination researcher, he set off on the long mile to Redwood City to explain to Detective Katsumis about those missing lug nuts and the strange and terrible things that paranoia can do to you. If all goes well, sometime this holiday weekend Lewis will be visiting the owner of the white van to explain why Mr. Paranoia took him for a Mafia hit man. If the other driver accepts this mistaken identity in the true Christmas spirit, Lewis can reclaim his beloved car and get back trucking. If not, he says he is ready to face the music should the San Mateo authorities bring charges of hit-run property damage. His defense will be, of course, paranoia. Me, I'm a material witness.

[*San Francisco Chronicle,* December 23, 1978]

The Ten Days that Shook San Francisco

*T*HE REVEREND JIM JONES BEGAN HIS LIFE AS A PREACHER selling
spider monkeys on the streets of Indianapolis. He came to San Francisco
and mixed politics with religion. He died in a Guyana rain forest on
November 18, 1978, along with 912 of his followers. Thus began the
worst ten days in the city's history. This is the story of those horrible
days that began with the mass suicides and murders in Jonestown and
ended with the City Hall slayings of George Moscone and Harvey Milk
on November 27, and of the aftermath. It is the thesis of this essay that
the two events were related.

The operative bond between the Jonestown suicides and the City
Hall slayings was paranoia. The Reverend Jones, an itinerant preacher
whom indulgent Frisco had taken under its liberal wing, was a self-proclaimed Robin Hood who took from the poor to give to the poor. He
was so certain that the CIA, the FBI, the media, and the city's conservative seraphim were out to get him—a paranoia fueled by some advisors and his increasing drug use—that he pressed his flock into a mass
orgy of suicide and murder in his jungle paradise in Guyana. The city
will never free itself of the terrible vision of suicide-bent San Francisco
mothers lining up in Jonestown to feed cyanide-laced Flavor Aid to their
babies before drinking it themselves.

Supervisor Dan White, who campaigned for office making parsonish statements about the state of sin in which the city was living, came
to see San Francisco political life as "them" against "us"—liberal mayor
George Moscone and gay supervisor Harvey Milk conspiring with a
crooked communist vote-stealing preacher like Jim Jones to take the
city away from the Catholic blue-collar families of the San Francisco
where Dan White grew up. When he went to City Hall to kill Moscone

and Milk, White was not only avenging a perceived wrong but was, in his own twisted way of thinking, removing the remaining devils—Jones had already removed himself—who were making Old San Francisco disappear before White's very eyes. In retrospect, the pledge in White's 1977 campaign brochure for supervisor was a declaration of war that foreshadowed the Jonestown and City Hall tragedies: "I'm not going to be forced out of San Francisco by splinter groups of radicals, social deviates, and incorrigibles...There are thousands upon thousands of frustrated, angry people such as yourself, waiting to unleash a fury that can and will eradicate the malignancies which blight our city."

Paranoia has always been an American way of life. In San Francisco in November of 1978, it became an American way of death.

The thick paranoia that crept like the fog through San Francisco in the mid-1970s was by no means limited to the extremes of Jim Jones' left and Dan White's right. A reverse paranoia kept many liberals and political moderates from taking at face value the horror stories that had begun to surface about Peoples Temple, which by mid-decade had become a fulcrum of San Francisco's world-famous radical chic. While behind the scenes Jones psychologically and sexually abused his largely black congregation and the white power elite was running the Temple, leftist celebs trooped to the Temple altar. Angela Davis spoke from Jones' pulpit (she later expressed disgust at Jones' phony faith healings, occasioning a rift between the Temple and the Communist Party) and the Temple lent money to Indian leader Dennis Banks. Jones at the same time contributed money to First Amendment causes and used guerrilla tactics to try to keep the city's newspapers from printing questioning stories about his church. The Temple appeared to run one of the city's largest soup kitchens, a successful drug rehabilitation program, and a free medical clinic. From the outside looking in, Jones was doing the Lord's work.

He was also delivering the Lord's vote. Liberal politicians such as George Moscone and California lieutenant governor Mervyn Dymally were not unaware of the Temple's political clout—Jones could turn out hundreds of campaign workers at a snap of his unclean fingers. It became an article of faith in the western, conservative side of San Francisco—a faith to which Dan White belonged—that Peoples Temple members were bused in from upstate and downstate to vote fraudulently in the

1975 mayoral election in which Moscone defeated West Portal realtor John Barbagelata by the cat's whisker of one percent of the vote. More than two hundred ballot registration books were never turned in to City Hall, and the records of the 1975 election were removed from the office of the Registrar of Voters.

The Temple's liberal supporters were disinclined to take early criticisms made by the Savonarola-like Barbagelata (who as a supervisor authored a law to put pasties on the neon nipples of Broadway strip-joint signs) at face value because, at the time, revelations about the FBI's anti-left COINTEL program, particularly its 1960s campaign against the Oakland-based Black Panther Party, showed the Bureau had created phony communications among party leaders to cause disharmony and had planted critical press stories. You didn't have to be a conspiracy theorist in San Francisco in 1977 to view the sudden surfacing of bizarre stories about one of the city's most successful leftist churches with a modicum of suspicion.

Ironically it was the same possibility—of government undercover dirty work inside the Peoples Temple—that was burning Jim Jones' brain cells to a paranoid crisp. A series of unsolved trashings, a suspect firebombing attempt, and other attacks on the Temple's San Francisco headquarters (some believe Jones himself instigated them to scare the faithful into line) convinced the congregation someone was indeed out to get them, and after they fled to the safe harbor of Guyana, Jim Jones, with Mark Lane sitting at his right hand, talked more about CIA assassination plots than Fidel Castro ever did.

Critics of Dan White's botched trial—he got off with voluntary manslaughter and spent barely five years in jail—believe the Peoples Temple horror haunted the prosecution. Once White's defense threatened, however obliquely, to make San Francisco politics an issue in the trial, the prosecution steered away from raising the political conflicts between White and Moscone and Milk that might in a jury's view have contributed to the element of malice necessary to sustain a higher charge of murder—but might have also prompted White's defense to retaliate by raising the Temple's close ties to Dan White's sworn political enemies and other unsavory aspects of San Francisco liberal politics.

San Francisco in the late 1970s was a city bitterly and violently divided by politics laced with paranoia. Gays were regularly beaten on the streets and Frisco cops, in the days after the City Hall assassinations, showed up to work wearing "Free Dan White" T-shirts. Few in San Francisco ever dared ask why Dan White never said he was sorry.

THE PEOPLES TEMPLE BEGAN IN INDIANAPOLIS—a city where the KKK cross was known to burn at midnight and where Jim Jones daringly assembled a racially-mixed congregation. Jones' ministry enjoyed a somewhat contradictory reputation of excellently feeding and taking care of the poor while also taking their money. In 1965 Jones had a vision of atomic disaster and moved his church to Redwood Valley near Ukiah to escape the fallout. By 1972 he wanted his church in the cities where the action would be and purchased an abandoned synagogue in the wasteland of San Francisco's Fillmore District, a black ghetto suffering redevelopment, which gave it the look of 1945 Berlin. Jones acquired rent-free from the city several fenced-in empty acres adjacent to the old synagogue. These became the storing ground for massive shipments of supplies to the Temple's "agricultural mission" in socialist Guyana on the eastern tip of South America. The agricultural supplies included large quantities of handguns and rifles and poison. U.S. and Guyana customs agents inspected the crates but apparently did not discover any of the contraband.

When the Temple first opened its doors in San Francisco in 1972 the Jim Jones who later became a jungle recluse had been as omnipresent as the god he told the faithful he was. The good man was out feeding the hungry, "curing" cancer, caring for the elderly, saving drug addicts, doing the Lord's work with high visibility. Jones' church was unique among fundamentalist religions in that it not only offered the vision of a good life hereafter but the promise of a better life here on earth. His gospel was avowedly Marxist and his message revolutionary. While the cynical Jones had voted Republican and hobnobbed with Birchers in Ukiah, in liberal San Francisco Temple members became the vanguard in campaigns for progressive candidates. Assembly speaker Willie Brown, a pol who knows a good machine when he sees one, was one of the Temple's greatest supporters. Jones opened another temple in Los Angeles and by 1975 he was claiming that membership in his church had grown to more than twenty thousand people, although in reality it never boasted more than five thousand members. But Jones was on a roll. San Francisco mayor George Moscone appointed him chairman of the city's housing authority and the shades-wearing reverend was photographed with vice presidential candidate Walter Mondale aboard his jet.

The Temple's membership remained largely poor blacks, but it also attracted a significant number of guilt-stricken white middle-class liberals—businessmen, an ex–TV newscaster, even an assistant district attorney. Guilty liberals found the Temple attractive because members threw all their earthly possessions into the common pot for the common good. The least a member would do was give a fourth of his income to the church; many gave everything. The Temple was not just a religion, it was a way of life, and a lot of people thought it was the way of the future. Dr. Nathan Hare, a prominent black sociologist, was ecstatic about it. "There was good blues music, African dancing, professional-quality entertainment. You got caught up in the mood," he said. "Jones was soft-spoken and self-assured. He had a voice that was soothing. He spoke eloquently and with compassion. His themes were freedom and interracial harmony. He had his own style of socialism. Capitalists would be brought to the table. They would be persuaded to share the riches. If there had not been a racist society, there would not have been a need for Jim Jones. He struck me as quite healthy mentally, quite relaxed."

That was two years before the end. Another side of the Temple—darker than the dark side of the moon—was revealed by former Temple members who said Jones' method of keeping his troops in line was not fear of the Lord but fear of himself—coupled with a classic brainwashing program that included physical beatings, forced sex, total financial dependence, mentally and physically exhausting work, bad nutrition, forced sleeplessness, and the threat of execution if anyone strayed from the Temple line. Ex-members said many of the Temple faithful had gone so far down the brainwash path they no longer realized what was happening to them. These were the suicidal pioneers of Guyana.

One method Jones used to control his flock—this was particularly effective with his white middle-class members—was getting them to sign false confessions to crimes such as molesting their own children. To sign such a paper and give it to Jones to use as he willed was a required act of faith. One woman member told me Jim Jones was a real god who at "confession times" urged her to tell the most intimate details of her sex life and had her write down a complete account of every sexual experience she had ever had. Jones often counseled Temple women to use vibrators for sexual release since "the Temple had more women members than men," she said. Jones kept telling her she would wake up one day and find the whites had fenced off the black areas, but he would lead her to freedom.

Other ex-Temple members said Jones' interest in sex extended to establishing a "relationships committee," where he would decide which woman would have sexual relations with which man. Often he substituted himself as the best choice. His sexual appetites were egalitarian: he sodomized women as well as men. The irreverent preacher, who once instructed his faithful to use the Bible as toilet paper, preached that all good socialists must be sodomized. He used sex as a weapon of control, forcing heterosexual men to surrender to him sexually as an act of total submission. After such moments of homosexual sex, Jones had the man write him a letter thanking "Father." The letter was put in the man's Temple file to be read to the congregation if he misbehaved. A woman who violated his sexual commandments by seeing an unapproved man told me Jones tried to force her to engage in sex on the stage before the entire community. "The Reverend, he was really interested in revolutionary sex," one member said, after the disaster.

Jim Jones sold photographs of himself to the faithful that were supposed to protect them from assault, fire, and cancer. Each picture was good for only one disaster, so Temple members had to buy several if they wanted full protection. The photographic concession could bring in $2,000 to $3,000 on a good weekend. Former members said people were pressured into deeding their homes to the church, which would then sell them for cash. There was always a ready supply of blank power-of-attorney forms and deed papers at the Temple headquarters.

Jones didn't neglect even pocket change. On weekend bus trips, Temple members had to eat and sleep aboard the crowded vehicles and were constantly being hit up for cash. "Every time you'd get to sleeping good, they'd be coming around taking offerings," said one former member. "If you said you didn't have any money, they'd make you empty your purse and see if you could find any." Temple members who lived in church communes turned over their salaries to the church and received two dollars a week for living expenses. People did this gladly because it gave them a feeling of total commitment, former members said. Older members signed over their Social Security checks. Some $40,000 a month in Social Security checks went to the jungle settlement in Guyana. Over a million dollars in cash, checks, and gold was found stashed in the settlement.

Jones' insistence on getting every dime was more megalomania than simple greed. He wanted his followers to be totally dependent on him. Then he could be God. He asked members to address him as "Heavenly Father." Several times he told them he was the reincarnation of Lenin. In time, the sacrifice of worldly possessions was not sufficient to satisfy Jones' megalomania. He wanted the ultimate sacrifice. He wanted people to die for him. "Jim would get up on the altar and call out: 'How many in here will lay down their lives for me? How many in here will lay down the lives of their children? How many will lay down the lives of their wives?' And we would scream and jump up and down and yell: 'I will, Heavenly Father, I will,'" said a former member.

In the early 1970s, his mad paranoia fueled by critical news stories and by defections from the church, Jones began leading mock suicide drills. In one such drill, he called his followers to the church and harangued against the defectors. The congregation gave him the clenched-fist salute. "We are going to celebrate tonight," Jones said. Paper cups were brought in and wine was poured. Jones told everyone to drink. They did. He smiled. "You have just drunk poison and all of you will be dead in twenty minutes," he said. A man jumped up and said he didn't want to die. The church's disciplinary enforcers—Jones called them his angels—ran over and beat the man to the floor. Another woman who cried that she didn't want to die was shot point blank with a pistol by one of the angels. She fainted before she realized the bullets were blanks.

"Jim Jones always said, 'If they ever put me in jail or if I am killed, we are all to commit suicide, killing our children first, making sure they are dead, then killing ourselves,'" another ex-member said. Temple people came to believe it was better to die than to live in a world hostile to their leader. "Jim would say there was nothing to fear in death. He said there was nothing to it. He had people believing that even if they died, they would be reincarnated and come back," she said. Jones made the older members cash in their life insurance policies and give the proceeds to the Temple. He told them they didn't need insurance because they would not die. Ritual suicide drills became part of life in the Jonestown jungle community. The psychologically subservient members were subjected to long paranoiac harangues from the leader. Loudspeakers were placed in the fields so Jones could tell the faithful while they worked about the "conspiracy" against the Temple by the press and the CIA.

Jones was always talking about threats against his life. He told his followers he had cancer and would die soon. He said to die was beautiful. The ever-alert San Francisco press was particularly lax about the monster in their midst. The *Examiner* discontinued a series of articles by its then religion editor in 1972 after four of the articles ran amid vociferous Temple protests. And a *Chronicle* reporter who got some of the goods on the Temple's bizarre sadomasochistic practices and couldn't get them into his newspaper took the material to *New West* magazine, which published the first major report of this less-than-utopian side of Temple life in 1977. The *Examiner* ran critical stories at the same time. Jones retreated to his jungle stronghold in Guyana before the articles were even published and never returned to San Francisco. He resigned the housing authority chairmanship in a letter to Moscone dictated over shortwave radio from the jungle.

In his new isolation, Jones' paranoia overwhelmed him. His fanatically loyal angels became smugglers, moving the Temple's arsenal from the San Francisco yard to the jungle settlement. They also smuggled in barbiturates and other drugs Jones took in prodigious quantities and Thorazine he used to pacify Temple members terrified by his constant preaching of the coming race war and their destruction at the hands of their enemies. As Jones was preaching to his captive flock of "revolutionary suicide"—a concept borrowed from Black Panther leader Huey Newton—he was also ordering Temple members to take their children out of San Francisco schools and send them to Jonestown. Many children were sent to Guyana by Temple "guardians" without their parents' consent. Lawsuits filed by anguished parents got nowhere when Guyana authorities refused to interfere in what they called an American religious dispute.

Jones' feverish paranoia was exacerbated by the activities of Temple defectors, many of whom were as fanatical in their fear and hatred of their former leader as they had been in their devotion. Two armed attacks against Jonestown—believed to have been orchestrated by Jones—created a siege mentality in the settlement. The socialist paradise where young and old worked together to feed and care for the indigent became an armed camp of people waiting happily for Armageddon.

The Peoples Temple had two famous lawyers, Charles Garry and Mark Lane. They hated each other. While Lane seemed to encourage Jones' paranoia—telling Jones of a government conspiracy out to destroy the Temple—Garry appeared to discourage the paranoia. It was Garry, a courtroom streetfighter who has represented mostly leftist clients during his long legal career, who talked Jones into opening up Jonestown to a visit by a delegation headed by Congressman Leo Ryan of San Mateo, who had received complaints from concerned relatives of Temple members that people were being held against their will in Guyana. Garry thought the Temple would benefit by giving the world a look at "this beautiful place." He represented the Temple in many legal actions brought by ex-members who felt the revolutionary preacher had bilked them into signing over their property. The brilliant lawyer was aware of Jones' sexual excesses — Jones once told him he had sexual intercourse with sixteen Temple members in one day, fourteen women and two men—and the questionable financial practices of the church, but he thought Jones was not unlike others of the cloth in these matters and was genuinely impressed by the communal spirit and multiracial harmony of the Temple. He knew Jones was paranoid but didn't think him suicidal, let alone mass-suicidal. "I thought he was just another crooked preacher," Garry said to me a few days after the Guyana holocaust.

Mark Lane has thrust himself center stage into most of the great controversies of the last two decades—the Kennedy and King assassinations, Vietnam, and Wounded Knee. "He came into the Peoples Temple like a kamikaze operator," said Dr. Carlton Goodlett, a black San Francisco newspaper publisher who supported the Temple in his *Sun Reporter*. One of the bizarre stories of Peoples Temple is how Mark Lane got his opportunistic foot in the golden door of Jonestown through a cinema caper that turned out to be a chimera. Lane came to San Francisco and checked into a suite at the St. Francis Hotel and met with Temple representatives to discuss the potential movie and sent the hotel bill (which included $22.40 for a beard trim) to the Temple. The movie, by writer Donald Freed, who had worked with Lane on the Kennedy assassination flick *Executive Action,* was to be a feature-length film telling the inspiring story of Peoples Temple. The idea was loaded with sizzle—it would have a Graham Greene plot with Berlin Wall twists and be set in beautiful Guyana, where the CIA and other baddies were plotting against a group of idealistic Americans who had created a paradise away from home. Freed approached the revered film director Paul Jarrico, who did the classic 1953 lefty film *Salt of the Earth.* Jarrico had never heard of the church and dismissed Jones as a phony.

But the idea was sufficiently compelling to get Lane an invitation to the religious settlement in Guyana and to prompt a letter, dated August 22, 1978, in Jonestown, from the Reverend Jones to director Jarrico, in which Jones said it was his understanding that Jarrico was "currently negotiating with a major star to play the role of myself." After the suicides, Temple survivors told me about this strange project and I called Jarrico in Hollywood. He was outraged that his name had been invoked and said he never had any intention of making a movie about Jim Jones. But the ersatz movie ploy did get Lane into the thick of the Peoples Temple real-life disaster scenario. He was paid $10,000 by Jones and produced a report telling Jones that there was "a coordinated campaign to destroy the Peoples Temple and to impugn the reputation of its leader, Bishop Jim Jones," and the usual "suspect organizations" were the CIA, the FBI, the IRS, the FCC, the U.S. Post Office, "and their agents and employees." Lane recommended that the Temple undertake a "counter-offensive" by opening an "Embassy" in Washington, D.C., and suggested that for that purpose Jones rent a building Lane owned "on Capitol Hill directly across the street from the U.S. Supreme Court."

Temple defector Tern Buford told the *New York Times* that just weeks before the tragedy she told Lane that Jones had gone mad and Jonestown was an armed camp full of drugs and guns where people were being held against their will. That was not what Lane told the public at press conferences before Ryan's trip. Lane continued to hit on his theme that the CIA was out to get Jones. Lane's actions may have helped raise the paranoia level at the settlement to the higher decibels.

Charles Garry thought the fact-finding visit by Congressman Ryan had been a "public relations triumph." He said Ryan had been impressed by the Temple's agricultural achievements and the advanced jungle medicine it was giving the natives. He said that even though a Temple member had put a knife to the congressman's throat and had to be restrained just before the group left for the airport, Ryan would have given a good report about the Jonestown settlement. According to Garry, Lane asked: "Why would the goddamn fool come down here without security?" Garry, the idealist, responded: "Why would he need security here?" Garry thought it no big deal that fourteen people had elected to leave with the congressman. He didn't consider that a significant number in a settlement of more than nine hundred.

Jim Jones saw it ghastly different. He knew the defectors would tell about the guns and drugs and that would bring an investigation that would bring down the Temple walls. As Garry was telling his client how well things had gone, a Temple hit team was at the jungle airstrip trying to kill the visitors and defectors.

Jones then called his congregation together for the last time. The dedicated doctor who administered jungle medicine to the natives diluted the cyanide in grape Flavor Aid and mixed it with tranquilizers. The children were given it first, the way Jim Jones had always said. Babies were fed the deadly brew   it was squirted down their throats with syringes. Some of the reluctant adults were given injections of the poison. The armed angels stood guard to make sure all joined the death ritual.

Word reached Jones that many of his intended victims had escaped. The congressman, three newsmen, including *Examiner* photographer Greg Robinson, and one Temple member died in the shooting. Lane and Garry, meanwhile, had been taken to a distant part of the compound. Two Temple guards said good-bye, smiling. "We are going to die a revolutionary suicide as an expression of protest against racism and fascism," one said. They seemed genuinely happy. Lane saw an opportunity to escape with their lives. "Then we'll tell your story," he said. The guards seemed to think this a capital idea—someone should survive to tell the story of the glories of revolutionary suicide—and they let the lawyers flee into the jungle. There took place one of the great scenes in the spotted history of the law. The two famous barristers spent the night huddled together for warmth in the cold, wet jungle. Garry says that Lane during the long night bragged to him that he had brought cough drops with him, which he ate at lunch instead of the cheese sandwiches that were served to the Ryan party because he suspected that the sandwiches might have been poisoned. Garry, who had eaten a sandwich, asked Lane why the hell he hadn't told him it might be poisoned. "Because we weren't speaking," he says Lane told him. Lane later denied that account.

Jones was found dead with a bullet in his head, although it remains a mystery if Jones shot himself or was shot by someone else. His long-suffering wife, Marceline, took poison. So did his mistress, Maria Katsaris. The Temple dogs were killed because Jones had preached that animals, too, had an afterlife and the members wanted their pets with them. A few of the faithful waiting to drink the poison saw their comrades writhing in agony on the ground and escaped into the jungle from the guns of the angels. "Whom the gods would destroy they first make mad," Garry said, emerging from the jungle. When Mayor George Moscone heard what had happened in Guyana, he vomited. At the San Francisco Temple a group of survivors were secluded in the Geary fortress.

ON NOVEMBER 27, THE NINTH DAY after Jonestown, Daniel James White, ex-cop, former paratrooper, hero Frisco fireman and superjock, an All-American boy from everybody's favorite city, strapped on his police special .38, loaded his pockets with extra hollow-point bullets, and went to City Hall to settle some political differences. Two weeks earlier, White, thirty-two, of Irish build with a pretty-boy face, had impetuously resigned his seat on the Board of Supervisors to devote himself to his hot potato stand near Fisherman's Wharf. Now White, as conservative as a priest's suspenders, was asking Mayor George Moscone, who was George Bush's typical card-carrying liberal, to reappoint him. The mayor invited White into his private sitting room and poured two drinks. When Moscone told him that he would not give him his seat back, White shot him in the chest and the upper right arm. He then walked over to the wounded politician and pumped two bullets into the right side of his head, execution-style. The drinks were never touched.

White crossed the marble expanse of City Hall to the other side of the building, where the supervisors have their offices. He reloaded his gun. Harvey Milk, the gay supervisor, had an office not much bigger than the closet he had come out of many years earlier. Milk was forty-eight, short and bubbly with charm. He was not a single-issue politician and had forged progressive alliances with many heterosexuals. Of the eleven members on the Board of Supervisors, Dan White had been the lone vote against Milk's gay civil rights ordinance, which the mayor had signed with a lavender pen handed him by Milk. White knocked on Milk's door and asked to see him for a minute. The gay man and the straight man walked across the hall to White's old office. White shut the door. Milk was heard to cry out, "Oh, no!" White shot him three times in the chest and stomach and back. The executioner then fired two bullets into the back of Milk's head.

White, an unchurched Catholic, left City Hall and went to St. Mary's Cathedral to meet his wife before surrendering at Northern Station to cops who were his old friends and former comrades in blue. That afternoon a reporter standing by a police radio heard cops singing "Danny Boy" and whistling the Notre Dame fight song over the police frequency. The "night of dark intent" that Robert Frost saw coming to the Pacific seemed to be falling on San Francisco. As news of the City Hall assassinations spread, people stood on street corners staring ahead, as if waiting for imaginary streetcars.

That November evening forty thousand people, mostly gay, moved slowly down Market Street to City Hall in a solemn candlelight march like the procession to a cathedral. Instead of the Gregorian chant, there was a lone trumpeter playing "Blowin' in the Wind." On the steps of City Hall appeared Joan Baez, who greeted the mourners with "Amen" in dirge tempo. The mourners heard the chilling, challenging, posthumous words of Harvey Milk: "Let the bullets that rip through my brain smash through every closet door in the nation." About a year earlier, in a moment of extraordinary premonition, Milk, the city's first gay supervisor, had taped a message for his followers were he assassinated.

The huge crowd walked offstage into the wings that Black Monday night as silently as it had entered. Almost six months later to the day, on May 21, another Monday, there was another march down Market Street and another massive nocturnal gathering of gays outside City Hall. This time, there was a riot. Gay men and women poured into the streets, peas from the pod of outrage, shell-shocked by the verdict delivered late that breezy summery afternoon by a jury of Dan White's peers. City Hall was trashed, a dozen police cars were burnt to melt-down, and property damage reached a million dollars. The cops counterattacked busting heads, and it became a gay Selma.

The conservative ex-supervisor had shot down the liberal mayor and the gay supervisor in cold blood, but the jury found him guilty of voluntary manslaughter. With good time, he spent only five years, one month, and nine days in jail and walked out of Soledad Prison on January 6, 1984, the year of Orwell. His wife visited him regularly in jail and he even got to make a baby. (After little more than a year of freedom, White committed suicide by asphyxiating himself with his car exhaust in his basement on October 21, 1985.) In the precision of the cliché, Dan White got away with murder. There's another cliché that applies here: It could only have happened in San Francisco.

NEAR A STREETCAR STOP AT DOLORES PARK, overlooking the 1791 adobe Mission Dolores, the basilica minor of California, the words were spray-painted in jagged foot-high letters on the concrete wall: KILL FAGS! DAN WHITE FOR MAYOR. Homophobia was a kissing cousin to San Francisco's paranoia.

White's friends and family, and a large part of the city of his nativity, have come to accept what Dan White did as incontestable fate, like one of Edward Gorey's childish misfortunes. The explanation favored by San Francisco officials for the City Hall executions is that they were a "senseless tragedy." There is another explanation, one the prosecution did not offer the jury. Listen to the voice of San Francisco undersheriff Jim Denman, who guarded White in city jail the afternoon he surrendered: "It all seemed very fraternal. One police officer gave Dan White a pat on the behind when he was booked—sort of a 'Hey, catch you later, Dan' pat. Some of the officers and deputies were standing around with half-smirks on their faces. I heard later they were making Harvey Milk jokes. The joke the cops were telling was that Dan White's mother says to him when he comes home: 'No, you dummy, I said milk and baloney—not Moscone!' The attitude of the cops seemed to be that Dan White had done something they were not unhappy about—some of them seemed elated—and they seemed in no way upset with him. To a lot of these cops Dan White was a hero."

During White's trial, the sympathetic portrait the defense presented to the jury was of a tormented man with rollercoaster emotions who was deeply depressed the day of the shootings. Denman says this was not his prisoner. "He was super-controlled. There was nothing in his face or in his body posture to indicate any emotion. There were no tears. There was no shame. He was polite, purposeful, and deliberate. A couple of weeks before he had been a supervisor and now he was in jail and it didn't seem to bother him. You got the feeling that he knew exactly what he was doing and had no remorse. It was a real macho type of thing."

Denman was not called as a witness for the prosecution, even though he says he told San Francisco district attorney Joseph Freitas about his observations of White in prison. Denman believes he was not asked to testify because of "political decisions" made by the district attorney's office. "The prosecution did not want to go into the connection between police attitudes toward gays and Dan White's state of mind," he said. "That which was left unsaid was what this trial was about. If White's typically paranoid cop attitude toward liberals like Moscone and gays like Milk had been brought out at the trial the jury would have received a totally different picture."

Dan White's botched trial—some critics used the word "thrown," but assistant D.A. Tom Norman, who prosecuted White, insists he shot with both barrels—had a lot to do with the politics of paranoia that seized San Francisco in 1978. "After the Peoples Temple violence the national press made immediate connections between what happened and San Francisco's liberalism. But nobody seemed to want to make that connection between Dan White and the antigay and reactionary side of San Francisco. That never seems to get into the papers. The more I observed what went on at the jail the more I began to stop seeing what Dan White did as the act of an individual and began to see it as a political act in a political movement."

"What scares me about the City Hall murders is that they were so much like Jonestown," said gay journalist Randy Alfred. "They were both cult murders. In Jonestown it was a suicide cult, in San Francisco it was a cop cult."

"This is the first bad thing that Danny ever did," a friend of White's said after the City Hall murders. The prosecution allowed the jury to share this view of the killer. "Background" and "hardworking" were buzzwords used repeatedly by the defense when describing their client; they were code: read "white" and "straight." The defense argument was that such a nice kid from such a good working-class Frisco family wouldn't shoot anyone, let alone the mayor, unless something snapped inside. There was a further, subliminal argument: the victims somehow deserved it. White was portrayed as innocent as a Jamesian heiress. The defense suggested to the jury that White's exposure to the dirty world of liberal politics had led to his becoming unglued. The leftist Peoples Temple which had helped put both Moscone and D.A. Joe Freitas in office had exploded like a dark star, and the political fallout was dirtying up White's victims. In paranoid, schizophrenic San Francisco, Moscone and Milk, the liberal and the gay, somehow came to be seen by some as the bad guys.

For the prosecution not to present any evidence of White's political and sexual loathings was like going after James Earl Ray without suggesting he hated blacks. In one of prosecutor Tom Norman's favorite phrases, "a kid out of law school" would know such testimony is the coin of malice, motive, and premeditation that must be tendered by the prosecution to buy a first- or second-degree murder conviction. The lawyers call this establishing a state of mind. Instead, this jury heard that Dan White *liked* his gay victim. "Harvey's office was right across the hall from Dan White's. He could see right in. When you went in to see Harvey he looked away like you were poison. He hated us," said Wayne Friday, a close friend of Milk's. "If I made some campy remark walking down the hallway—like commenting on some well-fitting pants—Dan would stop and glare, really glare. His lip would be curled. It was almost scary," said Cleve Jones, a former City Hall aide to Supervisor Milk.

Five days before his death, in a tape-recorded interview with political consultant Jack Davis, Harvey Milk said, "Dan White is a stone homophobe. He's dangerous." The jury heard none of this and said after the verdict that they had considered—as the judge had instructed them—Dan White's character and background, and found him the "moral man" the defense had painted. The prosecution had no witnesses to the contrary.

Yet a detailed look at Dan White's life shows an All-American Boy movie that worked only in freeze frame: in action, he was all walking contradictions. Inside the fearless competitor—the band played the theme from *Rocky* at his campaign rallies—was a bully, a man who used a street gang to hassle his political opponents, a man quick to threaten

violence, a man who plotted revenge against his enemies, real or imagined, with the one-track mind of a vacuum cleaner salesman. Inside the
superathlete and devoted husband and father was a junk-food junkie and
Irish Catholic mess who would sleep in a sleeping bag instead of with
his wife, a lazy slob who would send the baby to the babysitter while
his wife slaved at the hot potato stand, and sit home unshaven stuffing
his face with Twinkies and feeling sorry for himself. The man of action
never finished anything. He left high school before graduation and went
from the army to the police to the fire department to politics—always
striving for an "A" in manhood, and always ending up with an "incom-
plete." The only thing he ever finished was the lives of George Moscone
and Harvey Milk.

"Dan was always threatening people and pushing them around," said
Bob Barnes, a San Francisco machinists union official who ran against
White for supervisor. Barnes and other candidates told tales of White
on the campaign trail that are out of Huey Long. White packed neighborhood meetings with a gang of black youths known as the Sons of
Sunnydale to disrupt other candidates' speeches. Gang members went
everywhere with White during the campaign—"It was like Jim Jones
with his bodyguards," one community leader said.

White's tape-recorded confession, which moved the jury to tears,
was a model of self-service. "I wanted to serve the people of San Francisco well, and I did that," he said. White said that he was anxious to get
his job back because of the outpouring of support from the people in his
district, but that was a lie. By the time he quit, the local boy who made
good had almost no support left in the old neighborhood. In Chairman Mao's phrase, Dan White had dropped too many stones on his own
foot. He won with black support, but he was no sooner in office than
he called for vigilantes to patrol the streets and berated the press for
failing to routinely identify the crime suspects by racial characteristics:
"If they're white, say they're white; if they're black, say they're black; if
they're Chinese, say they're Chinese," said White the Orator, sounding
eerily like the racist nineteenth-century Frisco sandlot politician Denis
Kearney, who stained the city with chants of "The Chinese Must Go."

Once in office, White was rarely seen in his old neighborhood. He
became the representative of the powerful Police Officers Association (POA) on the board, holding the thin blue line on pro-police and

antigay issues. When he changed his vote to No on a key business tax proposed by Moscone, he was welcomed to the world of big-business fundraisers, and Pier 39 developer Warren Simmons made it possible for White to become a capitalist by getting him his hot potato stand. Dan White went downtown and never came back.

For the prosecution to tear down the Old Town good-guy image of Dan White would have been to shatter the vestigial image of San Francisco middle-class respectability. After Jonestown, this would have been psychologically devastating for the city and politically unproductive for D.A. Freitas, who was coming up for reelection. White's defense lawyers first announced that, in exploring what prompted their client to go for his gun, they planned to explore what were euphemistically called "social and political pressures that offended White's sense of values." This was a thinly veiled warning to the prosecution. It never happened because the prosecution accordingly adopted a strategy that pleaded only the facts of the shooting and stayed away from the question of possible political motivations.

A prolonged debate over White's character and political motivations would have brought out matters the San Francisco Convention and Visitors Bureau—and not a few prominent politicians—would have undoubtedly preferred to leave in the closet. The antigay feeling in San Francisco was but one thing. There was also the very sore point of the Peoples Temple political alliances with the city's liberal establishment, including Freitas, who hired Jim Jones' right-hand man, Timothy Stoen, as an assistant district attorney and put him in charge of the investigation of the 1975 election in which the Peoples Temple was suspected of importing votes for Moscone. Somewhere in the Temple archives there was even a faith-healing film into which Jones' stalwarts had spliced footage of San Francisco's liberal seraphim—Freitas, then sheriff Richard Hongisto, and black assemblyman Willie Brown among them—giving the Reverend Jones their political blessing. The only question in the trial was why—and only the defense had an answer. The poor man had eaten too many Twinkies.

Freitas defended his handling of the case by arguing that White's mean character and paranoid political beliefs "weren't relevant" to the prosecution. Veteran criminal lawyers laughed at that. "Once the defense brought in White's good character as part of his defense, the prosecution could introduce anything in his background on rebuttal. It's ridiculous to say that stuff couldn't be relevant," one lawyer said. "This just wasn't a normal prosecution." San Francisco in 1978 wasn't a normal town.

IT IS SUNDAY NIGHT IN MID-OCTOBER in the city, almost ten years after Jonestown. The high tide of paranoia has receded. At Max's Opera Café, yuppies stuff their perfect faces with corned beef sandwiches. At a front table, chomping on ribs, sit the Odd Couple of 1988, John Barbagelata and Tim Stoen, the yin and yang of the cultural and political differences that split Frisco a decade earlier. In the mid-1970s, Barbagelata attacked the Peoples Temple and Stoen defended it. In the intervening years since Stoen defected from the Temple, they have become friends, but wary friends. They are still arguing about the Temple.

Barbagelata is living proof of Thomas Pynchon's theorem that just because you're paranoid doesn't mean you aren't being followed. When he lost the mayoralty to Moscone by an electoral sliver in Frisco's Chicago-style election of 1975, he began an investigation into rumors that the Temple had bused members in to vote illegally. Barbagelata, who had friends in high places in the SFPD Red Squad, unearthed all kinds of dirt about the Temple's involvement in welfare fraud and theft of members' property, let alone electoral fraud. Moscone's officials were deaf to these charges, and when Tim Stoen, a former key leader of Peoples Temple and the consigliore to Jim Jones, was appointed a San Francisco assistant D.A. and named to investigate the Temple's role in fixing the election, Barbagelata threw up his hands and gave his material to *New West* magazine, which printed the exposé of Jones the San Francisco papers had avoided and hastened the reverend's flight to South America.

Lawyer Stoen was of such faith that he sold his Porsche and gave the cash to Jim Jones when he joined the Temple. He rose to sit at the crazed reverend's left hand and fended off all legal claims against Jones' acquisitive brand of Christianity and headed off press exposés. "When Freitas hired me he said he wanted me to handle the press for him the way I had for Jim Jones," said Stoen. Barbagelata frowned. Stoen only split when Jones accused him of being a CIA agent and held, and ultimately murdered, Stoen's son (for whom Jones had persuaded the accommodating lawyer to sign a piece of paper saying Jones was the real father) in the jungle paradise. Yet Stoen, lawyerlike, continued to defend the Temple against Barbagelata's attacks. "People's lives were enhanced. I had a lot of ecstasy there," Stoen said.

Barbagelata would have none of this. "You worked for a man who was the devil," he said. "I stabilized Jones. I kept a Jonestown from happening in America," Stoen replied.

"I know more about the Temple than you do," Barbagelata said, confronting Stoen with a Temple bus driver who had admitted driving phony voters into town during the election in 1975. "I didn't know that," Stoen said quietly.

"Let's face it, Tim, you were just an asshole for a while," Barbagelata said.

Stoen, downcast, made little waves in his wine glass with a red plastic straw. "So I was, John," he said.

"Well, we all make mistakes," said Barbagelata.

[*San Francisco Examiner*, *Image* magazine, November 6, 1988]

Gayslayer!

*I*N HIS CLASSIC STUDY OF AMERICAN DEMOCRACY, *The American Commonwealth,* Lord Bryce remarked that the political situation in California was both peculiar and dangerous. That was in 1888. It was more so in 1978. One result of the tragic events of November 1978 was to put to rest the conceit that Southern California was the cradle of all California craziness and violence. This was a view of some longtime standing. In the thirties, George Creel, a San Franciscan of the old school who was FDR's patronage honcho for California, despaired of the Golden State's political future: "Northern California offered no problem, for there hard-headed, hard-working native sons and daughters were in a majority, but when I crossed the Tehachapi into Southern California, it was like plunging into darkest Africa without gun bearers."

Creel's observation became conventional wisdom. The bifurcation of California into sane and zany, North and South, has been constantly reinforced by the types of cracks that are the raw stuff of dictionaries of quotations. Bertrand Russell remarked that Southern California constituted "the ultimate segregation of the unfit." The image of Los Angeles was that of a cultist's paradise, a sun-kissed Land of Mu inhabited by frantic utopians, swindling real estate promoters, daft clergymen and clergywomen, surfboarding astrologers, and other infectious boosters who believed in the ultimate perfectability of hype. San Francisco, on the other hand, was a city of amiable sin whose citizens dined on pasta stuffed with reasonableness and allowed harmless movings and shakings around the cultural totem pole—beats, hippies, topless dancers—to flourish in an atmosphere of tolerance.

That was the way it was. S.F. and L.A. As different as Don Juan and Rube Goldberg. Then, in November of 1978, everything suddenly,

unbelievingly changed. San Francisco became the macabre capital of
the world in a way that none but a madman would have dreamed. A
preacher whom the indulgent city had taken under its liberal wing, the
Reverend Jim Jones, a self-proclaimed Robin Hood who took from the
poor to give to the poor, led more than nine hundred of his Northern
California followers to death in an orgy of mass suicide and murder in
a Guyanan jungle. While the city was trying to shake the unshakable
vision of suicide-bent San Francisco mothers lining up in Jonestown
to feed cyanide-spiked Flavor Aid to their babies, the Reverend Jones'
many politically well-placed former supporters here were trying to
explain how they had turned deaf ears to warnings that the man they
accepted as a saint was a devil.

Before anyone in San Francisco could make a farthing of sense of
the cultish self-destruction, Mayor George Moscone and gay supervisor Harvey Milk were assassinated in City Hall by ex-supervisor Dan
White, who had campaigned for office making parsonish statements
about the state of sin in which the city was living. The dream of San
Francisco reason had bred monsters. During that fated November the
city's prideful image as a citadel of civility and tolerance collapsed into
a layer of hell reserved for perversions of that special incubus called the
California Dream.

Decades of certified kookiness in Southern California had produced
nothing like the death, carnage, and virulent insanity that came out of
Northern California during the 1970s. Since the early 1970s, political
violence has been a fact of Bay Area life—urban guerrillas, cults with
guns, bombings, assassination attempts, mass murders, mass kidnap-
pings, and suicides with metronomic regularity. Compared to this grim
recital, Southern California's legendary "nut cults" of the thirties, forties,
and fifties seem the stuff of nostalgia. The great "I Am" with his benign
neon sign advertising his get-rich gospel of wish fulfillment and "concentrated energy" seems quaintly out of Oz. Aimee Semple McPherson may
yet become a belated heroine of women's lib; she did the job of shucking
the faithful far better than mere men like Elmer Gantry.

L.A.'s reputation as an incubator for crackpots blossomed in the days
when Los Angeles was the "white spot" of the nation and the town was
run as a fiefdom by the Merchants and Manufacturers Association and
the *Los Angeles Times,* whose editorial policies in the thirties so infuriated

Upton Sinclair, the eternal crusader, that he wrote: "It would seem better to turn loose a hundred thousand mad dogs in the streets of Los Angeles than to send out a hundred thousand copies of the *Times* everyday." Sinclair's questioning of the *Times'* enlightenment came against a background of bread lines, the Dust Bowl migration, Cossack police tactics against labor, wholesale foreclosures on homes and small farms, old ladies clawing at garbage cans, and angry torchlight parades of the shoeless and the hungry who could find no room at the poorhouse. In this hothouse environment flourished a remarkable combination of romantics, radical social reformers, and talented swindlers who attempted to forge solutions to the economic crisis outside the pale of orthodoxy—Technocrats, Townsendites, Social Creditors, Fourth Cyclers, Silver Shirts, Ham and Eggers. Carey McWilliams, who wrote the best book on the Southland, *Southern California: An Island on the Land,* liked to quote Emma Harding, the historian of spiritualism, who concluded that cults thrive on the Pacific coast "because of the wonderful transparency of the air, the heavy charges of mineral magnetism from gold mines which set up favorable vibrations, and the still-living passions of the 49ers which create emanations."

Whatever the cause of these audacious quests for utopia, they are endemic to California. But the recent shift of California's seat of oddball activity to the North has proved, in the topical phrase, to be bad karma. San Francisco's media-hyped reputation for tolerance attracted thousands of disturbed people who brought their own troubled heads to where the psychic action was supposed to be. The line between acceptable craziness—always indulged in San Francisco—and violence proved frightfully thin. One remembers that Charles Manson began recruiting followers in Haight-Ashbury. People in the Bay Area have trouble distinguishing one mass murderer from the other. Who can recall whether it was Herbert Mullin who killed thirteen or Edmund Kemper who killed eight in Santa Cruz, and which one of the two thought he was part cannibal? San Francisco already had its own suicide cult years before the Peoples Temple, only it wasn't called a cult. It's called the Golden Gate Bridge.

When spiritually anemic people band together, the cement that binds them is, usually, paranoia. They create a reality for themselves to replace the reality they don't like, and when their new reality invariably begins to crack, they tend to crack, too. The politically charged Bay Area imbued many of its indigenous cults almost by osmosis with a sense of radical or racial theory, which geometrically increased both paranoia and a messianic sense of purpose, which in turn increased the potential for violence—as a defense against imaginary enemies, or in ideological combat. Whether it was the robot-like Zebra killers shooting down whites on sight in the streets of San Francisco, or the lumpen Lenins of the SLA, or Jim Jones and his cup of poison, the decision-making process, or lack of one, was woefully the same.

WHAT FOLLOWS IS ONE MAN'S OPINION. A lot of people may not like it; I'm not so happy about it myself. But as a fourth-generation San Franciscan and a journalist who knows this city intimately, this is the truth as I see it.

Dan Rather, who is not often stimulated to hyperbole, called it the crime of the century when Dan White walked free after spending barely five years in jail for two murders. The nation watches San Francisco and wonders. The double assassination is supposed to be just one of those weird things that happens here. San Francisco doesn't dwell on why Dan White never said he's sorry but prefers to think good thoughts about Joe Montana. The blame for Dan White has been put on just about everyone and everything but San Francisco herself. The infamous prison sentence that had all the sting of a Confirmation slap has been called variously the fault of a) the jury, b) the "diminished-capacity" defense, or c) the legal system. In no way was San Francisco to blame. This city on the earthquake fault is otherwise no fault.

Some liberals have fallen out of their trees to blaspheme the legal concept of diminished capacity which in pre–Dan White days they idolized. Supervisor Harry Britt was on national TV on *Nightline,* preaching against the abominations of the shrinks. When Ted Koppel correctly asked Britt if he would deny the avenue of psychiatric defense to a fellow gay who gave Dan White tit for tat, Britt looked confused. San Francisco has simply avoided dealing with what really happened. This is understandable; if you're a pretty city, you don't want to roll over and let the world see your nasty underbelly.

THE MOST COMMONLY USED WORD about San Francisco was once "fun." Suddenly it became the nastier three-letter word, "why?" From the Guyanan *Götterdämmerung* to political assassinations to the exoneration of a mayor-killer and a gay Selma, 1978 and 1979 were the most emotionally devastating years in San Francisco's fabulously spotted history. Some judgmental elements among the Bible thumpers advanced the theory that San Francisco was collapsing internally, as with rot, from its fabled liberality. This was a difficult proposition to sustain in a town where harassment, violence, and even murder had become, among many, acceptable "solutions" to the considerable matter of homosexuality. Former supervisor Dan White was a hero to a lot of people in San Francisco, not all of them in unrespectable quarters.

The story of how this happened in a city synonymous with tolerance is the story of San Francisco's failure to live up to its easygoing reputation in a time of immense cultural and economic change—most of it centered, or to old Irish Catholic San Francisco seeming to center, on the great gay migration to the Golden Gate. In the last decade, more than one hundred thousand homosexuals have heeded Horace Greeley's advice. In a city whose population is shrinking toward seven hundred thousand, this has created social and economic pressures that underlie a gusher of violence—little reported except in homosexual newspapers—against the San Francisco gay community. The number of beatings, murders, rapes—the thrill gang-rape of Charles Lewis is but one gross example—trashings, mutilations, bombings, and arsons has been building since the early seventies. By 1977, a decade after the famous hippie "summer of love" in the Haight-Ashbury, gays were experiencing a summer of terror in the cradle of the counterculture.

Rat packs of homophobic punks, mostly white or Latino teenagers, prowled gay neighborhoods by night in search of victims. This antigay violence was at its most frenzied in 1977 A.B., the year of Anita Bryant, when gays organized patrols—one was called the "Butterfly Brigade"—for their own protection. A gay man cannot feel safe alone on San Francisco streets at night. Most street homosexuals carry police whistles to summon help in case of attack. In an average month thirty to forty muggings and stabbings by gangs of street toughs preying on gays are reported. Many gays are reluctant to call the cops because they encounter little sympathy, and often outright hostility, from responding officers.

Homosexual assault seems on the lower rungs of the ladder of crimes Frisco deems serious. The situation is not without its analogies to the familiar feminist complaint about condescending "you probably deserved it" attitudes of cops toward rape victims.

This is a young gay man talking the night of the riot, as high flames from burning cars lit the City Hall dome in an eerie, flickering orange: "You're seeing the people's anger—gay people's anger. Dan White getting off is just one of a million things that happen in our lives: the beatings, the murders, the people driven to suicide by the hostility of straights. We're just not going to take it anymore. Dan White's straight justice is just the last straw. We're not just a bunch of fairies. We can be as tough as they were in Watts." He and a friend rolled a torch of newspapers and went off to set fire to another police car. "Just tell people that we ate too many Twinkies. That's why this is happening."

Since the deaths of Moscone and Milk, their protector and their champion, gays in San Francisco have complained of increasing police harassment under the less liberal regime of Moscone's successor, Dianne Feinstein, whom gays with decreasing affection began to call the Ayatollah Feinstein. Moscone was barely in his grave when the cops raided the Mabuhay Gardens, a punk nightclub police had been itching to bust, and crashed the Crystal Hotel in the Tenderloin, where they subjected the drag-queen tenants to the ministrations of nightsticks. "Why should you care? They're just a bunch of fruits," the sergeant in charge told the owner of the hotel.

Moscone had frowned upon police poking their clubs into the business of consenting adults. Mayor Feinstein seemed to hear the sound of another drummer. In an interview with the *Ladies' Home Journal,* the attractive, ritually bebowed lady mayor said: "The right of an individual to live as he or she chooses can become offensive—the gay community is going to have to face this."

"Can you imagine Dianne telling blacks that certain aspects of their behavior were offensive? No way!" said a gay activist who does not normally read the *Ladies' Home Journal,* as he put the magazine down in disgust.

Mayor Feinstein's tightening of the screws of propriety upon the city, the continuing antigay street violence, and what Harry Britt, the gay whom Feinstein appointed to fill out Milk's supervisorial term, called "blatantly antigay attitudes widespread in the San Francisco police department"—all this was social kindling stacked to burn. When Dan White got a five-year walk for the dumdum-bullet execution of two popular progay public officials, it was like the pull of the moon upon the waves: San Francisco had the nation's first major gay riot.

GEORGE MOSCONE ORDERED THE COPS to handle the gays with lavender gloves. This was an order not enthusiastically received among the rank and file. The liberal mayor also appointed a reformist-minded chief from outside the force, Charles Gain, the first "outsider" in half a century to head the clique-ridden, Irish Catholic–dominated San Francisco Police Department, which was operated mainly on the buddy system; promotions could hinge on which parish you belonged to and other Irish tribal rites, and departmental policy was often settled in conversations on the church steps after Sunday Mass. The new chief's attempts to modernize the department, which, professionally, has been compared to an unaccredited college, were met with Russian front–type resistance from the troops. The most bitter opposition to Moscone and Gain's new-age policies came from the San Francisco Police Officers Association, known as the POA, a union with some of the cultish overtones of an Orange Lodge, which powerhoused the notorious police strike of 1975 in which many cops destroyed police cars, slashed tires, waved guns, and otherwise behaved like goons. Even before he got to the jail and received a welcome fit for Lindbergh, ex-cop Dan White was the political hero and great white hope of the POA.

POA members were active in White's 1977 law 'n' order campaign for supervisor, and the winner became the cops' champion on the San Francisco Board of Supervisors. White's vote was key to delaying a multimillion-dollar settlement—ferociously opposed by the POA—of a lawsuit brought by Officers for Justice, a group of black policemen. The suit sought to end the department's traditional racial discrimination—so blatant that critics have complained that San Francisco's police department was less integrated than that of Montgomery, Alabama— and to make financial amends for internal racisms past. White saw the SFPD's white mainline as the last bulwark against the takeover of San Francisco by the radlibs, a.k.a. Moscone and Milk. "Once they've taken over the law-enforcement mechanism of San Francisco, they've got the city cold," White told an approving columnist for the Hearst *Examiner* who shared White's reductionism about what ailed San Francisco.

When White gave up his board seat for his hot potato stand on Pier 39, the police heavies put enormous pressure on him to change his mind and ask the mayor to tear up his resignation letter; without White's vote, the bad guys would win. The head of the POA was standing at White's right hand when the happy supervisor told the press that Moscone had promised him he could have his job back. POA members were the leading protesters when Moscone changed his mind about giving White back his seat, in part because of pressure from supervisor Harvey Milk against giving a free ride on the merry-go-round to the city's most homophobic politician. That was when White, his sense of personal betrayal amplified by his sense of us-against-them, strapped on his old police .38 and set off for City Hall to talk politics man to man.

THE BULK OF THE POLICE FORCE is still made up of cops who, like Dan White, are the native sons of second- and third-generation Irish and Italian working-class families. The San Francisco they grew up in is vanishing before their eyes, and with it the dependable value structure of church and family to which so much of gay life is anathema. Before it became self-conscious and self-important and began to object to being called Frisco, San Francisco was a nice place to live. It was a place where the Mission District Irish didn't know their stick houses were Victorians and cable cars were merely things to go home on; in the Old Town the sound of dice in cigar store back rooms was street music and twilight was effulgent with the gleam of splendidly iced martinis from the Mark's Lower Bar to Coattail Molloy's, where the cemetery workers drank; the unofficial mayors were the McDonough brothers, who, from their bail bond factory at Kearny and Clay Streets, regulated all business that was best done after dark while the cops drank next door at Cookie Picetti's; an old sport named Shanty Malone was king of the publicans, a place named the Fly Trap had great food, "high-rise" meant elevator, God was in His heaven, and Joe DiMaggio was coming up to bat with the score tied in the bottom of the ninth.

That San Francisco, like Yeats' romantic Ireland, is with O'Leary in

the grave, done in by successive invasions of tourists and plastic com-
mercialism; by swinging singles who work in the new skyscraper corporate headquarters downtown; and finally by the gay population influx.
To old Irish San Francisco, the world was turning like a worm.

The homophobia characteristic of Dan White and many of his police
force comrades does not lend itself to the simple pop-psych explanation
that their uptight manhood is threatened by so many people coming out
of the closet all at once. There is a hard economic edge to the San Francisco homophobic backlash that voids any simple Freudian answer. The
way many see it, immigrant gays have been used to reverse-blockbust
low-rent minority neighborhoods. Young gays fresh to town generally
get lower-paying ribbon clerk–type jobs, but two or three men sharing
a flat can pool their paychecks and come up with a rent that a working-
class nuclear family can't match. As the houses are renovated, the rents
continue to rise and the poorer gays who pioneered have to move out
and into the next neighborhood, where they encounter increasing hostility from black and Hispanic families vying for affordable housing. Economic homophobia is not limited to whites of the stripe of Dan White.

Dan White's stereotypical view of gays—one shared by many San
Franciscans—was that they are all liberals, libertines, and real estate
speculators. The political reality is that the gay world has the same
conservative-liberal splits as the straight world. In 1978 there were three
gay Democratic clubs in San Francisco, and two Republican clubs. The
Alice B. Toklas Democratic Club, the largest, refused to endorse Harvey
Milk in his various tries at public office because the streetwise Harvey
wouldn't kowtow to Democratic party hacks. The economic reality is
that gays are caught in the same rent spiral as other San Franciscans.
Harvey Milk himself had to close his Castro Street camera store after
his landlord tripled the rent.

When Dan White was campaigning for supervisor he would talk
about people like his parents, who had lived and worked in the city all
their lives and now were unfairly being driven out of town by rising
taxes and rising rents. And it was clear who he believed was at fault.
That was when he would say he was not going to be forced out of town
by "social deviates." His campaign slogan was "Unite and Fight with Dan
White." He pledged to himself to sweep the sand off the beach.

"By choosing to run for supervisor, I have committed myself to the confrontation which can no longer be avoided by those who care," said White, an ex–Golden Glover. When Dan White walked into the room at a campaign gathering, the band played the theme song from *Rocky*.

FRISCO COPS CAN PLAY ROUGH. One police chief who had crossed his men was taken for a boat ride on the bay and, according to legend, fed to the fishes. That was more than half a century ago, when the West was wild, but there remain perhaps as many cowboys as gangbusters in the current Frisco force. In 1979 a bunch of boys in blue commandeered a motorized cable car for a bachelor party, crashed a lesbian bar, and got into a fist fight with the girls. Richard Hongisto, the former sheriff of San Francisco, now a supervisor, used to carry a gun in the bay city like the sheriffs of old, according to his former second in command. But his was hardly the traditional reason: "Dick wasn't afraid of the prisoners, but he was really concerned that someone in the police or sheriff's department would try to kill him," said James Denman, the former undersheriff of San Francisco.

Before he was elected sheriff, Hongisto was a San Francisco policeman. He was the only white cop to join the black Officers for Justice. His liberal postures made the law-enforcement old guard hyperventilate. Some of the hot air came out as death threats. The threats became so heavy, Denman said, that Hongisto kept a sealed letter in his desk, which he told his undersheriff to open in the event of his sudden death.

Within the police department, threats of bodily harm to Chief Gain were almost as commonplace as bathroom pornography. The force was not with him. In 1979 he had his picture taken, out of uniform, at the annual Hookers' Ball, a San Francisco sybaritic gala. This photo, along with the chief's likeness encircled in telescopic rifle crosshairs, was on station house bulletin boards. George Moscone—bucking enormous police pressure—refused to replace the despised reformer with someone acceptable to the POA. Thus the mayor, too, became an object of police blood oaths. Margo St. James, the founder of COYOTE, the San Francisco–based national organization of prostitutes, said that she had received a telephone call in the summer of 1978 from a friend in the police department who predicted that "Moscone will be dead before Christmas." There was a lot of loose talk about offing the mayor among the hard-noses on the force. "They have a perverted poisonous anger and a paranoia that gives them a sense of themselves as above the law," said Denman, who believes these police attitudes shared by White should have been introduced by the prosecution to give the jury an alternative theory of the ex-cop's motive for the murders. "The prosecution wasn't about to take on the cops," he said.

THE HALLMARK CARD IMAGE of San Francisco is a place at the foot of the golden stairs, a sophisticated city of amiable sin whose hill-dwelling citizens indulge beatniks and flower children. But there is an argument to be made for the proposition that the true patron saint of San Francisco is Savonarola of Florence, rather than Francis of Assisi. Contrary to San Francisco's tolerant reputation, the city fathers beat up on the beatniks, hassled the hippies, and arrested the topless; in the late seventies San Francisco spent millions shutting down nude encounter parlors while violent street crimes such as rape went on apace.

The 1975 municipal elections reflected Frisco's latent schizophrenia. George Moscone was elected mayor by 4,315 votes, one of the thinnest margins in city history. San Francisco had split amoeba-like in two; the upper-income liberal and the new gay enclaves voted for Moscone, as did the majority of black, Latino, and other ethnic poor areas; the remaining half of the city was Dan White turf—the working-class families who had resisted the flight to the suburbs and remained to watch in bewilderment as swinging singles bars mushroomed on Union Street and the gays took over Polk Street and then Castro Street, which became the Great White Way of Gay America. The 1975 elections gave San Francisco a liberal triad: a new mayor, sheriff, and district attorney, all supported strongly by the gay community. This was viewed by some as a takeover of city government tantamount to revolution. The plot thickened with the adoption of the Moscone-supported supervisorial elections by districts, which in 1977 brought to City Hall, in one corner, Harvey Milk, representing the Castro; and in the other, Dan White, representing the God-fearing blue-collar people of the Outer Mission neighborhoods.

As the political tensions in town increased, so did violence against gays. Mayor Moscone strongly defended his gay constituency. He offered a $5,000 reward for the capture of three youths who had stabbed to death a gay city gardener on a quiet neighborhood street while yelling "faggot, faggot!" Moscone blamed the murder of Robert Hillsborough on state senator John Briggs, the Southern California paladin who was preaching the antigay gospel of Anita Bryant. The week before Hillsborough was stabbed, Briggs had called a press conference on the steps of City Hall to denounce San Francisco as a sexual garbage heap because of its gay lifestyle; the words "Sodom and Gomorrah" were used. This was June of 1977. Dan White was busy writing his pamphlet with the now famous statement about not being run out of town by "sexual deviates."

DAN WHITE'S SAN FRANCISCO is the unpicturesque southeastern flatlands where the city meets the slurbs. This is the home of Joe Six-pack. The area has more savings accounts than the other areas of San Francisco, fewer newspapers delivered, and the lowest voter turnout. The neighborhoods—heavily Catholic, ethnically Maltese to Samoan, hardworking, and no-nonsense—are the last reservoir of the blue-collar ethic in a romantic city lately tilting toward narcissism. People out there still call chicken breasts "white meat" because they don't wish to mention the anatomy. The music is Lawrence Welk and the libraries stock pulp westerns of the kind that took Dwight Eisenhower's fancy. "There's nothing prestigious out here. People just belong to the church and play bingo," said Mary Brook, the publisher of a neighborhood newspaper.

When the grand wizards of San Francisco district elections apportioned the city into more or less natural geopolitical districts, the neighborhoods that seemed to fit in nowhere else became District Eight. It was the only district without an established political leader. Dan White, an ex-cop who had joined the fire department, suddenly materialized, a genie rubbed from the lamp of the unknown, to fill the void. The candidate was cut of Frank Merriwell cloth. The second son of a large (nine children), popular, local family—his father was a hero fireman—Dan White was a high school legend as captain of both the football and baseball teams. An injury kept him from the New York Yankees farm system and a baseball career. He joined the army, went to Vietnam, came home in 1967 to join the police department, then in 1974 became a fireman. In 1977, he ran for supervisor.

Dan White has been called, admiringly, a born competitor. He entered the Golden Gloves competition at the advanced age of twenty-nine, and, Rocky-like, went the distance, even though he was in the ring against a champ. He had a pretty Irish wife, a schoolteacher from another well-known neighborhood family. White campaigned door-to-door, with help from off-duty firemen and cops. The good word about Mrs. White's boy was put out by the "mothers' club mafia" in the Catholic parishes. Dan was everybody's favorite son. Said a political writer during the campaign: "If Dan were a breakfast cereal, he could only be Wheaties." Coming out of nowhere, White thundered to easy victory like some happy client in a Bobby Zarem press campaign. His politics were simple: He was against the bad guys. "We've got to stand up to the criminal element in this city and tell them we're not going to take it."

THE SEMANTICS OF HOW TO CHARACTERIZE the prosecution are at best imprecise. There have been arguments over whether the case was "blown" or "thrown." A word frequently invoked is "fix," although in San Francisco it is subject to as many interpretations as the King James Bible. "I'd say there's been an informal or a subconscious fix," said San Francisco Charter Commission member Jack Webb, an ex–police inspector. "The prosecution clearly had an affinity for Dan White—it's just not like the police to go hard on one of their own."

"Fix! That's strong language. But the prosecution certainly stayed away from certain malcontent aspects of White's background," said Jack Berman, a prominent San Francisco criminal attorney who was later appointed to the bench. Berman said he wouldn't call it a "fix—not in that sense. Not a corrupt fix. If anything it would be more of a prejudiced fix."

Much of what was left out of the Dan White trial is told, for the asking, in District Eight. Before the trial, I spent two weeks on Dan White turf interviewing his former supporters. I came to the conclusion that the truth about Dan White had been very thinly harvested. The Dan White I learned about was something other than an All-American Boy, unless one considers certain black aspects of the Nixonian paranoia and vindictiveness as quintessentially American. "Dan White had a little-boy way about him," said Mary Brook, who published the *Portola District News.* "He could plead and beg to get what he wanted, and if he didn't get it he could be a perfect brat. He could be mean and down-right frightening."

Dan White was as humorless as an Iranian tribunal. He was never in half fun and full earnest, as the Irish like to say, but always in full earnest. He suffered from a mental arthritis that kept him from bending to see anyone else's point of view. He admired the tough-guy Bay Area intellectuals, like Jack London of Oakland, the health faddist he-man who suffered from a terminal case of macho, and Eric Hoffer of San Francisco, the late longshoreman-philosopher, a hawkish Plato to the TV generation, who once explained that he had rejected Marx without reading him because "Marx never worked a day in his life."

The White jury said after the verdict that they had considered—as the judge had instructed them—Dan White's character and background, and found him a "moral man," as in the portrait of the young man the defense had painted. The prosecution had no witnesses to the contrary. District Eight had plenty.

GOLDIE JUDGE WAS IN HER SWEETS SHOP on Leland Avenue. She was sitting at one of the black plastic tables smoking a cigarette and sipping coffee from a styrofoam cup. There was red-and-white ticking on the walls. Giant ice cream cones hung from the ceiling like sugar stalactites; her partner, Mr. Bercival, was behind the candy counter, piecing out treats. Goldie Judge was talking about Dan White. Judge had been White's first campaign manager. She quit after the candidate called her up at 4 a.m. and wanted her to make him a hero. Fireman White had just rescued a mother and daughter from a burning apartment house. He wanted the campaign literature to reflect his brand-new heroism. Goldie Judge thought that was getting a little afield of the issues. "It was all ego with him," she said. "He was in it just for the ego."

Judge had a problem with White on his first campaign brochure, the piece of agitprop where the candidate talked about ridding the city of "social deviates." (The brochure was later redone with the offending words modified.) "I kept asking him what he meant by that but he would never answer the question. After a while it became clear he meant gays. His whole campaign was antigay."

His first campaign manager described White as a bit of an ingrate and a snob. "He never contacted his supporters after the election. He never thanked anyone." When the defeated candidates, in the good-loser tradition, offered after the election to close ranks behind White for the good of the neighborhood, White's reaction was "once agin' him, always agin' him"; he would have nothing to do with them. "The only thing he seemed interested in was getting even with the people who hadn't supported him," Judge said. Judge resigned in mid-campaign: "I didn't like all these cops constantly hanging around the campaign. When he was a supervisor he ended up representing the cops more than the people out here. When he quit and then announced that he wanted his job back, there was hardly a person from the neighborhood at his press conference. But who was standing next to him? The cop who was the head of the policemen's union."

White's former friends and supporters described him as a man with a pugilistic temper and an impressive capacity for nurturing a grudge. Former classmates at Woodrow Wilson High School said he would pick fights—often with blacks. At Riordan, a Catholic high school White attended before transferring to public school, one of White's classmates was Herbert Mullin, who grew up to become a Santa Cruz mass murderer. White told a psychiatrist hired by the defense that he and Mullin "used to talk a lot about boxing."

"Dan was always threatening people and pushing them around," said Bob Barnes, a San Francisco machinists union official who ran against White for supervisor. Barnes and other candidates tell tales of White on the campaign trail that are out of Huey Long. White packed neighborhood meetings with a gang of black youths known as the Sons of Sunnydale, who would disrupt other candidates' speeches and in general march around the breakfast table for Dan White. "One of White's men would give a signal and the kids would start jeering when somebody else was talking," Barnes said. "He thought he was above the law." Gang members went everywhere with White during the campaign—"It was like Jim Jones with his bodyguards," one community leader said—and tore down the signs of other candidates. Bob Barnes said he was physically threatened when he protested these tactics to White. "There was a lot of violence during the campaign. It was like *Clockwork Orange*," he said.

Ray Sloan was the out-of-town campaign manager White hired to replace Goldie Judge. He later became White's City Hall aide and political mentor. Sloan recalled fondly that White had won over the Sons of Sunnydale by "getting it on with them." Said Sloan: "One afternoon Dan just took off his coat and got in their football game and played like the devil. All of a sudden here was this white guy—the only white guy—in the game. The kids were impressed." Residents of the predominantly black Sunnydale housing projects in District Eight tell another story. They say White bought the black youths' allegiance with beer busts and promises of jobs he never delivered. "He was always throwing parties for the boys. There was drinking," said Donna Phillips, former director of the Sunnydale Community Center. "I don't think Dan White liked blacks—but he wasn't above using them for muscle," said the former secretary of the Sunnydale Community Coalition, Mary Brewer, who is white. Brewer said that after the election White abandoned his black boys. When the promised jobs never materialized, "the kids said it was just another white man's promise."

People in District Eight are still talking about the night during the campaign the Nazis came to cheer for Dan White. There were four of them. The two men had swastikas in their lapels. The women had swastikas on silver chains around their necks. The Nazis were all wearing "Unite and Fight with Dan White" buttons. Bob Barnes asked White's campaign people to ask the Nazis to leave. This request was denied, Barnes said. He said one of the Nazis tried to recruit his son, twenty, who is gay: "He told them what they could do with their pink triangles," Barnes said. People in District Eight were reminded of that night when a woman wearing a Nazi armband showed up at Dan White's murder trial to root for the defense. "We call him Gentle Dan," said the Nazi.

Gary O'Rourke was in the Boy Scouts with Dan White. He said his childhood friend grew up to be a "bully boy." The ex–Golden Glover appeared to consider violence a tool of the political trade. His aide, Ray Sloan, was involved in several roughhouse incidents, including a City Hall shoving match with a Samoan princess. The head of Catholic Charities in San Francisco, the Reverend John J. O'Connor, wrote to the Board of Supervisors to complain that Sloan, with his boss' approbation, had verbally abused two Catholic social service organizers while trying to oust them physically from a gathering. Their offense was that they wanted to lobby against one of Dan White's pet projects. White's reaction was to recommend his aide for a merit badge. "I told White he was inciting people and that it could lead to violence, and he said something like, 'Well, if that's the way it is, then that's the way it is,'" said Tony Fazio, one of the complaining church leaders.

"You must realize," said Dan White, in his campaign call-to-arms, "there are thousands upon thousands of frustrated, angry people such as yourselves waiting to unleash a fury that can and will eradicate the malignancies which blight our city." Dan White built his political base on the fears of crime-shy residents, much as a century before in San Francisco, Denis Kearney, a sandlot agitator, built the Workingman's Party on the slogan "The Chinese Must Go." "White had an uncanny ability to stroke people's insecurities. He helped people hate. He's the scariest person I've ever heard give a political speech," said San Francisco consumer activist Kay Pachtner. Gary Yose, a District Eight community organizer, originally supported White for supervisor, but then opposed him when, he said, he discovered that the ex-cop politician's goal was "to build a mass white reactionary political movement."

According to those who knew him, White's personality was erratic; he could be a begging friar or a traffic cop at rush hour. There was about him that peculiar quality Lewis Carroll once tried to describe as "uffish," which he said was the state of mind when the voice is gruffish, the manner roughish, and the temper huffish. There was also something thuggish about Dan White. He once pursued a community leader all the way home and pounded on his door like a cop, demanding he turn over a mailing list to White because "I'm a supervisor." Many people recalled White, at campaign meetings, giving his "I know who my enemies are and I'm going to get them" speech punctuated by fierce glares at the audience. He was known for an evil eye. He barged into a big meeting of neighborhood people opposed to his reappointment as supervisor and his eyes were the metaphorical daggers. "If looks could kill," said Steve Rabisa of the Communities of the Outer Mission Organization, "I would be a dead man."

IT WAS THE LUNCH RUSH AT THE HOT POTATO STAND on Pier 39. The place was packed. The curious came along with the hungry. The pall of a murderer-owner had not discouraged the pursuit of the perfect champ fry, and Ray Sloan, Dan White's right hand, was separating the Bakersfield from the Oregon spuds like a jeweler sorting diamonds. Pier 39 is an unloved tourist trap bulging ticky-tacky out into the San Francisco Bay. Practically everything about Pier 39 came to be investigated by the city. There were allegations that the city was being fleeced out of a million bucks a year in rents and charges, that port officials were "bought," and that sweetheart deals for restaurants and shops went to the politically influential. Sloan said Dan White got his potato stand through political connections.

Sloan was White's partner in the fast spuds business. He said the business opportunity came to them through the intercession of mayor—then supervisor—Dianne Feinstein with her friend, developer Warren Simmons, the maharajah of Pier 39. Feinstein, who owns a hotel and does not have to water the soup at home, was concerned about the financial well-being of her young political protégé. San Francisco supervisors then earned a paltry $9,600 a year. "Dan had to quit his job at the fire department after he was elected and Dianne wanted him to have some outside income. Simmons happened to have a spot left at the pier and things worked out just fine," Sloan said.

There were some problems. Supervisor White came in for political flack after he appeared before both the Arts Commission and the Bay Conservation and Development Commission to praise Simmons' huge tourist come-on as the best thing to happen to the bay since the Golden Gate Bridge. Pier 39 was nowhere near Dan White's district. Those with suspicious minds accused White of being quick to do the bidding of his sugar daddy. When people in his district made inquiries, the word went out that White no longer had a piece of the stand but that it belonged to his brother. When the *Bay Guardian*, a local consumer-lib weekly, called White to suggest a conflict of interest, "White told us the [potato stand deal] was off," the *Guardian* reported. Later, it turned out that White had become an owner of record. "We each put up $20,000 to get in—me, Dan, and Dan's brother," Sloan said. Nowhere during his trial was it pointed out that the All-American Boy might be a fibber.

White was no sooner in office than he fell down the rabbit hole of big bucks. The candidate of the outsiders ended up on the lap robe of the fat cats. In the wake of Proposition 13, which cut property taxes almost in half, George Moscone had a plan to increase city business taxes to make up for lost revenues. Supervisor Dan White was the swing vote. He first voted for it; pass, 6 to 5. The next week, on a mandatory second reading, he changed his vote; fail, 6 to 5. Shortly after White reversed his field, Warren Simmons threw a fundraiser for the supervisor. White wasn't running for anything. It was one of those non-election-year checkbook show-and-tells where men of property gather to let a fellow know he is appreciated. San Francisco's corporate royalty was well represented. Their support for Mr. Clean never slackened. White's last financial statement read like the morning line of San Francisco capital—contributions from the banks, department stores, billboard interests, realtors, corporate giants like Bechtel and Standard Oil of California, and high-rise developers. About the only high rise in White's district is a church steeple.

While Dan was being noticed by the big boys downtown, his constituents in the flatlands began to complain that he was ignoring home base. "After he was elected Dan wasn't around the district that much. He went downtown and stayed there," said Goldie Judge. White took any such complaints as instances of rank disloyalty. He was, at any rate, listening to other voices. One was that of Ray Sloan, who, according to Sloan, was busy talking to White about the possibility of the freshman supervisor challenging George Moscone for mayor in 1979. "We thought the money was there," Sloan said. White was interested. "He would have been a hell of a candidate," said Sloan.

White's constituency began to narrow from his original broad base of support in District Eight to the special interests of downtown and, of course, the cops, many of whom live out of the city. "Dan White was the man the POA went to on the board," said Frank Falzon, the cop who took his confession. A proposed citizens' complaint review board to monitor complaints about police operations had wide support in District Eight, although not for the usual liberal reasons. People out there thought the cops weren't responding fast enough when they called them. Dan White was the swing vote on that. He shocked his supporters by voting against it; fail, 6 to 5. This was the POA's wish. Dan White had voted for No. 1.

While he was trying to convince the mayor to reappoint him, Dan White was reported at a City Hall copying machine, running off letters to generate support. He couldn't muster any troops. When he met the press, White was flanked by cops and spear carriers for the downtown real estate crowd. They were the only ones eager for him to get back on the board. He'd sold out his people and was tasting the ashes.

Studying the financially grubby underside of White's sterling public image is instructive for understanding San Francisco's split personality and the dirty little secrets that were covered up in the City Hall murders. It is an article of political faith in certain quarters that the "dirty politics" of the town goes on between liberal bedsheets and that the good and pure families of the city suffer financially the burdens of blacks on welfare and socially the antics of gays. "Good people from good backgrounds" was the way his lawyer kept describing White's purity to the jury, without any objection from the prosecution.

THERE WAS CARROT CAKE AND WHITE WINE. The Alice B. Toklas Democratic Club was meeting at the Dovre Hall, a gabled building with a French-sounding name that has been home to a Norwegian lodge but is now owned by liberated women. Downstairs is Paddy Nolan's bar with a clientele of Irish laborers and Italian and Mexican garbagemen. It is your basic San Francisco building. Alice is usually nice to the straight politicians who come to curtsy to the gay vote. Tonight there was the gritting of teeth. The speaker was Joseph Freitas, the district attorney of San Francisco. Freitas is a modish dresser and man about town known to intimates as "Disco Joe." He once sued to challenge Wheaties to prove its claim that it was Bruce Jenner's breakfast of champions; he also called a press conference to attack a department store's preteen underwear ads as kiddie porn. He had politically cultivated the gay community and, until the Dan White trial, was a straight dear to most gay organizations. Now he was trying to explain why it wasn't his fault that Dan White got away with murder.

The D.A. blamed the jury, who he said had succumbed to "emotionalism." Then he blamed California's "diminished capacity" defense. The suggestion came from the audience that the fault lay not in the defense of diminished capacity but in the prosecution, which, among many omissions, had failed to present to the jury any evidence of White's homophobia. "We did a background on Dan White and came up with no hard evidence of his being antigay," replied Freitas, who was hit with hisses thick as hail. The D.A. retreated. This time he blamed the cops. "The investigation of witnesses is a function of the police department,"

he said. Freitas said he had been "informed" that all witnesses relevant
to the prosecution were interviewed. Over the thunder and lightning
of boos and obscenities names were yelled out, names of people with
stories to tell of Dan White's antigay antics. The D.A. did not take notes.

Anne Kronenberg, Milk's former administrative assistant, a lesbian:
"Dan White always acted nervous around me. He couldn't relate to me
as a 'normal woman.' He was always ill at ease around gays, and particularly so around Harvey. Harvey in his nine months on the board became
a hero to a lot of people—and not just gay people. He enjoyed politics
and was successful at it. Dan White became increasingly withdrawn and
uptight. I think he was jealous of Harvey, I really do." A San Francisco
fireman who worked with Dan White: "He was a very moral person
who was outraged by gays." Robert Barnes Jr., in 1978 one of the few
out-of-the-closet gays in District Eight: "Just the way he looked at you,
you could feel the strange air. It was like he had feelings that he was
having trouble handling." Harvey Milk, five days before his death, in an
interview with gay journalist Jack Davis: "Dan White is a stone homophobe. He's dangerous."

White's homophobia went beyond stares. He religiously voted
against gay causes and opposed federal funding for a proposed gay community center in the nation's largest gay city. The only exception to
White's slavish devotion to the wishes of the cops was his vote—the
only one on the board—against closing Polk Street, the gay left bank,
for the homosexual rites of Halloween. The cops wanted to close the
street to aid crowd and traffic control, but White, so straight he was
out of a Robert Service poem, didn't think the city should in any way
encourage gays doing their thing on the street. The stern straight supervisor stopped speaking to the happy gay supervisor: "Harvey tried to get
along with Dan, but after a while Dan just stopped talking to him," said
Anne Kronenberg.

Milk assigned one of his aides, Dick Pabich, to talk to White in his
place. Pabich became Milk's John Alden: "Harvey was always saying
to talk to him and explain things and give him a chance to learn. It
obviously didn't do much good," he said. Pabich would sit in White's
office and talk for hours about matters gay. "He kept asking me what we
wanted—'Do you want everybody to be like you?' he would ask. When
I said gays just wanted acceptance, he kept giving me advice—'Don't be

so far out of the closet.' He said that gays being upfront—which was the essence of Harvey's style—was 'antagonizing' people. He claimed that 'many other supervisors' felt the way he did about gays, but that they were politically afraid to admit it. He said the others didn't have enough guts. 'I know that—and you know that,' he'd say. All the time it was as if he wanted to say 'you faggot,' but it was like his mother had told him to be nice, and he was straining not to say it. He really wanted things to go back to the way they were before gays came to San Francisco. Talking to him, I realized that he saw Harvey Milk and George Moscone as representing all that was wrong with the world," Pabich said.

When both were new on the board, the two freshman supervisors maintained a banter, bittersweet in retrospect, about their sexual preferences. "Harvey used to say to Dan, 'Try it—you'll like it,'" Ann Kronenberg recalled. The relationship changed to White's frigid silence after the board voted to establish a treatment center in District Eight for emotionally disturbed adolescents. The project was a favorite of George Moscone, an advocate of mental health programs, who was concerned that San Francisco was shipping its disturbed children out to psychiatric warehouses in other counties. Dan White had been on a crusade against the idea. He thought he had Harvey Milk's vote—gays, after all, don't have children. Milk voted with the mayor, and White never forgave him. Supervisor Quentin Kopp was in the board chambers during the vote. "When Harvey voted against him, Dan just kind of stared at him and said, 'Well, I see the leopard never changes its spots,'" Kopp recalled. The White-Milk antagonisms were known to many people I talked to at City Hall, and these weren't just Milk's friends. Ray Sloan recalled the feud: "I don't know if they ever talked again after that mental health vote—right up to the day Dan killed Harvey."

Frank Falzon, the veteran homicide inspector who took White's controversial "friendly" confession—"Can you relate these pressures you've been under, Dan, at this time?" was one of the not exactly Star Chamber questions—said that he and his partner put in 480 hours on the investigation and that they treated White's case as professionally as any other. That may be part of the problem. Cops just aren't conditioned to dig up dirt about homophobia. But Falzon is a rigidly honest cop and his investigation was far more thorough than the D.A.'s prosecution—which failed in the trial to develop evidence that Falzon had uncovered about

White's antagonism toward Milk. The prosecution devoted its considerable resources to proving what the defense had already stipulated: that Dan White took a gun to City Hall and shot two men dead. The only question in the trial was why—and only the defense had an answer. The prosecution was thick with an attitude that, loosely translated, is part of the cop mindset: Why do anything more to one of your own than he has already done to himself? Dan White had, after all, confessed; his wife and child were already going to suffer; why drag him, and the city everyone loved, through more muck?

To get a verdict other than the one that shamed San Francisco, the prosecution would have had to take on the cops. This it was clearly not inclined to do. The prosecution's attitude is captured in an incident in the office of prosecutor Tom Norman, whom Joe Freitas chose to try the case. Norman is low-key and thorough and as predictable as a flea collar. He's been working with cops like Frank Falzon for almost twenty years; they're his friends; he drinks with them after work. Before he was selected as White's prosecutor, Norman told a prominent trial attorney that he hoped he didn't get the assignment because he felt "sorry" for White. When a reporter suggested to him that he might have to beat up on Falzon, he reacted as if she had suggested he beat up his mother. The reporter was Linda Schacht, who was covering the trial for a San Francisco television station. She went to Norman's office one afternoon during the trial and told him about the talk in the press box that the prosecution was either blowing the trial or throwing it. Norman seemed genuinely taken aback. He asked her what he possibly could have done that he hadn't done. She began counting on her fingers, backward.

Despite Norman's objections (overruled), inspector Falzon was put on the stand by the defense. He had answered the question about his opinion of Dan White's character before the unfortunate Twinkie binge: "A man among men," Falzon said. This, for the prosecution, was the stuff of disaster, like a Perry Mason denouement. Falzon was not only the friendly voice on the twenty-four-minute tape-recorded confession, which moved five jurors to onion ring tears when Norman played it in court (the tape ended with Falzon thanking White for "the truthfulness of your statement"), but he was the chief investigator for the prosecution; as such he sat at the head table with Norman every day in full view of the jury. The state's star investigator became the defense's best character witness. Schacht asked the prosecutor why he hadn't tried to blunt the emotional impact of the almost Dostoyevskian tape on the jury and Falzon's positive testimony about White by going into Falzon's close relationship with the accused, police attitudes toward gays, POA support for Dan White—the works. "Falzon's family was in the court-room, so there were questions I didn't want to ask him," Norman said.

"Judgment calls," D.A. Joe Freitas said about the prosecution's strat-egy, when angry gays at the Alice B. Toklas meeting nailed him to the cross of fact. It was a judgment call when the prosecution excluded minorities such as blacks and Asians and gays from the jury—this in a town 50 percent nonwhite and one-sixth gay—and came up with a solid-gold, all-middle-class, mostly Catholic, District Eight–type jury of family people sharing Dan White's values. It was a jury of the mur-derer's peers. The majority of the women jurors were the same age as Dan White's mother. One juror was a retired cop, another the wife of the cook in the county jail—but a gay man from a police family was excluded. The prosecution went along with the defense's desire to keep gays off the jury—"Imagine if Harvey Milk had been a black supervisor and the defense tried to keep blacks off the jury!" a gay activist said. Prosecutor Norman barely used his jury challenges. The White jury was speedily selected out of the first panel. (But the D.A.'s office, in an encounter-parlor prosecution, took the time and trouble to go through three panels to get the hanging jury it desired.)

It was a judgment call to allow the defense to steamroller the jury with hired-gun psychiatric testimony (the defense had three psychia-trists and one psychologist). This enabled the defense to give the jury Dan White's sob story without putting the accused on the stand. The prosecution summoned only one psychiatric witness, and his testimony was largely shot down by defense attorney Douglas Schmidt. (Norman has said in his defense that he didn't know until too late that a psychiatric defense was coming, although Dr. Roland Levy, the prosecution's psy-chiatrist, testified at the trial that Norman had wanted him to see White immediately—the day of the murder—because Norman told him that a psychiatric defense in this kind of murder case was common. Inspector Falzon also said that he told Norman—after Norman suggested he have a pretrial lunch with White's lawyer, Douglas Schmidt, to see what the defense strategy would be—that a psychiatric defense was coming.)

It was a judgment call when the jury was left believing the defense's explanation that White reloaded his gun "by instinct"—because of his military training—before he went in search of Harvey Milk. If that were so, as Paul Krassner has asked, then how come he didn't reload *after* shooting Milk? It was a judgment call when the prosecution did not challenge defense testimony that Dan White was a walking, Twinkie-stuffed mess in the days before the shooting, despite the many witnesses who would have testified that right up until Bloody Monday he was as normal as a Big Mac. Ray Sloan visited White on Saturday. White was in fine spirits. They talked about football. Sloan talked to White on the phone Sunday night about business. "He seemed fine," Sloan said. Supervisor Quentin Kopp also talked to White on the telephone Sunday night. Kopp said that White sounded more together than he'd ever heard him. "If Dan White was as depressed as the defense psychiatrist said he was before he went to City Hall, then shooting these people sure seemed to clear up his mind," said his jailer, Undersheriff Denman, who had found White as relaxed as a Grant's Scotch ad, just hours after the murders.

District Attorney Freitas' final refuge was in lawyerisms. He said that not one comet in the entire galaxy of political and personal facts about Dan White—his rabid homophobia, his bitter political feud with Moscone and Milk, his condoning of violence in political situations, the dirty truth about his so-called political purity and innocence—would have been admissible in court. "Those things weren't relevant to the trial," Freitas said. Several accomplished criminal lawyers have said that the D.A. must have been inhaling swamp gas to argue that. "Once the defense brought in White's good character as part of his defense, the prosecution could introduce anything in his background on rebuttal. It's ridiculous to say that stuff couldn't be relevant," one lawyer said. "This just wasn't a normal prosecution."

ON THE ALL-NIGHT MOVIES IN SAN FRANCISCO, a car salesman in double knits was offering a free six-pack of Twinkies to anyone who came in to test drive an RV. Thus San Francisco assimilates its tragedies.

Dan White's bullets have changed the leftward drift of the city on the earthquake fault. Since 1979, it has been back to dead center. Mayor Dianne Feinstein, who uses the buzzword "lifestyle" the way Richard Nixon used "national security," surrendered to the POA and fired Charles Gain, Moscone's reform-minded police chief who painted the police cars baby blue. Gone is George Moscone, who did not look the other way when a gay couple crossed the street. Gone is Harvey Milk and the coalition of the minorities and the poor and the gays that he was forging. The night of the City Hall riot, the crowd chanted above the wail of dying sirens in burning police cars, "Dan White—hit man for the New Right."

People keep talking tough in Frisco. There are Dan White clones. A former police captain running for sheriff tells a luncheon audience, "We have to get after the weirdos and miscreants who've been putting our city in a bad light." An official of the POA describes the police-gay situation as "a political confrontation." The gays, making new enemies since the riot, are losing old friends. The late Charles McCabe, a *Chronicle* columnist who championed gay rights back in the straight sixties, wrote after the riot that gays must adopt a strategy of "low public visibility" if they are to keep their advances. In other words, back to the closet. "The closet is no longer a guilt-ridden cell. Today it is, as a man's home should be, his castle," wrote McCabe.

The Friday afternoon before the Dan White verdict, while the jury was sequestered in a stuffy room in the unlovely Hall of Justice, arguing and snacking on white sugar foods, D.A. Joe Freitas (who later lost his bid for reelection), was at a society gala on Alcatraz—a men's fashion show benefiting the Police Activities League. The D.A. was surrounded by cops in Charles Jourdan boots and Nino Cerruti jackets. People were eating escargot in truffle sauce by candlelight in the main cellblock. The sun set, and across the water the city was embers.

"DAN WHITE NEVER ATE A PRISON DINNER the whole time he was in San Francisco County Jail. He dumped it in the toilet. He had roast beef sandwiches and Dreyer's ice cream and Cadbury chocolate brought in. He was out of his cell every night sitting in the nurses' office with his feet up on the desk sipping a can of Coke and talking on the phone as large as life. He had linens on his bed while the other prisoners had to sleep in their jumpsuits. He was very demanding and got everything he wanted and never said thanks. He never showed a sign of remorse for the killing he did. He was spoiled rotten."

This is an intimate picture of Dan White's life in jail, drawn by a woman who saw him almost every day while he was in county jail. Later she visited White frequently at Soledad State Prison. Dan White wrote many letters to her, expressing his opinions and plans for the future. It is not on the whole a pretty picture. It is the portrait of a killer without apparent remorse who has become a macho hero to some cops because he gunned down a gay supervisor and a liberal mayor. "Policemen would come in to visit Dan almost every night when he was in county jail. A bunch of them wore their jackets zippered up and when they saw him they would unzip and expose their Dan White T-shirts. This helped Dan's morale a lot," said his friend, a nurse who took care of him in county jail. White had taken agricultural courses while in prison. "How does the moniker 'Farmer White' sound to you? Ha!" he wrote his friend in a letter dated April 30, 1980.

Although White was described in press accounts at the time of his trial as wearing a blank mask in court, he appears to have been concerned about the intricacies of his defense—he told his friend that he had to lose twenty pounds so the jury would think he looked "debilitated." He was also a press watcher with a moon-sized ego. "Don't let Herb Caen see this letter, he doesn't think I should have any friends, Ha! Ha!" he wrote in one letter. He even read the fringe press. He complained to his friend when she visited him in Soledad about an article published in an underground newspaper by a former prisoner who claimed he had seen White in the showers and described him as having a small male sexual organ. "Dan said to me, 'My God, don't they have anything better to put in the newspapers than to talk about the size of my penis,'" she said.

Dan White's nurse friend and pen pal worked in the county jail atop the Hall of Justice at Seventh and Bryant Streets in 1978 and 1979, before and during his murder trial. There she met White. And there she was charmed by him. "He was a pretty one," said his nurse-confidant. "Every night before he went to bed he was always out of his cell in the nurses' room, brushing his teeth and combing his hair and shaving himself at the mirror."

I met her because she was a character in a play. The play is one of those "docudramas" where all the characters are supposed to be real. It was called *The Dan White Incident,* by Steve Dobbins. It has since aired on national television. A lot of what was laid out is the story San Francisco has never wanted to hear about Dan White. The actor who played former undersheriff Jim Denman hushed the house with a soft-spoken exposition of the antigay, macho police subculture—"the choirboy syndrome"—that made Dan White a hero to many boys in blue. In the play the nurse was named Jenny McAllister, which is close enough to her real name. She is introduced schlepping roast beef sandwiches into jail every day because Dan White, it is said, wouldn't eat the prison chow because he feared some gays working in the kitchen might want to poison him. The actor playing Dan White glowers at Jenny if she forgets to tell the deli to hold the tomato.

Jenny lives in a Dashiell Hammett–era apartment house on lower Nob Hill. Her apartment is as neat as a surgical instrument. She is a hearty Irish lady from Northern Ireland with a brogue you could gargle with. She keeps her letters from Dan White in a manila envelope. There are some twenty in all. Jenny is a pleasant and candid woman with a big heart. I asked her how she had got to be such good friends with the man who made a shooting gallery out of City Hall. "Well, you know, he's Irish, and he's got this pretty-boy face on him, and he's got this way of asking for things that it's hard to refuse." Other former friends of the defrocked supervisor have made similar observations about the upside of his personality. "He asked me for the same thing every day—roast beef sandwich on white bread, lettuce and mayonnaise, no tomato, Cadbury's chocolate, Dreyer's vanilla ice cream, fruit—oranges and bananas—and the evening paper. He threw his prison supper in the toilet."

She got to see the downside of Dan White's personality when she made a mistake. "If I stopped at some store that didn't have Dreyer's ice cream and brought it [another brand] to him, he would refuse to eat it. The same thing with the chocolate—if it wasn't Cadbury's, he'd throw it on the ground. One Good Friday I brought him a special shrimp casserole because of him being Catholic and all. He made a face and said he didn't want it and sent out for chicken." I asked the nurse if she had ever been repaid for bringing the man almost nine months' worth of roast beef sandwiches and such. "No," she said.

"Dan White had just about every privilege you could imagine, and he took advantage of every one," his nurse friend said. "Twice a week another nurse brought him fresh linen and pillowcases for his bed (prisoners aren't supposed to have sheets), he had special visiting hours later than anyone else, and policemen were always stopping by to see him. He had a private shower all by himself—the guard walked him to the shower every night and the other prisoners would line up at their cells and yell at him. He got tea served to him every night and played chess with the guards and sat around making phone calls from the nurses' office and the guards' office free as a bird."

Dr. Tom Peters, a physician with the city health services who was the nurses' superior, said he, too, had heard about White's friendly treatment in the San Francisco jail. "Sometimes it's unavoidable that interpersonal relationships will develop between staff and a prisoner," he said. "But I'd say that in this situation the line was crossed over inappropriately by members of my staff." Peters said he had spoken to the nurses about doing special favors for White, but it was a difficult situation to monitor because of the "general air of favoritism" toward White on the part of the prison staff. "That sort of favoritism will normally accrue to an ex-cop," he said. "In White's case, I'd say there was an element of homophobia involved on the part of many guards who approved of what he had done."

The nurse said the thing that bothered her about her friend was that he never exhibited any remorse for what he had done. She said that during the trial White confided in her that he was worried the jury might take the fact that he took the time to reload his police special .38 after killing Moscone and before killing Milk as an element of premeditation; and that it might bring a verdict of second- or first-degree murder, which would have resulted in a far longer prison term than the voluntary manslaughter charge under which he eventually was sentenced. "The closest he came to saying he was sorry was to say to me—he said it kind of flippant—'I guess they were nice guys; too bad it happened,'" she said.

Nurse McAllister and another Irish nurse who took care of Dan White in county jail often went to visit him after he was transferred to Soledad. They met on Sunday mornings outside St. Boniface Church on Golden Gate Avenue, made the long drive to Soledad, and spent the afternoon with White in the visitors room, exchanging chitchat. The two nurses made the trip about every other month. "One day we were sitting at the visitors table talking and this man came over and asked Dan for change for the Coke machine. When he left Dan said, 'That's Sirhan—that Kennedy fellow,'" she said. "He said they talked about a lot of things."

If Dan White's letters are any guide, life in Soledad wasn't exactly durance vile for him. He wrote that he spent "most of my time in my cell, reading, studying, typing, and exercising." He said he was able to "maintain good physical condition" by "weightlifting, handball, basketball, and limited jogging." White was able to indulge his penchant for solitude in state prison. He wrote on November 7, 1979, that he had a private cell with his own television set—"a real luxury. Now, I do not have to sit in a common area with the other inmates. They are constantly bickering about which program to watch. I can stay in my cell and watch programs I enjoy without any hassles. The television set comes with an earphone so I am able to block out most of the noise that pervades this wing. I am receiving the *Chronicle* (plus some Irish newspapers) and have been trying to follow the trial of the two men charged with killing [Lord] Mountbatten. Their trial is rife with political implications and I wonder if they will be treated fairly..." White always managed to keep abreast of his case. "There are legal manouvers [*sic*] being tried to prevent me from getting a sentence reduction," he wrote his friend on August 11, 1980. "These state lawyers are tricky fellows; just when you think you've got them, [like a greased pig] they slip away on a technicality..."

One of White's greatest dreams, according to his nurse friend, was to father a child while in jail. "He kept saying all the time, even back when he was in county jail, that 'Charlie's got to have a playmate,'" she said. (Charlie is the first child of Dan White and his wife Mary Ann.) In this wish he succeeded. His friend shared in his joy. "He was proud that he had got her pregnant in Soledad. He was bragging one day when I visited him that if you could do it in Soledad you could do it anywhere," she said. She also shared in the family's sorrow when the Whites' second child, christened Rory, was born retarded. "Dan never said much about it. He just said that Mary Ann was taking special classes to learn how to take care of the child."

White tried to gain a few months on his scheduled release date in January 1984. He wrote his friend that he got a six-hour-a-day, five-day-a-week job in the laundry of the protective custody wing at Soledad.

His job was to hand out clean laundry to the troops. Under a work-incentive program at Soledad, prisoners could have additional time subtracted from their sentences for working full-time. "These extended hours reduce the amount of time I can devote to personal projects, but the extra work will be worthwhile," White wrote on August 30, 1982, because "I may receive a four-month sentence reduction." White said he hoped to get out in September or November of 1983. However, White ran into trouble with the boys at Soledad. They apparently gave the raspberry or worse to the man handing out their linens. "I am no longer working as a laundry porter," he wrote in November of 1982. "It became too much of a hassle dealing with the characters in this wing. I could not eat meals or walk in the yard without being pestered. I am relieved not to have to suffer their importunities any more."

The nurse's last letter from Dan White was dated February 2, 1983. White noted that in a short time he would be out of prison. He was thinking of the future. "I am still going to buy you drinks and dinner in Ireland one day," he wrote his friend.

DAN WHITE IS ARGUABLY one of the more successful assassins in the history of violent America and he is without question the luckiest. He blew away George Moscone and Harvey Milk and sent the city backward in a political direction he favored and did barely five years for the double murders. The assassin was patted on the back by cops in jail, slept on linen sheets, dined on roast beef sandwiches, and otherwise led the life of Reilly in prison. Although he presented a psychiatric defense at his trial, in prison he received no therapy or psychiatric treatment; he was stone-straight normal. While behind bars he fathered a child.

He was pampered on parole. It was first announced that he had to get a job, but he never worked. He was allowed to vacation in Tahoe and attend the Olympics in Los Angeles (he went to the boxing matches). In the fall of 1984, shortly before the assassin was released from parole, the San Francisco chief of police flew to Los Angeles and met secretly with White to urge him not to return to San Francisco—his original goal—as it might be dangerous for him.

By the middle-class standards he so reveres, White is fairly well-off. His house in his old district has increased in value and his hot potato business is profitable. His wife kept her job teaching in the San Francisco public school system. His large Irish family has gathered around him.

District elections, which brought Dan White and Harvey Milk to City Hall, are gone. Gays now have enough political strength to elect a supervisor citywide, but they no longer have Harvey Milk. San Francisco remains the biggest queer-bashing town in the world. The number of street attacks continues to average thirty to forty a month. The only change is that the cops have begun to treat gay bashings as a crime rather than a sport.

It is an exercise in confusion to attempt to understand the City Hall murders outside the context of violent homophobia in San Francisco and the deep political division in the city. In an interview after the trial, prosecutor Tom Norman said he could not understand the criticisms that he had done something wrong. "They talk about [how Norman should have put on] a political trial. I don't even know what that means," he said. By that logic Norman could prosecute Sirhan Sirhan without mentioning the Middle East.

The pretrial threat by Dan White's defense to make the social and political climate of San Francisco an issue in the trial effectively kept the prosecution from developing the very issues—albeit politically embarrassing ones for the city—that could have given White the motive required for a murder conviction. Jurors said after the verdict that they had been waiting for the prosecution to say something bad about Dan White's character. But all they heard was that he was the All-American Boy who somehow snapped. So Dan White got away with murder. And he never even had to say he was sorry.

[From *Gayslayer!: The Story of How Dan White
Killed Harvey Milk and George Moscone & Got Away With Murder,* 1985]

Halloween in the Castro

*T*HAT DAMNED INFERNAL END of Daylight Saving Time! It was 6 a.m. yesterday, but already it was 7 a.m. real time and the girls in the Castro had developed a terrible thirst waiting for the bars to open. The girls were lined up at the front door of the Pipeline before the first light. They were in need of a drink. The rain had made a mess of their mascara, and the tall brunette in the black ostrich-feather hat and flowing pink peignoir was having a terrible time trying to adjust a boob that had slipped inside his purple leotard. The doors opened and the rush was on and so began Day Two of Halloween in the Castro.

The inside of the bar looked like a scene out of a possessed-child movie. There was a monk with a scarecrow face, a buxom old thing in a mustard wig wearing a red dress wrapped in chains, and a Raggedy Ann in a long flowing gossamer robe over a daring black lace slip who wore pink plastic curlers in his red wig. There were two real girls in the party whose costumes competed with the boys for cleavage and two six-feet-tall wet rabbits talking to each other in Dutch. This year, Halloween has been a three-day celebration in the Castro, and you'd think that these people didn't have a care in the world. But people celebrating Halloween in the Castro had plenty to worry about. In this midst of their finery, the drag queens were all wearing whistles around their necks—the kind of whistles you call the cops with. Halloween in San Francisco can be a time of terror at a time of laughter.

Last year, gangs of homophobic punks ran wild in the Castro. There was a gang from Hayes Valley numbering more than fifty, a big gang of WPODs from the Sunset, and smaller gangs from the Mission. They acted like Marines out to get themselves some Cong. Many of them carried clubs and some carried knives. They swept through the crowd, pushing and shouting, and trashed stores. A worker at Marcello's pizza parlor got his head busted open by a bottle when he tried to stop them. The cops were nowhere to be seen.

Fag bashing in San Francisco has become increasingly violent and brazen. It's a dirty part of this supposedly tolerant city that the cops, until recently, have tended to make less than a priority. Now there is a new captain at the Mission Police Station, Vic Macia, who has declared gays off-limits to punks. This weekend his officers have been working with the lesbian and gay volunteers who will be out in force to patrol the streets tonight. This year, the Castro is ready for the punks of Halloween.

"Can you read me, Ellen? This is Gale. Please report your position."

"This is a radio check, Gerry. Can you read me? This is Gale."

Gale Shapiro was wearing a fluorescent red flak jacket with a flashlight taped to the sleeve. She was leaning against a fire hydrant at 18th and Castro with a walkie-talkie in her hand, contacting the troops. This was ten o'clock Saturday night. She was coordinating some thirty street monitors who patrolled the Castro. There will be more than one hundred of them out tonight. A heavy percentage of the monitors were women. In the Castro this Halloween, the boys are in drag and the girls are in flak jackets.

The constant walkie-talkie patrols gave the Castro an oddly military ambiance. They were greeted for the most part as heroes. When a man wearing nothing but pewter paint and devil's ears jumped out of a doorway brandishing a pitchfork at the monitors, he was admonished by another man in a plumed hat for disturbing the troops. "I'm glad to see you on the street," he told the monitors. He remembered last Halloween.

"The frightening thing about Halloween is the number of people on the street who aren't here to celebrate," said Diana Christensen, the director of Community United Against Violence, which worries about lesbian and gay safety from its offices above Castro Street. Their door is marked by a first-aid sign. Ms. Christensen said that street violence against lesbians and gays has been on the increase all summer. "The attacks have become more severe. Weapons are used more often—bats, clubs, knives, and even guns," she said. In one incident in late August a group of twenty or so men from the Catholic gay group Dignity were assaulted after a picnic in Sigmund Stern Grove by an equal number of punks, macho and drunk, who blocked their cars and threw rocks at them and hit at them with sticks, shouting epithets like "Take your AIDS and get out of town, faggots."

Inside the Castro defenders' command post, there were coffee and cookies and lots of volunteers looking at a wall map of the city with colored dots marking attacks on gays, and the dots were lumped the heaviest, not surprisingly, in the Castro. As lesbians and gay men came in and out of the crowded office putting on their flak jackets to go patrol, sitting at a desk manning the hotline was another volunteer, Father Anthony McGuire, the pastor of Holy Redeemer Catholic Church at 18th and Diamond. The Catholic Church in the presence of Archbishop John R. Quinn has had its tiffs with gays recently over what is or is not sin, but Father McGuire said differences over the interpretation of theology had nothing to do with seeing that people in his parish were safe walking on the streets. "Five members of the parish have volunteered as street monitors," said Father McGuire.

The Catholic priest shook his head and said what has been happening to gays on Halloween is downright un-Christian. I think the naked silver guy with the pitchfork down the street would agree.

[*San Francisco Chronicle*, October 31, 1983]

Just a Regular Guy who
Puts Rice in His Bra

"…And a policeman invited me home! He said, 'I'd really like to take you home and get it on with you,' and I said, very properly, quote unquote, 'Well, I don't think I have quite the right plumbing for you,' and he said, 'You are a broad aren't you?' and I said, 'Of sorts, this evening.'"

—From the book *Forbidden Fantasies*

*A*T MIDNIGHT FRANK DYMECK finished his shift on the switchboard at the hospital and scooted right home. He had to be up early to get ready because tomorrow was his other job.

Getting ready: In the morning, Frank shaved and then patted on his Estée Lauder moisturizer and his liquid foundation and then the blue eye shadow and the purple and then the white and when his eyes were rockets blasting out of his head he topped them with gushy brown eyebrow pencil and put on the wonderfully fluffy Revlon eyelashes and powdered his glistening cheeks like they were a baby's behind. Last came a kissy smear of Italian pink lipstick.

That was his face. Now came the hard part. Frank had to wiggle his 235 pounds into black Danskin pantyhose, the kind they make for big and beautiful women. There was another giant wiggle and a shrug into the all-in-one corset and bra. Over this went his mother's beloved old black slip. Then he put on his French maid's black dress with the taffeta borders and his black natural-curls wig and the white knit gloves and rhinestone earrings and the pillbox that his mother made. Frank stepped into his size 12 black patent-leather pumps with white lace bows from Tall Girl on Grant Avenue and he was ready for the job. He was off to serve breakfast in bed to a banker's wife in Marin County.

This is Halloween, and on Halloween a lot of people in San Francisco dress up. Some dress up more than others. Frank is one of those. This story is about Frank, and some other people who will be out on the streets tonight dressed in strange and beautiful ways. They are called, in street language, drag queens. Most, but not all, drag queens are gay.

This is also about Frank's mother, Ada, who lives with her son and makes his dresses. She made his French upstairs-maid outfit. It took eleven yards of material. Frank and Ada live in a dear little cottage house on a slope of Bernal Heights. Their dining room affords a splendid view of the spires of St. Paul's. Frank puts his face on—he calls it "pounding" makeup—at the dining room table with his back to the view. He uses a stand-up mirror strong enough to bounce a beam back to the sun. Ada watches this with a motherly gaze. When his face is transfigured, they both go into another room where Ada helps her son get into his dresses. Even in Frisco this could be considered a strange living arrangement. They make it seem natural, even sweet. "Mother always said she wanted a girl—and I said I was the girl she never got, in true heart," says Frank.

Ada's husband was a long-distance trucker. They lived in Williamsport, Pennsylvania, where Frank grew up. Ada is a perfect wiz with a sewing machine. She used to buy dolls and makes dresses for them, as a hobby. Her bride doll won first prize at the Pennsylvania State Fair. When her husband died a few years ago, she moved to S.F. with her son. I asked her if she had made dresses for him before she moved here. "Oh, no," she said.

There was the inevitable question about the bosoms. "Oh, I made them," she said. "I just took some material and zipped them up on my sewing machine." Frank's bosoms, it was discovered on further inquiry, are filled with Uncle Ben's converted rice. "We've always used rice," Frank said. This was after an unfortunate experience with macaroni. "The macaroni elbows kept pinching," Frank said.

Frank has been doing his French maid number for two years. He serves breakfast in bed, does cocktail parties, dinners, or what have you that needs camping up. Most of his customers are straights. "I think the straight audience appreciates it more. Most gays get so jaded," he said. Just last Saturday night at the Beaux Arts Hall, Frank had a horrible experience when he encountered an entire table of men dressed up as French maids. His indignation knew almost no bounds.

These drag queens sure do like to boogie. I know. I went boogying with Frank last Sunday. Among the stops was a roller skating rink on South Van Ness where Supervisor Quentin Kopp was having a political bash. Frank slipped out of his pumps and into skates and got out on the floor and began disco rolling with Kopp, who, on skates, is like the Tin Woodsman on 'ludes. The Upstairs Maid wasn't exactly light on her feet, either. They made a lovely couple.

It became part of the inescapable logic of the evening that we would proceed out Third Street to the premises of Sam Jordan, the mayor of Butchertown. Sam was hosting a sparerib barbecue contest. The proceedings had been a bit delayed due to the fact that the entry of Jordan's archrival, Paddy Nolan, the mayor of the Mission, had been accidentally thrown in the garbage. Nolan was marinating his ribs in his secret Irish BBQ sauce—a half gallon of white wine, a can of Ragu, and a can of minestrone soup—in a big green garbage bag, and one of Sam's kids had mistaken it for real garbage. The crowd at Jordan's went wild over Frank. Beautiful black women kept coming up and squeezing his bosoms and saying theirs were bigger than his. "I was afraid I'd spill my rice," Frank said.

Frank was dancing up a storm and gaily autographing the pictures of himself in drag he carries around in a little briefcase for a host of admirers when the real world interfered. He came running up with his eyes bulging out of his tricked-up face. "Somebody ripped off my case!" he said. He ran out into Third Street, where a lot of people were sitting in parked cars. Frank began running up and down the street beating on car windows with the large feather duster that he carries, demanding to know if those inside were the ones who ripped him off. One guy got out of his van and asked Frank if he'd like to buy a new Sony TV for fifty bucks. I suggested that hot pursuit in full drag with a feather duster for a weapon on Third Street at midnight was not the best way to deal with this matter, but Frank was not to be dissuaded. It took an hour to calm him down enough to get him into a cab out of there. "Why me?" he kept saying. "I'm a minority."

Barry Shapiro is a streetwise photographer who has spent much of the past two years shooting Frank and friends for a book on San Francisco drag queens. The book, done with photographer Mike Phillips and writer-cabbie Mark Joseph, has just come out. It's called *Forbidden Fantasies*, and, like drag queens in the flesh, seems to be freaking a lot of people out. There's something about drag queens outrageously playing with the male-female roles that provokes a lot of yikes from people. According to the queens the authors interviewed, this reaction is far from limited to straights. A lot of gays are freaked out by drag queens. The idea that three straight guys could do a book on drag queens and get to understand their weirdness and appreciate them as people and become friends with the likes of Frank is a lesson about straight-gay relations in this town, as opposed to the curled macho lips in North Beach bars or the looks of horror at parties frequented by the USF Irish Mafia type when the dreaded word "gay" is mentioned.

The drag queens that the authors found living all over town—from the Excelsior to the Haight to Hunters Point—will be out tonight in full flower. Some will be dressed as pumpkins and eggplants and some will be dressed as the Raiderettes. One dresses up as Wonder Woman—"I always had an attraction for Amazons"—and another goes out in Jackie Kennedy drag. Most all of them are gainfully employed in straight-type jobs—from bankers to Catholic school teachers. (Frank is a switchboard operator at a local hospital and on his days off volunteers as a reader for Lighthouse for the Blind.) "What we found out is that they're all just people, like everybody else," Shapiro said.

Frank recently did the sixteenth birthday party for Shapiro's daughter. The girls loved it. He put on his face in front of teenagers, and one of them lent him her eyebrow pencil sharpener. Then he put on his dress and did his thing. "The girls said it was the nicest party they'd ever been to," said Frank's mother, Ada, proudly. Kids aren't freaked out by the same things that grown-ups are.

[*San Francisco Chronicle*, October 31, 1980]

Zap Turns Twenty

*D*ORI SEDA, A.K.A. D. SOMERSET SEDA, A.K.A. SYLVIA SILICOSIS, had long straight hair and peachy-mayonnaisey skin and kumquat eyes behind glasses as big around as a D-cup brassiere and an inviting gap between her front teeth the size of the kick-starter on a Harley hog. Dori was the first woman to die among the underground Bay Area cartoonists who took the comic book, once a wholesome American art form, into the chasms of depravity and hipness that define the sixties in burnt-out cells of memory and kept it there to assault eighties sensibilities with outrageous comics twenty years after *Zap* contributed to the national patrimony such professional deviants and turkey necks as Mr. Natural, the Fabulous Furry Freak Brothers, Trashman, Mr. Peanut, the Checkered Demon, and an entire barnyard of unwholesome hand-drawn characters whom you would never want to get near your bedroom, not even in a bad dream.

Dori Seda was the latest *underground* artist to surface. She was at once the finest cartoonist to enter the neo-*Zap* spectrum and the first to go through the narrow door and, according to the famous R. Crumb, the hey-boparee-bop-to-counterculture controversialist who pushed her ascendency into the seraphim of underground comics artists, may have been the most talented of the lot. She died in February at the ripe age of thirty-six of complications from silicosis acquired in a previous incarnation as a potter, an incessant cough further complicated by the suicidal consumption of many packs of cigarettes a day and an insomniac lifestyle that whether it was Dori drawing or Dori playing with her dog Tona, who was always snorting her socks, or Dori playing with her cat Dracula or Dori playing with a man or Dori working at her straight job as a bookkeeper for Ronzo E. Turner—the connoisseur of evil geniuses who, as proprietor of Last Gasp Comics, continues to publish whoopee pillows in the form of forty-four-page comic books with names like *Weirdo* and *Zap* and *Wimmen's* and *Cannibal Romance* and *Commies from Mars* and *Anarchy*—no matter what she was doing, Dori was always staying up all night and pouring down maybe twenty brewskis. She thought of the sun what most people think about ants, as a nuisance to be avoided.

Dori Seda was as skinny as the tip of a Bic and in body deportment the polar opposite of the caricaturistic "wimmin" in Crumb's cartoons, which feminists find so outrageous—fat ladies in colored smocks and mini-Amazons with greedy sexual appetites, rock-like thighs, bicycle buttocks, and breasts that belong on Mt. Rushmore. If you think Crumb's wimmin look funny, you should see Crumb, who looks for all the world like an anorexic Charlie Chaplin, a walking string bean wearing a straw hat and a tie narrower than his nose and a drugstore clerk's Sunday suit made in 1954, with a pencil mustache on his shriven face and tortoiseshell glasses that weigh more than his head. But for all the feminist agitprop about Crumb's antagonism to women, the artist has been unchauvinistic about female talent. His second wife, the talented cartoonist Aline Kominsky, is the editor of his magazine *Weirdo*, which has showcased the best women cartoonists of the eighties. Crumb immediately saw Dori as *Zap*-compatible talent.

Dori had a winning giggle and a hoarse laugh that often tumbled into a barrage of deadly coughs and the ability—common to the *Zap* school—of poking relentless, savage fun at the human condition, beginning with her own. In the sixties, when most everyone among his Haight-Ashbury contemporaries was blitzed out of their gourds on potluck dosages of low-grade pills, Crumb somehow remained sane enough to as evenly caricature the hipster white revolutionaries as the porcine-faced cops who routinely busted their faces. Dori Seda similarly managed in her art to make fun of her own sex life and the eighties sexual perk-and-turf battles.

A short time before her unexpected death, I met Dori at the redneck Jay'n Bee tavern, a cop bar with the badges of SFPD retirees hanging in positions of honor on the walls. *Zap* publisher Ron Turner and I were there discussing what, if anything, could be expurgated from the celebrated raunch of *Zap* that could be printed in the Sunday newspaper in honor of the socially significant event of its obtaining twenty years of age (first issue: February 1968) and selling over two million copies. The Jay'n Bee was an unlikely venue for a femrad, sexual liberationist artist, but Dori, who popped in to show Turner some work in progress for her next book, blended right in with the boys, ordering up a few brewskis and chattering charmingly about her compulsive relationship with her dog Tona, a black Doberman, who was constantly at her side and always getting into the laundry pile and snorting her socks and otherwise sticking his nose where it didn't belong, including her sex life, in embarrassing moments she has hilariously told in her comic strips. When she decided that Tona needed a new home, she placed this hand-drawn ad:

CLASSIFIED AD SECTION

58 PETS

FREE DOG TO GOOD HOME. OVERWEIGHT DOBERMAN WITH A CHRONIC SKIN CONDITION. SMELLS BAD, AND LEAVES ECZEMA FLAKES AND DOG HAIR ALL OVER THE HOUSE. SPENDS MOST OF HIS LIFE WITH HIS NOSE IN HIS BUTT. IF YOU WANT THE DOG, OR IF YOU HAVE ANY COMMENTS ABOUT THIS BOOK, PLEASE WRITE TO:

DORI SEDA

If you asked Crumb why he supported the idea of Dori Seda getting published, he would, Bible-spouting fool, most probably say, "Sufficient unto the day is the evil thereof." "Dori the person is a seething, barely controlled nut-case coming out of her skin. Dori the artist is patient, orderly, keenly perceptive, reflective—you might even say wise and reassuring. How does she do it?" Crumb wrote in an introduction to Dori's *Lonely Nights,* published in 1986.

There was an impromptu requiem for Dori at the party March 11 at the San Francisco Art Commission Gallery honoring *Zap*'s twentieth anniversary and the publication of *Zap* number twelve in June. With the exception of expatriate Gilbert "Fabulous Furry" Shelton (who now lives in Paris, where he oversees his comics published worldwide in fourteen languages), all the original *Zap* movers and shakers were there: Crumb, Rick Griffin, Victor Moscoso, S. Clay Wilson, Robert Williams, Spain Rodriguez, and Don Donahue, the first publisher of *Zap*, with whom Dori lived the past few years. When she died, Dori's second book of comics was two-thirds done, and Turner said he hopes to bring it out this year, with memorials from her *Zap* friends filling the pages she left blank.

[*San Francisco Examiner*, *Image* magazine, April 17, 1988]

The Crazy Never Die

STEADMAN WAS WAITING FOR ME in Cookie Picetti's Blue Star Café. The artist's hands were in angelic repose around a glass of Scotch. The rest of him was a rattled venetian blind. His vest hung open over a blue dress shirt that had escaped the laundromat. His eyes looked like wet firecrackers that had somehow been trapped in his head and were looking for a way to get out. The sight of me, he said, brought back memories too horrible to endure.

This was on a drippy gray day in the 1980s. Cookie's was a magnificently inelegant Frisco cop bar; the clientele included generous helpings of defense attorneys, judges, mailmen, bail bondsmen, poultry salesmen, and the drinking press. The buffet part was simplicity itself: if you wanted a burger you banged on the back door to get the attention of the cook in the Chinese restaurant next door. The front was cracked blue tile dulled with the grim patina of diesel bus exhaust. The air inside was forever stained a permanent nicotine yellow. A framed page of dialogue from a *Dragnet* script—Ben Alexander, Jack Webb's sidekick, asked where they should go for a drink in Frisco and Webb says Cookie's, where else do the cops go? In this midst of this living wreckage of old San Francisco stood Ralph Steadman, arguably England's greatest living artist, trembling at the bar next to a naked-to-the-waist mannequin of Freud, with whom he said he had been sleeping.

The artist made his hands into a claw and cradled his large head something like a condor egg in a monster's nest and shook involuntarily at the very mention of the name of the Beast, Hunter S. Thompson. Steadman insisted I was at fault for ruining his life by pairing him up with Thompson, that Beast, by sending them to cover the Kentucky Derby. His psychedelic Sancho Panza adventures with Thompson had driven him into four years of intense therapy and an unhealthy relationship with Freud. He blew his nose in a bar rag. "You got a big honker," Cookie said.

Steadman was still crying over the shoes he had lost at the America's Cup races in Newport, Rhode Island, some ten years previous. It was all Thompson's fault, and by extension mine for sending Steadman and Thompson to Newport for the America's Cup Races on assignment to do mischief for *Scanlan's Monthly,* a magazine unloved by the Watergate White House. Thompson had fed him LSD in fishcakes and sent him underwater like a hairy porpoise with a can of spray paint clenched in his teeth on an aggressive mission to spray "NUKE THE POPE" in red on the lead yacht, which was white. The previous assignment I had given them, "The Kentucky Derby Is Decadent and Depraved," had ended in disaster, too, with Steadman losing his tools and having to draw in borrowed lipstick and eyebrow pencil and Thompson macing him for the fun of it. The artist ended up fleeing the country without his shoes, muttering that any money he got paid by *Scanlan's* for the aborted Newport mission would be danger money and vowing never to return to the United States.

Yet he did return, to fitfully collaborate with Thompson on books and "Fear and Loathing" articles in Vegas; Hawaii; Elko, Nevada; and other altered states, most of them published in *Rolling Stone* when the short-lived *Scanlan's* imploded after the Canadian Royal Mounties arrested an entire edition's press run, which was in trucks headed for the border, carrying an issue dedicated to guerrilla warfare in the U.S. Sometime after his morning-after morning in Cookie's, Steadman drew some monstrous portraits of Thompson, including a classic of its kind, revered, depicting a broken-footed Hunter in his director's chair during his reign of terror as night manager of the Mitchell Brothers O'Farrell Street Theater, a beloved San Francisco institution dedicated to the art of undressing in public which Hunter called "the Carnegie Hall of Sex."

Steadman said his latest recorded message from Thompson was: "Call immediately. Time is running out. We both need to do something monstrous before we die." Fast forward to 2005: Hunter wanted his ashes shot out of a cannon. A great funeral was what he wanted, he told his son. Then he sat in his command-post kitchen in Woody Creek, Colorado, and shot himself dead in the head. That was the end of my old friend, Hunter S. Thompson. But the end is only the beginning of his story.

His last column was a sports column, for ESPN's Page 2. He began his writing career as a sports writer and he came full circle to end it that way, quite brilliantly and most politically—Thompson was the fiercest critic in mainstream media of the Bush administration. He called Bush the "boy president," which was the kindest thing he had to say about him. That he was able to throw out these political slinging meanies only on a sports network was quite mainstream America to him. Hunter generally viewed corporate journalism through the same prism of suspicion that he used to pull the butterfly wings off professional politicians. He once told me that the sports box scores were the only part of a newspaper you could trust because "there are too many witnesses to the final score for anyone to lie."

Hunter Thompson's demise at sixty-seven last February of a self-inflicted gunshot wound at his compound in Woody Creek shook his friends and admirers in earthquake-prone San Francisco, a city that is still struggling to ascertain if it was Kool Aid or Flavor Aid that the Reverend Jim Jones of San Francisco served to his followers in Guyana, and why. Sudden death shakes this hang-loose city where life is taken so easily for granted. Thompson's favorite San Francisco hangouts were decked in gloom. The night of his death, in the back room of the Tosca, writer Tim Ferris and other Hunter close Frisco friends sat shivas with owner Jeannette Etheredge. Gavin Newsom, the mayor, sat in to hear the tales.

Recalled fondly was the story of the night when Thompson was stacking every brandy snifter in the bar in an increasingly unstable pyramid on a cocktail table. They were waving like a giraffe's neck. Hunter was concentrating on the task at hand. "I've got to get this vicious bugger up there," he said. Thompson could get pissed off faster than an unexpected East Coast thunderstorm, and he directed a sudden ire at a towheaded lad he had in tow, introducing him vaguely as "a cousin of the Kennedys who needs to have his tooth pulled." Thompson had sent out for pliers to do the job. "You touch that table and you'll eat every glass that breaks, you little puss-faced greaseball," he told the fat-lipped Kennedy. Hunter had to get that last glass up there. The understandably concerned owner told Hunter that if he put one more glass on top of the heap the "damn thing will fall down." Just one more glass, Jeannette, Hunter said. The hapless sore-toothed Kennedy touched the table to steady it, the idiot, and the glasses fell down with all the clatter of a drunk attempting to climb the Macy's Christmas tree.

Ferris, a Hunter bud and black hole expert who would frequently sojourn to Woody Creek to greet the dawn with Hunter outside examining the mysteries of the stars, had placed a hundred-dollar bill on the backroom pool table—the back room is the Holy of Holies of the old operatic bar where those not invited by Jeannette dare not to tread—as a coaster for a glass of Chivas Regal on the rocks, the drink that Hunter washed his teeth with each of his mornings, which were most other people's afternoons.

The next morning at the O'Farrell Street Theater, Hunter's other home away from home, the flags above the marquee were lowered to half-staff. The O'Farrell was Hunter's San Francisco office. He spent many moons there as the night manager on a prepaid assignment from *Playboy* about the sex industry, roosting on a high director's chair up in the wings where the spotlights were played on the girls on the stage below, learning the biz and watching the action. He had broken his leg in an indelicate backflip off the bar at the Tosca and it was in a Titanic cast. A bottle of Chivas Regal was in one hand and his dainty cigarette holder in the other. This was the nightly sight for years. He never wrote the article, of course.

A word about Hunter's friends: Tim Ferris has said that if you wanted to know who Hunter Thompson was you should check out his friends, the way the monument to London's great architect Christopher Wren at St. Paul's Cathedral states simply, if you seek his monument, look around you. Hunter, his good friend Ferris said, modestly, had great taste in friends. Hunter picked his friends, and they were legion, but it was never the other way around. Hunter had the not-so-eccentric attitude that there had to be something terribly wrong with anybody who *wanted* to be his friend—must be some sort of a goddamn suckup scumsucker wannabe bottom-feeder. Friendships to him just happened like the collision of atoms or the felt recognition of mutual madness certified by actions signaling same. One of Hunter's signature phrases was, "We are, after all, professionals," spoken often of a night, usually nights, of madness culminating in nifty and edgy writing, editing, and deadline-defying that the straight publishing geeks who had the keys to the asylum held as a matter of faith that the inmates could not perform. Hunter appreciated some of his saner friends, such as Ed Bradley or Jack Nicholson, though he would be ever ragging on and prodding them—

that was part of Hunter's charm—and by association drew them to appreciate the attractiveness of The Edge, that place Hunter was always heading but most feared to tread.

"Hunter knew where every ice machine was at every motel in San Francisco," said his good friend Jeannette Etheredge, the proprietor of the Tosca and one of Hunter's closest Frisco confidants. Tosca is to the San Francisco filmmaking set what Elaine's is to the New York glitterati. Hunter was not much into sleep at the routine hours and often of a night after the Tosca closed at the puritanical San Francisco hour of 2 a.m. and the nights' receipts had been tagged and bagged would take Jeannette out for what he called a "ride" in a top-down convertible or a Jeep—wild, daring, conversation-laden windblown rides in the night with the stars looking down in the predawn hours when the cable cars were still in the barn snoozing for the night and there was none of that Tony Bennett sentimental crap about little cable cars climbing halfway to the stars. Hunter's car was always well-stocked with provisions for a roader—a bottle of Wild Turkey, a six-pack of Heinekens in an ice bucket, and drugs in an enclosed inhaler lest the wind get in the way of progress. He once took Jeannette in a Jeep down the Coast Highway just out of San Francisco hard past the zoo and drove down a rough road to a beach below Pacifica where he did doughnuts in the wet sand with the Jeep in the dark before dawn intruded. He sometimes ran out of ice. One night out by the Cliff House he abruptly braked the car outside the Seal Rock hill and climbed out of the driver's seat without benefit of opening the door. He had to enter quietly because he had been banned from the inn for repetitive destruction of the premises. "When he came back, he had a new bucket of ice," said Jeannette. (Hunter always paid attention to detail. Once while having lunch with the Mitchell brothers, Jim and Artie, at the Washington Square Bar & Grill, my daughter Pia noticed that he had two watches on his hands. She asked him sensibly why he wore two watches. "Time is important," Hunter said.)

Hunter once brought a Mitchell Brothers dancer dressed in a guerrilla costume into Tosca for a drink and the movie crowd barely noticed. When he broke his ankle performing a ballet misstep on the top of the bar Thompson didn't want to go to the hospital, considerately fearing it might affect the bar's insurance rates, and insisted on taping the ankle himself with black electrical tape. Jeannette, who doesn't drink at all, accompanied Hunter on some of his epic S.F. binges. "He was always a perfect Southern gentleman," she said.

Action followed Hunter like a shadow from a scarecrow. I met him in the mid-1960s when I was editing *Ramparts,* a Catholic anti-(Vietnam) war slick. He was hanging around Frisco (yup, I know many residents h-a-t-e that word, but I love it; it recalls when Frisco was a real town and not the twenty-first insufferably p.c. version of sixties Berkeley it has become and brings up noir memories of piss and vinegar and strange stains on overstuffed couches in shabby Nob Hill apartments and Dashiell Hammett drinking like a fish and waterfront shanghais and real people drinking and eating the way real people did before California Cuisine reared its ugly snout dockside dice games and cops bribing and bars open all night and waterfront shanghais and...I guess you get my drift. *Ramparts* published out of an office on the lower Broadway strip. Hunter one night left his knapsack on the couch in my office when we went to dinner. At the time I had a pet monkey named Henry Luce. Henry got out of his cage and into Hunter's knapsack and opened many bottles of pills and gobbled the contents. When we returned the monkey was bananas and running at top speed along the railing above the office cubicles. He had turned into a ferocious, snarling monster and no one could pacify him. It took a day and a half for him to slow down. "Goddam monkey stole my pills," Hunter said.

Gonzo journalism—the unedifying concept of the reporter as the proactive part of the story, with equal emphasis on the imaginative and comic as the factual—grew out of the 1970 assignment I gave Thompson for *Scanlan's Monthly,* a successor magazine to *Ramparts* edited out of New York (with Sidney Zion) and San Francisco from advertising genius Howard Gossage's firehouse on Pacific Street. Gonzo started when Hunter called me from Colorado at home in San Francisco about 4 a.m.—a normal social hour for him—to say that he wanted to cover the Kentucky Derby, which was then but two days away. I said Okay, we'd send him tickets and money ("With expenses, anything is possible," Hunter frequently said), and find an artist to hook up with him. That of course would be poor, dear Ralph Steadman.

Hunter's high-and-low-jinks and his personal destructo-derbies have been portrayed by some as immature, but those sourpuss critics miss the point. Hunter was one of the sanest men I have known—suicide aside, but suicide can be a rational option, ask Clint Eastwood—his larger-than-life persona as part of the story was his way of shattering what he considered the myth of objectivity in journalism. He thought all media were biased, protected by layers of cautious corporate camouflage pretending to objectivity, and the only way a writer could express his well-founded political likes and dislikes was to break the mold of objective journalism and go for the wild thing; then editors treated you differently because they were either afraid of or fascinated by you. You had to be in a way bigger than the story to be able to tell the story, which in Hunter's case was the raw truth as the writer saw it.

A television journo asked me if Hunter had "forged a new path" in journalism. I thought about it and said, no, he had rather beaten his way back through the overgrown jungle of bureaucratic media to the original path of nineteenth-century journalism, when journalism was actually a popular, participatory sport and editors swore openly and imbibed freely and spat tobacco and carried guns and cussedly attacked politicians and other editors by name as varmints unworthy of road-kill. (Parenthically, the gloryhole days of American journalism which included the great muckrakers were before modern advertising as we know it; a publisher was previously dependent on the pennies or nickels of readers who actually wanted to read their sheet—with the intrusion of corporate advertising money subsidizing the price of a publication came corporate media and corporate caution and self-censorship.)

Thompson early in the Hells Angels book used this quote from Kierkegaard on journalism: "The daily press is the evil principle of the modern world, and time will only serve to disclose this fact with greater clearness. The capacity of the newspaper for degeneration is sophistically without limit, since it can always sink lower in its choice of readers. At last it will stir up all those dregs of humanity which no state or government can control." His own view was hardly more mellow. This at the end of *Fear and Loathing in Las Vegas*: "Agnew was right. The press is a gang of cruel faggots. Journalism is not a profession or a trade. It is a cheap catch-all for fuckoffs and misfits—a false doorway to the backside of life, a filthy piss-ridden little hole nailed off by the building inspector, but just deep enough for a wino to curl up from the sidewalk and masturbate like a chimp in a zoo cage."

Hunter's personal style of journalism blew a hole in the tin can of the profession and let in some welcome air. He has inspired a new generation of young journalists-to-be who had been less than called to a profession assuming the dull coat of armor of accounting. His the-personal-is-political-and-the-political-is-personal worldview was the seed path to the personal underpinning of blogging, which makes little pretense to harrumph "objectivity" but insists on telling the truth as the blogger sees scoundrels and professional humbugs. The galaxy of differ-ence between Hunter and the J-School mafia who carp that he at times made up facts—more precisely he fantasized them in the Mark Twain tradition—was that Hunter saw the political reality for what it was, the hog in the tunnel, and one can't say the same for the *New York Times* and the *Washington Post* support of the Vietnam War, or the *Times'* "objective" Judith Miller who promoted the myths of WMDs in Iraq.

Gonzo was born thirty-five years ago in the Bethlehem of the Ken-tucky Derby. The 131st running of the derby was spared the nettlesome presence of Hunter S. Thompson, who, suiciding himself in February, followed the belief of Lucius Beebe, a fellow champion of journalistic excess, that one should leave a party while it is still good. The wassails of the derby, both pageantry and personal, was the spore that grew the twisted gonzo branch of New Journalism and made the phrase "fear and loathing" an indispensable part of the American lexicon. This was no small matter, as even Thompson's detractors must allow that gonzo put a scar on the face of American journalism that a good many readers, many millions of them, found perversely attractive.

Thirty-five years ago in 1970 I assigned Thompson and a then-innocent English artist, Ralph Steadman, to cover the 96th running of the derby in the way that Thompson saw fit. He saw fit to mace Stead-man at the end of the article, which made "gonzo" more verb than adjec-tive. I was then coediting, with Sidney Zion, a magazine called *Scanlan's Monthly,* which was named after a much-disliked Irish pig farmer. In its short existence (it lasted only eight issues) it became, according to that magnificent informer John Dean, the most-hated publication of the Watergate White House. The cover of the issue in which appeared the seminal gonzo article, "The Kentucky Derby Is Decadent and Depraved," was a caricature of Nixon with a humongous fist punching his face in and delicate red headline type saying "Impeach Nixon."

Thompson had previously established a literary beachhead with his book recounting his year with the Hells Angels that was part first-person bemused freak-out, part groundbreaking sociology about the outlaw class in contemporary America. With the publication of the Kentucky Derby article in *Scanlan's*, Thompson and Steadman went on an unrivaled journalistic run on the gonzo gravy train. "Hunter ruined my life," Steadman said, almost gleefully, at Thompson's memorial soiree in March at the Hotel Jerome in Aspen.

What distinguished the Kentucky Derby piece from the earlier first-person New Journalism pioneered by Terry Southern and perfected by Tom Wolfe, an admirer of Thompson, was the hallucinatory stimulant-fueled novelistic attention given on a sporting assignment not to the horses but to the outdoor loony bin of boozed-up burgher spectators—the first look through the other end of the binoculars usually trained on the four-footed beasts. To get so down-and-dirty detailed, Thompson and Steadman became as wasted as the mob of fans, and a peculiar sort of truth, if not rough beauty, came out of the experience. *In vino veritas* never had a better literary test run. "We had come there to watch the *real* beasts perform," Thompson wrote. Thompson invented a phrase—the "whiskey gentry"—to describe the sports mob which rivaled Mencken's depictions of Bible-thumping preachers cooking souls like chicken wings in a frying pan: the derby fan was Everyman for the sports spectator-hooligan, "a pretentious mix of booze, failed dreams and a terminal identity crisis; the inevitable result of too much inbreeding in a closed and ignorant culture." Anyone who has witnessed an English soccer match or an on-court pro-basketball riot can swear to the cultural truth therein. "Teddible, teddible," said Steadman in Brit-speak.

Hunter Thompson burst into print in the first issue of *Scanlan's*, a magazine Sidney Zion and I rescued from the sinking ship of *Ramparts*, a former Catholic literary quarterly that had turned into a pirate craft of New Journalism cum New Leftism in the stormy seas of the late 1960s. We printed a piece by Hunter whacking the hell out of Jean-Claude Killy, which *Playboy* had assigned Hunter but then refused to run as it utterly exposed the hypocrisy and mercantilism and crude hypocrisy of the celebrity sport world. Thompson was elated that the "doomed" piece about "flackism in America" had been given new life. He wrote his editor at Random House, Jim Silverman, "Hinckle sounds happy with the notion of running the whole 110-page article, along with some correspondence from *Playboy*...and since he sent me a check for $1500 I guess I'm happy too. God only know what kind of magazine he has in mind, but if he can drum up anything like the old, high-flying *Ramparts,* I know I look forward to reading it. As an editor, Hinckle is one of the few crazed originals to emerge from the jangled chaos of what we now have to sift through and define or explain somehow as 'the 1960s.'"

That praise if praise it were was short-lived. As soon as he received the galleys Hunter wrote me a letter scorched on asbestos complaining that "it seems a bit rotten to cut the only part of the piece which partially redeems me...As it stands now, in your edited version, I come off as some kind of vicious, petulant drunk who slinks off at the end, muttering garbled slurs to himself...There is also the fact that, if anyone reads it calls me a mean, half-bright asshole for writing what I DID, I'LL NATURALLY SAY THAT 'HINCKLE CUT THE SENSE OUT OF IT.'"

Hunter was his own best critic—he was, in the old *New York World*'s slogan, "perpetually unsatisfied" (he wrote me after the derby article was published). But woe betide any copy editor who quoted or fucked with his copy—the only escape from his wrath was to get down and dirty with him on an all-nighter, share the pain, share the drugs, share the Chivas Regal washed down with copious numbers of Heinckens, order the room service, shoot the dart gun in the walls for stress relief...a creative process I have experienced numerous evenings unto bleary dawns.

Thompson kept suggesting wild and crazy things to *Scanlan's* because the magazine was in its own way—as was he—something of a throwback to the fantastic nineteenth-century western journalism of the days of the code duello. *Scanlan's* during its short shelf life was *his* type of mag. It established an early one hundred thousand circulation through a series of brilliant full-page newspaper ads written by Dan Greenburg headlined YOU TRUST YOUR MOTHER BUT YOU CUT THE CARDS (Sidney Zion's favorite phrase) and publishing articles such as an illustrated twelve-easy-steps article titled "How to Counterfeit Credit Cards and Get Away with It"; a detailed account of how the Chicago cops assassinated Black Panther leaders by John Kifner of the *New York Times,* a story that wasn't fit to print in his newspaper; journalistic pranks including reprinting the official newsletter of the South Africa mission to the United Nations in the magazine with the logo intact but the text dramatically changed and then mailing the lookalike phony to the regular recipients, printing on the back cover a slick ad running in national magazines promoting tourism to Germany with the headline "Next Time Think Twice about Germany" over lovely photos of German castles and river valleys and Bavarian songstresses in costume—we left the ad entirely intact down to the coupon to send to the German Tourist Board for further information, changing only two of the photos—with a Sieg Heil salute picture and a photo of a Nazi beating a naked woman with a whip (after a considerable uproar in the advertising world, the advertising program was canceled). Agnew called a press conference to claim the letter was a fabrication. *Scanlan's* was impishly ahead of its time with Robert Crumb covers and a 33 rpm record bound into the magazine of a recording of Special Forces soldiers torturing a suspected Viet Cong agent, so readers could play it themselves and hear the truth about U.S. use of torture.

Hunter saw weaponry to be an important connect to his campaign for sheriff of Pitkin County and a new circulation base for the magazine. He had thought it through in exacting detail. He wrote: "The nation is full of potential bomb-throwers & snipers who know *nothing* about the technical aspects of their chosen Trades. I think we should help these people, and I can think of no better way than to capitalize on my new-found conduits into the official Police Establishment. We can drive the fuckers crazy by discussing the pros & cons of all their newest weapons—small but important things like the fact that Army Surplus gas masks are no good against the new 'improved CS.' And addresses of companies which make the new masks, so freaks can rip them off. Given the rude temper of these times, I daresay this is a stroke of fucking genius. We can create, with Raoul Duke, a virtual clearing house for information on all forms of violence. Answer all questions, dispense strange advice of all sorts…and meanwhile keep a fine tap on The Police Chief & other cop books, in order to expose everything they come up with. Also things like 'How to Seize a Floating Rib, How to Choke a Vicious Dog'… & other small items like 'Why Slash Tires When It's Easier to Cut Off the Inner Tube Stems.'"

Hunter was both a tad paranoid and practical about the weaponry gambit. "No doubt the FBI would visit you very soon after the first column appeared, so you'd have to protect my identity if at all possible. In fact, I decided to use my well-worn pseudonym, Raoul Duke, so as not to blow my cover with The Police Chief & all the various agencies, supply houses, etc. that I've written to, asking for information and weapons. If I signed this piece of any other with my right name, they would soon have me blacklisted at every corner of the Police Establishment. But now, since I've already established myself with The Police Chief, I suspect the rest will be easy. We could actually order police weapons, and test them, then publish the results. We could buy a fucking pepper fog machine & test it in Golden Gate Park at a Shriners' Picnic."

Scanlan's was observably schizophrenic, with a constant tug-of-war between its offices in San Francisco and New York, both Left Coast smartass and a throwback to the Damon Runyon–Ben Hecht school of journalism. It was financed by a public stock issue in which the red herring announced that there was absolutely no possibility that *Scanlan's* Literary House had a chance in hell of making money. In the first issue we printed on the cover the check from the underwriter, an over-the-counter IPO genius named Charlie Plohn, stating in a front-page editorial that we wanted everyone to know where we got our money, from the gullible, greedy public, and there were not among the many small investors who peed into the *Scanlan's* pot enough souls who could get together to agree on anything, so *Scanlan's* was Fiercely Independent.

The masthead listed as publisher: The Late Howard Gossage. Gossage was the maverick advertising genius—among other things he invented Marshall McLuhan, although Marshall preferred the word "discovered." Gossage's answer to that was, "Marshall, we don't know who 'discovered' water, but it certainly wasn't a goldfish." Gossage was an anti-advertising advertising man. He was always biting the hand of the industry that fed him, telling advertisers that they were responsible for the poor state of the media by rewarding mediocre publications with advertising just to reach consumers. He died tragically and young, shortly before the first issue came out. *Scanlan's* adopted his philosophy of publishing—Gossage had been a longtime consultant for the *New Yorker* and *Scientific American*—which was: no cut-rate subscriptions through mass mailings, make it good and charge what the sucker is worth, let the reader pay his way, and don't be subsidized by advertising because then you become dependent and lose your own freedom of the press. Gossage's sidekick was Gerry Feigen, a wisecracking proctologist with a Jerry Colonna handlebar mustache who cross-indexed dirty jokes on cooking cards. Gossage and Feigen played key roles in trying to keep *Ramparts* afloat when I was editing it during the Vietnam War craziness. Feigen was on the board of directors of *Scanlan's*. We had quite a crew.

Gonzo journalism did for psychedelics and pharmacological recreation what Macaulay did for the Whigs. But it transcended that marginal if memorable fête, fermenting a new way of seeing and expressing political realities—the hog *was* in the tunnel—that cautious corporate journalism, cursed by the cult of objectivity, could not approach without permission from the J-School mafia. In New York terms, it brought back the glory days of Beck's Artists and Writers Restaurant (formerly Club), where a wizened bartender fed cracked corn to imaginary chickens behind the plank and Stanley Walker, the old *Herald Tribune*'s great city editor, proclaimed cirrhosis of the liver as the occupational disease of great reporters (now the occupational disease is carpal tunnel syndrome and the difference shows in the vitality of newspapering). We have the Kentucky Derby of thirty-five years ago to thank, if thanks be given, for gonzo journalism. The telly reminds us that this is also the twenty-fifth anniversary of CNN. If you had to choose between them, would it be the sheep or the goat?

[*The Argonaut*, December 2005]

Maoists
in
Limerick

Russia's Underground
Political Pornography*

"Oh, stop making excuses for depravity."

—Lermontov to Pushkin, 1830

SUPERGIRL OKTYABRINA SLOWLY STRIPS DOWN before the USSR's official portrait of Lenin. Her assignment is to turn the old boy on, and to hell with socialist realism. Oktyabrina, love child of the October Revolution, crudely mixes what—for want of a less offensive translation from the contemporary Russian vernacular—we must call boobs and ass with traditional Marxist history in the pursuit of her comic strip mission: the pornographic mockery of the Soviet state.

Largely Barbarella yet part Tugboat Annie, Oktyabrina is no Cold War wet dream of Al Capp's but the indigenous (if remarkably Americanized) creation of a shadow group of Russian intellectuals and artists who, in their disgust with Soviet society, have opted to go underground and fight dirty. In uptight, officially puritanical Russia the antics of Supergirl Oktyabrina are received—in daylight, anyway—with a sort of shocked and bemused disbelief that might be suggested as analogous to the reaction of television watchers in a Brooklyn bar if by chance Pat Nixon broke wind on Johnny Carson. Even in the most swinging of communist parlance, Oktyabrina is no lady.

Scene: The Gobi Desert. Oktyabrina is fighting on the side of the Red Chinese lackeys against the Russian imperialists. She has no difficulty getting laid, but has big trouble building a fire: "A whole day I have to be satisfied with raw meat until the yak dung will be dried for the fire," she complains.

Scene: A Sioux Indian reservation. The Russians have sent in secret agents to whip the Indians into fighting a war against the American gentry occupying their land, but Oktyabrina, playing Jane Fonda to her own Barbarella, rolls over for the braves and blows the Kremlin plot.

*Coauthored with Joel E. Solkoff

Scene: Madagascar. The island is crawling with Russian and Chinese agents vying for first place in line to exploit the natives. Oktyabrina, rotating her private parts like a hula hoop, wins the day for the Third World by, literally, screwing everybody else.

Scene: Southeast New Guinea. The American sailors are bugging the local headhunters, so Oktyabrina helps the cannibals do their own thing to the navy.

Oktyabrina has been putting out like this for ten years, but an Iron Comic Curtain has kept her salacious exploits from competition with Dick Tracy. Or was it James Bond?

> "He gazed for a moment into the mirror and wondered about Vesper's morals. He wanted her cold and arrogant body. He wanted to see tears and desire in her remote blue eyes and to take the ropes of her black hair in his hands and bend her long body back under his. Bond's eyes narrowed, and his face in the mirror looked back at him with hunger."
>
> —*Casino Royale*

RIGHT THERE, IN ONE OF THE RANKER PASSAGES in the paperback library of male chauvinism, we have the curious genesis of Supergirl Oktyabrina. Russian sailors, true to a seafaring tradition transcending any narrow political interest, carried copies of Ian Fleming's adventuristic and sexploitative novels back to the motherland in the late fifties. As "smuggled works from the West" have a way of doing in Russia, James Bond books floated to the top of the pile of reading of the bored and generally well-to-do young intellectuals who were to become the hard core of Russia's underground dissenters in the sixties.

There is a little of the Aztec princess and a pinch of a Nordic god in Oktyabrina's origins, and there is a crude cosmetic coating of Little Annie Fanny in her appearance (the sailors brought in *Playboy*, too), but her soul belongs half to the romantic, escapist, and bizarre strains in nineteenth-century Russian literature and half to Vesper, the scrumptious superlady double agent sharing top billing but the bed bottom with James Bond in *Casino Royale*. The Russians, in creating their fantasy character composite, succeeded in doing for Vesper's memory (Fleming, naturally, did away with her after vanquishing her) what even an occupying women's liberation force could never accomplish with Fleming's publishers—they freed Vesper from her subservience to James Bond.

Supergirl Oktyabrina travels as freely as Tinker Bell and lays more men than Catherine the Great, and all on her own terms. When she is roughed up a little, it is all for a good political point. In one episode, *Pravda* is given a left jab when Oktyabrina is carried off by a gorilla right on the cover of one of those hard-to-get Russian underground publications and raped on the inside pages. (Russian copyright law may be rather lax in this regard, as this is not at all unlike an episode in *Casino Royale* wherein Vesper gets kidnapped and Bond puts forth this traditional "just like a woman" male stream-of-consciousness: "...for Vesper to fall for an old trick like that and get herself snatched and probably held for ransom like some bloody heroine in a strip cartoon. The silly bitch.") Following Turgenev, the contemporary Russian antipolitical pornographers are true to the tradition of strong women in Russian literature. The end result of the rape seems totally within her control, and she comes out on top politically: the cover picture of the gorilla carrying away our heroine is slugged with a standing headline redundantly familiar to *Pravda* readers: "The Life of the Party."

Oktyabrina thus has a heavy pedigree, but no observable parentage. Only two members of the widespread groups which created and sell (in limited editions at a hefty five new rubles a copy) her offensive exploits have, in the real Bondian tradition that the group follows, surfaced: one is locked up in a lunatic asylum (an effective KGB method of disposing of dissenters without too much fuss) and the other has made his way to the West and is now trying to sell the printed exploits of Supergirl Oktyabrina to, surprise, *Playboy* magazine. The remainder of the membership of the PPP might as well all be named Lamont Cranston for all the KGB has been able to find out about them, which is all the more extraordinary since PPP magazines of regular frequency are published in Moscow, Kiev, and Tbilisi, in Stalin's homeland of Georgia.

In the loony bin and very out of favor is PPP's Lydia Borisovna Gall, adopted daughter of Anastas Mikoyan, who is also out of favor but not that much, and whom devotees of *Time* magazine's current-events quiz may remember as a top Kremlin aide in the Khrushchevian era of relatively good feelings (circa 1954–61). Young Lydia was one of the privileged and disenchanted Russian youths who pioneered the subversive publishing movement centered around Supergirl Oktyabrina. It has no formal letterhead for obvious reasons, but is generally known as the PPP (Peredavaya Politicheskuyu Pornogrefiyu), which translates fairly literally as Progressive Political Pornography. The other known PPP member is a young Czech filmmaker named Peter Sadecky, who left home clandestinely in 1967 with a laundry bag jammed with some five thousand PPP drawings, ranging from Oktyabrina's comic strip exploits to compromising and scatological drawings of revered Russian figures from Lenin to Brezhnev. Sadecky is both close-mouthed about his former compatriots and guarded with his treasury of Oktyabrina drawings, which, perhaps, he hopes to have published in book form in the West and which he has offered to *Playboy*. But the journalistic honors for discovering Oktyabrina must go to an unlikely candidate, the literary supplement of the conservative Paris daily *Le Figaro,* which treated French intellectuals to Oktyabrina's grim but girly visage in 1968. An enterprising leg man apparently found copies of the Oktyabrina comic strip floating around Paris salons amid other underground literature pouring out of Russia. Hugh Hefner, you have been scooped at your own skin game by *Le Figaro Littéraire.*

"Erika makes four copies,
Not much, but enough.
For the time being let
There be only four copies,
It's really enough!"

—Alexander Galich, underground ballad in praise of *samizdat*

ERIKA IS A TYPEWRITER. She is a rather disappointing typewriter if you are an aesthete of typefaces, as typewriters manufactured and used in the Soviet Union have a dreary sameness of print. That turns out to be a plus because the Erika celebrated in the sub rosa ballad of the otherwise orthodox playwright Alexander Galich is among thousands of machines used to turn out carbon copy volumes (the KGB has discovered that it can't trace even the freakiest characteristics of a particular typewriter after the first carbon) of literature forbidden by the Soviet authorities. The amazing flow of this underground communications system, which includes tape recordings of Western songs, secretive exhibitions of avant-garde art, and microfilmed copies of books and manuscripts both smuggled into and out of the USSR, is lumped together in the Russian *samizdat,* a word which is a dirty pun played at the expense of *Gosizdat,* the more or less camp abbreviation for the Russian state publishing house, Gosudarstvennoye Izdatelstvo, which is to monopoly communism what the telephone company is to monopoly capitalism. The *sam* part means "self" in Russian. To avoid tedious linguistic analysis, the coined word is adequately, if loosely, translated as "we publish our own thing."

The *samizdat* movement is largely a boom product of the hardening of the Russian cultural arteries in the Brezhnev-Kosygin era, following Khrushchev's thumping de-Stalinization campaign in the fifties which aborted in the early sixties, somewhere around the time Dean Rusk looked at Khrushchev eyeball to eyeball. The *samizdat* underground railway functions as a sort of combination domestic and foreign intellectual Pony Express for less-than-favored literature. It has, for instance, brought Orwell's *Nineteen Eighty-Four* into the Soviet Union and Alexander Solzhenitsyn's *The Cancer Ward* out.

The Soviet government, even in its tough-minded state, has adopted a relatively tolerant attitude toward *samizdat*—at times suppressing it, always watching it, occasionally toying with it. While Mondadori, the Italian publisher, was secretly negotiating for permission to publish *The Cancer Ward*, it is reported that the KGB arranged for a *samizdat* copy of the novel to surface in England. As long as the Russian authorities retain some measure of control, *samizdat* undoubtedly has its own peculiar value to the regime on the intellectual homefront—it provides a sort of perverse release valve for the pressure-cooker tactics of the official censorship bureaucracy and maintains the patina, and the eternal breast-fed hope of Soviet intellectuals, of free literature and free thought in the Soviet Union.

The *samizdat* tradition has become so voguish that it has begun to inbreed. It makes jokes in *samizdat* about itself, utilizing a sort of urbanized *New Yorker* ennui. One popular story has a Russian bureaucrat returning home from a trip and discovering his wife feverishly typing out *War and Peace*. When he asks her why, she explains that their teenagers won't read any book that isn't a poorly typed carbon copy.

> "Active resistance is nonsense. They would crush us like fleas and would boast of this as historical justice. Take flight into dreams and don't give a damn about ideals. To the Party slogan, 'All energies for the establishment of Communism,' we reply just as dogmatically, 'All energies for copulation with Maria Ivanovna.'"

> —statement of the PPP

THE PPP MOVEMENT REPRESENTS a distinct stylistic break with the mainstream of Russian intellectual dissent in this century. It is unreasonable, crude, and nihilistic. Its literary and political manners are such that the bravest of Russian writers, who have been willing to suffer the rigors of Siberian labor camps or outright imprisonment and death for their liberal views, would find the PPP decidedly uncomfortable if not completely repugnant. For the liberal movement in the Soviet Union is, in fact, liberal: it accepts the legitimacy of the Soviet state and its institutions as constituted, but sees the need for reforms and progress within the delicate channels established by the uncodified but mutual consent of the Communist Party bureaucrats and the left and right elements in the central writers' organizations. In that sense, most Russian intellectuals are not willing to go for broke because going for broke—in most cases—means losing Russia. Thus Boris Pasternak openly begged Khrushchev not to expel him from Russia when the Party went on the warpath over his receipt of the Nobel Prize, and Alexander Solzhenitsyn writes his novels "for the drawer" in the certainty that, one day, the liberals will again gain the upper hand in the intellectual world, as they did under Khrushchev.

The PPP's break with this tradition of civility and liberalism represents a serious intellectual chasm in Russian society. Just how serious a political question it may become rests on the extent of the PPP's membership and the scope of the influence of its nihilistic sensibilities; that is at the present more of a matter for cultural than political detective work. The fact that the KGB has been unable to root out the PPP in a decade of trying means, in the most cynical interpretation, that the PPP is a KGB propaganda ploy to vulgarize and discredit legitimate intellectual dissent, which is an unlikely alternative since the PPP literally shits on Brezhnev. The other alternative is that the movement is simply too widespread and organizationally amorphous to track down. In that case, the KGB may be no more efficient than the CIA, which would explain everything.

The established facts about the PPP would hardly fill a sketch pad for an Ian Fleming chapter. Centers of its activity have been variously reported in Leningrad, Moscow, Kiev, Tbilisi, and Kishinev. Its hardcore membership consists of some one to two hundred sons and daughters of the educated middle class, some of them formally artists, writers, and poets, most of them informally so. They represent a cosmopolitan spread of nationalities: about one quarter Russian, the rest of the stock from Georgia, Armenia, the Ukraine, and central Europe. One harbinger of the trend of cultural if not political dissatisfaction in the Soviet Union is that many of the alleged centers of PPP influence (and the strength of the broader *samizdat* movement) lie in the scientific and technological circles of Russia rather than in the universities. (One of the KGB's rare discoveries of an actual illegal printing press—hot type and all—was traced to the engineer-officers of a Russian submarine who were turning out *samizdat* over vodka.)

The PPP allows one story about its origins. It goes that its alliterative name had birth during a Soviet filmmaker's extracurricular tour of Greek houses of ill repute when he noticed with his camera eye that the Greek letter "pi" was painted three times on some establishments' exterior walls—a symbol as universally recognized as the three balls of the American pawnbroker. The Russian letter for "p" was so similar to the Greek "pi" that inevitably the pi-pi-pi became the PPP. That story is representative of the quality of American Legion convention fun that is recurrent in PPP humor. That is, of course, the PPP's heritage from the West. And for that Supergirl Oktyabrina thanks you, Al Capp.

[*Scanlan's Monthly,* May 1970]

Maoists in Limerick and
Other Pogroms of Modern Ireland

"We give the people what they want."
                    —Limerick mayor Stephen Coughlan

"When the mob poured out from Mount St. Alphonsus after
Father Creagh's speech, the first and nearest Jewish home
was my father's. They broke the windows and smashed in the
door. When our family, as I was told, took refuge in an upstairs
room, they smashed everything they could lay their hands on.
For months Jews were starved into submission and beaten.
My sisters, aged seven and eight, were the sole sources of food
supply."
                    —Alderman Gerald Y. Goldberg of Cork

*T*HERE ARE SOME PEOPLE who go to Ireland by submarine, but they
shouldn't. Roger Casement, the famous Irish patriot and pederast,
rowed ashore in Kerry in 1916 and came to only grief. Sean Russell,
the Irish Republican Army leader whom Franklin Roosevelt locked up
in Detroit when the king and queen of England visited America, died a
natural though unpleasant death aboard a German submarine just one
hundred miles from Galway in 1940. It remains unproven that it was
an atheistic sea power which brought six Irish Maoists by underwater
means to the riverport of Limerick last Christmas. However, there have
been nothing but demented goings-on in Ireland since.

The right-wing IRA moved to the left; the left-wing Labour Party
moved to the right; the Maoists were bombed, stoned with rocks, and
then shot at in Limerick; the two most prominent ministers in the Irish
government were arrested for gunrunning; the mayor of Limerick gave
an anti-Semitic speech and was defended by the son of the former Jewish lord mayor of Dublin; an old-fashioned gang of bank robbers had the
run of the country like Jesse O'James until the banks were all closed

down, indefinitely, by a strike in which most of the tellers forsook settlement and went away to England to count British money instead; the prime minister announced that contraception was up to the individual conscience, then Irish Customs began seizing packages of spermatocidal jelly which colleens had hastened to order by mail from abroad; Bernadette Devlin lost her image as Joan of Arc, an image replaced in the conservative Irish press by that of Rosa Luxemburg.

Other terrible things have happened also, to which we shall proceed, and the sophisticates in the Baggot Street pubs in Dublin this once agree with the black-coated ladies standing at the bars of the one-room grocery stores in the poor villages of Connemara: Ireland has not been in such a condition of fantastic chaos since the Civil War of 1922. The country made more sense in the mad days before the Second World War, when Brendan Behan took up the study of infernal machines under the great explosionist James O'Donovan at the IRA's finishing school in Killiney and then went off to do in the British before the Germans got to them.

But unlike the Civil War, or the Rising of 1916, when—even though it was Ireland—events could be traced to a definable start if not to a discernible conclusion, contemporary Ireland is a wonderful witch's cauldron of boiling Guinness into which one can put a ladle all night long and always spoon out a different crisis. Take care not to get burnt, and we will have potluck with the Maoists of Limerick.

[ECHOES OF THE INTERNATIONAL
MIDDLE-CLASS MAOIST CONSPIRACY]

It should come as a surprise to none but the Irish that Maoists come in a variety of colors and often derive from good middle-class stock. Sophisticates of Dublin, where Maoism was launched in the land of saints and scholars in 1965 at that hotbed of radicalism, Trinity College, got that picture early and watched somewhat bemusedly as the Maoist ranks swelled during the last five years to a total of twenty. In that period the Maoists' Internationalists/People's Rights Organization/Irish Revolutionary Youth managed to promote a modest anti-imperialist riot during the visit of the Belgian royal family in 1968 and to set up small bookstores in Dublin and Galway. Recognizing that having propaganda outlets only at universities in the Irish equivalent cities of New York and San Francisco left something to be desired in terms of class analysis, a small contingent of the Dublin Maoists made a fateful decision last fall to locate in the southwest market town of Limerick, the better to infiltrate the workers. This was in the Irish tradition of bravely attempting the improbable under circumstances that make it impossible.

Limerick is a quintessentially conservative city. Its population of fifty thousand is more semi-proletariat than middle class, and the town is all but completely run by a Catholic cultural and social chain gang called the Arch Confraternity of the Holy Family. In addition to staging bingo games and four-nights-weekly devotional sessions at which attendance is taken, the Confraternity has successfully harassed Limerick's only discotheque as a suspect source of wet dreams and sent flying squads of purity vigilantes into the back rows of movie houses to break up couples.

An ancient city at the mouth of the River Shannon's estuary, its face distinguished by bridges and battlements and pockmarked by warehouses and rundown homes, Limerick in recent decades has suffered compounded frustrations in the decline of its port and the accompanying indignity of existing in economic somnolence in the shadow of the nearby Shannon Industrial Estates, where most of Limerick's working citizens are employed. But this was all dough for the doughnut to the Maoists, who were led to this promised land of cultural exploitation and economic depression by Arthur Allen, a typical Irish Maoist who turns out to be the son of one of Ireland's wealthiest textile manufacturers. Young Allen and his compatriots took jobs in the Industrial Estates, began to publish a small newspaper which they handed out to workers in pubs, and were immediately and widely rumored to have been put ashore from the submarine of an unfriendly foreign power. But they worked hard and saved their money, and, acting just like the characters in a typical capitalist success story, shortly after Christmas they opened a Red bookstore in the heart of Limerick on the mistaken tactical assumption that they were fish in water.

The Maoists thus became bait for the hook of the mayor of Limerick, Stephen Coughlan, a sportsman who has been known to go fishing with a Gatling gun. Mayor Coughlan, whom even the reserved *Irish Times* was moved to call "The Bad Seed" for his role in the dirty business that is to follow, was looking for something with which to snare the rank and file of the Irish Labour Party, for which he holds the parliamentary seat from Limerick in the Irish Dáil. He accordingly instituted a vicious pogrom against the naive Maoists and was so successful in inculcating fascism in his city and party that, had he been Hitler, it would have been unnecessary to burn the Reichstag.

The mayor's sense of urgency was prompted by high dudgeon, but also by alarm at the attempt of a Dublin cabal of left-wing swingers and socialist sophisticates to take over the ideological direction of the politically and intellectually rudderless and rural-based Labour Party. This group included the American left's hero, Dr. Conor Cruise O'Brien, returned to Dublin to make domestic political hay; Dr. Noel Browne, a prominent psychiatrist and left-liberal thinker; and television personality David Thornley.

A word here about Irish politics, because the players are more interesting with their programs. It would not be controversial to say that there has been no such thing as an Irish left, or even the rudimentary analysis to develop one, since the death in the Easter Rising of the brilliant Marxist and nationalist James Connolly. Twentieth-century Irish politics have subsequently been largely a politics of oligarchy, the ruling parties either satisfied with Ireland's semicolonial status with Britain or unconscious of it. The only serious political issue in Ireland has been what was historically argued as the "national question"—that of the "free statism" (accepting, to varying degrees, the evils of some bond to Britain and a temporary separation from the six counties of the North) as opposed to "republicanism," a term which used to mean the total and absolute separation from England of a reunited Ireland, but in contemporary politics is subject to as many definitions as "democrat." With the simple caution not to repeat this indiscriminately while drinking in Ireland, we must make the outrageous deduction that the basic political difference between the two dominant Irish parties, Fianna Faíl (seventy-five seats) and Fine Gael (fifty-one seats) is twenty-four seats. Both parties are centrist and pragmatic, and both share the same essential biases: pro-Catholic, pro-capitalist, anti-British (but practical about it), anti-ideological, and therefore anti-leftist. In the exercise of these biases Irish politicians range from middle-of-the-road to extremist, which defines, more or less, their political position. And there you have it.

That being the extent of the political game at home, there was little
else for an Irish liberal intellectual like Conor Cruise O'Brien to do but
join the foreign service and travel, which he did, or give speeches for
the likes of Eugene McCarthy in America, which he also did. But here
he is, back again, and why? For one thing, Ireland is a great place to live,
but you need something interesting to do or you will go bonkers after
a while. Conor Cruise O'Brien's attempt to assume political leadership
in the Labour Party (he won a seat for Labour in the Dáil in a Dublin
by-election) reflects the belief of many Irish intellectuals that there is a
new potential in Ireland to develop social and socialist issues in politics.
This new soil, they hope, is the product of fertilization from the long-
range effects of the belated but final acceptance of the Irish government
of the need for industrialization and economic planning (which came
decades late and barely, but hardly in time to save the west of Ireland
from complete ruin) and the accompanying broadening of education
necessitated by the continuing urbanization. Right or wrong, that analysis is, at any rate, partially the cause for the salivation by certain intellectuals at the thought of the discombobulated but at least up-for-grabs
Labour Party. Part of our story is how they fared in their idealism, for
it was the presumption of making a leftist experimental farm out of his
grassroots Labour Party that set Mayor Coughlan off and running over
the Maoists.

[GETTING A LITTLE HELP FROM THE
REDEMPTORISTS AND THE NEO-NAZIS]

Having just invested all that money in their little Red bookstore, it
is of course understandable that the middle-class background of the
Maoists would have some vestigial influence on their first big political
decision in Limerick. They voted, democratically, not to participate in
a planned protest against the Limerick visit of the Springboks, South
Africa's whites-only rugby team. The Springboks, on a tour of Ireland,
had been met with pickets, boos, boycotts, and fistfights virtually everywhere they went. The Maoists felt that it was too early in the game to
endanger their presumed standing in the community and their property
by showing up at what was certain to be a violent protest in Limerick.

Subsequent events taught the Maoists a lesson about where prudence gets you on the left. They boycotted the demonstration but were blamed for all the trouble anyway, an accusation which led directly to the burning of their surplus property of little Red Books. That learned 'em.

Stephen Coughlan, who runs Limerick as a feudal fiefdom, promulgated in his wisdom that the Springboks would be welcomed in Limerick. So Limerick gave the racist rugby team a welcome. Coughlan thus socked it well to his intellectual enemies in the Dublin wing of the Labour Party who had played key roles in organizing the protests against the Springboks. Conor Cruise O'Brien lectured the Irish press on the application of pure political principle, suggesting that the national newspapers should not report the activities of such a racist organization. Ironically, the Dublin papers would soon have an opportunity to throw that demanding question of principles back at Dr. O'Brien when he was faced with resigning from the Labour Party or staying in an organization that had by then formally included Mayor Coughlan's penchants for fascism and anti-Semitism under its umbrella of permissible political principles. Not to keep you in suspense, Dr. O'Brien stayed in. And the Irish papers, run by gentlemen, didn't even raise the question.

Mayor Coughlan was helped by his two favorite Limerick organizations in preparing a proper welcome for the traveling racist ball club. That would be the Arch Confraternity, run by the traditionally reactionary Redemptorist Order, with whom Coughlan has close personal and political ties, and another cooperating organization known as the National Movement, a largely illiterate Limerick group of amorphous purpose whose literature is clearly inspired by that of the American Nazi Party and whose behavior is modeled after Ireland's infamous "Blueshirt" fascist movement of the Fine Gael in the thirties.

The *Limerick Leader,* a newspaper that sees eyeball to eyeball with the mayor, was also right on with a front-page banner that read "WELCOME BOKS." When the team left town with every honor but palm leaves strewn before their feet the *Leader* headline read: "STRONG SILENT TYPES FLY OUT." The Arch Confraternity made sure its six thousand members were out on the streets to wave a good Irish hello to the South Africans, some of whom had taken to wearing raincoats while in Dublin to avoid sudden expectoration showers. And the National Movement did its civic duty by parading its members with signs that read "SUPPORT SOUTH

AFRICA'S WHITE PEOPLE." The Movement men also beat up the few out-side agitators who traveled down from Dublin to protest, and that was where the Maoists—even though they weren't there—got in trouble with the Lord. And it was a Jesuit who framed them.

It is instructive to study this incident because it gives a good example of the effective cooperation of church and state in modern Ireland. We must rely on accounts in the Limerick press because we could obtain no comment from the agent in question of the Society of Jesus, who, in pursuit of his priestly duties, attempted (and missed) a flying tackle of an anti-Apartheid youth who was fleeing the National Movement's attack force. The priest's missed tackle was nowhere as myopic as his story the next day that he had been set upon by a band of Maoists who knocked him to the ground, spat on his priestly presence and that of God within him, and otherwise verbally and physically abused the Lim-erick Arch Confraternity itself.

[ANTI-SEMITISM CAN MAKE FRIENDS AND INFLUENCE COALITIONS]

Things then happened to the Maoists faster than the eye can read. The Redemptorists revenged the downed Jesuit at Sunday Mass in a hellfire sermon which condemned, without definition, the Maoists' "Tin Gods." Mayor Coughlan arranged for all six Maoists to be fired from their jobs. The *Limerick Chronicle* warned: "The number of Maoists in our midst can be estimated at more than 200 and the number is growing." Women threw stones at the bookstore. The mayor warned all Limerick's pub owners, in writing, that a person who would serve a Maoist a drink must be presumed to be a Maoist sympathizer, at the very least. The bookstore was firebombed.

The *Limerick Leader* wrote in an editorial: "We say that the Irish Revo-lutionary Youth Movement must be crushed in Limerick and they must be run out of this city without delay." The Christian brothers preached a sermon. The bookstore was bombed again. Coughlan issued a for-mal statement: "As Mayor of Limerick I wish to alert the people to the dangers of the insidious propaganda by left-wing agents of a foreign power…" A speeding car loosed a shotgun blast into the now charred bookstore; the charge was aimed at the place where head Maoist Allen usually sat—but he wasn't there that day. The mayor formally allowed the neo-Nazi group to present a petition against the Maoists at the Limerick Corporation meeting; the petitions, signed mostly by Catholic workingmen who were told to sign by the priests at Arch Confraternity meetings, said in no uncertain terms that Nazis do not like communists. So much for the Maoists.

Coughlan's open support of fascist attacks on a leftist group brought bloody screams from the liberals in the Labour Party. The mayor of Limerick replied that the Maoists deserved all they got. "I could see this coming all along," he said, with a measurable tone of proud civic prescience. Even wishy-washy Brendan Corish, the Labour Party leader, who happens to be a drinking and racing buddy of Coughlan's, found that reply a little impolitic of the mayor. But he cringed at torrid suggestions that Coughlan be tossed out of the party. Division in the ranks, and all that. Then there was the ever-present question of a coalition with the opposition right-wing party, Fine Gael, where Coughlan had considerable support. Finally, Corish came up with an Irish compromise: a vapid motion of criticism of the Limerick mayor was passed overwhelmingly by the Labour Party's Administrative Council at their March meeting, along with a highly vitriolic condemnation of those troublemaking Maoists...

And what more could one man do to his party? Just three weeks later, the Irish papers were filled with reports of a massive split in the Labour Party over Mayor Coughlan—but it was not about the Maoists. Almost everyone had forgotten about those poor persecuted fellows by then, because the mayor had taken on a slightly larger minority: the Jews. Addressing the convention of the Credit Union League of Ireland, the mayor allowed to the delegates that credit unions were very good things because Jewish moneylenders of old in Limerick, whom he referred to as "bloodsuckers," used to take terrible advantage of the good Catholic citizens of his town.

As the delegates looked on in what observers described as acute disbelief, the mayor continued in a familial manner: "I remember when I was a very young boy, and I am practically sixty years of age now, the problem of the Jews in Limerick. A Father Creagh, in his courageous way, declared war on the Jews at Killooney Street. The Jews at that time, who are now gone, were extortionists. At the time Father Creagh declared war on the extortionists, he had the backing of everybody in the city of Limerick." Many delegates began shouting at the mayor to shut up, some using less-than-polite phrases. The mayor registered surprise at this reaction and immediately volunteered one case that he knew, when the Limerick Jews took the bed right out from under a pregnant woman because she couldn't pay her debt. The meeting broke into a general melee; the mayor broke into tears, and the delegates reconvened to note with alarm the mayor's anti-Semitic remarks and formally denounce his analysis.

The campaign of Father Creagh's that brought tears of affection to Mayor Coughlan's eyes was, in fact, nothing but a pogrom. Father Creagh, a quite mad Redemptorist priest who wanted to punish the Jews for killing Christ, in 1904 whipped up Limerick Catholics to a point where they beat Jews on the streets, broke into their homes, and abducted their children. Eventually, some two hundred Jews fled the city. The *London Observer* called the incident "one of the most infamous episodes in recent Irish history." The *Irish Times* was moved by Mayor Coughlan's remarks to worry in print about the latent anti-Semitism in Catholic Ireland, a concern reinforced by the reaction of the official church. The archbishop of Cashel and Emly remarked that he "did not judge that the situation warranted the issuing of a statement." The archbishop of Limerick at first had no comment; later he issued a statement that seemed to whitewash the mayor.

Mayor Coughlan issued an apology which itself is a candidate for the collected speeches on anti-Semitism. He said that some of his best old friends were Jews, that he apologized for using the word "bloodsucker," and at any rate had only used it in reference to dead Jews, not live ones, that his mother once helped some Jews get into a tennis club in Limerick, that criticism of him for anti-Semitic remarks was part of a left-wing conspiracy against him within the Labour Party, and that, anyway, the Labour Party should be "big enough to contain all shades of opinion, for this is the essence of democracy." The Jewish community in Ireland at first reacted sharply. But within a few days, it amazingly began to seem as if some of the mayor's best new friends were Jews. The chief rabbi hastened to accept Coughlan's apology, Jewish businessmen wrote him letters of praise, and when alderman Gerald Goldberg of Cork, whose father was beaten in the Limerick pogrom, dismissed the mayor's apology as unsatisfactory, Ben Briscoe, the son of the former Jewish lord mayor of Dublin, attacked him as "a man with a very large chip on his shoulder."

Meanwhile, back at the Labour Party disciplinary proceedings, Mayor Coughlan stood accused of embracing the trinity of racism, fascism, and anti-Semitism. He said calmly that he gave "the people what they want," and reminded everybody that the party had fared disastrously in the last election, for all its big-shot left-wingers. The vote was 16 to 10 to "warn" rather than to "discipline" the mayor. Six key party members, including the financial secretary, resigned in protest. Dr. O'Brien, who resigned his United Nations post in Katanga over his principled sense of anti-imperialism, stayed in the party. When last heard from, he was giving law-and-order speeches in Dublin in an attempt to topple the wobbly government of Prime Minister Jack Lynch to make way for that coalition government with the right-wing Fine Gael. Perhaps he might be named foreign minister and thus be able to get out of the country again, back to the real world of principled politics.

As we walk away from the wreckage of the Irish left which is now in as many pieces as the statue of Lord Nelson (a graphic reminder of Ireland's British past which you used to have to drive around on O'Connell Street until the IRA rubbed it out with a dynamite eraser in 1966), let us bid an awed farewell to Mayor Coughlan, who, according to the *Irish Times*, had just taken "three days off from municipal duties to attend Killarney races in his private capacity as a bookmaker."

[THE FOLLOWING IS INCOMPLETE BECAUSE IT HAS UNDERGONE CENSORSHIP BY THE GOVERNMENT OF IRELAND]

The preceding is a reasonably complete review of feature-length pograms now playing in Ireland. But there is other late-breaking news from the island republic which has put the government uptight. The IRA has split into Red and Green armed amoebas. The Red, dominant in the South, is seriously Marxist and is going slow on the traditional IRA politics of guns, concentrating on developing socialist programs for Ireland. It remains willing, however, to punctuate its proclamations with bullets. The Green IRA, closest to the traditional republican anti-British military force, is concentrating its activities against English soldiers and Ulster Protestants in the besieged northern six counties.

This development in the IRA is a matter of serious concern to both liberal and extremist republicans in the government. Prime Minister Jack Lynch, who is betting his career that Britain will be able to handle the crisis in the North for him, knows that the Green IRA forces in the North are being financed by prominent members of his own party. On the other hand, the extreme pro-Catholic and pro-capitalist republicans in Lynch's party don't like his reliance on the British and are most disturbed at the idea of the new southern IRA becoming Marxists with guns. Blowing up the British is fine but, as the Red IRA did in 1963, blowing up an American fishing boat in Galway as a symbol of exploitation by foreign capital is quite another thing to conservative republicans. These tensions, largely unreported, undoubtedly played an exacerbating role in the extraordinary occurrence last month when Lynch unexpectedly fired his two most prominent cabinet ministers, Charles Haughey and Neil Blaney, at 3 a.m. Eric Ambler time and had them arrested the next day on charges of gunrunning.

The Irish government, on June 4, officially refused to release a press cable filed to *Scanlan's* by Proinsias Mac Aonghusa and supplying details important to this analysis, on the grounds that the contents of the cable threaten national security. It was the first act of formal censorship in the Republic of Ireland since the Second World War.

> "The Prime Minister is guilty of the greatest treachery of which an Irishman could be guilty."
>
> —former government minister Kevin Boland

> "This is a party of ignorance and fanaticism which has fallen on their heads and will fall on our heads and the heads of the people."
>
> —Conor Cruise O'Brien

[*Scanlan's Monthly*, July 1970]

A Patriot from Esteria*

*T*HE JUDGE WAS SURPRISED. It was to be but a routine pleading by a routine gangster. His name was Johnny Roselli and he was, by reputation, a rather bad fellow. He had run numbers and broken legs and leased wires for the mob in Chicago, Las Vegas, and Los Angeles for the better parts of half a century. The latest crime for which he had been found guilty was that of cheating at cards. Roselli's card-cheating was not of the garden variety. He drilled peepholes in the gilded ceiling of the card room in Beverly Hills' exclusive Friars Club and spied down upon the celebrity gin-rummy players below, sending electronic signals to his confederates at the card tables who took unfair advantage—in the aggregate of some $400,000—of club members of the cut of Phil Silvers and Zeppo Marx and Harry Karl, the millionaire shoe man otherwise known as Mr. Debbie Reynolds.

The judge had given Roselli five years. There were many in the movie colony who considered this permissive treatment for a man caught cheating the pants off Hollywood's finest. Yet Roselli had petitioned the court to reduce his sentence. This petition was not supported by his former friends Dean Martin and Frank Sinatra, who had put their countryman up for membership in the Friars Club and were trashed by him.

Roselli had not appreciably improved his manners since he fled Eliot Ness and moved west to become a "muscle man" in the Hollywood extortion rackets of the forties. It was this unreconstructed past, together with the bizarre nature of Roselli's petition, that contributed to U.S. district judge William P. Grey's considerable surprise on the afternoon of July 6, 1971. The mobster's lawyers rose in the brightly lit, antiseptically modern federal courtroom in Los Angeles and dramatically requested that Judge Grey reduce their client's sentence for card-cheating

*Coauthored with William W. Turner

on the grounds that this one-time associate of Al Capone was an unsung hero of the Cold War—a secret American patriot who had risked his life attempting to assassinate Fidel Castro for the CIA.

The silver-haired gambler was fashionably dressed for his day in court in a neat dark-gray suit and a red turtleneck sweater with a gray stripe. He sat attentively at the defense table, the diamond-brightness of his gambler's eyes softened by stock dark glasses. Roselli politely declined to answer the judge's prompt questions about the CIA on the grounds that he was sworn to secrecy under a national security oath.

The United States Attorney bounded to his feet; to call Mr. Roselli an American hero was to mock the Alamo. He pointed a prosecutor's finger at the dapper, hawk-faced offender—alias Filippo Sacco, as he was born in Esteria, Italy, in 1905, alias Don Giovanni, as he was known to his Mafia cohorts—a man known to keep the company of the likes of Bugsy Siegel, Frank Costello, Meyer Lansky, Anthony (Little Augie Pisano) Carfano, and Lucky Luciano, a convicted extortionist of over $1 million from Loew's, Fox, and Warner Brothers studios, the stylish front man overseeing the mob's Los Angeles–Las Vegas gambling axis, a frequent invoker of the Fifth Amendment whose one brush with respectability was a stormy marriage to actress June Lang. "Your Honor," declared U.S. Attorney David R. Nissen, "this man is a menace to society." Yet, according to government documents, this was the man the Clandestine Services of the United States had drafted to murder Fidel Castro.

In their haste to establish their client's bona fides as a patriotic assassin, Roselli's lawyers were to put into the public record certain names and facts that they perhaps should not have. The name of William K. Harvey was one. William Harvey was a ruddy-faced giant of an intelligence agent who headed the covert action or "dirty tricks" section of the CIA in the early fifties. He was in residence at the Berlin station in 1956 at the time of the fabled "Berlin tunnel," which the CIA dug to tap the telephone lines of Soviet military headquarters in East Berlin; the Russians eventually discovered the tunnel and it became something of a minor tourist attraction.

In 1959 Harvey was assigned to the interdepartmental agency team which made up the command of the Cuba Project. While his colleagues planned the Bay of Pigs invasion, Harvey plotted perhaps his biggest dirty trick—the assassination of Fidel Castro. In furtherance of this goal he recruited John Roselli. The gangster graciously refused the usual CIA contract operative's salary, asking only that some expenses be paid by the government. The expenses were never totaled, but they embraced high-speed motor launches, handcrafted Belgian hunting rifles with "sanitized" bullets, poison capsules, and comfortable quarters in far-flung hotel suites. Roselli worked for Harvey from 1960 through 1963, during which time he ramrodded six attempts on the life of the Cuban premier. This was done at some risk to the gambler's life and limb; once his speedboat was sunk from beneath him by the Cuban navy. Roselli's lawyers held the courtroom spellbound with fantastic tales of domestic intrigue and Caribbean derring-do that ranged from the Desert Inn in Las Vegas to the Fontainebleau in Miami Beach to the Hilton in Havana and implicated both the Chicago crime syndicate and the Howard Hughes business empire in clandestine United States intelligence operations.

Washington has found it expedient in the past to cooperate with organized crime. Lucky Luciano helped keep the labor peace on the East Coast docks during World War II and was subsequently released from the penitentiary for conduct unbecoming a gangster. Meyer Lansky, at the behest of Naval Intelligence in 1944, paid a special visit to his old associate in the businesses of liquor and gambling, Fulgencio Batista, to deliver the bad news that Franklin Roosevelt desired Batista's retirement from the profession of president-dictator of Cuba. And there have been other accommodations. But the employment of Johnny Roselli was the first known time, even off the record, that the government has attempted to utilize that aspect of the syndicate known in the pulps as Murder, Inc.

Roselli's fifties gambling connections in Havana made him a natural for the assignment. In 1960 he still had excellent contacts within the politically controlled cooks' and bartenders' union, whose pension funds, in pre-Castro days, were used in building the Havana Hilton in the same manner as Teamster pension millions have been invested in gambling-connected edifices in the states. His union cronies put Roselli in touch with a chef in the kitchen of the presidential palace in Havana; this was a vital connection, for Roselli's first assignment from the CIA was to poison Fidel Castro.

Among the documents used to support the mobster's contention that he had served his country as a special operative of the CIA were FBI reports viewing with alarm the close working relationship of the *capo*-mafioso with the intelligence agency. The ever-resourceful FBI had followed Roselli to Miami Beach, where it discovered him holed up in the swish Fontainebleau Hotel with two high-level CIA agents; all three registered under fictitious names. The FBI identified the CIA men as William K. Harvey and James "Big Jim" O'Connell. While rooming with the CIA pair, Roselli caucused with his old Mafia confederates in the better nightspots along the Miami Beach strip. Unable to restrain its curiosity, the FBI approached the gambler and attempted to recruit him as an informer about the CIA's domestic monkey business. Roselli refused, and the rebuffed FBI increased its surveillance.

Posing unconvincingly as a Wall Street lawyer whose clients sought revenge on Castro for confiscating their Cuban holdings, Roselli preened about Miami recruiting Cuban exiles for his project and availing himself of the remaining mob pipelines into Havana. There are indications that the syndicate was more deeply involved in the assassination maneuvers than the singular presence of Johnny Roselli might imply. Roselli was known, for instance, to have enlisted the aid of Sam Giancana, the Chicago rackets boss, in lining up hit men inside Cuba. And, true to his word, Roselli ponied up most of the expenditures—amounting well into the six figures—himself; it is doubtful he would have spent the money or the time on the project without the blessing of the mob seraphim.

One is loath to question the patriotic motivation of the syndicate, but it should be pointed out that if the joint Mafia-CIA venture to murder Castro had been successful many advantages would have befallen the party of the first part. The return of its Havana gaming tables and ancillary graft would have been true manna from heaven for the mob. It is a fundamental assumption of syndicate theology that the Lord helps those who help themselves first, and the Mafia overlords were fully prepared to take advantage of the miraculous sudden death of the puritan Cuban leader. Roselli's first hit was timed to coincide with the Bay of Pigs, and on the eve of April 17, 1961, waiting in Nassau, in the wings of the theater of the invasion, was Lansky lieutenant Joe Rivers—with a stable of gaming technicians ready to reactivate the casino equipment and a stash of cash to grease the wheels, just in case a miracle came to pass.

The poison the CIA concocted to do in Castro was an innocent-appearing liquid in a small capsule; it was slow-acting, killing in three days, by which time all trace of the poison would have left the victim's system and a physician of average competence would be forced to diagnose the cause of death as a heart attack. On March 13, 1961, at the Fontainebleau Hotel, Roselli delivered the capsule with Fidel's name on it to a Cuban courier. By prearranged route; the courier was infiltrated into Cuba, making the crossing from Miami in a fast boat manned by an armed crew, and delivered the vial to a chef in the presidential palace in Havana. Then the conspirators had nothing to do but wait. Their expectations soared when it was reported in the Cuban press a few days prior to the invasion that Castro was ill with an undisclosed malady. However, on April 17, when the scattered invasion force stumbled ashore at Cochinos Bay, Castro had dramatically recovered and ably directed the defense of his island.

The poisoners in Miami were agonizingly uncertain about what had gone wrong. They elected to try again, this time with a larger dosage. Three weeks after the Bay of Pigs, Roselli slipped a triple-strength capsule to another Cuban courier. The courier was landed in Cuba but never heard from again and Castro, as far as is known, never had another sick day in his life.

Roselli checked out of the ill-fated Fontainebleau and into a motel on Key Biscayne. There he organized a more traditionally Mafia-hit attempt using crackshot Cuban exiles with power launches as seagoing getaway cars. The CIA provided Belgian FAL rifles equipped with sniper scopes and communist-made ammunition. The syndicate man complained that he would prefer good American weapons, but the CIA boys insisted on foreign arms, explaining that it was standard "sanitation" procedure in such matters; should the assassins be captured, all precautions must be taken to avoid the "Made in USA" stamp on their mission.

Twin powerboats were used on the assassination team's midnight run to Cuba. Roselli rode one boat to make sure that his charges did not waver in their treacherous resolve, and it was here that he got wet. A Cuban patrol craft discovered them close to shore and tore the bottom out of Roselli's speedboat with .50 calibre machine-gun fire. The mobster jumped overboard and was pulled aboard the second boat as his sank. The launch full of assassins outran the Cuban patrol and raced back across the moonlit Caribbean to Miami.

Roselli thereafter became a strictly landbound plotter, engineering another three attempts on Castro's life during the next two years. He was abetted in these by his CIA "control," in the persons of agents Harvey and O'Connell, who provided the bucaneering gangster with special two-way radios tuned to Castro's security channels. Roselli's other marksmen managed to hit the island, but they never got near enough to Castro to draw a bead on him. The attempt that came closest was the last. In March of 1963 a trio of Roselli's men were arrested while setting up their homicidal apparatus on a Havana rooftop across the street from a public building where Castro was scheduled to visit. Other attempts were planned but never carried out, and in June of 1963 Harvey told Roselli that the CIA was washing him out with an "E" for effort. "I did it all out of patriotism" is all that Roselli, supremely faithful to his national security oath, will say. Harvey, now retired and living in Indianapolis, is similarly tongue-tied, except to say that he has a "high regard" for Johnny Roselli. There are, after all, not that many mobsters who take a bath for the CIA.

Roselli's lawyers had one more stroke to complete this portrait of the gangster as James Bond. The CIA operative who originally recruited Roselli was one Robert Maheu—the right-hand man of Howard Hughes and the boss of the recluse billionaire's Nevada gambling interests. The patriot from Esteria sat demurely at the defense table as his attorneys extolled his high-blown business relations with Howard Hughes and his patriotic if murderous undercover work for the secret government of the United States. Surely here was a man who deserved the mercy of the court. The surprised judge said he would take the CIA material under submission, although he expressed some judicial misgivings as to its relevance to a $400,000 gin-rummy swindle in Beverly Hills.

Johnny Roselli was sent back to McNeil Island Federal Penitentiary without getting time off for his good behavior in the Caribbean. His unsuccessful attempt to cash in on his CIA connection caused a flurry of coverup activity that presaged the Watergate tentmaking that would occupy many of the same disinformation artists a year later. As pious as the mafioso had been about keeping his blood oath of silence, he had said enough in open court to imperil the shadow alliance of the underworld, big-business, and United States intelligence operations that was the nexus of the Cuba Project. These alliances did not prosper in the harsh light of day. When Johnny Roselli sang his assassination song as if it were "The Star-Spangled Banner," a good many normally patriotic people did not stand up.

In Robert A. Maheu's office high above the Las Vegas strip, the telephone jangled annoyingly. Maheu answered with a sigh. It was the fifth call in thirty minutes from Los Angeles reporters. Would Mr. Maheu care to comment on the statement made that afternoon in federal court that Mr. Maheu, the manager of the Howard Hughes holdings in Las Vegas, was also a CIA bag man who had hired a notorious mobster to do in Premier Castro of Cuba? Bob Maheu was a short man with a round face and receding curly hair and the pleasant gaze of a Rotarian Santa Claus. He was a former FBI agent, former head of an international public-relations and private-investigation firm that put his "Old Boy" FBI contacts to profitable use, and a devout Roman Catholic and family man. He was paid $500,000 a year by Howard Hughes. One of his duties was to lie if necessary.

There were certain matters that Mr. Hughes wanted in the press and others that he did not, and it was Maheu's charge to see that the earth revolved around his boss. When Hughes wanted the world to know that Hughes Aircraft had built Surveyor II, Bob Maheu arranged it, despite a NASA rule prohibiting product identification in the space program. At Cape Kennedy, Maheu hired an RCA employee who played Scrabble with the astronauts; later, out in space, one of the new American heroes just happened to let the name Hughes Aircraft slip out during a moon walk back to his craft. Maheu was usually successful. His one failure of record was in 1960 when Hughes instructed him to delay a story about a $205,000 loan to Richard Nixon's brother Donald, but Drew Pearson, the feisty Quaker columnist, refused to be reasonable. There was but one other task at which Bob Maheu labored in vain: Johnny Roselli didn't kill Fidel Castro.

Robert Maheu had been a contract employee of the CIA from the mid-fifties. Like most CIA operatives he is loath to talk about even what he had for breakfast while on a CIA expense account. But in 1974 Bob Maheu broke radio silence about the Mafia-CIA joint venture to do in Castro in the same forum that Johnny Roselli chose—in court. His motivations were not dissimilar from Roselli's. Maheu had suffered a stunning falling-out with his billionaire boss—Hughes convened a

bizarre telephone-hookup press conference to unkindly depict his former employee as "a son of a bitch who stole me blind"—and Maheu's
lawyers had responded with a $17.5 million slander suit. It was by way of
establishing the sterling attributes of Maheu's character that his lawyers
questioned him in court about his government service, albeit service in
the secret government. Maheu disclosed that in late 1960 or early 1961
he undertook, with Hughes' permission, a "very sensitive assignment"
for the CIA. The assignment was the elimination, for reasons of compelling national interest, of the communist, contrary ruler of Cuba. In
this high purpose Maheu recruited a gangster and introduced him to his
friends in the CIA. Maheu remained deeply involved in the operation
for two years, and made several trips to Miami with Roselli in pursuit
of their mutual goal.

The red flag raised by Johnny Roselli's late-blooming attempt to take
refuge in patriotism encompassed substantially more than the controversial politics of assassination. It involved the interlocking of secret-
intelligence projects with private gain that was the way of life of the
Cuba Project. Howard Hughes, as we shall see, was up to his uncut
three-foot fingernails in such practices. Even Johnny Roselli got a piece
of the action. The mobster, introduced to the Hughes court via the back
door of the CIA, came to perform some business functions for the billionaire that were not to be sneezed at.

As Maheu recalled it, Roselli provided the "grease" for Hughes' entry
into the starry world of Las Vegas gambling. Said Maheu, delicately: "I
told Mr. Hughes that I thought I had found a person fitting the background that he had requested me to seek, to wit, a person who had
connections with certain people of perhaps unsavory background as
described to me by sources in the United States government agencies...
the FBI and CIA." The problem was that the hygiene-frantic Hughes
wanted to rebuild the entire ninth floor of the Desert Inn as a germ-
proof haven for himself before he would settle down in Las Vegas to
play Monopoly. The proprietors of the Desert Inn were the intractable
gentlemen of Cleveland's Mayfield Road gang, who were unenthusi-
astic about the remodeling, as the ninth floor was reserved for private
accommodations for the casino's high rollers. Exhibiting the diplomatic
skills of a Mafia Kissinger, Roselli was able to intercede on Hughes'
behalf with the Cleveland people and convince them to give the bashful

billionaire his way. Hughes liked the ninth floor of the Desert Inn so much that he decided to buy all the others, and Roselli helped arrange the sale, pocketing a $50,000 "finder's fee."

There were thus several matters to be covered up on that July afternoon of 1961 when Bob Maheu was being beseiged by the newspapers. Howard Hughes of course did not desire his business dealings with Johnny Roselli reported on the financial pages; the CIA understandably preferred that its liaison with the syndicate remain an in-house secret; and Maheu, for reasons which will shortly become clear, could not afford to have himself or his boss linked to the CIA. In the days of the pre-Watergate press, when national security was not a phrase of levity, and power was still presumed to be practiced by responsible men, the bold lie was a more effective exercise in prevarication than it may be today. So Robert Maheu answered the reporters' preposterous questions about his and Howard Hughes' ties to the likes of Johnny Roselli and to the CIA. He summoned all his soft-spoken authority in reply: "I will not dignify such a story by even commenting upon it," he said. And it worked.

In the course of a two-year investigation of the Cuba Project, the authors have conducted more than seventy interviews with persons who worked for the CIA or had first-hand knowledge of CIA activities— ex-CIA agents and contract operatives, exile Cuban commandos, American paramilitary specialists, private arms brokers, sources in organized crime and in law-enforcement intelligence. Based on their accounts— supplemented by corroborative research—we have been able to piece together a broad outline of the CIA's plans to murder Castro. As far as we have been able to trace them, assassination attempts were made over a five-year period—from 1961 to 1965. In addition to Johnny Roselli's round half-dozen tries, there were at least another five CIA-connected plots to take Castro's life. In all but one, CIA recruiting and equipping of assassins was done in the United States. The agency used the U.S. naval station at Guantánamo Bay in Cuba as an infiltration base in three assassination efforts. The last agency-supported plot for which we have been able to establish independent verification was in February of 1965 and involved E. Howard Hunt, then on "deep cover" CIA assignment in Spain, playing out his last Cuban hand before Watergate.

The dimensions of the CIA's participation varied in each plot. But in all eleven instances CIA personnel provided technical equipment, funds, and transport to the conspirators. Many details of these dark activities are still lost in the cloud cover over the agency's covert operations, but enough facts have now been established to afford an overall view of the CIA's deployment of assassins in the Cuba Project.

The CIA prefers to keep its successes secret and rarely comments on its failures, even in its own defense. The one exception to this mute rule was the Bay of Pigs. In the aftermath of the disaster that was the agency's Dunkirk, CIA director Allen Dulles took the then unprecedented step of replying to the agency's critics. He denied that the CIA had expected a popular uprising on the island coincidental with the invasion, as many of the CIA's critics had asserted. "We were expecting something else to happen in Cuba…something that didn't materialize," Dulles said. He did not elaborate.

What the CIA expected, according to reliable intelligence sources, was that when the invaders landed, Fidel Castro would be dead—and his island in leaderless chaos. It was hardly a matter of wishful thinking. The CIA supported two separate but equally unsuccessful assassination plots timed for the eve of the invasion. Johnny Roselli's poison capsule was the failsafe alternative lest the main plot fail. The primary assassination plan involved ranking Cuban government officials and military men who were secretly members of Unidad Revolucionaria, a coalition of anti-Castro factions inside Cuba working with the CIA to develop underground support for the coming invasion. The conspirators planned to kill both Fidel and his brother Raul. The chief assassin was Commandante Humberto Sorí Marín, a revolutionary hero who had been with Castro in the Sierra Maestra.

In an interview with the authors, a man who knew the assassins and both their intended victims described the CIA's role in the plot. Andrew St. George, a journalist who was with Castro in the Sierra and who later had extensive contact with the CIA and exile Cuban commando groups, said that the CIA infiltrated four operatives into Cuba to join the Sorí Marín conspirators. The agents were caught red-handed meeting with the plotters when a routine Cuban security patrol quite accidentally came across a clandestine gathering of the counterrevolutionaries a short time before the invasion-assassination target date. St. George said the CIA supplied the assassins with cases of plastic bombs the Cubans call *petacas.* The conspirators planned an incendiary attack in downtown Cuba to create confusion to aid the assassin's escape.

The *petacas* were smuggled into Cuba on the *Tejana III*, a converted subchaser outfitted by the CIA with concealed deck armaments and exhaust mufflers. It was part of the fleet of heavily armed converted patrol craft and supercharged pleasure cruisers the CIA operated in the Caribbean until approximately 1965 as an ersatz "navy" servicing the agency's anti-Castro operations. The *Tejana III* was the main transport for the assassins and their CIA connection. The vessel would pick up the conspirators—many of them *commandantes* wearing their revolutionary uniforms—from small boats off Cuba by night and spirit them across the Caribbean to Marathon Key off the U.S. mainland for conferences with their CIA mentors and then return them to Cuba. The CIA did not run the *Tejana III* as a very tight ship. Several paramilitary sources readily identified it as a CIA craft and knew of its service with the Sorí Marín conspirators. In another vein, the captain of the *Tejana III* once complained to a journalist about having to take CIA agents water skiing in the Caribbean.

The key figure in the twin assassination attempt, Johnny Roselli, never knew he was part of a double-barreled plan. In the terminology of what E. Howard Hunt has referred to as the "Clandestine Services" of the United States, he did not have the need to know. And when Roselli, after his initial miss, carried on with the aid of Chicago Mafia overlord Sam Giancana in another five hit attempts, the agency again set up a parallel series of assassination efforts—this time out of the U.S. naval station at Guantánamo Bay.

Before turning to the Guantánamo assassination plots, it would be instructive to consider the manner in which the extraordinary story of the gangster and the CIA was surfaced. It is an object lesson in the elusive alliance of powerful businessmen, the CIA, and organized crime that is recurrent in many domestic CIA operations—particularly its Cuba operations.

Roselli's relationship to the CIA was first reported by Jack Anderson in 1971. His account was strenuously denied by the CIA at that time. Anderson said he could not disclose his sources, but insisted that they were extremely reliable. Former assistant U.S. attorney David R. Nissen, who prosecuted Roselli for his high-stakes card-cheating, told the authors that an off-the-record interview with Roselli, then in the penitentiary, was arranged for Anderson in 1971 by Edward P. Morgan, a former FBI man who is the Washington, D.C., attorney for Howard Hughes. Anderson's subsequent columns about the gangster's CIA exploits were then introduced in court by Roselli's lawyers as proof of his patriotism in the unsuccessful effort to reduce Roselli's prison sentence for his Friars Club conviction. By having the columnist indirectly tell his story for him, Roselli could attempt to influence the court with his government service while still nominally keeping his oath of secrecy.

Howard Hughes' involvement in CIA anti-Castro operations may extend beyond Robert Maheu and Johnny Roselli. Several paramilitary experts have told the authors that a mysterious Caribbean island called Kay Sal, leased by Hughes and adorned with "Keep Out" signs in the names of the Hughes Tool Co., was used during the sixties as a frequent jumping-off point for anti-Castro commando raids against Cuba. (Kay Sal is located in the Bahamas chain some thirty miles off the coast of Cuba.)

The last known time that the mob and the CIA cooperated in an attempt to hit Castro was in the spring of 1963—Roselli's last try. But there are some indications that the syndicate carried on alone for a period. The involvement of Howard Hughes' attorney in an apparent attempt to aid an imprisoned mafioso could stem from Hughes' business dealings with Roselli, in which the gangster received a $50,000 fee for helping Hughes acquire a prime Las Vegas gaming temple. But that would ignore Hughes' close or organizational ties with the CIA. Underworld sources believe that individuals in the CIA used the Hughes organization to pay off a marker given the gamble that the agency would do what it could to help him in difficulties with other government agencies; if so, the CIA did it in a way that was fully deniable and, accordingly, when Jack Anderson published the story of the CIA's dealings with Roselli, it denied it.

The CIA's serial failures to assassinate Fidel Castro in eleven attempts over five years are due at least in part to Castro's determination not to play sitting duck. The wary Cuban premier has developed the instinct of self-preservation into almost an art form. During his visit to the United Nations in 1960, he warded off potential poisoners by sending his bodyguards out to buy food from different restaurants, which Castro

selected each mealtime by a different number—such as "seven"—
which meant that the bodyguards had to pass seven restaurants before
entering the next one. But the CIA's assassins never got near enough to
test Castro's vaunted luck. The agency's assassination plots were foiled
by double agents Cuban intelligence had planted in the circle of CIA
conspirators.

In 1961, while mobster Johnny Roselli was still playing out his string
of attempted hits in a futile effort to fulfill his contract with the CIA,
the agency initiated several well-plotted schemes to eliminate the revolution's leaders. The new plots all centered in the United States naval
base at Guantánamo Bay, on the southeastern shore of Cuba. These
assassination attempts were carried out with the cooperation of the
Office of Naval Intelligence, according to reliable sources in the intelligence community. ONI had earlier worked closely with the CIA, using
the Guantánamo base to infiltrate CIA agents into Cuba prior to the Bay
of Pigs invasion.

The first plan was to shoot Fidel's brother Raul, the head of the
Cuban armed forces, when he appeared at a revolutionary celebration in
Santiago on July 26, 1961. A key participant in the conspiracy was Luis
Balbuena, a former theatrical booking agent who was a Cuban employee
of the naval base. Balbuena was identified in a Miami Police Department
intelligence report as the "contact between United States Naval Intelligence and the Oriento (Province) underground." The Miami authorities
said Balbuena had been "involved in an attempt to assassinate Raul Castro." The assassination was supposedly to be followed by a staged shell-
ing of the navy base to make it appear the Cubans were taking reprisals
for Raul's death. Cuban intelligence uncovered the plot, and Balbuena
took sanctuary in the naval installation, where he remained for several
months before being transported to the American mainland.

A second Guantánamo conspiracy ended on September 25, 1961,
when Cuban police arrested twelve men who had been preparing a
bazooka barrage—zeroing in on the speakers' platform at the Havana
sports stadium where Fidel Castro was due to orate. One of the arrested
conspirators was Luis Toroella. In his recent book, *Inside the Company,*
ex-CIA officer Philip Agee wrote that he had trained an agent named
Luis Toroella to penetrate Cuba from Quito, Ecuador, where Agee was
stationed. Agee wrote that he did not know Toroella's mission because

the CIA's Miami station was giving the agent direct instructions by radio.

A month later, Cuban G-2 smashed a third assassination plot in which the would-be triggerman had been infiltrated into Cuba from the Guantánamo base. The regularity with which the Guantánamo-based plots were being discovered by Cuban counterintelligence convinced the CIA that a double agent was operating at the base and further actions were called off.

While there have been reports of a good many other CIA plots to kill Castro, the last CIA-connected attempt for which the authors have been able to establish independent verification was in February of 1965. A prime mover was Manuel Artime, a Bay of Pigs veteran known in Cuban exile circles as the CIA's golden boy because of the alleged favoritism displayed to him by CIA agents organizing the invasion brigade. Artime is now a well-to-do Miami businessman. But until 1965 his stock and trade was rougher stuff. He headed a Cuban exile commando group headquartered at secret bases in Costa Rica and Nicaragua. Between 1962 and 1965, the CIA underwrote Artime and his men terrorizing the Cuban mainland to the amount of some $6 to $8 million.

The Madrid assassination plot was to be coordinated with a lightning raid by Artime's commandos to take power in Cuba. The architects of the conspiracy were Artime, a Cuban Army major named Rolando Cubela, and several CIA agents in Madrid. One of those agents was E. Howard Hunt. Hunt's participation has been ascertained from reliable intelligence sources and from Cuban exiles intimately involved in Artime's operations.

Artime and Hunt have been close friends since they worked together organizing the Bay of Pigs invasion brigade. They were the Odd Couple of the invasion planners, set apart from the others by their distinctive blend of conspiratorial style and conservative politics. Hunt became the godfather to one of Artime's children, with much the same ideological and religious motivations that led William F. Buckley Jr., another former CIA agent, to become the godfather to Hunt's children. When Artime was released from Castro's prison after the Bay of Pigs, Hunt was the first person he visited; when Hunt emerged from his distressing Watergate months in prison, the first person he went to visit was Artime.

E. Howard Hunt resigned his position as chief of covert action of the CIA's Domestic Division in 1964. Early in 1965 he traveled to Madrid. In his recent autobiography, *Undercover*, Hunt wrote that he had to resign from the CIA and become a "contract agent" of the agency to undertake a "delicate but hardly time-consuming political action assignment" in Madrid. At that time, Hunt's good friend Manuel Artime was in Madrid arranging the assassination of Fidel Castro.

The CIA provided the conspirators with $100,000 in pocket money and a special marksman's rifle scope and silencer. Major Cubela smuggled the assassination equipment home to Cuba in a diplomatic pouch. He had it with him when he was arrested on February 25, 1965, along with other Cuban conspirators. It was later revealed at Cubela's trial that the plot had been undone by a Castro double agent named Juan Felaifel, who had been working as a CIA agent for the past three years in Miami. Felaifel had sacrificed his cover to expose the conspiracy. The double agent had passed eight CIA lie-detector tests and participated in seventeen CIA missions into Cuba from Florida while earning his pay from the agency.

In 1971 the operative question about the CIA's own politicalization of the hit-man tradition was asked in a Los Angeles courtroom. The question was raised by Johnny Roselli's lawyers, who argued that the gangster deserved a quality of mercy from the court because of his government service as a CIA assassin. The judge was not impressed.

"I don't see where Mr. Roselli is entitled to any brownie points," he said.

[*City of San Francisco*, September 9, 1975]

An IRA Woodstock

*O*N A MORNING GRAY AND BLACK, Bobby Sands' mother came to church. The funeral got there before her. Thousands of people gathered silently on a slight hill. She didn't look up. She had watched her son die by inches and her face was a map of grief. Don't feel sorry for the hero, feel sorry for his mother.

Bobby Sands died on a Calvary of his own choice. His last days were incredibly painful. His mother had held his hand as he lay dying. She walked into the church with the carriage of a sad queen.

Yesterday Belfast woke to silence. The night before there had been riots and burning. The town was tense and shopkeepers were crabby. The weather was clammy and the sky darkened as crowds gathered for the funeral.

St. Luke's Church was in Twinbrook Estates, which is Roman Catholic. A mile down the road the Royal Ulster Constabulary had put up giant screens around the houses in a Protestant estate, and the Protestants couldn't watch the Catholic mourners walk by. You could not pass a street without seeing a gun. A British solider with a machine pistol stopped me outside the Catholic area. I showed him some pieces of paper and he let me go by. "It looks like rain," I said. "Right-o," he said. Behind him was a battered gray Land Rover with a square hole in the rear door so soldiers could stick their guns out in a riot.

In Catholic South Belfast every store was shut. In the window of a closed meat market a pro-IRA sign was pasted next to yesterday's special. Schools were out and Catholic girls in blue sweaters and plaid skirts and white socks were on the streets. Double-decked buses went by with black flags of mourning waving out the window. Everyone was going to the funeral.

Twinbrook Estates is a new housing development of gray and tan buildings. The church was new, and people stood in the mud outside where the grass had never grown. Wives stood on top of husbands' shoulders. There was no way to see in the mass of humanity, and the crowd on the hill above the church was the first to see a lone bagpiper playing a dirge with all the sadness of Ireland, leading Bobby Sands' coffin toward his grave. Behind him was the empty black hearse with an Irish Scout on one side and on the other an IRA guerrilla fighter wearing combat fatigues and a green face mask. He carried a gold bugle. On the top of the hearse were folded Bobby Sands' black military clothes and his beret. The crowd reached twenty thousand before it left the church for the five-mile walk to the cemetery. But as people came out of their houses along the route, the black flag-waving crowd stretched back two to three miles and swelled to at least seventy-five thousand. When they finally reached Milltown Cemetery in Andersontown, the entire center of town was jammed with people. Throughout the three-hour funeral march, British Army helicopters kept crisscrossing over the procession.

I walked with an old IRA man. Jerry O'Daugherty, from Derry, is a walking Barry Fitzgerald. He wore a tweed overcoat with a black arm band and a gray hat that he says he had in the 1916 rebellion. His friends call him "The Bird" because he escaped from prison so many times. O'Daughtery himself was on a hunger strike for fifty days in 1943. Outside the cemetery, in front of a closed supermarket, three IRA combat men fired a military salute over the coffin of golden wood. The order to fire came in Gaelic. The mass of people in the streets and on the long, gradual slope leading into town was absolutely silent. The procession moved ahead into the large cemetery, which was a forest of gray Celtic burial crosses. It took an hour and a half for the last people in the long line of marchers to reach the cemetery.

At the gravesite, in a soft slanting rain, Mrs. Sands sat on a stiff chair in front of the grave, which was piled with heaps of flowers. A priest said the Rosary in a quivering voice that sounded like a mourn at the Wailing Wall. Then the speech came. The man who was Bobby Sands' campaign manager two months ago when he was elected to Parliament from his hunger striker's bed in prison was chosen to give the Requiem. Owen Carron was his name. He had black hair and black glasses and a short beard and a chin as straight as an engineer's slide rule. He spoke directly to Mrs. Sands. "Your son is indeed a hero," he said. "He has joined the ranks of Ireland's patriotic dead. You are the epitome of the generations of generations of Irish mothers who watched their sons go out to fight and die to end British rule. Bobby Sands was a very ordinary young man in this city who at the age of eighteen decided he could no longer accept second-class citizenship. He fought against the British. He died rather than be branded a criminal. He is the symbol of the moral right of the Irish people to struggle for self-determination. Because of his death, Irish Republican prisoners will never wear the British prison uniform or do prison work." Then Carron paused and leaned over the microphone and said to Mrs. Sands, whose face was streaked with rain, "Your son's sacrifice has not been in vain." Applause like thunder rolled across the cemetery.

The family left but the mourners didn't. After the funeral, lines of people stood in the rain for hours to pass the grave. As I left the cemetery five young girls stood arm in arm before his grave. They each took a flower from a wreath as a relic from a saint. I walked from the cemetery down the Falls Road, which has become the symbol of the most besieged of the Catholic areas of Belfast. There was half-light, and in the distance were the towers of downtown Belfast. The Falls had had a riot the night before, and houses and stores were still smoking. Glass, brick, and burnt-out cars filled the streets. An old woman was standing in the doorway of a little brick house. I stopped and asked her if she could tell me how to get to Belfast.

"This *is* Belfast," she said.

[WATCHING A RIOT BREAK OUT IN BELFAST]

Last night the riot started early. I was sitting in the Ashley Lounge on the Lisburn Road, a high-tone Protestant thoroughfare in Belfast. The news came over the telly shortly after 6 p.m. that Francis Hughes, the second IRA hunger striker, had died. "Good," said the man next to me. He spat on the floor. I left to be with the Catholics.

The unreality of Belfast is that everything is so close. If you can imagine San Francisco's Haight-Ashbury District being all Protestant and the Castro being all Catholic and the Richmond being half and half, with cops on patrol everywhere and an occupying army standing around street corners in military fatigues with M-1s in hand and everyone totally paranoid, you can begin to imagine Belfast. Five minutes from the Protestants I was among Catholics and being frisked by cops as I passed through the barricades of the central city toward the Falls Road, the largest Catholic ghetto. I stopped and had a drink at a Catholic bar for courage. I had to walk through a wire cage to get into it. Most of the Catholic bars in Belfast were bombed out years ago, and the remaining few are surrounded by wire cages. In Belfast, if you drink in a Catholic bar you look out at the world the way monkeys do in a zoo.

I walked through the street barricades into Divis Flats, an area of ticky-tacky high-rise apartments and burned-out brick buildings that begins the Catholic ghetto of West Belfast. The air was already smoky from fires. The first corner I passed, four British soldiers were hugged against the buildings with rifles pointed upward. It looked like Vietnam, except on the same street old ladies were walking and children were eating ice-cream cones. Normality and terror are together in this city like the fork and the plate.

In the Lower Falls, the barricades were already up. Kids were dragging bed springs and hunks of corrugated metal roofing and clumps of barbed wire to block off the street. An old man said to me this is the Agro Corner. This is where in the regular rioting that ripples Belfast the Catholics stop the British. The madness of the normality of it all was that as the preparations for riot went on, life went on. Black taxis, which are the only transportation from downtown Belfast to the ghetto—city buses no longer dare to come here—would slow down at the barricade where a car was now on fire and drive up on the sidewalk while kids pulled aside rubble so they could pass.

The sky was dark blue turning black and all over the street kids were putting on ski masks. Some masks were alpine blue and others striped red and white and some black with white tufts. All had eyeholes. A boy next to me was ripping up a gray Irish sweater and passing the pieces out to his friends. They cut eyeholes and put the handmade masks over their heads.

This was a community riot. Two girls were sitting on a bench with an old man. Behind them was a burned-out building. The two girls looked to be no more than eleven or twelve. They were putting stocking cap fuses into milk bottle gasoline bombs. The old man told them when they made a mistake. A third girl came up to help them. She put a ski mask over her face. If you didn't see the pigtails sticking out from her mask, you would have a perfect picture of one of the terrorists you see in the newspapers.

A reporter from an American wire service was next to me. Some kids came up and tried to sell him one of the plastic bullets that the British shoot at rioters. He'd already bought one. He'd been here for weeks. I asked him why he thought the British would send troops to Falls Road since it was obviously a totally Catholic enclosed area preparing to riot against troops. "It's part of the ritual night game here," he said. "Everybody plays out the trouble." When I asked him his name, he didn't want to give it to me. The press here is as uptight as the population. American reporters, since one got exposed for exaggerating, are trying not to have opinions.

All of a sudden the American reporter was running away. Two gray armored cars—called "pigs" by the rioters and the cops alike—crashed through the barricade and came down the street. Gasoline bombs flew like red hail. Hundreds of kids were running every which way and guns were fired from the armored car. I ran with some of them down a side street. As the armored car passed, I could see the snout of the gun, waving back and forth, shooting plastic bullets the size of jumbo hot dogs. One hit a young woman across the street from me. She lay on the sidewalk bleeding and a Catholic volunteer ambulance came and took her away. The people on the street said her name was Pauline Donnelly.

Everyone went back to the main street. Kids there were sharpening long sticks waiting for more British in the dusk. Another armored car went by shooting. A kid named Brian yelled at it: "Your mother was a hamster." There was smoke from burning cars and the sounds of sirens and people smashing curbstones to make rocks for throwing.

The streets were now full of people waiting to riot. The unemployment among Catholics on the Falls Road is so high that there is little else to do anyway. There was a sense among the people tonight that the death of the second IRA man was different. The IRA had controlled rioting after the death of Bobby Sands, and street demonstrations were said to be largely connected to kids being paid by French television newsies to attack the cops for good film. Tonight was the beginning of something different. Sands was an IRA volunteer, but the people here said that Hughes was a military IRA heavy. They spoke of him as part General Patton, part Superman, who had carried the war against the British in Derry. He was captured, they pointed out, in military uniform, not civilian clothes. As his life was not peaceful, people I talked with said what would happen from tonight on would not be peaceful.

The armored cars came down the street again shooting. Now the street was ablaze with firebombs. I found myself flat on the sidewalk next to a young boy. He had on a green-and-white stocking mask. When he got up he took it off and gave it to me. "Maybe this will fit you," he said. "It's too big for me." His face in the dark was full of freckles and he had a smile like an American toothpaste ad. His mask smelled of sweat and gasoline. Then the kid was gone, running after the tank that was far bigger than him. I watched him and the big ugly machine disappear around a corner.

[UNDER ATTACK WITH IRA MOURNERS]

The old bus from Belfast wheezed over a lovely hill in the manicured wilds of mid-Ulster. Below were rolling hedged fields and trees that looked like parsley in the distance and maybe five hundred cops, bottle-green dots amid the heather. "Jazzus, at least the Indians let the cavalry bury their dead," said a little Irish kid with a nose full of freckles pressed against the window.

This is the story of the hassling of an IRA funeral. It began with the attempted hijacking of the casket by the authorities and ended with the stoning of mourners by a Protestant mob. The woman in the bus behind me ended up in surgery after her head was bashed in by a rock. I was on a bus with people from the Lower Falls ghetto of Belfast who were going to the burial of hunger striker Francis Hughes last Friday as other Catholics go to Lourdes. The English called him a terrorist and a suicide artist, but to these people he was a war hero and a saint.

Mrs. McGarr, a lady of seventy-five years, frowned as the bus was stopped at a roadblock of armored Land Rovers and Saladin minitanks sealing off the southern Derry village of Bellaghy. Royal Ulster Constabulary cops in their green uniforms packing American-supplied M-1s stood across the road with their thumbs hitched into their flak jackets. Three British Army paratroopers in camouflage fatigues lay on the grass at the side of the road with their rifles pointed toward our bus.

I was looking out the window and found a Brit paratrooper in a green beret staring unpleasantly back. "These people torture you in life and then they want to pound you into the grave," said Mrs. McGarr. She cradled a clear plastic cross filled with red roses in her lap. Her frayed blue coat was covered with yellow petals that had floated down from the funeral wreaths jammed into the overhead baggage rack. We passed two more military checkpoints. When we were stopped a third time a man with a walrus moustache and a B-movie British accent got on the bus and told us to get out and walk. We were two miles from Bellaghy.

We made our way uphill along a backcountry road past an occasional farmhouse. A cold wind blew away the sun's warmth. There were aspects of Lourdes to the procession. A kid with one arm and twisted legs was pushed along in a wheelchair by a bent old man. A Mrs. Hanary, who was wearing a bandanna as white as her hair, trudged along lugging a huge floral wreath in each hand; as we walked on the bows began to dip in the mud. "You all right in the legs, luv?" a man asked. She nodded yes. "The Black and Tans and the B-men and the UDA and the pick of the British Army couldn't get these flowers away from me. I'm puttin' 'em on the grave meself," she said.

At the top of what the Irish call a wee hill was a view of fields spread over the ground like a green patchwork quilt around Bellaghy. From every direction rivers of people poured down the roads toward the Hughes family home, where the open casket of the shrunken-faced hunger striker had been waked. People were jumping fences and running over fields, and the crowds made deep trenches of humanity in the Derry countryside. A confused French journalist asked how big he should say the crowd was; I told him to write that it looked like an IRA Woodstock. You may have seen glimpses of the funeral on the TV news: the bereted and masked IRA honor guard in green khaki uniforms and Sam Brown belts, the coffin draped in the tricolor of the Irish Republic, the military salute fired over the casket as Irish women stepped forward from the crowd snapping open black and yellow and red umbrellas in the sun to protect the identities of the men firing from the British Army surveillance helicopter whirring overhead.

At the graveside, a prominent San Francisco Bay Area republican, Charlie Laverty of Richmond, was consoling the mother of the dead twenty-five-year-old IRA commando who always fought the British in a military uniform. Laverty is an upholsterer who left his Irish homeland in 1958 after serving time during the forties as a political prisoner.

"And how does it feel to be the mother of a saint, luv?" Laverty said to Margaret Hughes.

"Ah, I'm sure he's in heaven," she said. "He died with a smile on his face."

"Sure it 'tis, he's a saint just like the people on the pedestals in a church," said Laverty, who has a brogue as thick as Irish bread.

Mrs. Hughes was holding her son's military beret and black gloves tight to her breast. She took my hand. "Would you like to touch my son's gloves?" She touched my hand softly to the gloves as to a relic.

Laverty, who is "a sort of cousin" to the Hughes family, was with them during the unseemly tug-of-war over the body. This is how Laverty relates the events that took place on the same day the pope was shot. "We got to the Foster Green Hospital in Belfast at 2:30 p.m., the time the authorities had told us we could pick up the body. The family had brought a new oak casket and they changed him from the wooden one into that. All his brothers and sisters and relatives were there and we all said a prayer. We were just about to lift the casket when an RUC man came in and said wait a minute, there'd been a change." A while later two other RUC men appeared and announced they were taking possession of the dead hunger striker's body. "They said something about arresting the remains under the Flags and Emblems Act," said Laverty. "We told them no way they were taking Frankie's body." The family and relatives rushed into the small room holding the casket and crowded round it, protecting the dead from the cops with their bodies.

After hours of negotiations, Laverty said, the Hughes family agreed not to take the body through the Falls area. "They said they'd give us an escort part of the way to Bellaghy," he said. The hearse escort turned out to be a military convoy of the dimensions that broke Patton through France. Laverty said the cops had allowed a Loyalist mob to gather at the hospital that hooted and jeered at the mourning relatives.

The procession had been traveling several minutes when a line of policemen suddenly blocked off the road just after the hearse passed.

The Hughes family poured out of their cars to watch helplessly through the police line as RUC men surrounded the hearse, which was the proud property of Danny and Tom McCusker, brothers, co-owners, and undertakers. When the cops tried to get the keys from Danny, who was behind the wheel, so they could drive the hearse away, the undertaker said "over my dead body" and swallowed the keys.

The arrival of some unlikely Galahads, an American TV crew, put a stop to the "body-snatching attempt," Laverty said. This is not the type of film the British like to have on the news at eleven. After further negotiations the cortège was allowed to proceed again, the co-owner of the hearse having another key. About five minutes later the hearse was stopped again, "for no apparent reason," outside a Protestant estate where angry Loyalists who had gathered began to throw rocks. The cortège finally reached the tree-lined driveway to the Hughes home in Bellaghy six hours after originally scheduled.

After the funeral, there had been a two-mile hike back to the bus and then an hour's delay before the cops let it take off. Buses stretched along every road. More than two thousand buses had brought people that day from all parts of Ireland north and south—to bury the man the British had dismissed as a "terrorist."

On the trip back to Belfast, I thought about a conversation I had had at the funeral with two IRA men. I had told them that many Americans couldn't understand how they could allow their best men to starve themselves to death. They reminded me of Irish history, where the IRA has had its greatest victories in the violence it has suffered, rather than the violence it has meted out. The 1916 Easter Rising, when a small group of men seized the Dublin Post Office and proclaimed an Irish Republic, was by and large not a very popular act. It was Britain's cruel execution of sixteen men, with the wounded James Connolly shot strapped in a chair, that inflamed public opinion and led to England's eventual loss of the southern twenty-six Irish counties. The IRA men believed history would repeat itself, and the English would lose their hold on the northern six counties because of the growing public resentment north and south over the deaths of the hunger strikers. The one thing the Irish people won't stand for is Irishmen being murdered by the British, one of the IRA men said. "Call it a race memory or what you want, but we're seeing 1916 happen all over again."

The bus fell silent as we neared the town of Portglenone, which was a ten-to-fifteen-mile detour from the most direct route through the nearby Catholic town of Toomebridge. Portglenone is largely Protestant. "They did this on purpose, just to give the Loyalists a whack at us. They're spoiling to see some trouble, they are," said Seamus McAllister. They had blocked the Hughes funeral from proceeding directly to the church through the center of Bellaghy, which is some 80 percent Catholic, and forced the procession to take a three-mile detour through back roads to avoid what they called "the possibility of fomenting sectarian violence." Now they had routed a caravan of almost one hundred buses from a Belfast Catholic slum through a strongly Loyalist area.

"There's going to be pandemonium here, I can see it," said a woman sitting across the aisle. We were the third bus through. As we passed people glared at us from doorways. We got out of town safely, but the bus behind us was not so lucky. A hail of rocks trashed its windows and Mrs. Donnelly, of Harrogate Street in the Falls, was taken to the hospital with a head injury when the bus reached Belfast, and had her head operated on to relieve pressure from the wound. The buses farther behind were also stoned. People on them said the cops, who were all over the streets, did nothing to discourage the trashers. But when one of the stoned buses stopped and some men from the Falls got off to chase the rioters, "the cops started shooting rubber bullets at us and forced us back into the bus," said Fra McCann, a former H-block blanket man who was on the stoned bus.

As our bus neared Belfast, they took up a collection for a tip for the bus driver. I asked McAllister why they were doing that, since the driver was a Protestant: Catholics rarely get such jobs in sectarian Belfast. "Oh, we're not like that," said McAllister. "The poor man deserves a wee tip."

A bus inspector was standing at the entrance to the Falls. He got aboard and told the driver: "Everybody gets off here. You go back to the yard. They can walk the rest of the way." A flash of anger seared through the bus. A dozen angry men at the front of the bus screamed at the inspector. They had paid for the bus from the Belfast "Muni" and it would bloody well take them home to the ghetto. "It's either that or we'll burn it right here," a young man with flushed cheeks said. There was no question that he meant it. The inspector walked rapidly backward.

In the Falls, little kids were already dragging the jetsam of other riots together to form street barricades for the night's activities. When everyone was off the bus, the kid who had threatened to burn it told the driver he'd ride escort with him to see him safely out of the ghetto. "Otherwise one of these kids might stop you and burn the bus," he said. Not everyone here is into tit for tat.

[*San Francisco Chronicle*, May 8, 13, and 20, 1981]

The Crime Against Cuba

RONALD REAGAN IS A LIKEABLE LIGHTBULB SALESMAN with an empty shoebox for a brain. The only thing we have against him is that he is in the White House. Otherwise he'd be relatively harmless. Right now he's the most dangerous man in the world. He's hunkering to make war with Cuba.

The economy has gone the way of a dollhouse in a mudslide and the Great Communicator dearly needs a diversion to keep the grim reaper of public opinion from his door. From all available signs, he's settled on starting a street fight with Cuba. American intelligence is under no delusions about the ability of Cuba to fight back; the revolution hasn't survived twenty-two years because they're pushovers. Yet there is unnerving evidence that Washington is planning to unleash the so-called Cuban exiles—CIA-spoonfed drug traffickers and professional throat cutters who have made a Belfast of Miami—against the island of Cuba and to intervene militarily, via client armies under tinhorn generals, in the revolutions in Nicaragua and El Salvador—revolutions the Cuban people are committed to defend. This will mean one hell of a shoot-out in the Caribbean. Ronald Reagan looks at a map of Central America and he sees the OK Corral.

The dog barking at his master's voice in this derring-do scenario is Alexander "I'm-in-charge-here" Haig, the secretary of state who bears a certain resemblance to a daffy dowager. Haig's role has been to enunciate the Great Communicator's Latin American policy. This he has done so clearly that public doubts have been raised about his sanity. The Reagan administration's policy has been to bully and sabotage Cuba and through threats and economic and military support of goon squad governments such as that of El Salvador to turn back the clock of social progress; it is at least consistent that we have a Republican administration of the Coolidge model whose policy upfront is to make the world easy pickings for the United Fruit Company.

The urgency now is in the escalation. Although much of this has escaped the attention of mullahs of the national media, this is what has been happening: Reagan has green-lighted the hardhat boys who ran the CIA's still little-known secret war against Cuba, which ran the gamut from assassination to counterfeiting to biological warfare and was the occasion of sin for the marriage of the CIA and the Mafia. The Miami CIA station, which during the freebooting sixties was the largest CIA station in the free world, has been hurriedly restocked with low-floating logs from the espionage swamp. Redundant spooks have been demothballed out of retirement, former Cuban CIA operatives released by Castro during the Carter détente with Cuba put back to work, and the word from Miami is that some of the face cards of the bellicose sixties Miami station may be back in the game. These include such high trumps as Eugenio Martínez, the veteran CIA boatman and Watergate bungler, and Ted Shackley, the former Miami station chief who before his recent retirement from the agency distinguished himself by running interference with government investigators for Wilson and Terpil, the dropout CIA agents who became rent-a-spooks for Libya.

The new troops have a lot of backup. The government has installed high-tech listening posts outside Homestead Air Force Base and at the 1961 Bay of Pigs command post on a former navy base in Key West to bug phone calls to and from Cuba and snoop on internal communications on the island. New financial and business fronts for covert actions against Cuba have been set up, new resources made available in the terrorist Cuban exile groups which are once again foaming at the mouth in training camps from Southern Florida to Southern California. The Reagan administration's pious stand against "international terrorism" is two-faced; it is opposed to left-wing terrorists such as the Red Brigades or the PLO, but provides a sanctuary and intelligence support in the United States for the Cuban exiles who form the hit-squad core of an international right-wing terrorist network; these brutes are guns for hire of Latin American nations who want to kill off their exiled dissidents (remember the Orlando Letelier bombing in Washington, D.C.); and they murder the more moderate Cuban exiles in the United States with the abandon of a pigeon shoot. The bums who blew up a Cubana Airlines jet, killing the entire Cuban national fencing team, have openly bragged about their friendly relations with the CIA. In Reagan's myopic worldview, these killers are not terrorists.

Reagan's squeeze on Cuba is double-whammied. The exiles will be allowed to go ape on one front, while Haig's Ultimate Solution to the problem of legitimate social revolution in Central America is put into action across the Caribbean sea. Haig still thinks he's a general. He hardly can open his mouth but that the word "invasion" doesn't pop out. There was a lot of loose talk about military action against Cuba for supplying the rebels in El Salvador, until the State Department's embarrassing white paper on the subject crumbled into confetti.

Now we hear mutterings from Haig about not ruling out military force against the Sandinista government in Nicaragua—this from the same man who, when he was licking Henry Kissinger's wingtips, gloated over the secret bombing of Cambodia. Haig still thinks that the Soviet-run communist cell was the seed of revolution in Nicaragua, although most people who read anything other than Evans and Novak know that the village Catholic church was the unit of that revolution and remains the basis of its broad popular support. Maybe General Haig should invade the Vatican.

What the demented cowboys in the White House appear to be planning for Nicaragua is apparently not the Marines-type landings of 1896, 1899, 1910, 1911, and 1926. Vietnam forever devalued that coin with the American public. We have instead a crafty plan to use surrogate forces to do Washington's nasty work. While that swell anti-Semitic gang that runs Argentina will no doubt be willing to serve, the most likely possibility appears to be the formation of some Central American NATO using the mass-murderer governments of Guatemala and El Salvador as lynchpins. There is already the sound of muffled oars at night. The United States is quietly beginning to train the bloody-handed troops of the El Salvadoran military regime and is scheming a way to turn Guatemala into an arms and munitions manufacturing center to escape congressional controls over military sales. There are plots afoot to manipulate Honduras into this little war game.

It is not outside the realm of imagination to see this ersatz NATO go to the aid of the wretched El Salvadoran government, or start a beef with Nicaragua, which would call on the Cubans to help, which they would, and ultimately Argentina and possibly Venezuela and Panama and the like would jump in on the other side and we would have the beginning of World War III right on our own doormat in Central America. The word "doormat" is not ill-chosen, as that is the place where imperial America has traditionally wiped its feet.

Columnist Mary McGrory has observed that Cubans like everything about America except its government. This is something they share in common with many Americans. Yet if Reagan gets his way with the war he is cooking up, we would not be surprised to see the Cuban patience with the catburglar government ninety miles away wear thin, and the war come home to America. As sure as Reagan has uncorked the CIA by executive order, the country will become increasingly a land of paramilitary targets; if you live near one that you know of, move. As for Guantánamo, it won't last the length of a Monday-night football game.

America has robbed Cuba of many things, including the name of its own revolution. What our history books call the Spanish-American War was the Cuban-Spanish War for decades before. Cuban casualties and Cuban generals won the war. All Teddy Roosevelt and his yahoo boys did was run recklessly up a hill and kick some easy ass. The story has been downhill from there. From the Platt Amendment, which gave the United States license to interfere in Cuban self-determination, to the notorious alliances of American businessmen and American politicians with corrupt Cuban politicians who became filthy rich looting their own island, the history of our Cuba relations is a sorry example of American corruption and gangsterism making a mockery of American idealism.

From 1960 onward, the United States has attempted to economically starve our ill-used island neighbor off our shores, to isolate them diplomatically, to assassinate their leaders. That none of this has worked does not make it right. Emerson once said that in America when a mistake reached sufficiently grandiose proportions it was accounted an achievement. The way the Reagan administration is going, escalating the crime against Cuba may be its only achievement. The word for this is not diplomacy; it is thuggery. His own grandchildren will hate him.

[*Frisco*, February 1982]

Dateline: Cuba

*T*HE KIDS CAME LAUGHING DOWN THE STREET in Old Havana. They were singing a catchy little song in Spanish. "Is Reagan gay? Ask the USA" was the refrain. Havana is no longer an *American Graffiti* junk-yard of fifties cars, but certain things are not subject to change. One is the traditional Latin machismo attitude toward gays. Another is a certain view of the American presidency as the lair of a deranged eagle, although this is severable from a widespread feeling of friendship for the non-governmental American. I spent four weeks on this communist island, and no one said boo to me.

The popular media image of Havana as a Sargasso Sea of cannibalized Studebakers and Dodges and Plymouths is what you might call slightly exaggerated. Instead, it looks more like a Toyota ad. The streets are full of newish Russian Ladas, Argentine Fiats, and Polskis from Poland, a version of the VW dreamed up under a toadstool. The only time warp I experienced was when the spanking-new Cubana Airlines jet landed at Jose Martí International Airport in Havana with Glenn Miller doing "Little Brown Jug" over piped-in U.S. Muzak.

The Cuban revolution saved Havana's skyline from a fate like San Francisco's. When George Raft woke up with a hangover in the Capri Hotel on New Year's Day of 1959 to find the bearded ones smashing up his gaming rooms, the Mafia was building a wall of high-rise casino hotels that would have cut Havana off from the sea. The revolution that also kept Havana from becoming a Caribbean Las Vegas left it a human-scale city of classic stucco homes and apartment houses in whites and pastel blues and grays with red-tiled roofs and landscaped thoroughfares and parks. The only garish American note in post-revolution Havana is the huge blue neon sign atop the former Havana Hilton—now renamed the Havana Libre—which spells out Free Havana, beaconing like an impolite finger in the night toward the hostile USA ninety miles away.

From the roof of the Capri Hotel, you could hear the music from the loudspeakers of the government building on the street below. It was a medley of the Beatles' "Hey Jude" and Harry Belafonte's "Island in the Sun." When it comes to American music, Cuba is as eclectic as KABL. The sky was overcast and puffy like a gray bruise. The pool atop the Capri was crowded with sunbathers hoping for a break in the Caribbean clouds. A honeymooning Cuban couple huddled together for warmth; the woman was pretty and wore a full-bodied red bathing suit of the cut that was daring in early Doris Day movies. Next to them were a group of Spanish stewardesses in bikinis, and next to them a slick-haired Russian businessman in tropical shorts who was making notes in a morocco-bound notebook with a silver pencil.

"Americans are crazy," a Canadian businessman sunbathing in the haze was saying. "I've been coming down here for twenty years and making good money." He said his company sold the Cubans paper and chemicals and salt. "When they have hurricanes they run out of salt," he said sipping the rum of his Cuba Libre and puzzling over the sacred mysteries of Washington foreign policy. "Everybody does business with Cuba but the Americans," he said. "The Americans say Cuba is Russia's puppet, but look at all the business America does with the Russians. If you do business with the master, why not with the puppet?"

A Russian built like a tree stump walked into the pool area and stopped short and stared at the Astroturf around the swimming pool. He wore a T-shirt with Russian comic book characters on it and long black leather trunks. His skin was as white as talcum powder. He took a thick toe out of his sandal and poked at the Astroturf on the deck like a deer nudging grass. He picked it up and peeked underneath. "Why, he's never seen Astroturf before," the Canadian said. He tried to explain in broken Russian what Astroturf was. The Russian smiled and offered us Russian cigarettes. They were sort of like smelly Lucky Strikes. When I tried to get him to talk about Poland, he gave me a ruble as a souvenir and walked away.

"We are not like the Chinese. We don't tear down the monuments of our past," said a Cuban diplomat. We were driving down an elegant, tree-lined boulevard of Paris dimensions, past a showstopper monument that made the Lincoln Memorial look like a Cracker Jack prize. It had been erected in honor of the past presidents of Cuba—a very select club of embezzlers—by one of the grander thieves to inherit the former presidential palace. The diplomat laughed: "He was nicknamed the Shark because when he stole he splashed a little around to others."

The crew that Castro kicked out were no minor-league thieves. The story of the Cuban government before the revolution is simply the story of the theft of a nation. "I know of no country among those committed to the Western ethic where the diversion of public treasure to private profit reached the proportions that it attained in the Cuban Republic," former U.S. ambassador Philip W. Bonsal once said. One minister of education of that era was asked how he had managed to get some $30 million out of Havana to Miami in just over two years. He answered, "In suitcases."

We drove along the Malécon, the elegant highway that curves along Havana's seawall, to the old city, through narrow streets once walked by pirates, to the Floridita, where by popular legend Hemingway helped the bartender invent the perfect daiquiri. According to the 1950s *Esquire* article framed on the wall, the Floridita is one of the great bars of the world—in the company of the 21 in New York, the Shelbourne in Dublin and, this is news, the Pied Piper in San Francisco.

Like San Francisco, Havana is a city of restaurants. The Floridita is one of Havana's finest public rooms, an eating arena of glistening mahogany and ancient murals and curtained doorways. Old-timers say that nothing has changed since the revolution—the waiters look like thirty-year veterans of the likes of Jack's or Luchow's in New York, and bartenders who served Hemingway still stand behind the plank. It is amazing that nothing has changed because the government owns the restaurants; imagine the Washington Square Bar & Grill run by Dianne Feinstein.

What is different is the clientele. Where the silver-spoon set once exclusively dined, now the workers eat. There is something exhilarating, like seeing a Warren Beatty leftie movie, about watching guys in coveralls chowing down at lunch in a white-tablecloth restaurant being served by red-coated waiters. In the midst of this workers' paradise, I thought I spied a couple of capitalists. They were sitting at a table by the wall and acted like they had held it for decades. One had heavy cuff links and a shiny suit; the other an expensive blue polo shirt and sunglasses. They looked for all the world like the type of rich émigré Cubans you see in Miami Beach. All around, workers and their families were chewing and chatting, but those two seemed oblivious. "Oh yes," the Cuban diplomat smiled. "You see, we still have some bourgeois who stayed—we aren't as bad as Reagan says. We aren't against people having property—we're against them using it to exploit other people. They didn't participate in the revolution but they didn't do anything against it, so we don't hold it against them. We let them keep their homes; if they had several houses, we gave the extras to poor people but paid them the market price. If we nationalized their business, we pay them for it for life. They live quite comfortably that way. They have no need to work. They live in the old world—for them, there has been no change."

[BLACK MARKET TAPES AND OTHER SURPRISES]

The black marketeer was so excited he was letting his fish get cold. His long fingers caressed money as he talked. We were sitting at a restaurant counter in uptown Havana. He was telling the American about a deficiency of the revolution. He said he once had sixteen pairs of shoes in his closet and someone in his apartment building ratted on him and citizens with stern faces came and took fifteen away. He was left with only the alligators on his feet. This to him was a deficiency of the revolution. I said that in the four weeks I'd been in this economically blockaded city most of the people I met had shared the sensibility that everyone should have one pair of shoes before anyone had two. He shrugged and chugged at his beer. In Cuba, it is said, you are for the revolution or against it.

Cuba is in one respect a right-winger's paradise: all the able-bodied men have to work. Have a job or go to jail. The black marketeer didn't have a job. "I'm in the private sector," he said. A cardboard box full of tape decks was at his feet. "I procure what people can't get," he said in fractured English. He hacked at his cold fish like a sugarcane cutter. This was a busy man. He asked if I wanted another beer. I did. "Beers cost sixty cents. But you can't drink at the counter unless you order food. So I'll order a beer for you on my tab and you pay me eighty cents for the convenience," he said. Capitalism is alive and well in Cuba.

The black marketeer, who said he was a religious man, said that God had sent the recent plagues that have infected Cuba's tobacco and pigs and cattle and given the island's children dengue fever. Punishment for stealing his shoes. Most Cubans I have met here are of the opinion that the CIA had more to do with the plagues than God. But I told the black marketeer that I understood what he meant: when I went to school, the Jesuits taught me that homosexuality was the cause of earthquakes.

He left with his tape decks. An old Cuban man wearing a white rain hat had been sitting next to us at the counter. When he paid his check, he silently handed me the twenty cents the man in the private sector had scammed. In Cuba, you are for the revolution or against it.

Before the revolution of 1959, there were two Cubas. One was Havana, America's brothel, the empress city of organized crime, a *Guys and Dolls* Disneyland of gambling, prostitution, drug trafficking, abortion rings, and other immensely profitable sleazy activities. A large part of one million Havanans made their income one way or the other off this dreck. The other Cuba was the rest of this long, thin island, as large as the state of Tennessee, where five million people lived in huts. The illiteracy rate approached 50 percent and the children who survived the acid test of poverty grew up with parasitic infection and malnutrition.

The revolution confiscated the large, mostly American-owned landholdings and gave the land to the peasants and built housing and schools and hospitals in the country. Today the life expectancy in Cuba is seventy-two, rivaling that of advanced industrial nations; there is no unemployment; everyone has at least an eighth-grade education; rent is a maximum of 10 percent of your income; movies and concerts are the equivalent of a dollar; sporting events are free; public transportation is a nickel; and all workers get a month's vacation where the government picks up part of their tab at hotels or beach resorts. This may be communism, but some people like it.

Herbert Matthews of the *New York Times* once said that the Cuban revolution was one of the most poorly covered stories in the history of the American press. Maybe ditto for the great refugee exodus of 1980 from the port of Mariel. The press viewed it as a sign that Castro's regime was collapsing. The view you get here—and I heard this not just from Cubans but from foreign residents who are keen Castro watchers—is that Fidel snookered Jimmy Carter into taking a load of welfare cases and hustlers into the good old USA.

Over a million Cubans marched down the Malécon to demonstrate their displeasure with the one hundred thousand who left (Cuba's population is ten million), but from the government's standpoint there were singular advantages to the exodus. Castro relinquished a good deal of his prison population to the care and feeding of the U.S. taxpayer, and the migration allowed a way out for the most disgruntled segment of Cuban society: an estimated thirty thousand of those who left were gays, a good number of whom came to San Francisco. Although the Cuban officialdom has recently relaxed its attitude toward same-sex sex, this remains a decidedly machismo society where gays see greener grass on Castro Street than in Castro Cuba. Most of the straights who left were less traditional political refugees than they were consumer refugees— seekers after the designer jeans and other flotsam of the Good Life advertised on American television. After midnight, Havana television sets can pick up the Florida channels. People stay up late here.

The irony of the great migration is that Castro has repeatedly said that anyone who doesn't support the revolution is free to take a hike. The wrinkle is that the American government controls the spigot of immigration. It was when Carter decided to open the floodgate and let everyone who could swim come to Florida that Castro emptied the hedgerows of Cuban society. Many of the types who came by boat to Miami you would not be quick to invite to your neighborhood Tupperware party. According to Cuban police statistics, after the 1980 flock of refugees left for the United States, street robberies in Havana dropped by 50 percent.

"How many Cubans are for the revolution? That's the question everybody asks. Even after twenty years here I still can't say exactly—but there's no question that the majority of the Cuban people support it. Otherwise the government could never survive. Let's face it—for most of the workers, this country works," Lionel Martin said. Martin is the dean of Havana's foreign correspondents. He went to college at Berkeley and got into journalism and went to Cuba in 1961 and wandered into the Bay of Pigs waving his KPFA press card and has been here since. "I absolutely never thought I'd be here this long," he said.

Cuba is an island of surprises. What you expect to see before you come here is not necessarily what you get. You don't expect, for instance, to hear a lot of people openly mouthing off against the government on this communist island. But that's what you hear. "Criticizing the government is a national pastime in Cuba," Martin said. Martin is Reuters' man in Havana. We were sitting in the living room of his office, on the top floor of a seaside apartment building with an iffy elevator. A teletype was chattering in the next room. "What they're really paranoid about here is becoming another Poland," Martin said. Cuba's leaders are quick to criticize the Polish Communist Party, which they say screwed up royally, became fat and bourgeois and out of touch with the people. The Cuban government is going to extraordinary lengths to make its brand of mass democracy work. The columns of the state-owned newspapers have been opened to criticism, there are popularly elected municipal assemblies to bring grassroots opinions into party-decision making, and all factories have regular "production conferences" where workers criticize the managers.

A premium is put on party leaders hanging out with the people. In this as in most all things in Cuba, Fidel Castro sets the example. He frequently flies around the country in a helicopter, dropping in unannounced on farms and factories where he slaps the boys on the shoulders and asks if everything's going all right. This is a caudillo with an ear to the ground of public opinion. A couple of years ago, Castro read the riot act to the C.P. Central Committee, accusing party officials of indulging in "privileges" such as renovating their homes or bringing luxury items back with them from foreign travel. As the novelist Gabriel García Márquez once said, Cuba is one big family that shares the same secrets, and within days the entire island was talking about Castro punching his own windbags in the stomach.

This revolution has a sort of New Deal willingness to experiment and screw up and admit the mistake and try something else. When they make a mistake it can be a dilly. About ten years ago I was asked to visit Cuba but I declined to go because the government in a fit of puritanism had shut down the bars on the theory that bars were bad influences on workers and dens of spies, to boot. I sent them a letter saying that there was no way I was going to a country where the workers couldn't drink; it wasn't my idea of democracy. The move proved as popular as Prohibition in the United States, and the government eventually surrendered to the thirst of the people and reopened the saloons. "We goofed on that one," a Cuban diplomat told me, over a drink.

Although most of the Cubans seem to feel free to criticize the government's means, criticism is not indulged about the goals of party policy. I heard no one, for instance, criticize Cuba's presence in Angola, although to be fair that seems a popular national commitment. Ask most any Cuban why they have troops in Angola, as I did when I visited a school and a factory, and you will hear, with a quiet pride, that Cuba will not live with its back to the struggles of other countries. Cubans feel a special kinship to Angola because of Cuba's African heritage. They say they were asked to come there to help fight the CIA and protect Angola from invasion by South Africa. The kids and workers I talked to all said with genuine enthusiasm that they wanted to go over and help out if they could. They sounded like Yanks anxious to get Over There and beat the Hun.

THE AMERICAN WOMAN CAME OUT of the department store shaking her head. This was a big store on Fifth Avenue, which is Havana's equivalent of New York's. "I can't believe it," she said. "There's nothing to buy." The American visitor was accustomed to the cornucopia choices of consumerism. "I had to wait in line outside and then they let us in six at a time. A matron took us one by one to look at the goods. It was more like going to a museum than a department store. The things they had in the window were the only things they had, and there were only four things—slacks, two types of sweaters, and a bathing suit—all sort of dull East European polyesters. They had these same items in all the racks on the main floor in different colors—but all the same clothes. The women went around looking at different-colored slacks and saying, 'Do you think this would look nice on me?' just the way American women talk when they're shopping. It was amazing, really amazing."

Cuba is an ecologist's heaven. There are no throwaway containers—the maids in my hotel carried cleaning fluid in empty Havana Club rum bottles—and no competing brands of toothpaste or aspirin. You go to the store and buy one of it, and that's it. There is of course no advertising; Havana billboards sell political ideas instead of new, improved formulas. Packaged consumer goods are virtually unknown (the hotel I stayed at served canned Romanian tomato juice as a luxury), and food items such as meat and fresh milk remain rationed. Toilet paper is doled out like gold leaf. A woman told me that the bathroom attendant in a fancy restaurant's ladies room handed each customer *one* piece of toilet paper. The Cubans I spoke with who bitched about life's inconveniences under the rigors of the American economic blockade seemed to accept the situation as a burnt offering for the next generation. "I know my children are going to grow up educated and healthy and that's worth a few sacrifices," a Cuban friend said. "What the hell—we've learned to live without cornflakes," he said.

[AN EVENING IN HAVANA'S PACIFIC HEIGHTS]

The man of the house was an elegant revolutionary. He wore white linen slacks and a gray cashmere sweater over a purple silk shirt and he had wild, frazzled white hair like Einstein. Pablo Armando Fernández had just come from an afternoon at the opera. Dinner guests were expected. We drank rum out of crystal glasses and talked about firing squads.

We were in Miramar, the Pacific Heights of Havana, a neighborhood of wide, tree-lined streets and stately homes that is set off from the commercial center of the city by a slow-flowing river. Most of the people who were rich enough to live in Miramar left Cuba when Castro came to power. Their mansions are now embassies or state office buildings or have been rehabbed into workers' apartments. Pablo was one of the exceptions. He came from a wealthy family, but he thought the revolution was a good idea. He still lives in the same house he did before the revolution and there are still Picassos on the walls.

It was a typical Havana society evening. Dinner guests began arriving. There was Ailina Sánchez, a singer with the Havana opera and a movie star, and her husband, Ronaldo, a journalist for a Cuban military magazine. Ailina sat down at the piano and rendered the music of Bola de Nieve, a Cuban Cole Porter, a thin black man with a shiny, bald head who wrote incurably romantic verses and was the rage of Paris and New York cabarets in the forties and fifties. We sat under Picassos in wicker furniture with bright flowered upholstery. Ice for the drinks was on a table in a silver bucket with silver tongs. The talk was of music and politics. Havana's beautiful people wanted to know what made Berkeley tick. Alas, to some questions there are no answers.

There was delicious gossip. Cubans love to gossip almost as much as they love their tiny cups of sweet, black coffee, which is half sugar, and it is a wonder anyone on this island has any teeth at all. The gossip was about Barbara WaaWaa. When she came to interview Fidel Castro she arrived like Queen Ozma of Oz with an entourage of shakeup men and TV technicians and producers and gofers. The interview with Fidel lasted more than four hours. The one-hour program, with time out for commercials, that was shown on American television displayed Ms. Walters as the equal of the bearded one, giving him the old socko questions, hitting him up about his love life and such. "Where do you sleep?" she asked. "I have many houses," he answered.

After the show screened in American primetime, Cuban television perversely showed the entire four hours of the interview with all the gaffes and swear words and Barbara WaaWaa adjusting her nose and such. This became a subject of great amusement on this communist island in the sun. One memorable answer left on the cutting-room floor was when Ms. Walters asked Castro about his sister, who had defected to the United States early in the revolutionary game. Castro did not answer in the circumspect manner of your usual head of state. Castro leaped up on the screen like Dwight Clark catching the touchdown pass against Dallas and gave an impassioned oration, saying, "What sister? I have no sister. What does the same womb have to do with kinship? I have a million sisters. Women who stayed here and struggled to make the revolution work, they are my sisters."

"Before the revolution," Pablo was saying, during dinner, "even Batista could not get into the beach clubs because he was of mulatto blood." This was former president Fulgencio Batista, the Little Tojo of Cuba, a former army sergeant who decked himself out in white suits and high heels and spent his evenings watching American horror movies and gained himself a reputation as a bit of a torturer. Pablo told me a story about the daughter of his family's cook. He told it with tears of joy in his eyes. He had known this girl as a child. She was a Caribbean black. Before the revolution, she would have been a cook, like her mother, he said. Today, she was the principal of a high school. "Anyone who knows anything about Cuba knows that this would have been impossible without the revolution," he said.

The color hierarchy of pre-revolutionary Cuba has been totally dismantled by the Castro regime, and the status of Cuban blacks has changed as radically as that of Cuban women. Before the revolution only 10 percent of women were in the labor force—and that included the prostitutes. Women stayed at home in the traditional role the church and machismo men have cast them. It has taken the full twenty-one years of the revolution to get men—and women—to gradually accept the idea that a wife could work and the kids go to a daycare center. Now a majority of Cuban women are in the labor force, although women are exempt from the "bum laws"—have a job or go to jail—that apply to men. Some feminists think that amounts to discrimination.

The dinner wine was imported Romanian red. Ailina Sánchez, the Cuban beauty, raised her glass and smiled with teeth whiter than new sheets. She is a product of women's lib, Cuba-style. Ailina is married, has a child, and is able to pursue a full-time career because the state educates and takes care of her kid during the daytime. Cuba is today what America might become if the enthusiasts of the ERA have their way—there is full-time free childcare, equal jobs for equal pay, abortion on demand, easy divorce laws, and the streets are safe for women to travel at night. Still, women have problems with men here. Ailina acted in a Cuban movie called *Portrait of Teresa,* about the problems a young woman who works in a factory had with her typical machismo piggy husband coming to grips with her independence; she ended up dumping him and signing on a lover. A divorced woman at the table said that was great for a movie, but she had trouble finding available men. I had the feeling I'd heard this conversation before.

The Cuba I have read about in most American press accounts has been colored gray and grim. I found it more yellow and red and white and blue. Havana has a cultural life that could never be summarized on a Ronald Reagan three-by-five card. There are little theaters galore, big-league ballet, symphony and opera, cabarets and revues, a booming film colony that has created a nation of movie junkies, a publishing industry that has spewed out some five hundred million books since Castro took over (the first commercial book printed on the revolutionary presses was a huge rerun of *Don Quixote*) and a profusion of literary, political, and satirical magazines.

A Communist Party official was sitting next to me at dinner. He was chatty. I mentioned that I had spent the day before visiting a cigar factory and had been surprised to learn that the workers got bonuses and other quasi-capitalistic wage incentives. Of course, said the man from the C.P. The revolution wasn't above adopting some aspects of capitalism that worked. He said Havana even had farmers' markets where what the farmer produced above his state quota was sold at free-market rates, allowing people to get around the rationing system.

"One of the first things the revolution did was to make public telephones free. We found out that didn't work. Kids would sit around all day talking on the phone." Now, he said, the phones cost a nickel. "You can't give people something for nothing. They just don't appreciate it," said the communist.

[NO AMERICANS, BUT IT'S STILL FUN]

The other night at 2 a.m., there were at least two hundred thousand Cubans throwing a heat on in Havana. They were drinking beer out of cardboard cups the size of popcorn cartons and partying along the Malécon, the broad boulevard that gracefully arches the great seawall built by the Spaniards. The sea surges strongly into Havana's inner harbor, and waves broke against the old stone wall and spray splashed wickedly into the foam on beers in people's hands. A few blocks up the Malécon at the U.S. Interest Section, formerly the U.S. Embassy, a lone diplomat was peeking out a window of the squat ugly building, but he didn't come out to play.

Havana has always been a party town and, contrary to the popular impression, communism has not turned this red island gray. The city still parties toward the dawn in bars and cabarets and nightclubs and— this week, during a carnival celebrating the Cuban revolutionary holiday of July 26—in the streets. Instead of the likes of Errol Flynn and George Raft hogging all the fun, campesinos from the countryside now get in on the act. At the Bodeguita del Medio, the famous restaurant in the cobblestone-streeted old town, where Hemingway drank his mojitos and the poet Nicolás Guillén wines and dines his friends every night, ordinary Cubans were jammed into tables alongside tourists from Canada, Mexico, Spain, and Czechoslovakia. There were no Americans. It is difficult for an American to get to Havana these days, as Ronald Reagan in his wisdom has made this fun city in the other country discovered by Columbus virtually off-limits, the way the Moral Majority would like to blockade San Francisco. The isolation of this island from continental America has contributed to an anti-Cuban hysteria as prevalent as was the anti-Spanish hysteria whipped up by the Hearst press in the 1890s.

The porter at the Miami airport looked at me as if I were the illegitimate son of Lenin when I asked him to take my bags to the plane heading for Cuba. It is a charter job that operates twice a week, sometimes. The passengers are either spies or Cubans who fled to the consumer society and are returning to visit relatives, carrying plastic bags full of spray deodorants and other amenities of civilization unavailable on the blockaded island.

The revolution has ended racial discrimination and poverty in Cuba and, except for an ill-advised period in the sixties when it closed down the bars for a time (Fidel Castro likes to talk candidly about the revolution's mistakes—and that was one), it hasn't repressed the Cuban sense of fun. A night in Havana is like your average night in North Beach with Hunter S. Thompson.

Earlier in the week, Mayito García Joya, a Cuban photographer and cinematographer, was speeding in his little Russian-made car along the Malécon under a full moon, talking a mile a minute while driving. We stopped at a fancy restaurant in an old mansion and scored a bottle of rum by greasing a waiter's palm. We were on our way to Mayito's home in Miramar, the Pacific Heights of Havana. It was one o'clock in the morning, and the party was just beginning. The home of Mayito and his wife, Marucha, also a photographer, is sort of a no-pay Elaine's where Cuban artists and filmmakers gather to discuss Cuban politics, American politics, intellectual gossip, and whether Ronald Reagan is really crazy or just loco. This week the visitors included the Nobel Prize–winning Colombian novelist Gabriel García Márquez, a frequent traveler to this island, whom the irreverent Cubans call "Gabo"; Cuban filmmaker Tomás "Titón" Gutiérrez Alea, who made the much-acclaimed film *Memories of Underdevelopment*; and fellow photographers such as the mischievous Rigoberto Romero, an award-winning photographer of Cuban street life.

Havana has gone VCR crazy, and Mayito and Marucha are not immune to the disease. They have a couple of VCRs and IBM PCs; Cuban artists are hot for the latest technology. A popular form of home entertainment here is to watch taped American movies on the VCR. The latest American films are available through underground video clubs where members swap VCR tapes like baseball cards. Friends and relatives living in the United States will tape a film as soon as it appears on cable TV and mail it to Cuba—and within a week they multiply like rabbits, with hundreds of copies in circulation. On Saturday night, American films are shown on Cuban television, and most of the country stays home to watch the latest Jack Nicholson flick. "I've seen more American movies in Cuba than in the United States," an American woman living here told me. Havana was a cosmopolitan crossroads trading city long before New York or San Francisco existed, and Cubans today have an almost insatiable need for information. Contrary to its image as a closed society, Cuba is alive with curiosity and gossip.

We sat outside in a hot night cooled slightly by northeast trade winds. Jaime Sarusky, a novelist and American history buff, dropped by to join the discussion. He said he was writing a novel about Nicaragua a century ago when Vanderbilt owned it almost in fee simple. He was a gentle man with eyeglasses perched like a bird on his nose. He had questions about San Francisco. What about the gays? "It's crazy—but one of the strongest criticisms recently against Cuba is that we have been persecuting homosexuals. But in Cuba we don't have a law like your Supreme Court upheld against kissing in the privacy of the bedroom." The man had a point there.

The conversation went on to discuss how the revolution has tried to redress the typical macho Latin American attitude toward gays. Textbooks condemning homosexuality had been changed, etc. There was in all this conversation not an ounce of hostility toward Americans, despite the fact that successive U.S. presidents have attempted to kill Fidel and overthrow the government. Rather, there was a curious sort of affection for the United States. They just wanted to know what was going on. It would not be in character with the man, but if Fidel Castro ever wished to restrict the news in this most curious of nations, he would face a revolution.

It was 5 a.m. and the street lights of Havana burned orange against a dawning-blue sky. Mayito drove me back along the Malécon to the Hotel Capri, the former home of George Raft. The restless ocean splashed against the seawall. "Don't call me before noon," Mayito said. This is the country that Ronald Reagan thinks is poised like a dagger at the heart of America?

[CUBA LAUNCHING NEW WEAPON: A RUM SUBMARINE]

We stood on the shore at the edge of the rum factory and looked out to sea, to where the submarine would go. The east coast of Cuba still has scar tissue from the ravages of last year's hurricane. But where there is rum, there is hope.

A bulge of concrete that stuck out like the burl on a redwood had been added to the rocky shore. Its size was misleading; it extended deep into a subterranean lair. "Here we will load the submarine," said the director of the rum factory. His mustache, thick as the bristles on a toothbrush, quivered in the afternoon trade wind. There was a Captain Nemo glint in his eyes. A Cuban submarine? CIA analysts will no doubt take note.

"It took us three years to make the submarine. We launch it on August 15," said José Manuel de la Osa, director of the Havana Club distillery, the world's largest rum factory. Its famous elixirs are exported to all the world except the continental United States, where Señor de la Osa is forbidden by the remaining logic of the Cold War from selling Cuban rum to American aficionados. The rum submarine, Señor de la Osa declared, would never fire a shot in anger. Alas, its purpose is not to break the American delivery blockade and deliver rum but to dump it. The rum submarine has no torpedo tubes, he said, because it is an ecological weapon, albeit one out of the imagination of Ayn Rand.

As we walked through the streets of the Cuban distillery, which is as large as a small town, the director proudly pointed out newly laid pipes leading to the sea from acres of huge rum warehouses. Through these the waste from the distillation process would flow directly into the belly of the submarine and then be expelled three thousand feet deep, four hundred miles out at sea, like drinking men's depth charges. The visiting American wanted to know why they would waste anything about such good booze. Cuban rum has a one-of-a-kind taste that makes your tongue knock at the roof of your mouth. Couldn't it be made into alcoholic chewing-gum or something useful? The rum boss made a face. What is left over after the rum is made is a nasty bit of business, an extremely unpleasant blend of liquid and goo—sort of an alcoholic atomic waste. It presents a great disposal problem. If you leave it on the ground, the birds get drunk, or worse; if you throw it in the ocean, the fish get stoned; if you bury it, you create a quicksand of booze end-products. He said they had been making the best of a bad situation and dumping it offshore, but the Cuban environmentalists were after him and threating to arrest the rum factory. The Lord's cops are everywhere, even in Cuba.

We reached the air-conditioned oasis of the director's office. He had a desk as large as a football field that was lined with bottles of rum in all the flavors of Jell-O. The giant Cuban rum factory has also begun producing orange- and lemon-flavored vodka and a blended whiskey called Old Havana. The director's eyes flashed over the display of his wares like Gene Wilder in *Willy Wonka and the Chocolate Factory.* "Where do you wish to begin tasting?" he asked. The visitor suggested it would only be democratic to go from right to left and taste them all. No, he was in a communist country, make that left to right. I insisted that the director join me, explaining that it was an Irish custom. "I'm not sampling alone," I said.

"We begin," said the director. Halfway through the samples—I believe it was between the Ron Arecha Extra, which had to be sampled twice, and the Licor Diabólico, which sent smoke out your ears—he admitted ruefully that elemental capitalist logic had dictated the imaginative solution of a submarine to dump the rum at sea. "A small submarine was the most cost-efficient," he said as we went to work on the rum chartreuse. "A ship or a seagoing barge would have been more expensive, not only to construct, but because of the workers required to dump the rum waste overboard."

There was, most exquisitely, Cana Santa, a sugarcane-based version of the miraculous Fernet, the bitter herb liquor that has kept generations of North Beach citizens cured of every ill from a bad stomach to menstrual cramps. The meanies of the Reagan administration have halted its importation on the ridiculous ground that it is more medicine than drink, and home health care is declining rapidly. The Cuban version is as sweet as Fernet is sour, but cures the same ills.

Later, the director took out the keys to the kingdom and took me to the Frankenstein Room. This was the inner sanctum of the rum factory where new products are created, a room in the tropics kept as cold as a meat locker with tile floors and rows of testing booths partitioned like places you take your driver's license test and shelves full of giant mad-scientist-type bottles. When I asked whether this was the Frankenstein Room, the Cubans, who have watched so many old American horror films they know them by number, understood immediately. Technicians in smocks began bringing in their inventions in clear bottles marked only with paper labels with chemical formulas handwritten on them. There was a copy of Japanese scotch that was not worth copying, a Cointreau based on Cuban sugarcane that would put hair on your tongue, and a blend of light and dark Cuban rums that had achieved critical mass that they were thinking of marketing under the name Havana Gold. If it ever made it to the states it would wipe Tequila Gold off the shelves.

At the end of a most unusual afternoon in the Pearl of the Antilles, I made an impassioned plea to the director, on humanitarian grounds, to find a way to bring the Cuban version of Fernet into San Francisco, where supplies of life-saving liquid are dwindling alarmingly. Impossible, he said, sadly. The law forbids...I looked longingly toward the sea. What about the submarine? I said I knew a perfect spot in Half Moon Bay where bootleggers used to land their wares.

If you happen one day to see a Cuban submarine surface in Half Moon Bay, don't shoot. It's carrying medical supplies.

[CUBAN ARTISTS, WRITERS, PHOTOGRAPHERS CAN'T GET U.S. VISAS]

They must be dangerous people, these Cubans, since so many of them are banned from visiting the United States. "I am one of the banned," said photographer Mario Díaz as we were sitting at a state-run roadside restaurant, a marvel of fifties non–art deco that looked like a gas station in a James Dean movie, on a seaside highway outside Havana. Cubans sometimes love to wait to the last minute to tell you things. We were traveling in search of a banned person to photograph. I told Mario the photographer that he could have stayed home and shot himself in the mirror and saved us a hot drive in the noonday sun.

Mario had two days' growth of hairs, and in the humidity of the Cuban summer the limp growth stuck to his face like tiny wet shoelaces. Cameras hung on his chest like bandoliers. To me he looked like your typical photographer. I asked how in the world he got himself banned. "People in New York arrange show of my photographs there," he said. "My photographs go to New York. When time comes for me to go, my visa is denied. I stay." But why him? What had he done to offend Ronald Reagan? Mario lit a cigarette from a box of spaghetti matches no longer than your thumb; small is big in Cuba. He shrugged. "I took photographs."

I have seen Mario's photographs, which are first-rate—moody, ethereal shots, many of them with the Cuban flag as a theme. This is hardly subversive for a Cuban; American photographers I know have made small fortunes out of portrait series with the American flag popping up in unexpected places, from cleavage to a hardhat's lunch pail.

And later in the afternoon: "I do not think I will be allowed into the United States this year. I am invited to Duke University for a conference on film, but I do not think I will get visa," said Tomás Gutiérrez Alea, known to most everyone as "Titón," one of Cuba's most provocative and internationally famed filmmakers. This was in the living room of Titón's second-floor flat in Havana, all glossy Swiss-white, cool in the Caribbean heat as the white enamel on a strip of film. His wife, Myerta, one of Cuba's most popular actresses, served tea on bone china. There was polite laughter about the latest American ban on Cuban artists. But there was also concern. Titón has been on the political rollercoaster. He was first banned from the United States in 1973, then welcomed to America in the later seventies. His film friends in San Francisco include Francis Ford Coppola and Tom Luddy, and he was honored, in the flesh, at the San Francisco Film Festival in 1979. He said to say hello to his Frisco friends because he figured as long as Reagan was president—what was that he'd heard about the man going for a third term? was it possible?—he'd never see them again.

The director of the famous Cuban flick *Memories of Underdevelopment* was last in the states in 1985. That was just before Reagan started up Radio Martí, and Castro responded by canceling the landmark migratory agreement that allowed relatively free travel between the two nations closer than cousins, and the much-desired (by the United States) return to Cuba of the several thousand junkies, lunatics, and assorted criminal degenerates that sly Fidel had palmed off on square Jimmy Carter in 1980. Radio Martí is an especially silly exercise in expensive propaganda because all of Havana tunes in to Miami radio and TV stations at night, where they get a stronger dose of consumer society hype than the hacks of Radio Martí can ever hope to provide. "I can't understand how people in Washington think we are a threat to the United States—Cuba is so little, so poor, so small," the balding filmmaker said in what seemed genuine puzzlement. "It is so ridiculous."

We had a polite discussion about this question that has reduced many political scientists to pop psychologists. Why is it that a Washington that can readily cut deals with Communist Russia and Communist China remains so off-the-wall about tiny Cuba? Perhaps Cuba's becoming the first successful socialist state in all of Latin America is seen by D.C. as not only a dangerous example but an act of parental defiance? Whatever the logic, we are spanking the bright children of Cuba, and punishing Americans, and mutual understanding, in the process. American artists are welcome in Cuba—Jack Lemmon was recently lionized there. But Cuban artists denied entry to the United States under Reagan's rules of order range from Arturo Sandoval, the great Cuban trumpeter who regularly jams with Dizzy Gillespie, who was refused permission to do a gig in New York, to the Cuban folklore expert and Afro-Cuban cultural historian Rogelio Martínez Furé, famed for his Saturday-afternoon rumba sessions in swinging Havana. Despite being invited to the United States under a Ford Foundation cultural grant, he was declared persona non grata by the Reagan administration.

Some Cubans think there is in these arbitrary cultural bans between two countries with such close historical ties an element of jealousy by Reagan's strong supporters in the Cuban exile colony in Miami. While businessmen, doctors, lawyers, and the like left Cuba after the revolution to plot counterrevolution in Miami, few artists left the island. The U.S.-supported Cuban counterrevolution has produced guns, but not culture. When I was in Florida recently a Cuban McDonald's—McCafé Cubano—opened in Little Havana, but otherwise the exiles have little indigenous culture—song, film, music, writers—to boast of. Ersatz

Cuba in America must still get its kicks from the nonstop rhythms of the Big Island. A case in point is Harry Belafonte's plea last week to the State Department to grant a visa to the pianist-composer José María Vitier, whose jazz group is the hit of both Cuba and Europe. Vitier is no doubt political—he wrote the theme music for a popular Cuban TV serial pitting the CIA vs. the Cuban DGI (guess who won)—but his hot music is nonetheless ripped off in Little Havana by Cuban exiles who even play it on elevator Muzak.

When I left filmmaker Alea's, I stopped at the home of the widely traveled Cuban poet and novelist Pablo Armando Fernández. He immediately began tearing out his long white hair at the thought-stoppage Reagan had installed by banning dangerous Cuban artists from America. "The most beautiful artistic relationship that ever was happened between Cuba and the United States," he said. "Just a short time ago we were so close to being good neighbors again. If that ever happens, we will be the best friends ever. What can we Cubans do to help?" You're a great poet, I told him; write a poem about it. But how will America hear my poem if its ears are closed? he asked. I told him that outside the White House, America's ears may be perfectly okay.

[A MIRACLE IN CUBA: THE CATHOLIC CHURCH AND CASTRO ARE TALKING]

There is a miracle happening in Cuba, and it isn't loaves and fishes. The Roman Catholic Church and the Marxist-Leninist government of this big island have gone from an extended period of hostile silence to actual schmoozing. To just about everyone's surprise, including many of the priests involved, the Communist state and the Catholic church are finding themselves in sync.

This has many implications for Latin American politics, not the least of them the increasing isolation of the hawkish cardinal of Nicaragua—Miguel Obando, the unofficial pope of the Contras—from the larger body of ecclesiastical opinion of the Central American Catholic bishops. Obando is the darling of the American news media for his criticism of the Sandinista government as commie and unholy, but from the larger Latin American perspective the man is a lonely crank totally out of step with his fellow churchmen. The archbishop of San Salvador, who is the head of the Central American bishops, for instance recently condemned the $100 million voted to the Contras at the same time Cardinal Obando was nodding assent.

The liberation theology syndrome—in which the Catholic Church, with some static from the Vatican, is positioning itself as "the option for the poor" in Latin America—is familiar enough to readers of American newsweeklies. But Cuba is an entirely different situation that doesn't fit the pattern. Most Latin American countries have the poor and the oppressed—as St. Paul said, they are always with us—and the Catholic Church joining the side of the poor, rather than the oppressors, is the theological story of this century. But that is old news. What is new is what's happening with the church in Cuba. Cuba doesn't fit the Latin American model. For whatever good or evil backers or detractors of the Castro regime may say of contemporary Cuba, the fact is that compared to the rest of Latin America, Cuba has less poverty (I've never seen a beggar on the streets here and everybody seems to have a job), better health facilities, and more schools than its peer nations. That may be great for the Cubans, but it left the Catholic Church with few options on this island. It at first didn't go along with the revolution—neither, by the way, did the Communist Party—and when the revolution triumphed, the church was sort of left in the woods. The revolution had left the church without a social or revolutionary purpose. "Liberation theology," a priest friend here told me at dinner the other night, "has little meaning to Cuba because Cuba has already been liberated in terms of the goals of eliminating poverty that the gospel espouses."

When I visited Cuba five years ago I spent some time with the secretary of the Cuban bishops, Monsignor Carlos Manuel de Céspedes, when the church-state situation was rather dicey. He said the church wasn't leaving Cuba but it didn't feel particularly welcome. Five years later, at a conference of the Cuban Catholic Church held here in February, Céspedes, who was the chief spokesman for the conference, told the delegates—who included American bishops and a representative from the pope himself—that the church had gone from silence to dialogue with the communist government and that everything was coming up theological roses. Where five years ago the Cuban government was censoring church pamphlets, today the government is giving the church money to print them—whatever the content.

A good deal of the credit for attitude toward revolutionary change in the Cuban church comes from a book that is now a best-seller in Latin America, *Fidel and Religion*, which is the transcription of a day and a half of frank religious and revolutionary discussions between Fidel Castro and Father Frei Betto, a Brazilian priest. What they said shocked a continent. The priest asked Castro whether he considered himself Christian. Castro replied: "There are many people in the world today who call themselves Christians but do horrible things. Pinochet, Reagan, and Botha, for example, consider themselves Christians."

One of the more interesting personal facts about Castro that came out in the book-length interview was that he gained his sense of rebellion when his family sent him away from the family farm to go to school in foster-family situations. His foster parents applied unreasonable rules for his behavior so they could both brag to their neighbors that they were disciplining the kid in their charge and still collect the bucks from Castro's well-to-do farmer parents. Castro and the priest, Father Frei Betto, seemed to establish a communion on that point and went on at elaborate length in the discussion that made contemporary Christianity to appear more copacetic with communism than with capitalism.

More than a million copies of this book have been sold in Latin America and an additional four hundred thousand copies—a record-breaking edition of any single book other than the Bible—in Cuba. The idea of their conversations—that Christ was a revolutionary—was not particularly original. But Castro's statement to the priest that there are no "contradictions between the aims of religion and those of socialism" was what stirred the troops. This unexpected accommodation between the Cuban Catholic Church and the revolutionary regime stirred the Reagan administration's anti-Castro radio station, Radio Martí, to denounce meetings of American Catholic bishops in Havana last year and a convocation of the Cuban Catholic Church leaders earlier this year as being manipulated by the Cuban government. This criticism has segued into contemporary hot politics with the much-adored counter-revolutionary former Castro prisoner Armando Valladeras charging in a French newspaper interview that the Cuban church is in the control of the Communist Party and that Monsignor Céspedes collaborates with the Castro police.

These politicized criticisms of an anticommunist and until recently anti-Castro Catholic Church in Cuba have provoked genuine outrage against the Reagan administration's perceived attempt to smear Cuban Catholicism with the brush of Marxism. The head of the Cuban conference of bishops and other leaders of the Cuban Catholic Church have been most biting in their critique of what they consider American propaganda attempting to interfere with genuine progress in formerly strained Catholic-Communist relationships on this island. Priests I spoke with here were actually angry to hear on the Reagan-sponsored propaganda station, Radio Martí, that the Catholic Church—long so sternly anticommunist in Cuba—had succumbed to "government manipulation" and was accommodating "religious persecution" in Cuba. They were darn mad. They said from their standpoint there is no religious persecution. The totally unexpected, if uneasy, friendship between the formerly hostile Cuban Catholic hierarchy and the communist head of state of Cuba has roiled the already turbulent waters of Latin American Christian politics.

"I don't think we'll convert Fidel," a Cuban priest told me. "I don't think he thinks he can convert us to communism. But the way things are going, I wouldn't be surprised that he'd agree to be an altar boy."

[CUBA'S NEW CAPITALISTS REVOLUTIONIZE COMMUNISM]

Communism is making millionaires in Castro's Cuba, and the main man on this big island is—to indulge in understatement—rather unhappy about it.

"We have created a class of newly rich who are doing as they please everywhere," Fidel Castro said in a recent speech. By taking advantage of the revolution, he said, many Cubans are making more money a year under socialism than the average capitalist did under former president Fulgencio Batista. "The revolution has become too generous with certain people," he said, referring to farmers who sold a single clove of garlic for $1.50, making as much as $70,000 a year off an acre of garlic, or private truck owners who made upward of $200,000 a year hiring out their scarce trucks. A lot of Cubans, Castro said, are becoming "two-bit capitalists." One example Castro cited was a certain "vegetable grower" who had a farm, four agricultural workers, and two trucks—which he rented out to other farms, charging as much as three hundred pesos a day per truck (a peso is worth about $1.35). "He would earn at least four hundred, five hundred, or six hundred pesos daily," Castro said. "How much would he earn in a year? One hundred fifty thousand pesos! Incredible! Very few of the capitalists in this country were able to make three hundred pesos a day," Castro said.

Last month the Central Committee of the Cuban Communist Party launched a campaign against "negative tendencies"—this is the Cuban euphemism for creeping capitalism—that amounts to the strongest reassessment of national values since the flap over the failure of the 1970 sugar harvest to reach its goal. The campaign against the new millionaires began with a decision to close what Cuba called the "free peasant markets." This was a quasi-capitalist innovation where farmers, after delivering their quota to the state market where people buy their rationed goods, took their excess produce for direct sale to the public at whatever price the market would bear.

Quasi-capitalism is nothing new to Cuban socialism. People here do not rent their apartments—they buy them, through a twenty-year mortgage with the People's Savings Bank, which charges interest. (We are talking condos in Cuba!) The hysterics in Washington, D.C., who have decreed Nicaragua a totally Marxist state, forget that there is still private enterprise in Nicaragua and that Castro—citing some Cuban economic mistakes—advised the Sandinista government not to abolish all free enterprise but to maintain a mixed economy of state and private ownership.

In Cuba, there is a quasi-capitalistic work ethic: Workers get paid according to the quality and amount of the work they do—Castro said it doesn't bother him if somebody who works more makes more money—and this has given rise to what amounts to middle-class spending power in Cuba. The free peasant markets were one place were excess spending power could buy what it pleased. But apparently a bunch of greedheads jumped into the act, becoming aggressive middlemen who bought what they could from farmers at low prices and sold it at the highest prices possible in the markets—creating such an uproar from the state farmers' cooperatives that the whole experiment was kiboshed.

The phenomenon of some farmers getting rich while others toed the line has contributed, at least in part, to one change in Havana since I was here five years ago. Then, Havana was still *American Graffiti*, with every fifties car you could imagine—Studies, Olds, Kaisers, the works—on the streets. Today you see far fewer of the golden oldies. The streets are full of snub-nosed Russian and Polish economy-type new models. The golden oldies, people say, have gone to the countryside, where farmers with extra bucks have purchased them and finance repair rings specializing in old parts.

While defending the principle of merit pay, Castro has declared war on profiteering in the form of speculation or the high rip-off in the capitalist mode. In recent speeches, he has cited many examples—it isn't just a few garlic farmers and truck owners who are getting rich in Cuba. There is a black market in cars. Cars, which remain scarce, are allotted to people on the basis of need and merit, and it is not uncommon that a worker who gets a car worth fourteen thousand pesos is approached the next day by a pssst! type willing to pay twenty thousand pesos to take it off his hands. There is also an incredible profiteering boom in superscarce housing almost akin to what we call speculation in the states—where an enterprising Cuban will sell a house for cash, acquire building materials and lots, and build and sell for big bucks. Castro, no man for understatement, has called it "incredible" that a "profitable business of building, buying, and selling houses" could be set up within the revolution. He said six thousand houses had been bought and sold, American-style, with people making profits of thirty to sixty thousand pesos, which is a hell of a lot of moola in Cuba.

There are minor corruptions—from teachers earning money on the side tutoring candidates for the university, giving a kid whose parents have bucks a better shot than a poorer kid (a distinction the revolution hoped it had eliminated), to country doctors selling early-retirement certificates and a major street-vendors boom selling hot items otherwise unavailable in the U.S.-blockaded nation, from frying pans to brooms. Mini-capitalism seems to be busting out all over on this island. Castro said it was in part due to "a Cuban bent for chaos, anarchy, lack of respect for the law, and everybody doing what he pleases. That has been the basis for all sorts of shady deals and illicit ventures."

To keep control of the state enterprises that are getting out of line, Cuba is turning to an interesting application of the capitalistic method of cost accounting. This is to put the brakes on managers who have accelerated beyond the idea of making a profit—pay your way is the goal for state-run businesses—to make an ultra-profit, leading to the obvious temptations. "We should not be afraid of washing our dirty linen all at once," Castro said in one of several recent major speeches addressing the unexpected phenomenon of people getting rich off the revolution.

The man is a master of the parable. Consider how he extended the dirty-linen analogy. When news reports say that Castro spoke for three hours, and no one can figure out what he could say that would fill three hours, the answer is that he chats away thus: "We should not be afraid of washing our dirty linen all at once. If we store some of it away, our house will fill up with trash, our house will overflow with dirty linen; it is better to bring it all out and clean the house. We must air the house and air all our dirty linen—not just air it but wash it. So, this isn't a whim: The revolution needs to use all these methods." All of this public discourse, which is the talk of Cuba today, amounts to an extraordinary burst of self-criticism and open discussion of national problems that does not fit the stereotypical media view of Cuba as a typically closed communist society controlled by the Thought Police. On the basis of two visits to this island, I can say with impunity that that is not how the Cuban revolution works. There is rather a priority on grassroots involvement in decision-making and a readiness to criticize government officials and admit state mistakes. What many Americans who view Cuba through grim glasses forget is that this has always been a nation of traders interested in making a deal. Lest we forget, the Cubans traded the captured CIA Bay of Pigs invaders for baby food and aspirin.

[*San Francisco Chronicle*, March 8, 9, and 12, 1982, and *San Francisco Examiner*, July 27 and 30 and August 2 and 4, 1986]

Metropoly

That Commie-Rat, Alien
Harry Bridges: Today S.F.'s Hero

*W*HEN CLUBS WERE TRUMPS ON THE WATERFRONT, the cops bashed heads and smiled about it like circus fakers. The bashees were strikers who asked for porridge in their bowls. The blood-specked cobblestones of the Embarcadero were littered with the beat-up bodies. This led to the General Strike that shut down the town. The leader of the General Strike was Harry Bridges—portrayed as a Red, an alien, and a trouble-maker. What a difference sixty-seven years makes. Harry Bridges, the troublemaker who organized the historic 1934 General Strike in San Francisco, was celebrated Saturday as an iconic hero. A plaza in front of the Ferry Building was dedicated in his name by Mayor Willie Brown. And the cops who used to beat up longshoremen escorted ILWU members, in their rank-and-file uniform of white caps, hickory work shorts, and black jeans, in a memorial march down the Embarcadero. The white-caps were back on the waterfront in honor of the one hundredth anniversary of Bridges' Red, alien, troublemaking birth.

There haven't been that many white-caps together on the waterfront in quite a while. The cargo business went to Oakland long ago, and Local 2, representing waiters and tourist industry workers, has more members on the waterfront than Bridges' old Local 10 of the ILWU. But the spirit of labor-militancy-past walked the waterfront Saturday as those several hundred white-hats marched from the Ferry Building, its proud tower mugged in a retrofit shroud, to Fisherman's Wharf. Marchers were reading copies of the former Communist Party paper the *People's World*—not exactly a hot newsstand checkout item in San Francisco anymore—and recalling the grand old days of class struggle when the town had both bite and backbone. It was a time of class warfare in San

Francisco, with citizen vigilantes and scab strike-breakers and Red-scare bloodlust headlines in the city's daily newspapers.

What was recalled along the march was Bridges' seminal role as perhaps the first San Francisco internationalist. He presciently in 1936 led the ILWU in refusing to load scrap iron aboard ships going to Japan. He was one of the first union leaders to speak out against the Vietnam War, which led to a tumultuous beef with the old guard AFL-CIO cold warriors who supported the war. Willie Brown touched on Bridges' universalist viewpoint when he recalled how Bridges led the way to integrate the once-lilywhite maritime unions. But there was more history beneath the facts: The shipowners in 1934, when the maritime workers asked for a decent day's wage and working conditions, looked to blacks, who they previously would not deign to hire, as strike-breakers. Bridges, with the wisdom of the radical, went to the black churches in the Western Addition and the Bayview and prayed with the congregations not to join the ranks of the strike-breakers. He promised them that if the strike were successful blacks would be welcomed as full brothers in the ILWU and in waterfront jobs. They heard his plea, and Bridges kept his promise.

The ILWU of Harry Bridges was not even arguably the most progressive labor and social institution in the United States during the Cold War years. He was Red-baited to hell's outer regions for his now liberal efforts. U.S. Supreme Court justice Frank Murphy described the relentless efforts of shipowners and McCarthyite fifties opinion-mongers to deport Australian-born Bridges as "Un-American" as "a monument of man's intolerance to man." This historical box score was evened a bit Saturday with the return of the white-caps marching on the Embarcadero—without stepping in their own blood and with cops on bicycles protecting them from traffic instead of beating them on the head.

[*San Francisco Examiner*, July 29, 2001]

The Big Strike

*J*OSEPH ROUSH, A TRAVELING SALESMAN of tear gas, had been scouting the West Coast for six months, a cat to the canary. Roush's employer was Federal Laboratories of Pittsburgh, Pennsylvania, one of the nation's leading manufacturers of domestic munitions. Industrial warfare was its game, and in 1934 there were opportunities aplenty to play. "Labor difficulties are in the making all over the country...It looks to me like the year 1934 may be a very beautiful one for all our men," the vice president of Federal Laboratories, Barker H. Bailey, wrote to his traveling salesmen.

Federal Laboratories sold gas guns, gas ejectors, gas mortars, and a dazzling array of "protective devices," including submachine guns, revolvers, shotguns, bullet-proof vests, and even armored cars. In addition to tear gas the firm also offered something called more colloquially "sickening gas." Roush wrote back to his boss that the situation in California offered "nice, juicy strikes" which would create a healthy demand for the firm's products. He bragged that he had the market in San Francisco virtually tied up because he had himself in like Flynn with San Francisco police chief William J. Quinn by cleaning gratis all the SFPD's tommy guns. Capitalism is, however, full of surprises and Roush had not reckoned on the enterprising activities of one Ignatius H. McCarty, a salesman for Federal's archrival, the Lake Erie Chemical Company. It was to Roush's horror that he discovered that McCarty had beat him to the punch and obtained an order for tear gas from Chief Quinn. This set off a rivalry between the two munitions salesmen that was to reach a climax of sorts in July of 1934 that was exceptional by even the bizarre standards of San Francisco waterfront warfare.

As something of an on-the-spot demonstration device, the enterprising McCarty had begun accompanying San Francisco's finest to show them how well his wares worked on live targets. "Tomorrow we are going to have a hunger march here, and gas will be on hand, both by police and me. I am anxious for an opportunity to use our clubs and baby giants," McCarty wrote to his boss at Lake Erie. Such on-the-spot testing allowed Lake Erie to refine its product for more efficient use. "The cops here, when they hit a man over the head, are not satisfied unless he goes down and a good split occurs. Our clubs are too light for this purpose. Should you contemplate making them heavier, advise," the field-demo man wrote home. Roush took to his rival's sales tactic with a vengeance. So enthusiastic did he become in the demonstration of Federal Laboratory's arsenal that McCarty took professional umbrage: "[Federal's] discharge of gas was wholly unnecessary and merely for advertising purposes, as it occurred after we had driven the crowd back," McCarty complained to his bosses.

On July 3, rioting broke out along the Embarcadero as longshoremen attacked trucks that the employers had ordered to drive through the picket lines. Roush described to his vice president for sales how he was on the job, helping out the cops: "I started in with long-range shells and believe me they solved the problem. From then on each riot was a victory for us. During the middle of the day we gathered in all available riot guns that I had and long-range shells and proceeded to stop every riot as it started…I might mention that during one of the riots, I shot a long-range projectile into the group, a shell hitting one man and causing a fracture of the skull, from which he has since died. As he was a Communist, I have had no feeling in the matter and I am sorry that I did not get more."

It later developed that Roush's kill estimate was inflated; the striker he hit with his grenade launcher, James Eagle, a twenty-six-year-old longshoreman, 1) recovered from his injuries and 2) was not a communist. Nevertheless Roush's handiwork did not go unrewarded. The president of Federal Laboratories praised his bloodthirsty salesman in a rah-rah letter to his sales force as an exemplar of the "boys who have given their personal services to direct the activities of the police in the use of this equipment during times of emergency." The San Francisco Police subsequently made Roush a special officer of the department. To

McCarty went the lesser honor of honorary membership in the Police Officers' Association. One good turn deserves another.

[CLUBS ARE TRUMPS]

San Francisco cops used to buy their jobs on the force. In 1890, a patrol-man's position went for $400. Most of the takers were Irish Catholics, and their sons and relations followed them into the department. A certain ingrown sense of superiority and of "owning the force" natu-rally developed. With power went corruption. Shortly after the great earthquake and fire of 1906, a newspaper called the San Francisco Police Department "rotten to the core" and called for the wholesale firing of police officers to cleanse the force. No such process occured. Instead, Police Chief William J. Biggy, who had made modest efforts at reform, was taken for a boat ride by some of his men and his body was found floating in San Francisco Bay. Subsequent chiefs went along with the system.

In the late thirties, former U.S. Department of Justice agent Edwin N. Atherton conducted an investigation into corruption in the San Francisco force. Atherton found that an officer who sought to honestly enforce the law was regarded as a "snake in the grass" by his fellow offi-cers and his career was sabotaged. The Atherton Report's description of the state of the SFPD circa 1934: "We found that there were approxi-mately 135 regular old established locations in San Francisco where prostitution was carried on...12 resorts, plus several others on different streets, were within a radius of three blocks of the Hall of Justice. There were five houses in one block on this street and it was not unusual, in several localities, to find two or more in one block...Houses of prosti-tution have been so plentiful in a section of the North Beach area that tenants in some buildings have been forced to put signs on their front doors announcing the fact that they are private residences...In the past persons intending to open a house of prostitution were usually required to pay an initial or opening fee, which varied in amount but frequently ran from $500 to $750. At the same time the regular monthly 'payoff' was fixed and the time and manner of payment prescribed..."

The monthly fee for doing illicit business was distributed in a gentlemanly manner among the captains, lieutenants, and sergeants. This payoff was exclusively for the brass, which is not to say that management ignored the lesser breeds. Whorehouse operators were ordered to "take care" of the cop on the beat. Arrangements were made individually and tailored to the needs of each officer. The monthly "juice" to the beat cop ran about ten dollars a man, although some cops were known to take part of their "juice" out in trade. The Atherton investigation found: "Some of the officers of the crime prevention detail of the Bureau of Inspectors had made it a practice to harass, or 'roust' (to use the vernacular) panderers and other questionable characters in the so-called underworld until these worthies found it much more to their advantage to 'pay off.' The '$1,000 Vag' law, which enables the police to pick up a person for almost no reason, lends itself readily to 'shake-downs.'"

The Atherton investigation also found that San Francisco cops had mastered the art of the freebie, and expected as their due in life free meals, free drinks, and free admission to sporting events and theaters. The wife of one officer said almost in a manner of bragging that her husband got groceries, liquor, household goods, clothes, and medical, dental, and optician's services gratis. The report concluded that San Francisco police officers as a class "seem to feel they should be exempt from paying their way like other members of the community." With corruption went accommodation with the powers that ran San Francisco. Men of capital looked the other way when a policeman's palm was greased, and in return the cops functioned as a sort of private security force for the major industrialists. On the waterfront, they functioned as a private army. "Clubs are trumps" was the operative saying among policemen who looked upon striking workers as bowling pins to be knocked down. In this the cops were not totally out of control but rather were following the lead of the multimillionaire shipowner Robert Dollar, who said that the best way to end a strike was to send ambulance loads of pickets to the hospital.

[PEACE AND HARMONY]

There were two worlds on the waterfront: the employers' world and the workers' world. The difference between them was more than mere night and day. It was as impossible for them to get together as the hopeless love of the sun for the moon. This is the employers' view, as published in a dandy little work of agitprop, a pamphlet titled "The Pacific Coast Longshoremen's Strike of 1934" by the Waterfront Employers Union: "Earnings dropped unavoidably during the depression following the year 1929; furthermore, there was no means provided in the old system of hiring to prevent the disparity of earnings referred to above. On the whole, during this period of fourteen years, a satisfactory employment condition for longshoremen existed. During that period there were no disagreements and no strikes. On the contrary, there was a high degree of efficiency, and the men, generally speaking, were satisfied."

In the combative world of the waterfront, even pamphlets were in the category of tit for tat. The International Longshoremen's Association (the ILA)—the precursor of the modern-day ILWU—published its own version of waterfront reality in 1935. It was titled "The Truth about the Waterfront." We will leave it to the reader to choose between the versions of 1934 reality:

> In 1916, the longshoremen of this port, then organized in the Riggers and Stevedores Union, went on strike for higher wages and shorter hours. It was during this conflict that the shipowners, in an unsuccessful attempt to smash the union, imported hired thugs to act as strikebreakers. Three years later, in September 1919, another big strike occurred. This time the shipowners, who had been steadily preparing for it, succeeded, with the help of big business interests throughout the state, in smashing the longshoremen's organizations all up and down the coast. Locally, they then set up the so-called Longshoremen's Association of San Francisco and the Bay Region, a company union familiarly known as the "Blue Book."
>
> For fourteen years through their "Blue Book," the shipowners completely controlled waterfront conditions and prevented the longshoremen from organizing into bona fide trade unions. The shipowners are fond of referring to those years as a period of "peace and harmony" on the waterfront. It undoubtedly was from their point of view. To the majority of waterfront workers, however, it was a nightmare of inse-

curity, fear, and intimidation, brutal competition for jobs, long hours, low wages and—in the end—failure to earn a living...

[AFTER THE MAST]

Six days shall thou labor and do all
thou art able,
And on the seventh—holystone the
decks and scrape the table.

—R.H. Dana, *Two Years Before the Mast*

Meet some of the boys: Suitcase Larsen, Patch 'em Up Red, Ape Anderson, Overcoat Reilly, Dago Red, Pelican Robertson, One Round O'Brien, Forty Fathoms, Left Rudder, T. Bone, Hamburger Whitey, Spike Hennessey, O'Hoolee How Red, Lantern Jaw Creedon, Bones Crosby, Soap Box Shannon, Ham & Eggs, Fine & Dandy, High Hat Feeney, Lord Love a Duck, Coconuts Andy, Scrapper O'Brien, Long Nose Brady, Moon Face Gibbons, the Wandering Jew, the Kokomo Kid, Scar Face Gallagher, Freddy the Trout, Jeez Give Us a Nickel, the Wee Man, High Pockets Smith, Diamond Stew Rider, and Galloping Andy Flynn.

These are sailors all, who fought the good fight on land against the hell that had been made of life at sea. Sailors have traditionally been distrustful of landsmen, and they had good reason. On land they were shanghaied and swindled by crimps and boardinghouse operators; the fleecing of sailors was a growth industry on the old Barbary Coast. At sea sailors were regarded as chattel and forced to live like cattle. In *Two Years Before the Mast*, a nineteenth-century exposé of conditions aboard the Yankee vessels, Richard Henry Dana described the flogging of the seamen Sam and John the Swede by a captain more maniacal than Ahab, screaming, "If you want to know what I flog you for, I'll tell you. It's because I like to do it!—Because I like to do it!—It suits me! That's what I do it for!"

In 1911, California governor Hiram Johnson signed legislation repealing the fugitive sailors laws—which held sailors in a state of involuntary servitude, making a sailor who left his ship, i.e., quit his job, subject to arrest. The legality of sea slavery had changed but not the conditions. Mike Quin went to sea for three years. This is how he described the living conditions of seamen: "I sailed as a seaman for three years and know perfectly well what I am talking about. On one ship more than forty men were jammed into a 'glory hole' where the bunks were three deep, and hardly room between them to stand up to take off one's clothes. We were below decks, right on the waterline, so that unless it was clear weather the portholes had to be sealed tight and ventilation was non existent. The ship was at sea fifteen or twenty days at a stretch, and stayed in port only three or four days or a week at most. And during that time you had to put in your full hours, so shore leave was meager. On top of that, all forty men had to do all their washing and bathing out of a single fresh-water tap."

In 1934, seamen were still working fourteen- to sixteen-hour days, especially Sundays. Sailors had had their differences with stevedores in the past, and would in the future, but when the call went out from the longshoremen to shut down the coast, the seamen hopped aboard. Both seamen and longshoremen, Quin indignantly wrote, were unfairly regarded as "semi-underworld characters" by the writers of romances. The caste condition of maritime workers "is a matter of class discrimination and not material for the romantic pen," wrote Quin.

[ROBBING THE TAXPAYER]

The shipowners cried poor. But they were fat and rich, milk-fed by the American taxpayer. Mike Quin found out just how fat, and how rich, they were. The man was a muckraker who could hold his own with the likes of Upton Sinclair and Lincoln Steffens. He pawed through the shipping companies' financial records and dug into congressional hearings. He came up with an astonishing picture of a slothful and sinfully wealthy maritime industry indulged by compliant politicians and protected by a paid press. The maritime industry is subsidized by Congress to allow American companies to compete with foreign lines which have lower construction and operating costs. That was the concept. The reality, Quin found, was that American domestic shippers shared in those subsidies—while at the same time operating huge fleets under foreign flags.

Only the railroad barons robbed the country better than the shipowners. Quin's maritime history was that of a scandal and a boondoggle of proportions to blind the imagination. The shipowners' and shipbuilders' publicity machine whipped up a shipbuilding frenzy during World War I which resulted in the expenditure of almost $3.5 billion dollars from the public treasury to construct some three thousand merchant vessels—*after* the war. There was no conceivable need for these ships. "They were never delivered, but simply tied up alongside each other in a sprawling boneyard," Quin wrote. Much of this gigantic ghost fleet was eventually sold to the private shipping companies for less than ten cents on the dollar. Then in 1928 Congress passed the Jones-White bill to make things right, but instead it made them more wrong. The Jones-White legislation gave American shipping companies operating in foreign trade a mail subsidy of $30 million annually—the rationale being that American seamen were better paid than foreigners, giving U.S. ships higher operating costs. The law also created a $250 million revolving slush fund from which shipowners could borrow from the sugar bowl at low interest to build new vessels.

The whole thing was a license to steal. "The Dollar Lines, which employed Chinese labor on their ships at extremely low rates of pay, and had their ships overhauled in Chinese shipyards by coolie labor, were one of the heaviest beneficiaries of the bill," Quin wrote. Government bounties amounting to almost $100 million were paid to West Coast shippers alone during the thirties. This treasure chest did not go to maintain a high standard of living for the American workingman but instead took the wrinkles out of the shipping lords' bellies. A Senate committee investigated this domestic version of a robbery at sea and found that "money transmitted to mail contractors in constructive trust for American seamen has been diverted by the contractors to their own private profits for exorbitant salaries and unearned bonuses." The snooping senators discovered that many ships carried small cargoes and merely sailed back and forth to collect the subsidy. The solons declared it a "saturnalia of waste," and charged that many of the apologists for this outlandish system—such as the West Coast newspapers—were sharing in the wealth: "Many of its apologists have been shown to be those who have directly received financial profit, or those who, for various reasons, have been influenced by those who did directly profit from it. Not the least of these influences has been the millions of government dollars flowing through the hands of the immediate recipients, their associates, affiliates, subsidiaries, holding companies, and allies, into the treasuries of newspapers, magazines, and publicity agencies. Evidence before this committee has illustrated the existence and effect of these influences."

The shipowners poured subsidy money into a public relations arm called the American Steamship Owners' Association, which in turn poured it into newspaper advertisements extolling the merits of the system. The hand-rubbing was not limited to the purchase of space. A subsidiary of the Dollar Lines had investments in first mortage collateral trusts in, surprise! the Hearst Corporation. The shipowners' awesome publicity machine successfully hid a financial scandal perhaps unparalleled in the history of legal swindles. With these subsidies, the Matson Navigation Company operated profitably throughout the entire Depression. Yet Matson was one of the companies which said in 1934 that it could not afford to pay longshoremen and seamen a living wage.

[CAPTAIN X]

Captain X was a merry old soul, almost as wide as he was high, with the heart of a jackal and an ungovernable desire for Red meat. His name was Bakcsy, but he preferred the more mysterious Captain X. He bragged that he had claimed Big Bill Haywood's scalp during the War to End All Wars. He convinced the San Francisco Waterfront Employers Union that the headquarters of the "Red Network" that secretly financed the General Strike was not Moscow but Carmel—the home of the retired muckraker Lincoln Steffens, whom he regarded as a second Lenin.

Captain X, armed with a generous cash advance from the waterfront employers, went south to ensnare Steffens. He rented a house in Carmel which he bugged from roof to cellar—no little accomplishment as this was long before Science could conceal a microphone in a martini olive. He planted dictographs in every room in the house, including the loo, and even hid a dictograph in the Christmas tree come December. He called himself Captain Y. Sharkey, world traveler, gentleman of leisure, and generous host—and proceeded to liquor up every leftie in the Carmel Valley in hopes of pinning the hammer and sickle on the aging Steffens. When Captain X's guests departed, their fingerprints were lifted from the cocktail glasses and a coven of secretaries set to work transcribing the cocktail chatter, ever alert for the pink passages. He called it the "house of a million ears." When the local press exposed a "Red Trap" in the middle of stately Carmel, Captain X had to beat a hasty retreat. He, however, considered the expensive fishing expedition money well spent.

Bakcsy's was but the first of innumerable covert operations against organized labor and the left that had their genesis in the "Red Scare" tactics the press, the employers, and the cops used in the General Strike. "VIGILANTES DESTROY RED NESTS," read the applauding doomsday-type headline in the *San Francisco Examiner* when goon squads protected by police smashed the offices of the communist *Western Worker*, the Marine Workers Industrial Union, and other organizations suspected of receiving orders via wireless from Moscow. The cops hauled in every wino in town and announced that they had captured five hundred "Reds." The San Francisco Police Department viewed these exercises in low comedy as so succesful that Chief Quinn announced the organization of a permanent anticommunist squad.

Communist-hunting became a growth industry in California and helped the rise of Harry Bridges' self-proclaimed nemesis, Harper L. Knowles—the chairman of the Subversive Activities Commission of the American Legion. Knowles solicited statements from rival labor leaders that Bridges was a communist and encouraged paid perjury against Bridges during the government's many unsuccessful attempts in ensuing decades to deport the feisty labor leader. Knowles later headed Western Research, a shadowy organization in San Francisco which kept files on hundreds of thousands of labor agitators and other suspicious parties and sold them to private industry for profit. In the fifties and sixties Knowles' office became a heaven for FBI agents who would spend their lunch breaks poking through the card files. One of the clients of Western Research was the *San Francisco Examiner*.

[ALL THE NEWS THAT'S RED]

Westbrook Pegler once said that the Hearst press resembled a screaming man running down the street with his throat cut. The Hearst papers in San Francisco—the morning *Examiner,* "An American Paper for American People," and the afternoon *Call-Bulletin,* a circus sheet—were at their yellowest during the General Strike. The state of being yellow over red was an attribute shared during the strike by the city's one independently owned newspaper, the *San Francisco Chronicle.*

Paul Smith, the paper's boy-wonder financial editor, attempted to bring sense into the *Chronicle*'s strike coverage. The upperly-mobile Smith went on to become the editor of the *Chronicle* and later of *Collier's* magazine. During the General Strike he became a close personal friend of Bridges, although the two men remained on different sides of the labor-management fence. Smith never believed the canard that Bridges was a communist, a belief held almost maniacally by the most powerful employers in San Francisco. (Smith made a "conservative estimate" that San Francisco capitalists spent more than a million dollars trying to gather evidence of Bridges' party membership.)

Smith memorably described his encounter with Bridges on the eve of the strike. Bridges had given up talking to reporters as he had been misquoted so many times that he considered it a useless act; let them make up things on their own. A friend prevailed on Bridges to meet the *Chronicle*'s young financial editor, whose first question to Bridges was about the state of the class war in America: "Arching a thin eyebrow, he said, 'Kee-rist, you don't mean to tell me there's anybody on the *San Francisco Chronicle* who knows there's a class war in America.'"

Despite Smith's efforts, the *Chronicle* joined the Hearst wild dogs in anti-striker editorializing: "Through agriculture, transportation, and shipping, through the rail, food and steel industries—through the vitals of the Nation—American Communists, Moscow-directed, drive their strategic offensive for revolution and Soviet power in this country."

Other *Chronicle* headlines provide a glimmer of the reading matter the public was offered: "DOCKS FOCAL POINT OF RED PLOTTERS,"..."RED MANUAL DISCLOSES METHODS PURSUED HERE"..."VIGILANTES, POLICE DRIVES AGAINST COMMUNISTS SPREAD TO RURAL AREAS."

The disinformation continued through the end of the strike: "GEN-ERAL STRIKE CRUSHED BY DETERMINED CITIZENS; BRIDGES ADMITS FAILURE OF PLOT TO STARVE CITY INTO DEFEAT" read the *Chronicle* front page of July 19, the day the strike ended. This was thirties news-speak: no such thing had happened. The city had never been threatened with starvation—Bridges as the General Strike general manager, so to speak, had made sure that there were ample food supplies for everyone in the city. The strike came to an end, against Bridges' wishes, through the efforts of the conservative majority of union leaders on the strike committee who had resisted a general strike in the first place. But the strike had proved its point—the waterfront employers never again attempted to crush the union en masse.

And what would Mike Quin say of Harry Bridges, if he had to sum it all up? I think he would say, as was said of Augustus' influence on Rome, that Harry Bridges found the labor movement of brick and left it of marble.

[From *The Big Strike: A Pictorial History of the 1934 San Francisco General Strike*, 1985]

Uppie Goes to Hollywood*

*I*N HIS CLASSIC STUDY OF AMERICAN DEMOCRACY, *The American Commonwealth,* Lord Bryce found the political situation in California to be both peculiar and dangerous. It was certainly never more peculiar—and in the opinion of the leading citizens of the Golden State, never more dangerous—than during that Depression year of the impossible dream, 1934, when the vegetarian socialist and veteran muckraker Upton Sinclair captured the state Democratic Party and ran for governor of California on a startling platform—the creation of a separate but equal communist economy parallel to the teetering capitalist system. This was to be accomplished by turning over the state's foreclosed farmlands and idle factories to the 1.3 million Californians on relief to organize as communes and run for barter, with a separate poverty scrip replacing the dollar as the poor's medium of exchange.

The gubernatorial campaign of 1934 was the most bizarre, the wildest, and the most expensive in the checkered history of California politics; it was probably the strangest political campaign in American history. The bespectacled novelist and utopian schemer almost won on the strength of his will-o-the-wisp promise to "End Poverty in California"—and it took the unprecedented mobilization of the propaganda might of Hollywood to defeat him.

Hollywood's role as spoiler in Upton Sinclair's dream of ending poverty was not without its ironies. It was the final act in a twenty-year comedy-drama between the idealistic muckraker and the film capital. Sinclair was an object of controversy and hatred in Hollywood long before his gubernatorial campaign frightened the studios into announcing "contingency plans" to move to Florida in the event of his election. Sinclair experienced only disappointment in his dream of instructing

*Previously unpublished

Hollywood in some sense of social responsibility. First, a movie of *The Jungle* was botched (sabotaged, he said); then he almost died of apoplexy when his novel about J. P. Morgan's manipulation of the panic of 1907, *The Moneychangers*, reached the screen as a story about dope trafficking in Chinatown.

Sinclair fought back at the studios and their bankers by taking the side of the fallen film czar William Fox against the rest of Hollywood. He closeted himself with Fox and pounded out an epic biography that laid bare the financial highjinks of the movie industry in a muckraking detail that has yet to be equaled. Among the "polished villains" Sinclair excoriated was the man who was to prove his nemesis, Louis B. Mayer. Sinclair modestly titled this strident apologia, like a Hollywood extrava-ganza: "Upton Sinclair Presents William Fox."

The Hollywood apprentice could not resist trying the sorcerer's brew. Sinclair plunged into movie making. He wanted to produce the great socialist movie. He achieved instead the biggest boo-boo in the history of film. "Probably more ink has been spilt and more reputa-tions soiled over this picture than any other since cinema began," a critic wrote in 1934 of Sinclair's *Thunder Over Mexico*. Sinclair financed the great Russian director Sergei Eisenstein in a Mexican film which was to be a classic portrayal of peasant life. But after international intrigue and foibles which defy summary, it ended a financial and creative disaster, with the genius director Eisenstein in disgrace and the well-meaning socialist Sinclair internationally denounced as a capitalist hack. It was an unrivaled artistic misfortune. In fact, everyone lost except Stalin, who had his own reasons for doing dirt to both men.

Sinclair's final political showdown with Hollywood in 1934 was almost perfectly constructed as melodrama. The fast-moving story is packed with intrigue and betrayal, villainy and thrills, surprises and mysteries, and conspirators of high estate. The principal characters include some of the most famous men of the century in journalism, politics, film, and finance—William Randolph Hearst, Franklin Roo-sevelt, Louis B. Mayer, A. P. Giannini; larger-than-life cranks and eccentrics—Aimee Semple McPherson, H. L. Mencken; unexpected heroes—Jean Harlow, James Cagney; and unexpected villains—Norman Thomas, Charlie Chaplin. The story is played out against a back-ground of the Dust Bowl migration, labor violence and Cossack police, bread lines, colossal swindles, peonage and child labor, old ladies clawing at garbage cans, distress sales and foreclosures (some nine thousand in Los Angeles alone in the first half of 1933), and angry torchlight parades of the shoeless and hungry who could find no room at the poorhouse.

America was on the fine edge of madness in 1934, and nowhere was the madness finer than in Southern California; there the bubble literally burst in Eden. For the hundreds of thousands of lower-middle-class people who heard the piper's call to Lotus Land and migrated from the American heartland during the first quarter of the century, the Great Crash was, in a real and particularly bitter way, the betrayal of the American dream. It was these frustrated middle-class fundamentalists who provided the groundswell of support for Upton Sinclair's crusade. Five years before they had been spitting at Eugene Debs, but when the bankers pulled their mortgages like so many weeds in the backyard they became hell-bent for utopia on Upton Sinclair's socialist terms. The regular Democrats from whom Sinclair stole the party's nomination were as mystified as the Republicans at the Nathanael West–type caricatures who flocked to support the muckraker-turned-messiah.

The Democratic party leadership in California and in Washington, D.C., did everything in its power to keep Sinclair from becoming governor in their party's name. Even the state's labor bosses opposed Sinclair, and business and labor formed an unprecedented united front against him. Most large firms put notes in employee payroll envelopes the week before the election notifying workers not to bother to come back to work if Upton Sinclair were elected. All California newspapers were in hysterical and trenchant opposition; the *Los Angeles Times* announced that Sinclair was out to "Sovietize" California. Church pulpits throughout California became platforms for anti-Sinclair sermons. Every radio station in the state boomed out anti-Sinclair messages paid for by an unprecedented $10 million collected by terrified capitalists to defeat the mild-mannered radical. Highway billboards—a new form of political advertising invented by the anti-Sinclair forces—were monopolized with sensational warnings that Sinclair would destroy religion and the family and "nationalize" women and children. The campaign against Upton Sinclair was the beginning of the modern media political campaign of images and innuendo. Arthur Schlesinger Jr. called it "the first all-out public relations blitzkrieg in American politics."

Yet Upton Sinclair almost won. His campaign was the greatest instance of electoral social evangelicism in the history of the United States. Were it not for the extraordinary intervention of Hollywood, most political commentators of the time felt that he would have become governor of California. Bosley Crowther, a fan of the movie business, called it "one of the most deceitful maneuvers of the motion picture industry in public affairs." The campaign of 1934 kicked Upton Sinclair out of politics but put Hollywood in. The results can be traced through the blacklisting of the fifties. It enhanced the bifurcation of California between North and South and established the smear as a defining element of California politics that is with us until this day.

Metropoly*

AS IF THE CREATION OF SOME PERVERSE MASTER of idle pastimes, Oakland spreads out like a giant game board from the north shore mud flats of San Francisco Bay to the rolling hills of the coastal range. The game is "Metropoly," and, as it is played in Oakland, it must also be played by anyone living in any American city over 250,000 persons. The object is survival, and the obstacles are chronic unemployment, racial imbalance, cultural deprivation, economic strangulation, educational disparity, housing inadequacy, entrenched power, stultifying bureaucracy, and loss of identity.

Playing rules are simple. If you are among the substandard income families that make up 47 percent of Oakland's population, you wait your turn, shake the dice, count your spaces, and keep quiet. Go to jail when you are told, only pass Go when you receive permission. Pay your taxes. And above all, don't rock the board. The rules are more lax if you are one of the elite group which makes 99 percent of the decisions in Oakland. After all, you know the banker. Since the other players constantly have to land on your property, the rents they pay make it difficult to buy any houses or hotels themselves. Whatever property they do have will be the cheapest on the board, and the odds are that you will end up owning it too. The analogy is familiar, but it applies with dismaying exactitude to life in Oakland, California, where the game of "Metropoly" is being played on a scale slightly below the epic.

*A Ramparts *special report with the help of Robert Scheer, Sol Stern, Robert Avakian, William W. Turner, Saul Landau, James Colaianni, Leslie Timan, Maureen Stock, Denise Hinckle, and Anne Scheer*

[A GEOGRAPHY LESSON]

Oakland makes a nice "Metropoly" game board since it is an "All American City." *Look* magazine said it was, in 1955, and a plaque from *Look* hangs in Oakland's marble-walled City Hall to prove it. A red, white, and blue billboard reminds motorists of this honor as they speed along Oakland's perimeter on an elevated freeway that slices across depressed flatlands of marginal industry and decaying housing. The view from the freeway is a city planner's version of the seventh layer of hell: an ugly, squalid, depressing hodgepodge of commercial neighborhoods, smoke-deadened greenery, and neglected residences of Victorian design and Edwardian vintage. The dominant color is gray. At the turn of the century the flatland area was a well-manicured community of bright gingerbread architecture that provided suburban housing, via ferryboat, for the more vital, if more sinful, city of San Francisco across the bay. But Oakland was doomed by its own geography. Its flatlands provide a natural base for industrial expansion of hilly San Francisco, an expansion that assumed forest-fire proportions as the twentieth century pressed on through the catalytic periods of World War I and then World War II.

In the boom period after World War I, port facilities, heavy and light industry, stores and storage tanks crowded the flatlands, without comfort of zoning or planning, and the residents fled inland, toward the pretty hills that mark Oakland's boundary to the east and south. Middle-class workingmen's homes were built by the score between the waterfront and the hill slopes, but, within decades, only the sacrosanct hills were free from unchecked commercial blight. Pockets of minority settlements became etched into the flatland topography—chronologically, Irish, Germans, Portuguese, Chinese, Italians, Mexicans, Indians, and Negroes. Illegally subdivided old homes afforded cheap housing, and as a tremendous influx of Negro workers came to Oakland to work in the shipyards during World War II ("imported," an Oakland official said, "by the Federal Government from the South"), the racial characteristics of the ghetto became well-defined. Thus, race begins at sea level in Oakland. Some ninety thousand Oakland Negroes, constituting almost one quarter of the city's total population, are jammed into restricted and blighted flatland areas on both the east and west sides of the city. As the height above sea level increases, the population becomes paler. The attractive, sylvan hill areas are reserved for expensive homes for whites. There is integration in Oakland, but it is basically the integration of necessity forced upon poor Negroes and whites alike by their economic status.

Oakland's unemployment is twice the national average, its Negro unemployment rate even higher; it is the fifth-largest city in California, but its welfare caseload is the second largest. A city planner estimates that Oakland needs to spend $80 million annually to keep the ghetto from the boiling point, but the city is administering less than $1 million in an ineffectual poverty program, in which the poor are excluded from participation. The men who run Oakland have disassociated themselves, even geographically, from the acute problems of the city. The mayor lives in the chic Claremont Hotel in Berkeley; the police chief in the racially restricted Oakland hills. Business and civic leaders also live outside the congested, depressing cityscape—or above it, in the hills. Or in Piedmont, a Caucasian mountain-city of upper-class homes surrounded on all four sides by Oakland. Their contact with the ghetto consists primarily of driving through it on the way to work. Business-dominated official Oakland's answer to the growing civic crisis occasioned by a massive minority influx, chronic unemployment, and the flight of the racially insecure, home-owning whites to the more distant suburbs is, basically, more industry—and more police. If only the people in the ghetto could somehow be wished away, Oakland would make a truly splendid industrial park.

["A SPECTRE HAUNTING OAKLAND"]

Oakland's leaders see a twofold spectre haunting their grimy city: the fear of an explosion from the ghetto within, and an invasion of "outside agitators" from the adjacent sprawling Berkeley campus of the University of California. Both fears were combined last fall when the Berkeley Vietnam Day Committee (VDC) scheduled an antiwar march from the campus through Berkeley and on through the Oakland ghetto. It provoked a confrontation that set in bas-relief, before an incredulous nation, the tinderbox condition of the great Oakland ghetto and the cantankerous, running-scared mentality of the city's leaders. Oakland's anguished reaction to the prospect of anti–Vietnam War demonstrators marching through its public streets underscores the fear and confusion with which Oakland leaders view the intellectual Berkeley community.

Oakland's ruling mentality is basically Deep Southern: conservative, Protestant, dreary, friendly to those who accept their perspectives, vindictive toward any who challenge them. The permissive, sexually open, blatantly intellectual Berkeley community constitutes an alien and dangerous world which the Oakland Establishment is incapable of understanding and must inevitably view with suspicion. The student activists are considered beatniks, savages, communists—ne'er-do-wells who must be kept from disturbing the normalcy of Oakland. Oakland has had its native rebels, but for relatively short periods of residence. Gertrude Stein was a native, but apparently left home shortly after becoming ambulatory. "The trouble with Oakland is that there's no THERE there," Miss Stein said. Jack London, also Oakland-born, ran, disastrously, for mayor on the Socialist tickets in 1901 and 1903. But Oakland has forgiven this indiscretion; it named a waterfront nightlife square in London's honor. It is doubtful that the new breed of rebels plaguing the Oakland leaders will ever be treated with such nostalgia. They will not become expatriates but will remain and insist on rubbing the world, and the ghetto, in Oakland's face. They want to remake society, and since Oakland is one of the worst examples of American society, they consider it a good place to begin.

Approximately one hundred anti–Vietnam War protest marches were held in cities across the country on October 15 and 16. A Berkeley-Oakland march began in Berkeley, but it never made it into Oakland. Blue-uniformed Oakland police were massed, in a scene reminiscent of Selma—tear gas guns and billy clubs out—at the Oakland city limits sign, as some fifteen thousand marchers approached from Berkeley on the night of October 15. The demonstrators were turned away, and blocked again the next afternoon as another march attempted to tramp upon Oakland streets.

OAKLAND'S SINGULAR INTERPRETATION of the constitutional right of freedom of assembly was based upon numerous rationales: the danger of marching at night, possible traffic congestion in a daytime march, the city's professed inability to protect the marchers from possible, but undefined, dangers. Essentially, it was based upon the incontrovertible fact that Oakland is afraid. It is afraid of a Watts. Life in Oakland's slums is so oppressive that Oakland Negroes have been known to suggest, sarcastically, a move to Watts to better their lot. (The Los Angeles riots, through a masterful public relations stroke by mayor Sam Yorty, are always called the "Watts riots"—as if Watts was anything but Los Angeles' prime area of Negro restriction; but if the Oakland ghetto explodes, the city cannot escape the appellation of the "Oakland riots.") It is afraid of outsiders, of intellectuals, of "agitators." It is afraid of anything that might upset the delicate status quo. In short, Oakland officials are afraid of the city they govern.

The VDC originally planned to engage in massive civil disobedience by means of a sit-in at the Oakland Army Terminal. But as the march date came closer, enormous pressure was brought against civil disobedience plans. Pressure from the University of California faculty, from state and national officials, but, mostly, pressure from within the VDC. A large proportion of VDC participants had been arrested in the Free Speech Movement sit-in at the university's Sproul Hall the year before, and the costly experiment of mass arrest made them fearful of the prospect of another long court battle that would divert energies from antiwar agitation to legal defense. The VDC met and revised its civil disobedience ideas: it would provoke no mass arrests. It would merely march to the Oakland Army Terminal. This decision was announced a week before the parade, but Oakland authorities continued to react publicly as if they were going to be forced to arrest over ten thousand people. It made it easier to be adamant.

Oakland's hysteria was painfully obvious during a series of lengthy and fruitless meetings as VDC representatives sought permission to parade. Chief of Police Edward M. Toothman accused the negotiators of wanting to instigate a riot which would be "more bloody than Watts." Mayor John C. Houlihan, running hot and cold between moderation and obduration, charged the VDC with being "disrespectful" to Oakland and eventually decided that the attempt to march was a "challenge" to the sovereignty of Oakland.

Oakland is the heart of Alameda County, and Alameda County district attorney J. Frank Coakley played the superpatriot. He attacked what he termed the "seditious and treasonous interests" of the demonstrators. He tried, unsuccessfully, to get a federal court to deny the marchers their constitutional rights. He issued ominous press releases based on Section 2387 of the United States Criminal Code—sedition; he worked with the California attorney general to threaten marchers with possible felony conspiracy charges; he made strange allusions to Berkeley officials "conspiring" with the VDC; he helped create a climate of crisis, whereupon California's easily influenced governor Edmund G. "Pat" Brown put the National Guard on alert, signed a paper in advance of the march declaring a state of emergency, assembled the preposterous number of thirty-two hundred law officers at Berkeley, and had the State Highway Patrol commissioner sleep on a cot in his office, just in case. Kent Purcell, chairman of the Alameda County Board of Supervisors, watched the massive police preparations and shook his head. "They're crazy, those marchers, but they're not going to push us around," he said. "We'll arrest ten thousand if we have to, and when the jails are full, we'll use the armory." This preparation was for the same sort of peaceful protest march that went unencumbered down Fifth Avenue in New York, and down streets of one hundred other less paranoid cities that same weekend.

[CHARGE OF THE HELLS ANGELS]

As the Oakland armed forces lined up on a Saturday afternoon in a Selma wall at the Adeline Street boundary to their town, a bizarre event with the most preposterous consequences occurred. Although the police armada was sufficient to stop eight thousand marchers from entering Oakland, somehow eight Hells Angels succeeded in getting around or through the police and into the ranks of the demonstrators. The Angels challenged the marchers to fight, ripped the loudspeaker from the rented truck that led the parade, roughed up a few demonstrators, and are accused of breaking the leg of a Berkeley police sergeant during the ensuing melee. The Oakland police had known the Hells Angels, who have a reputation for bad manners, were there—but did nothing to disperse them despite their often-professed fears of a riot. "Those guys got their constitutional rights, too," a police officer told one of the marchers who complained about the invading motorcyclists.

The story for the Sunday newspapers couldn't have been better if they had invented it. Hells Angels. Vietnam protest. Beards. Beatniks. Violence. Great copy. The Angels, the papers said, "broke up the march." This was not exactly true, since the eight thousand demonstrators could not have moved one inch farther without getting smashed by the Oakland police, but it served the unlikely purpose of making the Hells Angels, who used to be nothing but cancers, some sort of momentary, patriotic heroes. Thus, in the diffuse perspective events can take in the unreal world of Oakland, the Hells Angels came to represent respectable Americanism, while the marchers—professors, middle-class families with their children, students, veterans, ministers, all voicing their consciences—became the misfits of society.

A threat of the Angels to interfere with the second VDC march was extremely bad news, but Oakland authorities were curiously modest about the ability of their famous police force to stop the cyclists. This was an ambivalence displayed often during the great march crisis: they were fearful of another Watts in Oakland, but on the other hand gave the vague impression that they would almost welcome a riot. It would demonstrate the truth of what they had been saying about the "agitators," and, since the permit to march had previously been denied because of the danger of a riot, would prove their point. Southern police welcome violence over racial demonstrations for the same reason: it supports their rationales for keeping the "outsiders" out.

[A BUDDHIST AMONG WARRIORS]

Allen Ginsberg was stuffing his Christmas turkey. He was in his apartment in San Francisco, but he was talking about Oakland. "Oakland needs soul cleansing," the poet-philosopher said. "It is paranoid, but its paranoia is just a reflex in a small part of the overall paranoia and insanity that is gripping the world today." Ginsberg's analysis, Oakland officials will readily tell you, is something they can do without. They got quite enough of it last fall when Ginsberg self-cast himself as the man to bridge the human gap between Oakland, the Hells Angels, and the VDC. Ginsberg played his Tibetan silver prayer bells and sang Buddhist chants for the protection of the demonstrators before the first march and was justifiably worried about the second. Three days before the march he went on a peace mission to the Oakland residence of Sonny Barger, the Angels' Northern California president. Accompanying the poet were Ken Kesey, the novelist, who was against the war but also for the Angels, and Neal Cassady, Kesey's sidekick and the hero of Jack Kerouac's novel *On the Road.* Ginsberg later issued a hand-printed press release which told the whole story:

> "Ralph Barger, president of the Hells Angels, entertained Ken Kesey, Neil [sic] Cassady and Allen Ginsberg on Wednesday night in his home in Oakland. Also there were numerous Hells Angels. The conversation ranged from the Vietnam Day Committee March to Buddhist philosophy. The night was relaxed and friendly and ended in singing and dancing. Kesey said he was on the side of the Angels and that he wished all blessed. Sonny Barger said that the Angels' previous declarations of peaceful intent on the Vietnam March had been underplayed by the press…Barger explained the Angels' position as one of pro-Americanism and patriotism. Barger felt that a Communist victory in Vietnam would lead to a police state in America. Everybody present agreed that America was already too much of a police state. Some guests were sympathetic to the Vietnam Day Committee and explained that the march was an anti-war march, not a pro-communist march. That the majority of the marchers were equally opposed to a further growth of the police state. They also pointed out that the war was creating police state conditions everywhere. A Buddhist prayer (the highest, perfect prayer which says that the universe is an illusion) was chanted, as well as other high, holy songs. The host, Mr. Barger, put Bob Dylan's 'Gates of Eden' on the phonograph and also 'It's All Over Now, Baby Blue.' He also said he enjoyed Joan Baez's music. The evening ended with a collective sigh and the good wishes that other potential hotheads might find their way to conduct themselves with the same cool this weekend."

As a peacemaker, Ginsberg should commute between Washington and Hanoi. The Angels called a press conference to announce that, in the interest of tranquility, they would not attend the march on Saturday but would "go drink some suds" instead. Sonny Barger also announced that he had sent a telegram to President Johnson offering the services of the Angels, en masse, as "Gorilla" fighters in Vietnam. There was a feeling prevalent among VDC members that the Angels represented the "new wave of fascism," and were put up to their interference with the march by the desperate Oakland authorities. But Ginsberg said this is non-sense, that the Angels actually believed the marchers were mostly communists. The attitude of the Angels toward the marchers was not much different from the American public as a whole, he said. "The Angels are in the center of the American consensus," the poet said. "Didn't Vice President Humphrey suggest the peace marchers were dominated by Communists? Any misinformation the Angels get either about the war or about the march is from the mass media and is misinformation shared by the American public at large. After all, when the Angels very crudely announce that if we don't fight in Vietnam the Commies are going to start getting us in California, they only repeat a line which is expressed in more sophisticated fashion by spokesmen for the Johnson Administration." Ginsberg was critical of the VDC, also. He said they had no proper *upaya* (an Indian word, literally translated "method"). "In a situation surrounded with hostility, the VDC had no real means of transmitting wisdom," he said.

If to no one else, the VDC certainly had trouble transmitting their wisdom to Oakland officials. The city resisted plans for the second march down to the last final hours, although under orders from a federal judge to "reach an agreement" on the parade route with the VDC. Ex-senator William F. Knowland refers to Berkeley as the "Polish Corridor" through which the invading VDC marchers pass on their way to the strategic target—Oakland. The void between the two worlds of Oakland and Berkeley loomed immense in those fitful days of discussion before the march in mid-November. An exasperated VDC leader surveyed the gap: "What we didn't understand was that our frame of reference was so different from that of Oakland. When we think of the results of denying us the right to march we think of students, the liberals, the press headlines, the difficulty of talking about Vietnam, and the great ease with which discussion of Vietnam is related to the right to protest. But the problem was that the police and city manager are thinking about their responsibility to the merchants, the right-wing letter writers, and to people who give money to political campaigns, the Establishment interests. And to them, giving us a permit to march is appeasement and cowardly and they are not fulfilling their responsibilities."

Oakland, intransigent, went down to defeat before a federal court order. It is indicative of the city's mentality that, rather than deal realistically with a situation it disliked, it would make the federal government step in and force it to go along. This is the classic pattern of Southern resistance to civil rights progress. In Oakland, even if you can't shoot, you must stick to your guns.

[THE MEN AT THE BARRICADES: ASSEMBLYMAN DON MULFORD]

Absolutely the biggest day in assemblyman Don Mulford's life was on the seventh day of the Watts riots, when the telephone rang in his Oakland office. The call was long-distance; Los Angeles police chief William Parker was on the line. Parker invited Mulford to fly down and ride with the police through the riot-torn area the next day, an invitation Mulford accepted with alacrity. It is not every week that the police chief of one of the nation's biggest cities asks you, in person, to ride around with him and watch his town burn down. This was just Chief Parker's way of expressing his appreciation for Mulford's efforts in the California state legislature on behalf of policemen. For instance, Mulford is the author of a new law which makes it a felony to assault a policeman in California. He has always been strong on law and order.

Don Mulford represents the white and rich part of Oakland, but mostly he represents the eighteenth century. A Republican from the monied mountain community of Piedmont that overlooks the Oakland slums, his assembly seat is secure as long as he remains in favor of motherhood and the American flag. He has been very busy with the American flag lately because his district includes that part of Berkeley which is the University of California—where recent events have given him heartburn. The assemblyman is extremely concerned over the "agitation" at the university, his alma mater and also his wife's. He believes that the social protests on campus were "professionally organized" by people "oriented toward the Mao brand of communism." The assemblyman tells of his briefing by "security people" who told him the university is a sort of training ground for agitators who then move on to bigger and better things. Mario Savio, he points out (as if to prove his intelligence report), is now at the University of London.

Mulford believes that the VDC's attempt to march against the wishes of the Oakland police was a "threat of anarchy." He says the VDC used the campus to plan illegal acts in Oakland, and sees as many conspiracies at the university as the late junior senator from Wisconsin saw in the State Department. "I have in front of me a list of fifty-four incidents of illegal activities taking place in the classrooms on the Berkeley campus of the University of California," the assemblyman melodramatically told a startled junior chamber of commerce audience during the Vietnam protest hoopla. Alameda County district attorney J. Frank Coakley, a man who would like nothing better than to prosecute a good conspiracy on the university campus, had to tell Mulford that there was nothing to the "incidents," unless the legislator had more specifics. Mulford didn't.

[THE MEN AT THE BARRICADES:
DISTRICT ATTORNEY J. FRANK COAKLEY]

Gangbusters. That is Alameda County district attorney J. Frank Coakley. He is gangbusters against the Red Menace; gangbusters against murderers, armed robbers, and dope addicts. But he is not so gangbusters against civil rights violations. Or the crimes of corporations. Or police brutality. A hanging D.A. whenever he can be, Coakley believes in stiff punishment for ordinary criminals; he knows nothing of the sociology of crime. A prototype of the tough D.A. so favored in American cities, he is an honest, tough man who is hipped, lately, on two things: anti-communism and the young radicals at the University of California.

Coakley's debut in the prosecution business came in 1944, when he was a legal officer in the navy. A munitions ship blew up in the Port Chicago shipyard, about thirty miles north of San Francisco, and over three hundred people were killed. Most of the dead were Negroes who had been brought from the South to work in the yards. Fifty Negroes who had lived through the explosion refused to go on loading ammunition. The navy decided to prosecute them for mutiny, and Coakley got the case. He prosecuted it with a vengeance. It was the biggest mutiny trial in navy history. Coakley tried to prove that an organized conspiracy existed, beginning a long career of conspiracy-conjuring. In summing up his case he said of the fifty Negro sailors, "Any man so depraved as to be afraid to load ammunition deserves no leniency." And Coakley had his way. The fifty Negroes got no leniency from the court. They received sentences ranging up to fifteen years in prison. Thurgood Marshall, the present United States solicitor general, was at the trial as an observer and wrote a report in which he described the trial as an example of the navy's discrimination policy against Negroes. Whether it was a case of discrimination with Coakley or not it was clear that he had utter contempt for the sailors. Typical of the way he handled them on the witness stand was his interrogation of seaman Frank E. Henry: "Don't you know you're guilty of insubordination for not having called me 'sir'?" roared Coakley. Henry shook his head blankly.

Coakley's most dogged prosecution of a case as district attorney was the trial of an eighteen-year-old Negro shoeshine boy, Jerry Newsom, for the murders of a white Oakland pharmacist and his Negro assistant. Coakley's office strained through three trials to get a murder conviction—one decision against Newsom was reversed by the California Supreme Court, the other two ended in hung juries. Coakley's hunger for a conviction in the Newsom case led him into some strange activities. One of Newsom's attorneys discovered a hidden microphone planted in the visitors room in the county jail. The attorney raised a public outcry about it. Coakley was unabashed in taking full credit for having the mike planted. Of course, he explained that he had no intention of listening in on a privileged conversation with an attorney; it was just eighteen-year-old Newsom's conversation with his girlfriend that he was interested in. Said Coakley, the sleuth: "That mike was put there for the entirely legal purpose of helping to solve one of the worst murders in the history of the state."

Newsom's defense attorney was Robert Treuhaft, a left-wing Oakland lawyer who handled most of the police brutality cases during the fifties, when other local attorneys preferred not to antagonize the police department. The Newsom case apparently became an obsession with

Coakley, who has since carried a grudge against both Treuhaft and his wife, Jessica Mitford, Oakland's leading intellectual-in-residence. Newsom was eventually sent to prison on an unrelated robbery charge, and Coakley marked his calendar every year to send a letter to the Adult Authority stating, in effect, that Newsom should be treated as a murderer, not a robber, and never paroled. Civil rights groups developed an interest in Newsom's case and began to agitate for his parole. This infuriated Coakley. In one of his running letters to the Adult Authority, he hinted that the "brazen tactics" of the "Civil Rights Congress, the *People's World* [the then Communist daily], and other subversives" had somehow influenced the state Supreme Court to reverse the trial. Actually, the ground for reversal was the fact that the prosecution suppressed evidence that would have hurt its case—a police report of fingerprints (not Newsom's) taken from the druggist's rifled cash box.

During a 1960 state Assembly hearing on criminal procedure, Coakley took the witness stand to defend his handling of the Newsom case. The district attorney, a short, pudgy man with a winsome, red face, also took the occasion to announce the existence of another conspiracy. This time he linked Treuhaft and his authoress wife, who had been involved in civil rights activities, together with Treuhaft's law partner, in a plot connected with the "communist cause" aimed at discrediting the district attorney's office. The Alameda County district attorney's office is a large one, and Coakley infrequently takes an active role in trying cases. But when the Free Speech Movement developed at the university, Coakley saw a political hue of red. The district attorney felt certain there was a communist base to the FSM, and set out to prove it. Treuhaft was arrested in Sproul Hall during the big sit-in, and many people believe that Coakley wanted the arrest because he saw the political possibilities in getting Treuhaft (with left-wing ties in his background) linked with the students. Treuhaft was in Sproul Hall as an observer-attorney at the request of the FSM, and was in the pressroom talking to reporters when Coakley's deputy district attorney walked in. "Somebody is here who is not a member of the press," said the deputy. "Well, that makes two of us," said Treuhaft. The deputy D.A. looked at a sheriff who was in the room, and Treuhaft was arrested. The case is still pending.

Coakley's visions of conspiracy by no means ended with his discovery of the Treuhaft-Mitford axis. At one point in his running court battle against the VDC, Coakley suggested that the city of Berkeley itself was involved in some sort of cooperation with the VDC to "aid and abet" what he termed "seditious" activities. Gangbusters against Berkeley!

[THE MEN AT THE BARRICADES: THE KNOWLANDS]

The slogan on the editorial page of the *Oakland Tribune* says "Home Owned, Controlled, Edited," and that is about the truest statement ever printed in Oakland's leading and only daily newspaper. Oakland citizens call the paper "the old lady of Oakland" because it is so stodgy, but reportedly 50 percent of the people in Oakland who can read, read it. Yearly profits are close to $1 million. It is not fair to say that the *Tribune* is the most reactionary newspaper in California. It did, after all, support Goldwater for president whereas the *Santa Ana Register*, in the heart of Southern California's Orange County, refused to support the Republican candidate because they considered him too liberal.

The *Tribune* is now in the hands of former United States senator William F. Knowland. Knowland was a senator from California until he decided to come home and get beaten for governor, but he was best known as the "Senator from Formosa," because of his heavy-handed support of Chiang Kai-shek. He assumed the management of the paper from his eighty-one-year-old father, "Old Joe" Knowland, one of the wealthiest men in California and for decades the "biggest man" in Oakland. With the Knowlands at the helm of the *Tribune*, there is little "disharmony" in Oakland, and if there is, the paper doesn't report it. The *Tribune* doesn't admit to any race problem in the city, and is extremely proud of its role in promoting a huge new sports arena and a new museum, and in talking the public and the federal government into building an "Oakland International Airport"—a white elephant ever since it opened.

Knowland runs a tight ship. Pinkerton guards stand at the doorways of the *Tribune* building to make sure employees don't take home a paper without paying for it (ten cents). No "outsiders" are allowed into the *Tribune*'s library (known to late-evening television movie audiences as the "morgue") without a court order, though the availability of clipping files to the general public is considered traditional public service by most newspapers. Restrictive editorial policies have prompted much unrest among *Tribune* employees. Al Reck, a dissident city editor, staged a sit-down strike several years ago, then quit in disgust before he could be fired.

Knowland becomes upset if someone suggests that the *Tribune* runs Oakland. His view of the paper is that it just covers the news and states its opinions on occasion. That's it. In one sense, he is right. The *Tribune* and the Knowland family have been so powerful for so long in Oakland that they have succeeded in molding the type of city they want and establishing a system of priorities to their liking. The system seems to be working very well, and Knowland really has no further need to push people around. Needless to say, Knowland's list of priorities does not include any essential change in the city's social structure. Knowland is analogous, now, to an old baron preparing for retirement, his kingdom well-organized and running itself. He has disassociated himself from active state and even city politics, and spends his time tending to his newspaper and various civic boards, and his family—including "eight grandchildren and two 200-lb. St. Bernards." A friendly, congenial man with a gray crewcut and ruddy face, he is fond of saying that Oakland has achieved that euphemism of politicians, "progressive government."

Knowland's strong right-wing hand in running the paper is Paul Manolis, who was Knowland's administrative assistant in the Senate. Manolis is considered a very powerful man in Oakland because it is he who allows the ex-senator's wishes to be known to the Oakland Establishment. The new upsurge of social unrest in Berkeley has given Knowland his first genuine cause since Chiang began to talk about invading the mainland. *Tribune* front-page editorials have complained that radicals and beatniks are using the tax-supported University of California to stage assaults upon the city of Oakland, and have accused the VDC of working for a communist victory in Vietnam. Knowland even takes a strong hand in counting bodies at the demonstrations. (While most other Bay Area newspapers estimated there were fifteen thousand marchers on October 15, Knowland's paper reported the number as four thousand.) It could hardly be expected that the estimate of the ex-senator's paper would be anything but conservative.

[THE MEN AT THE BARRICADES: MAYOR JOHN C. HOULIHAN]

Shortly after the Los Angeles riots, a group of Oakland Negro leaders decided the community must take precautions to prevent a similar disaster in the tense Oakland ghetto. They asked Mayor John C. Houlihan for a meeting, a proposition to which Houlihan reluctantly assented. Before the scheduled meeting, Houlihan said at a public gathering: "Tomorrow I have to meet with the biggest bunch of kooks ever assembled in the city of Oakland." That is typical of the political style of Mayor Houlihan, called "Hooligan" by his detractors and "a fighting Irish mayor" by his supporters. Houlihan is touted as the "new face" of Oakland—a reform, energetic mayor, eager to deal with massive civic problems and, unlike the older and more conservative men who used to run the city, willing to work with the federal monolith. He is representative of the breed of American mayors who came into office in the post–New Deal period.

Houlihan is also considered an intellectual, a tenuous status made official by his assignment as a consultant to the high-minded Center for the Study of Democratic Institutions at Santa Barbara. The mayor loves to sit at the green-felt-covered conference table in the center's mansion atop a picturesque Santa Barbara hill and discuss the problems of the core city in America, and particularly what Oakland is doing in leading the way to solve them. Houlihan's trips to the center are reminiscent of the last days of Russian nobility just before the revolution. They would meet and academically discuss the serious problems of their country with no conception that the problems really were *serious*, and the country was about to explode. Houlihan and his former city manager, Wayne Thompson, who has since fled to higher ground and better pay as manager of a large Midwest department store chain, spent several sessions at the center last year talking about their city. The mayor and the city manager had some original contributions to make on the role of private enterprise in municipal management. Thompson said Oakland was curbing the "socialistic trend" of cities—socialistic things like running an emergency ambulance service. The job is better done under contract by private industry, Thompson said. He said he would like to see the fire department taken over by an insurance company, and some enterprising businessman open branch libraries around the city. Houlihan got kind of excited about that idea: "I can see where we would have to require that certain reference books be carried in that library and that library be open so many hours and so on and so forth," the mayor said, "but we wouldn't try to tell them what kind of books to have on the shelf."

One of Oakland's most essential fits of municipal genius was to hire out the garbage business. The city manager used garbage to make a point about his concept of how the modern city should be run. As the resident intellectuals of Santa Barbara listened in wonderment, Thompson said, "Look at some of the garbage department employees in other cities and you find a man who...you sometimes wonder, if he really has his heart in his work when he goes around picking up that garbage. He is a government employee and he doesn't appear to have much spirit. But come into our city, Oakland, and watch that garbageman. Boy, he just pounces down that street, his head is high and he is whistling and smiling and he really loves his job, for he is a part-owner of that company, and if you are ever out with him socially, he will invite you to go duck hunting at his duck club and that sort of thing. You won't find that in any other city besides Oakland."

Mayor Houlihan said that Oakland's unemployment rate runs between 4 and 5 percent above the national average because "we are the reception center for Southern migrants. Also eight thousand American Indians, whose chances for employment are very slim, have been deposited in Oakland," he said. The depositor is the federal government, which, in Houlihan's view, has done Oakland wrong in the past and is going to have to spend a lot of money to make good in the future. For instance, he is resentful of the fact that federal shipyards attracted tens of thousands of Negroes to Oakland during World War II—Negroes still in Oakland. "The federal government sent recruiters through the South and everybody they saw standing on the street corner, doing nothing, they went up to them and said, 'How would you like to go to California? All expenses paid, and you will make a lot of money every day.' They said, 'Well, I can't do anything,' and the recruiter said, 'They'll teach you...'"

THE UNDERLYING RATIONALE OF THE CITY administration is that no program can be viable unless it is instigated and administered at the

City Hall level. That is known in cruder language as "keeping the lid on." Listen to Mayor Houlihan at a City Council meeting. Under discussion is the request of some ghetto organizations to lessen racial tension by establishing a police review board: "We have only heard from the minority in the community and not from the majority who vote the members of the City Council and who pay the bulk of the taxes. We have an obligation to consider the wishes of the rest of the community, not the most vocal part of the community." Listen, also, to His Honor Houlihan on the question of who "controls" the poverty program: "We don't have machine politics in the West like they have in the big Eastern and Midwestern cities, so we haven't had the problem of control over the poverty money for the purposes of political patronage. Nevertheless, we control all the money. We [City Hall] must approve all the policies made by the poverty program."

Oakland doesn't have a machine. It has a computer. New city councilmen are appointed, click, click, very efficiently, when an incumbent steps down. There is rarely such a thing as an open seat in the City Council come election time. If a man is retiring, it is cricket for him to resign early so a kindred spirit may be appointed in his place and have the advantage of running as an "incumbent." Mayor Houlihan considers this "just damn good politics. If you have a good team doing a good job, it's easier to pick a man rather than go out and get an entire new person. I think it is a compliment that a man who is thinking of leaving will come and tell the council and give them a chance to replace him." Houlihan does not take umbrage at the suggestion that a club is running City Hall. "What's evil in a club? Both major parties have done it this way for years. I don't think it's evil. If we pick a bad man he will be defeated."

Houlihan calls Oakland a "well-integrated city." He is especially proud that the city recently retired a Negro fire captain and that there is a Negro captain in the police department. The pride in these two individuals is the key to Houlihan's attitude toward minority problems. He deals with "respectable" and "responsible" Negroes, the older, more conservative, middle-class, civil servant–type Negro, and he honestly feels that he is communicating with the Negro masses. Other, more militant and less respectful Negro leaders are *per se* irresponsible. They don't represent anybody. If there is trouble, it is explainable in the George Wallace syndrome: There is nothing wrong here. Our Negro people are good people. Trouble is the work of outside agitators—radicals from Berkeley, the dissident elements in the community.

In the city's approach to other problems of the modern metropolis, there is the same air of total reasonableness and a sense of grasping at straws. The city cannot cope with its problems; it looks to the federal government, to private industry. The leaders surround themselves with organizational superstructures and with activity: new agencies, a new sports palace, new buildings going up so the people in the hills can look down and feel that things are happening, that everything is all right.

[THE MEN AT THE BARRICADES:
POLICE CHIEF EDWARD M. TOOTHMAN]

Oakland Police Headquarters is in a sterile new ten-story downtown bastille next to a freeway. The big picture window in operations head-quarters on the eighth floor affords an excellent view of the ghetto, and legend has it that police officials gather there at dusk on Friday after-noons and pray for fog. If the fog comes in, as it often does from the San Francisco Bay, there is a deep relief among the constabulary. The fog cools things off; no Watts that weekend.

That is a quasi-apocryphal story but it represents the tension between the ghetto and the cops, just as the modern new building reflects the computerized mentality of Oakland's current police chief, Edward M. Toothman. Toothman prides himself on running a well-paying police force which recruits rookie candidates throughout the land from uni-versities with police science courses. The Oakland Police Department is considered something of a model force, and *Look* magazine, which thinks a lot of Oakland, wrote it up as such in 1962. This was nice for a change because the Oakland force used to be one of the most corrupt in the nation. In the late forties Oakland was worse than a small Southern town. The cops beat Negroes whenever they were picked up, and rolled drunks openly in the streets. The brutality became so blatant and the corruption so extensive that the California state legislature launched an investigation into the Oakland force. The police chief resigned under pressure and one officer was sent to San Quentin. A reform police chief named Wyman Vernon came in and pulled all the roots out of the department. He professionalized it. He was incorruptible; he laid down the law to his men. And, surprise for a police chief, he was genuinely concerned with civil liberties and civil rights. Like all good things in Oakland, Vernon didn't last. Toothman assumed office in 1959 and has had a difficult time filling his predecessor's footprints. A traffic specialist with academic credentials from the Northwestern University Traffic Institute, but with no deep understanding of social problems, the chief is honest and hardworking, though a rigid and insecure man who has difficulty accepting new ideas. He had, for instance, a good deal of trouble accepting a federal court judge's decision allowing Vietnam demonstrators to march on his streets. He called the decision "undemocratic," and complained that the judge wouldn't let the demonstrators go on federal property (the Army Terminal) but allowed them on Oakland property (his streets). Besides, Toothman said, there were tremendous traffic problems connected with the march.

The Oakland police chief, who once banned an issue of *Playboy* from Oakland stands, said frankly that he believed communists were behind the agitation at the University of California. He said his intelligence squad men know "every move the local communists make," and assigned his chief of intelligence to infiltrate the Berkeley-based VDC months before the march. A large, heavyset man, balding, with heavy eyebrows and basset hound bags under his eyes, the chief is annoyed by complaints of Negro organizations about police brutality and inefficiency. He denied a rumor that Oakland police don't answer calls in Negro areas. Every complaint is logged on an IBM card, he said, and "sometimes the police were accused of having too many men in the Negro areas." He said any claim of police brutality is thoroughly checked out by his Internal Affairs Department (but Oakland civil rights attorneys often advise their clients not to give information about alleged police brutality to the Internal Affairs Department because the depositions mysteriously turn up being used by the prosecution as incriminating evidence).

There are only nineteen Negroes out of over six hundred men on the Oakland Police Department. Toothman says he has difficulty getting "qualified Negro applicants." This is not difficult to understand. Being a Negro is bad enough in Oakland, but the cops are hated so much there that to be a Negro *and* a cop is almost masochistic. One Negro on the Oakland force who gets around a lot is Odom Sylvester. Sylvester is a captain, and Toothman is in the habit of bringing Sylvester along when-ever he has to meet with Negroes.

The chief brought Sylvester with him, for instance, when he met with the people who were picketing his home last fall. Toothman became very angry when some three hundred people showed up outside his residence high in the Oakland hills to bring home to the chief their demands for a police review board. He was so angry that he called his office and told forty-five cops to come out and bring their gas masks. Then he rushed outside and told Negro leader Eugene Stovall: "I won't be intimidated by you people." The chief was absolutely flabbergasted that the ghetto people would come up to the hills and picket his house. *His house!* He told Stovall of all the things he had done for "you people." He said he always consulted with "your leaders." And now, he waved his hand at the line of pickets; look what they'd gone and done. Stovall said that demonstrations acted as a pressure valve on the ghetto tensions and limited the prospect of a full-scale riot. "If the Negro community wants to riot, it's up to them," the exasperated chief said. Then he went back inside, leaving the forty-five cops and three hundred pickets in his front yard. It was clear that Toothman was visibly shaken by the encounter. In his own *front yard.* Pickets. Negroes. Unheard of. Upsetting. Out of line. Radicals. Negroes. And in his *own front yard!*

[THE POWER APPARATUS]

You had to ring five times, then the freight elevator came rumbling down, very slowly, and an elderly, thin-faced man with a gray crewcut opened the steel cage he operates in an Oakland office building from nine to five. His name is Ronald Cooley and he has had his ups and downs in Oakland politics for many years, both in labor activities and in the municipal machine. He semiretired to the elevator business in 1950, but he knows how power operates in Oakland: "No one runs for elec-tion in Alameda County; people are appointed...The Knowlands were always the big name in Oakland politics...but another big man was Earl Warren" (former governor of California, now United States Supreme Court chief justice). The back-scratching syndrome that keeps the Oak-land political wheels grinding smoothly is like a connect-the-dots game.

When you draw in enough lines you get the whole picture. From his long political memory Cooley sketched a few dots, taking Warren's local career as an example. The key position in local patronage is district attorney. The D.A. makes the deals. Warren, with the backing of the Knowlands, began his Oakland career as an assistant district attorney, an appointee of D.A. Ezra Dacoto. Dacoto later kindly stepped down to make room for Warren's elevation to district attorney. Not one to forget a favor, when Warren became governor he appointed Dacoto to the first vacancy on the Alameda County Superior Court bench. Then there was that little matter of Warren, as governor, appointing Bill Knowland to fill an unexpired term in the U.S. Senate.

The same merry-go-round pattern prevails in Oakland municipal politics. This sort of stagnation can go on because the Oakland voters are generally apathetic. The city itself is so depressing that it is difficult to get charged up over the idea of going to the polls to do something about it. Part of the reason for this stagnant politics in Oakland is the labor movement, Cooley said. Labor has big muscles on bread-and-butter issues, but never challenges the power structure. Labor leaders are conservative and generally satisfied with the status quo in terms of working conditions and wages. They are also secretly concerned about minority agitation for more union jobs for nonwhites.

IT IS DIFFICULT, and, if your Epicurean sensitivities are beyond the Doggy Diner, impossible to get a civilized meal in the downtown section of Oakland. There are no good restaurants. The area is so miserable that no one would venture there in the evening, and at lunchtime all of the important people downtown—the big businessmen, city officials, judges—eat at private clubs. This dining pattern is representative of the exclusiveness of Oakland's decision-making process. If you do not belong to the Elks Club or the Athenian Nile Club, or to one of the Masonic clubs, you are on the outs. You eat at a lousy sandwich shop and the guy having the chicken soup next to you is on the outs, too. Thus, decisions bearing on the future of the city are made by a small group of self-elected men—leaders in industry, some politicians, labor leaders, a few civil servants, members of social and civic boards. The mass of Oakland citizenry is supine, apathetic, and impotent.

There is a descriptive phrase for this singularity of collective decision-making: "power structure." A power structure is necessarily amorphous because power, like electricity, is invisible. All you can see is what it does. In Oakland, it maintains order. It keeps the boat from rocking, or even swaying. It is heavily business-oriented. When "Old Joe" Knowland's political machine began to decay a decade ago, the younger men who moved into the gap were business bosses. Unlike the old-style political bosses, they did not desire power for its own sake but to keep the community safe for the efficient functioning of business and industry.

It is not unusual to have a coalition of industrial and political leaders making the big decisions in American cities, but the situation in Oakland is entirely out of hand. Dr. Floyd Hunter, a respected sociologist who has extensively studied community decision-making, said that what stands for business and what stands for politics in Oakland have melded, fused, interlocked, and become undistinguishable. Oakland's City Hall is an "enlightened part of the civic machine of business bossism," he said. The city government has become a "coordinating effort for the business community." Big businessmen sit on the committees concerned with city policies. A city-manager form of government was installed to put municipal government on a "business-like basis." The people who run City Hall were responsible for getting the mammoth Kaiser Industries to headquarter in a skyline-dominating edifice overlooking the city's Lake Merritt. A necessary corollary of this is that Kaiser plays a very important role in city politics. (Henry Kaiser, an industrialist who was made largely by the largesse of federal spending, has eased the way for acceptance of federal aid for things like redevelopment. The Knowlands, junior and senior, still consider the proper functions of the federal administration to be limited to minting the coins of the realm and maintaining the armed forces.)

Dr. Hunter sees in the Oakland power structure the penultimate merger of the two vast systems of patronage in the United States: business and government. This pooling of psyches has produced the ideology central to all of Oakland decision-making: The panacea for all civic problems is to bring in more industry which will generate economic growth which will somehow, one day, filter down to the people in the ghetto. In the meantime, the poor must be kept, at a minimum of local expense, in a large, supine relief pool and prevented from creating any social unrest that might affect the climate for attracting new industry.

The power structure in Oakland has no formal apparatus, nor does it need one. A "lively communications circuit" of informal clearances and "cues" on policy decisions is largely handled by professionals in the business-oriented municipal government "who do not necessarily need to be told what to do or not to do, but through long experience in handling policy matters can anticipate, or are thoroughly convinced that they can anticipate, the reactions of the higher echelons of decision," Hunter said.

Despite an unwrinkled power apparatus, Oakland is a city in panic. The men at the top are fearful—and their fear drifts down through the labyrinthian channels of authority. It is a faint, uncertain fear, like the blip-blip-blip of a distant earth-circling satellite, that, somehow, something is drastically wrong with their city. Oakland's industrial plant is aging; a large portion of its commercial areas are already decayed. Industry has moved out because other cities can give them a better deal and, in any event, Oakland is a depressing place. (Ironically, neighboring San Leandro, which discourages Negro residents, is successfully wooing Oakland industrial firms by offering tax advantages Oakland cannot match because of its large Negro welfare expenditures.) The tax base is evaporating as white families, afraid also, flee toward the suburbs. And, though the men lunching at the Athenian Club seldom talk about it, the shadows cast by the thousands of able men standing idly on street corners get longer, and grimmer, each day. The Oakland leaders simply do not recognize the enormity of their problems. They do not even realize that the problems are bigger than they are.

[THE POVERTY SUPERSTRUCTURE: OR, HOW YOU CAN DRIVE A JAGUAR WHILE HELPING THE POOR TO RICHES]

Even in the hopeless world of the Oakland ghetto, there was a brief, shining moment of optimism when the great Johnsonian War on Poverty was promulgated. This was the program designed to begin closing the gap between the "Two Americas"—the America of the Oakland hills and the Oakland flatlands. That no economist or social critic of any stature ever took seriously the prospect of the program eliminating poverty in the nation—there simply wasn't enough money appropriated

—is understandable when you look at the funds that trickled down to Oakland. Dr. Floyd Hunter estimated it would take $80 million to *begin* to do something substantive about eliminating poverty in Oakland. The sundry social and welfare service agencies in the city estimated they needed $8 million *yearly* just to perform their jobs adequately. But the poverty program is allotting only $800,000 per year—and most of this money goes to the bureaucrats rather than the poor.

Despite such obvious limitations, the War on Poverty managed to spark the enthusiasm of those bounding optimists, the liberals. Their hopes were centered on the political possibilities of the program, a hope the *New Republic*, which should have known better, summed up: "The hope for the poverty program was not that it would wipe out poverty overnight but that it would begin to revive the instruments of representative governments which lie in wreck and ruin in the fast-growing Negro slums that now are the core of the American City." The sentence in the poverty program enabling legislation which caused such excitement said there would be "maximum feasible participation of the poor" in formulating and carrying out the poverty programs. The concept of involving the poor in the making of policy made the poverty program, as originally announced, the most far-reaching piece of social legislation since the New Deal. But what seemed a bold and radical plan for regenerating some life in the dormant slums of America is becoming, in the reality of big-city politics, just the opposite—the politicians and bureaucrats, instead of liberating the poor, are using the poverty program to strengthen their own entrenched positions. In Oakland, it happened faster than you can say John C. Houlihan.

From his prime list of "reasonable men"—the "responsible" leaders of business, labor, the social agencies—Mayor Houlihan appointed the members of a group called the Oakland Economic Development Council. The poor were not represented. The council adopted the city-run Department of Human Resources as its staff, whipped out a 180-page request for poverty funds, and sent it off to Washington. Only after the program was approved and the $800,000 was in the bank did the council set up the ghetto area "Advisory Councils"—the instrumentalities that were supposed to involve the poor in the program. But there was nothing for the councils to do. The program was in operation; the professionals had already decided what the poor needed.

Houlihan considers the poverty program one of the proudest accomplishments of his administration. On paper it is an exemplary program—the poverty superstructure is in place, the bureaucrats are spending their $800,000. But there is no intention of fulfilling the central idea of the poverty program: allowing the people to develop their own leaders and express their own needs. In fact, the constitution of the Oakland poverty program specifically prohibits the neighborhood councils from making any policy decisions. In this anal-retentive form of municipal management, everything must be kept within the safe City Hall structure. The officials are actually *afraid* of involving the poor. The important thing is to keep the machinery functioning smoothly; the poor might get out of hand and foul up the program being run for their own good.

HOULIHAN HAS TWO "REASONABLE" NEGROES in key jobs in the Oakland poverty program. One is Judge Lionel Wilson, a highly respected and intelligent jurist who is chairman of the Oakland Economic Development Council. He took the job only after he was assured by the mayor that he would be independent of City Hall. But there is no need for City Hall pressure, because the poverty program has done nothing to challenge the power structure, and Judge Wilson is not the person to take it in that direction. Wilson is a good and humane leader, but like most liberals in positions of responsibility, he tends to be skeptical about the possibilities of the poor organizing themselves. He views the rebels in the ghetto who are trying to goad the poverty program into becoming what it was supposed to be—an instrument for social change—as either naive or just plain troublemakers.

Dr. Norvell Smith, the city's director of human resources, is the very stereotype of the middle-class "Negro leader" painted by militant ghetto leaders. A light-skinned Negro with horn-rimmed glasses, wearing a tweed suit and a vest, Smith is forty-one but looks in his twenties. He said he was proposed for his position as the effective head of the poverty program by what he called "a majority of the established Negro leadership." Smith shares with Judge Wilson both a feeling of independence from City Hall and a limited view of the possibilities of the poverty program. He feels he has limited funds but does a good job with them. His biggest problems, the educationist said, are created by people who see the poverty program "as a means of obtaining power." Some of these people are the "bona fide poor" who want a voice in what happens to them (but can't have it). Now, that is legitimate, Smith said. But then there are the people "trying to use the program for their own purposes"—the radical and left-wing students who look upon Oakland as their laboratory, the wide spectrum of ministers and middle-class liberals working in the slums. It does not matter to Smith that their "purposes" are to make the ghetto in some measure livable; their "purposes" do not coincide with the limited aims of the bureaucracy he directs and are therefore not desirable.

Smith is very sensitive to the feeling in the ghetto that he is a bureaucrat who has no real feeling for the poor. He vigorously defends his neutral, administrative status: "I wear a Brooks Brothers suit and I drive a Jaguar but I have been working all my life. I am not a leader of the poor." Smith brands as "white interlopers" the white radicals who are working in the ghetto to organize the poor against the conservative dictates of the middle-class Negro leadership. He calls them the "white colonialist leadership."

Smith, who worked his way up the bureaucratic ladder in administrative posts in the Alameda County school system before getting the plum poverty assignment, believes the radicals are perpetrating a myth about the "so-called dignity of the lower classes." He thinks this is just so much nonsense. The only way to go, he said, is the good old middle-class way—just the way he did it. "My commitment is to make these people [the poor] middle-class. I want to make them acquisitive and aggressive and I want them to compete for the jobs that the people in the suburbs are now getting." The concept of a community of the poor or a political movement of the poor is distasteful to him—the label "good but honest poor" is something to be shed like dirty clothes, and, eventually, the people in the ghetto, with poverty aid and the Protestant ethic as spurs, may all be driving Jaguars like him. Or at least buying their underwear at Brooks Brothers.

A majority of the federal poverty funds for Oakland will go to the Inter-Agency project, the city's original and well-publicized vehicle to control the problems of the poor. What the project actually does is to coordinate the efforts of the many agencies whose programs don't get through to the poor anyway, and as far as the ghetto residents are concerned, the prime effect of Houlihan's pet project is to make more efficient the instrumentalities of their miseries. Before "coordination" a family might have been dealing with only one agency, but now they are harassed by two or three. While the essential need in the ghetto is for jobs, one-half of the funds requested are for education—and in Oakland, that means the federal funds will be spent for blatantly segregated education.

THE ALAMEDA COUNTY WELFARE DEPARTMENT performs two-thirds of its functions within the city limit signs of Oakland. The department is basically antiwelfare. Its caseworkers mechanically carry out their functions under the spell of a combination of the racist and nineteenth-century Gilded Age ethic—"the poor are lazy and immoral and undeserving." The attitude of most of the welfare workers is paternalistic, callous, and even brutal—characteristics usually increasing in degree with the number of years a worker has put in the department. The county is infamous for its cavalier treatment of the poor—peaked in Mack Sennett fashion by a series of sensational early-morning "bed raids" several years ago. Welfare workers, in the best tradition of Alameda County, would bang, at 5 a.m., on the door of a mother receiving "aid to needy children" because her husband had left her, force their way in, and look around the bedroom to see if the woman was sleeping with anyone other than her children. Recently the state investigated forty-nine cases of aid discontinued by the department, and found exactly forty-nine of them to be illegally and wrongfully cut off.

The director of the Welfare Department is Harold B. Kehoe, a chain-smoking, aging civil servant who is going to retire early this year and is very glad of it. Kehoe, who has devoted his life to not rocking the boat, has a kind of fey, naturalist ideology that involves the inability to understand why a man is not working, while at the same time recognizing that unemployment is the result of the improper functioning of the economic system. There are unemployed because there are not enough jobs; yet, one who is unemployed must have *something* wrong with him. He complains that welfare grants, especially for housing, are tragically insufficient for many families. But, he shrugs, "The state fixes the figures." What Kehoe doesn't say is that the county has the power to grant supplements to state welfare checks in case of need if it so desires. It doesn't.

Members of his staff, Kehoe said, are "embarrassed" to say they are social workers, such is the degree of the Oakland white community's distaste for the black poor. "When they went to a party or a bar they used to say they were social workers, but now they just do not mention where they work." Welfare workers who have tried to do something more than keep the lid on the dole and cut people off the welfare rolls at the slightest excuse have either quit in disgust or been fired. But, Kehoe says, "I haven't seen any anti-Negro feeling on my staff. In fact, we just conducted a probe and we did not find *any.*" Such are the mentalities involved in administrating the "dynamic" poverty program in Oakland. The attitude of the people who are supposed to be receiving the benefit of this enlightened munificence is represented by an elderly Negro sitting on the sagging porch of a weather-scarred apartment house in the East Oakland slum. "You are not going to get nothing done in Oakland until it burns to the ground," he said, with finality.

[THE GUERRILLA WAR: "ELLY" HARAWITZ STRIKES BACK]

Elly Harawitz got into the poverty business, underground division, two years ago. That was when she encountered a Negro mother of seven children whose welfare checks had been cut off because she was living in "unfit housing." The house was unfit because it had just about burned down and no longer had a roof on it, and the woman needed her next welfare check to move out and make a deposit on a home with a roof. An Alameda County welfare worker, with unfailing logic, told the woman that people who live in unfit housing don't get welfare checks. "I'm sorry, Mrs. Harper, but the longer you wait to move, the harder it will be on you." And it did get harder. It is easy for things to get harder when your seven kids' clothes have all been burned up and your bedsheets have burned up and you don't have any money to buy food or even to move into a flophouse with a roof on it. And then it became harder still, because it started to rain.

When Elly Harawitz, a petite, attractive, vital brunette of twenty-

five chanced to meet Mrs. Harper, she found her hysterical—and talking
even of suicide. Elly got the woman and her children some food, went
with her to the modern eleemosynary offices of the Alameda County
Welfare Department, and asked them what the hell they were trying to
do, anyway. "The social workers were uncooperative and cold. They had
no legal basis to hold the check. And when I asked the social worker why
it was being held, she replied 'to provide this woman with incentive,'"
Elly Harawitz said. When the welfare worker mouthed the word "incentive," Elly recalled, a small twitch began to flutter in Mrs. Harper's left
eye. "It is difficult to appreciate how deeply a person is affected by an
Establishment that is at best condescending and at worst punitive toward
those who depend on it for their survival," Elly said, in the bedraggled
stone front office she runs in West Oakland, two blocks away from the
well-scrubbed Welfare Department headquarters.

Elly calls her group the Welfare Rights Organization. It grew out of
her experience with Mrs. Harper and her realization that the people of
the Oakland ghetto will only be able to get civilized treatment from the
authorities when they band together and demand their rights in a united
front. Her organization provides legal aid and counseling to individuals
either cut off or ignored by the Welfare Department, and seeks to provide food and housing during the time when the person's case is being
fought out with the bureaucrats in charge of the dole. "We found that
when rights are fought for, and fought for by two rather than by one,
then it is possible to win something."

To win your rights in Oakland, if you are poor and Negro, you
should be Kirk Douglas or John Wayne or else it is going to be very difficult. As Elly Harawitz puts it, "Oakland is an absolutely stinking city;
it is just incredible. You can never find out who is responsible. When
you go to complain to the Welfare Department, to the School Board,
or at the City Council meetings, no one wants to see you. They don't
want to acknowledge your existence. Just try to find out who is responsible for something. It is a process of political education. You go to a
social worker—she is not responsible. You go to supervisor number one
and she is not responsible; then supervisor number two and she is not
responsible; finally you end up at the Board of Supervisors and they try
to pawn it off on somebody else, and then you see how this whole mess
is tied together."

The essential contradiction in Oakland's vision of a welfare state is that the human needs and the welfare eligibility requirements are in direct conflict. For instance, the average Alameda County monthly allowance for welfare housing ranges from thirty-eight dollars for a family of one to three persons to fifty-four dollars per month for families of ten or more. "The only way we can get anything from them is through a political organization. They must be pressured and shown that we can get a lot of people out to demand their rights. Then we can win something for the people," Mrs. Harawitz said.

The need for a political organization to gouge even substandard living conditions out of the Oakland authorities is far more than a physical need. It gives a new scope, and hope, to life in the ghetto. What kind of a life is it? Listen to Elly Harawitz: "A woman and her four kids were denied welfare aid because they did not meet Alameda County residence requirements. She refused to return to Arkansas, so the Welfare Department refused even to give her a food order. She had been living on the contributions of her neighbors for several months when we met her. By that time all the kids had puffed bellies. The oldest, a boy of six, had rickets. His legs were bowed, he limped, dragging one leg behind him, one arm was almost totally useless, his hands were always in his mouth, he drooled all over himself, and it seemed his brain was beginning to be affected by the disease. I remember sitting with this boy on a couch while his mother and a neighbor went to the church to try to get some food. We were looking through an old *Life* magazine, playing a game—I would point to a picture and he would tell me what it was. Around us the wall swarmed with roaches and we looked at ads for carpets and Cadillacs. This child had not eaten for days and we looked at a picture of kids licking their lips around a steaming bowl of Campbell's soup. So is this boy supposed to identify with those kids? Was *Life* magazine about his life? Could it ever be? How to measure his 'alienation' when he grows to adulthood?"

The Oakland Establishment has no conception of this sort of alienation from their white, insulated world. But it is just this sense of alienation, in growing proportions and under outrageous human conditions, that is leading to the almost certain explosion that will come if the Oakland ghetto remains as it is. Elly Harawitz's organization is working toward overcoming this sense of alienation by advocating an "adjustment" to society—but not the type of "adjustment" the educationists and other well-meaning, but naive, social theorists speak of. This "adjustment" is essentially different because it does not require acceptance of the very things that alienate the people. "Our group adjusts to the society by first reasserting its rights as members of the society and then trying to change the conditions which alienate them," she said.

ELLY HARAWITZ'S ORGANIZATION IS TRYING to do the things that the poverty program should be involved in—informing poor people of their rights, bringing pressure on public officials to change their astigmatic notions of how social services should be dispensed. For a few suspenseful days, the Welfare Rights Organization did provoke some excitement in Washington circles. Edgar Cahn, an aide to poverty program chief Sargent Shriver, wrote Mrs. Harawitz and expressed great interest in her organization. He spoke of incorporating some of her ideas into the poverty program; he suggested the possibility of flying a Welfare Rights Organization representative to a Washington poverty conference to report on its activities. He even implied the possibility of a grant to the Welfare Rights Organization so that it could expand its work. But Cahn's enthusiasm quickly cooled. The offer of a trip to the Washington conference was diplomatically withdrawn and further inquiries about the possibility of financial support were met with polite suggestions of going through channels. Somehow the word had gotten back that Elly Harawitz, or her organization, might be a little too radical, or just too eager and amateurish.

There is a final, ironic footnote to our story which bespeaks the failure of the official War on Poverty. Edgar Cahn, the man who had passed the word down to the Welfare Rights people, had in July 1964 written, together with his wife, Jean, an exceptionally perceptive article in which they warned of the danger that the poverty program could become a vast exercise in military-style bureaucracy, too cautious to fulfill its goals. In that article they called for a "civilian perspective" that would keep the program open for spontaneous, indigenous programs by grassroots people—precisely the kind of program that the Welfare Rights Organization is engaged in. Their article was prophetic—the dangers they warned of have come to haunt the Oakland ghetto. What

Cahn could not have anticipated, perhaps, was that he would be presiding over that process. But that is the way the liberal ball bounces in America.

[THE GUERRILLA WAR: A PARISH FOR THE POOR]

The Reverend Barry M. Bloom, an Episcopalian priest, had a penchant for startling audiences with this description of his environment: "I come from Oakland, the shitbox of the West." Reverend Bloom was one of the thoroughly unconventional clergymen who ran one of the most radical—and effective—grassroots organizations in the Oakland ghetto. It is called the East Oakland Parish, an interfaith movement for social and political action founded by clergymen who felt their churches had lost any relevance to the real problems of the poor. The clerics, who wear uniforms of black pants, turned-up collars, and black windbreaker jackets marked by the yellow insignia of the parish, are making life quite difficult for the Oakland Establishment. They believe they are following the example of the historical radical, revolutionary, and heretic named Jesus Christ. They call Christ their "corporate executive director" and think it will take them a long time to raise the qualitative type of hell he did.

The East Oakland Parish is one of the independent, underground poverty programs attempting to accomplish the virgin goals of the official War on Poverty. With the other guerrilla poverty organizations, the Parish people share a deep distrust and hostility to "downtown"—the official agencies and the bureaucrats and politicians who run them. The Parish makes its headquarters in an old bank building at 14th and Fruitvale Avenues, deep in the 80 percent Negro East Oakland flatlands. In addition to the eight clergymen (seven Protestants and one Catholic priest) who make up the Parish's board of directors and work at least one day a week in the ghetto, the Parish has two full-time community organizers and twenty-three students working part-time under a work-study grant from the University of California. They administer first aid to the entire gamut of the sores of the poor—debilitated housing and diets; lack of medical, dental, and legal services; no jobs and no job training; inferior schools and inferior schooling; broken homes; adult and juvenile delinquency in equal measures; and, worst of all, a lack of any power or organization to do anything to change their conditions.

But the Parish workers do more than parallel the paper projects of the official poverty program. They picket with the poor. They shoot pool with them. They actually *live* with them. Organizers for the East Oakland Parish make $200 a month—and live on it, and live in the ghetto. Organizers for the official program get $9,000 to $10,000 a year for the same type of job—and commute to work.

Although it is a phrase that is overused and underdone, it is "Christian witness" which the pastors in the East Oakland Parish are giving. The cornerstone of failure in conventional social service, they feel, is the "destructive condescension built into the staff-recipient or professional-client relationship." The converse proposition to this institutionalized welfare syndrome is the poor organizing and running their own war against their own poverty—and this is the proposition to which the Parish is dedicated. "In our generation the best way to accomplish this job seems to be through community organization—a technique for change, indeed, for revolution—whereby paternalism is throttled and the Lord is in fact free to help those who help themselves," said the Reverend Barry Bloom, now serving a Peace Corps stint.

It is unusual to find Catholic priests actively participating in radical social movements, but Father Savio Dindia is an exception. The young Franciscan priest, assigned to a Catholic high school in the ghetto, became one of the organizers of the Parish. "Because the Welfare Department is antiwelfare and the political power structure refuses to admit that this is a disaster area, the only solution is to organize the neighborhoods and create the power base necessary to get things done: control votes, get new people in to change the direction of Oakland," he said. Toward that goal, Parish volunteers registered over five thousand new voters, most of them Negroes, last year. Besides fighting the Establishment, the Parish has instigated programs designed to "shame the city into doing things": it started a dropout school and is planning a series of "Business Development Centers" to create jobs by helping small businesses to expand.

But, in the Christ-oriented approach of the Parish, it is the spiritual blight of the ghetto that must be combatted. This is a goal recognized by all the parish workers. Said Cheryl Arnold, a blond, heavyset, WASP-looking twenty-four-year-old volunteer, "You have a smooth-running machine downtown, but here in the ghetto there is so much apathy, and no feeling of life having any meaning. There is no connection with other people in the community. I think that's where the frustration and the anger come from." She was saying that Watts, aside from its physical deprivation, is also a state of mind. And it is the same state that Oakland is in.

[THE GUERRILLA WAR: WHERE THE ACTION IS]

Central Realty on Oakland's seedy Telegraph Avenue is a home away from home for those citizens who would like to abolish Mayor Houlihan. Among them are Jody Edmonson and Arlene Slaughter, who are principals in a wide-ranging ghetto organization called ACTION. This stands for the Alinsky Committee to Integrate Oakland Now. ACTION emerged last year from a seminar attended by Oakland ghetto leaders and run by Saul Alinsky, the professional radical. There is much excitement in the ghetto about the prospect of Alinsky moving into Oakland and taking over the war with the Establishment, and the people in ACTION are peppering city leaders with Alinsky's direct-action tactics to kind of pave the way.

Jody Edmonson is a tall, thin, and forcefully articulate Negro who is a co-chairman of ACTION; Arlene Slaughter, middle-aged, graying, tough, with a bit of the Jewish mother about her, runs the Central Realty office out of which ACTION moves. She wears a button with "We Try Harder" printed in Hebrew on it. The pair said that ACTION began after a series of City Council meetings on the tensions in the ghetto. Or at least what were supposed to be a series of meetings. Mayor Houlihan threw everybody out of one meeting, then kept cutting off speakers from the ghetto by arguing with them at a second gathering. At a third meeting, some three hundred people came to debate a proposal for a police review board. They should have stayed home, because the discussion lasted only three minutes and then the council voted overwhelmingly against any such board. At that, the three-hundred-member audience got up and marched outside singing "We Shall Overcome," and have been marching ever since.

ACTION is an umbrella activist organization that encompasses some twenty ghetto groups and stands ready to picket at the drop of a sign. It serves as the organizational channel for the increasing militancy in the ghetto, and for this reason it is shunned by the NAACP. That doesn't bother Arlene Slaughter much, who thinks the NAACP is composed of middle-class types who don't want to cause any trouble and have no influence in the ghetto. Strangely enough, that impression is shared by the president of Oakland's NAACP, attorney Clinton White. He warned the city councilmembers not to use their NAACP contacts to assure themselves that they had control over the Negro masses. White came right out and said that this was an illusion—that the NAACP had no importance in the ghetto.

ACTION is just getting going, and at the moment neither it, nor any other organization, has the following of large numbers of ghetto residents, Jody Edmonson said. There is no such animal as a "Negro leader," just now, in Oakland. "You can be a Negro leader for five dollars," he said. "I decided I would be one by going to the meeting of the Alameda County Negro Leadership Conference. It cost me five dollars to register. Unfortunately, only two other people showed up."

[THE "KICK-OUTS"]

All you need to understand racial segregation in Oakland's public schools is a pencil. Draw a square. Then draw a horizontal line across the top, about one-third down. Then divide the remaining space into three equal vertical sections. You have a diagram of how the Oakland school districts were gerrymandered for racial considerations. The horizontal portion at top represents the school district of the white hill area—the three vertical sections are the school districts running up to the hills through the largely nonwhite flatlands. This gerrymandering was done by the school board in 1961 and resulted in the establishing of the virtually all-white Skyline High School. The board also adopted an "open enrollment" plan which allowed parents to send their children to any school in the city—a practical criterion being if the parents had the money to transport their children every day to non-neighborhood schools. So the result of the open enrollment plan has been to allow middle-class white parents throughout the city to send their children to the Caucasian classes at Skyline High.

Oakland's style of segregated schooling, known to Latin scholars as *de facto*, has one other debilitating side-effect: that of economic as well as racial singularity. Many of the schools, particularly grammar and junior high schools, are of "one class, one race" constitution. The Negro bourgeoisie lives as far into the white hills as it can get outside of West Oakland—the symbolic home of the Negro poor. Thus there is little chance of a Negro slum child mixing with any of his economic betters, even those of his own race. "In a legally segregated Southern school you at least had more diversity," said Oakland Negro civil rights attorney John George. "Since all the Negroes in the area had to go to the Negro school, you had the sons of middle-class Negroes mixing with poor Negroes—but in Oakland the poor black know only the poor black."

The same incestuous pattern that marks Oakland's municipal office-holding is true of Oakland's school board—in spades. In the last three decades, twenty-one school board members have been appointed and only three first came into office by standing for election. The over-whelming majority of the appointees were conservative Republicans. Their choice for superintendent of schools was Stuart Philips. Philips has a concept of the melting pot which is barely post-Victorian. He scores any sort of "social engineering" which would lead to a "racial mixture" in the schools as "repugnant to me." Unrepugnant, of course, is the arbitrary zoning of Skyline High School: "I respect the freedom of choice which in an unregimented social area must result in a particular school being composed largely of one race or another." Speaking is the school superintendent of the city with one of the largest, most concentrated Negro populations in the nation.

Oakland school officials have their own unique version of "jug"— the traditional after-hours punishment period for errant students. Their version is to put the students, if they are Negroes, in the real jug—jail. Every Negro school in Oakland has a regular city police patrol, and Negro children who get in any way out of line are taken to the police station to await their parents. This practice fits in with an old Oakland school tradition known as the "kick-out." It is just like the dropout, except that the student doesn't do it voluntarily. Negro students, especially in their junior and senior years of high school, are discouraged or kicked out of school for being "stubborn" or "uncontrollable" or "uneducable." Suspensions are also legion for Negroes. Five days for smoking. Thirty days for playing with a firecracker. Ten days for coming to gym without a gym suit.

This crack-the-whip atmosphere in Negro-dominated high schools was documented in a 1963 study of Oakland schools by the California Fair Employment Practices Commission. "In a predominantly Negro high school the principal was almost completely discipline orientated," the report said. Principals boast about things like their school having fewer broken windows than other schools with as many Negroes. One Oakland high school principal told a state investigator that he felt it necessary to limit the number of activities which would require a large attendance by the student body, such as theatrical productions, because when Negroes got together they got what he termed "fever." He told the investigator that, when excited, Negro students could vent their feelings in "fearful ways."

When Negro parents try to become involved in school affairs they are treated no less cavalierly. A group of Negro mothers in the East Oakland ghetto picketed the Havens Court School to protest its disciplinary policies toward their children. They were so harassed and intimidated by school officials and the police that many of the mothers became frightened and dropped out of the organization. One of those who stayed, Mrs. Robinson, was awakened one morning at 2 a.m. by a burly Oakland police officer with a warrant for her arrest on a charge of assault and battery on a school teacher. Mrs. Robinson maintained that she never laid a hand on the teacher whom she had complained to about her child's treatment. Dr. Robert L. Nolan, an Oakland physician and former school board member who led a fruitless fight to get his fellow board members to even discuss anything as foreign as *de facto* segregation, considers the future outlook "very bleak" for Oakland schools. "Berkeley at least is making an effort to solve its problems of segregation," he said, "but Oakland, if anything, is trying to prevent a meaningful solution to this problem."

[THE SUPPRESSED REPORT]

Official Oakland has sometimes done very naive things, but in 1962 it outdid itself. The city hired Dr. Floyd Hunter to do a study on housing discrimination. A majority of the members of the Mayor's Committee on Full Opportunity, which did the hiring, didn't believe there really was any discrimination in Oakland and considered Hunter's Berkeley-based consultant firm a sort of super public relations outfit which would reinforce the committee's preconceptions. "They didn't know who we were or what I had written," Hunter said.

This was a major oversight because Dr. Hunter was just about the last person a city with an ostrich mentality like Oakland's should want around. A native American radical in the populist tradition, Dr. Hunter years ago wrote an extremely controversial sociological book on the community power structure of Atlanta, which had the denizens of Atlanta running record blood pressure counts. It can be reliably surmised that much the same reaction occurred in Oakland when Dr. Hunter dropped a 118-page bomb. Housing discrimination, he said in his report, existed in fully one-third of the city where both brokers and property owners were either acting in a discriminatory pattern or openly admitting they would if given the chance; his survey found that 60 percent of the whites in Oakland had prejudicial feelings, mostly against Negroes. But Dr. Hunter went even further. He came right out and said what was wrong with Oakland, and what had to be done to save it. The Oakland "civic machine," the sociologist said, needed its "social sights raised radically."

The city leaders were possessed of an "hypnotic inability" to think of racial problems in other than negative terms, and spoke "a local language full of clichés about achievement where little or none exists," he said. The more-more-industry panacea of official Oakland was a manifestation of "national economic anarchy and nonsense"; the city needed to jettison "cruel political clichés" about welfare and to institute "massive social solutions" to problems the magnitude of which Oakland failed to recognize. For starters, Dr. Hunter said it would be necessary to spend $80 million annually in order to advance the incomes of almost 50 percent of the city's population to "general community norms of adequacy." He said that Oakland was in such a physical mess it didn't need renewal—it had to be rebuilt, beginning with an expenditure of $125 million to replace just plain rotten housing. And he charged that minorities be allowed to play active roles in "all circumferences of government," most immediately and specifically the closed club of the City Council.

Well! Dr. Hunter's phone began ringing as soon as the first draft of the report reached City Hall. The city manager called to say there was no such thing as a power structure in Oakland. Members of the committee called to say that Hunter had gone a little too far, and offered the use of their garden hoses just in case he wanted to water it down. But Hunter stuck to his findings. The committee was fearful of showing such a radical document to the mayor, but Houlihan, with a Gnosticism that allows him to recognize social problems on an intellectual level but to be oblivious to them in the real world, accepted the report with equanimity.

Cooler heads, however, prevailed, and with its usual smoothness in handling such things, the city printed only 125 copies of the report, then destroyed the stencil. The 125 copies were as hard to find in Oakland as first editions of *Fanny Hill*. As word got around about the Hunter Report findings, the demand for copies reached a sort of howl. But this was the time of the campaign for California's controversial Proposition 14, which would make discrimination legal, and it was obvious the committee didn't want in circulation a report about the extreme discrimination in Oakland housing. After the election, and the defeat of the state's fair-housing law, the stencil was retyped and put back on the mimeograph machine.

[THE SHIBBOLETH MARCHES ON]

The foregoing chronicle is not to leave the reader with the impression that Oakland is not making concrete plans for future contingencies. It is. Just last fall, a high-ranking group of Oakland police officials met with a Los Angeles deputy police chief and discussed the problems Los Angeles cops encountered in handling Watts, and how Oakland could do a better job when their own Watts inevitably came. For one thing, the Oakland police were advised to get portable jails to facilitate hauling the rioters away quickly and thereby to leave the policemen on the scene to arrest more people. They also discussed extra-hard rifle butts, special colored helmets to identify ranking policemen easily during the melee, and the number of National Guardsmen that Oakland should call in.

Thus, Oakland prepares to meet its future. To survey this city of over 380,000 citizens, the second largest industrial city in the nation's most populated state, is like watching old March of Time film clips:

- Prohibition is enacted—it will never last—it doesn't.
- Hitler is a tough-minded democrat who is shaping up a sagging German economy—Germany invades Poland.
- Harlem is an explosive Negro ghetto; Harlem is bound to explode—Harlem riots.
- Negroes in California are better off than Negroes in the South; Watts has a high unemployment rate, but at least the Negro families live in pleasant suburban-type dwellings—Watts turns to fire.

These are the shibboleths we once lived by, and we now recognize them as shibboleths. At the very least we recognize the inevitable results. But in Oakland, in 1966, the shibboleth marches on. The ghetto is ignored. The leadership is blind. The worst may come—but all they can do is prepare for it. They can do nothing to stop it.

The tragedy of Oakland is not regional. It is a national tragedy. It is the tragedy of the American city bowing under the arthritic pains of the twentieth century. Yet Oakland, unbowed, refuses to admit it is sick. Its leaders mouth dry phrases about new coliseums and airports, a "professional" police force, "progressive" city government, "comprehensive" social service programs. But the malady is clear to even the casual visitor, an infirmity of such long duration that even Oakland's bed sores are visible. Ben Segal, an official of the Federal Equal Employment Opportunities Commission, came to Oakland recently, and went away aghast. "Oakland is a powder keg," he said.

Oakland cannot cure itself. Its problems are regional, and national, but it will take more than the federal government, in all its largesse, to provide the answers. Washington spends billions on aid to underdeveloped countries—but this is money, often literally, over the dam, if the administrative bureaucracies in those countries are unwilling to effect basic changes in the social and economic order. Like Monopoly, the analogy applies to Oakland. As all American cities in trouble, Oakland needs more than new federal programs and new industries. It desperately, essentially requires a revitalization, a redefinition of itself as a heterogeneous community. And this rebirth can only come, as the Phoenix, from the ashes of the ghetto. Only such a revolutionary awakening, stirring in the slums and accepted in the hills, can save Oakland from the deepening and eventually disastrous war between its two worlds.

Despite the singular obtuseness of its public officials, Oakland is not unique. It is America—it is the American core city. Oakland may be a funny place, but the joke is on all of us.

[*Ramparts*, February 1966]

The Cold Facts

*T*HE ROOM WAS AS COLD AS THE HIND SIDE OF HEAVEN, and Elizabeth Knight, who is seventy-nine and frail and wrinkled as a recycled dollar bill, wrapped herself in chilly blankets and showed how she tried to get warm at night, and it was no go. A match would shiver in this room.

This was Room 221 of the Aranda Hotel, on lower Turk Street, on Tuesday night. The room was the size of a steerage-class bathroom on a cruise ship. Clumps of wallpaper that had peeled way back, closer to the 1906 earthquake than the 49ers Super Bowl, hung from the ceiling like stalactites. An icy wind creaked in through the closed window, and in the corner a cockroach circled the basin of an old sink like an Olympic skater. Elizabeth said she had heat the night before, lukewarm heat hissing out of the radiator so slowly she had to stop turning the pages of her used paperback to hear it; but there had been no heat, she said, for six of the last seven cold nights. For that matter, she said, there had been hardly any heat for the past six months.

"She lies! She's a liar," said her landlord, Chris Patel, who had materialized suddenly in the hallway like a stage genie through a trapdoor. We were in the hallway because it was too crowded in the room for two people and the cockroach to stand at once. "The heat is on every night, six to eleven-thirty. Every night the heat is on," he said.

Elizabeth gave him the raspberry. "When I complained to him about the heat he laughed and told me that freezing was good for you; it kept you from getting heart attacks," she said.

"She lies like a rug," he said. Tenderloin landlord-tenant dialogues are frequently lacking in sublety.

Elizabeth Knight is one of three cold old ladies of the Aranda who are

mad as hell and aren't going to take it anymore. Last week they withheld their $99 monthly rent and said they won't pay until the radiators
are hot enough to roast marshmallows. A city ordinance requires that
landlords provide eleven hours of heat every day. The angry old ladies
of the Aranda say that they've averaged no more than an hour of heat
since last February, when the current management took over the 115-
room hotel. The other two protesting elderly ladies, Alice Fylstra and
Lillian Beazley, said that when they began complaining about the heat
the management offered to put electric floor heaters in their rooms—if
they wouldn't tell Elizabeth Knight. Divide and conquer. They refused.
"It was a pacifier, an insult," said Alice Fylstra.

The Aranda owners are part of the Patel clan who own perhaps a
thousand small motels and fleabag hotels in California. They are nothing
but experienced landlords and would be presumed to know when the
heat is on and when it is not. "The heat is on every night at six o'clock,"
insisted Chris Patel, who said he was a cousin of the owner, another
Patel. I asked him if the heat was on right now. "Of course the heat is
on," he said. "The old ladies lie." By now other people had come out of
their rooms and the hallway was crowded with tenants. This was becoming a scene. I asked if we could go see the furnace. "Of course," he said. "I
am right. Right is right. I know that." There is nothing like confidence.

We descended to the basement in an elevator lit by a yellow light.
The cement was spotless. It was the cleanest place in the hotel. The furnace room was at the end of a long concrete path lined by mothballed
mattresses. There was a danger sign on the door. We went in. In the middle of the room was a square green heater about the size of a Lilliputian
toaster. A large asbestos pipe wandered out of it into the ceiling. "See,"
Chris Patel said. "There's the furnace."

I went over to the squat green thing and put my hand on it. It was as
cold as a healthy dog's nose. I pointed out to the landlord that the furnace wasn't going. "It's going. It goes on at six o'clock," he said. It was
eight o'clock. This was like a segment from *60 Minutes*. Where was Mike
Wallace? I guided Chris Patel's hand to the cold furnace. He pulled his
hand back as if he had touched a hot stove. "My brother lights it every
night," he said. He went running upstairs to find his brother. Nick Patel
appeared and played with some switches; no good. The furnace stayed
cold. He came in with a torch made of newspaper and lit it and kept

poking it into the heater's innards like a dragon killer with a sword. Finally the thing belched into a sickly flame.

"See," said Chris Patel, triumphantly. "The furnace is on."

"You have no idea of the tyranny these old people live under in these small hotels. This one is little different than the others. They're afraid the managers will not give them their mail or hold up their checks if they complain," said Randy Shaw, a poverty lawyer working with the North of Market Planning Coalition. Shaw is paid through the Berkeley Law Project to make sure that the elderly living in Tenderloin hotels aren't freezing this winter. It's turned out to be a pretty busy job. "Most of these hotels cheat on the heat," he said.

"It's really brave for these three ladies to stand up like this," he said. The Tenderloin heat-man said that tenants in fleabag hotels are deathly afraid of being "bagged out"—you complain about something and you come home one day and your room is spiked shut and all your possessions are dumped in the hallway in big green garbage bags. Going to court over it isn't such a hot prospect when you're seventy and walking around with your earthly possessions in a garbage bag. "Our senior citizens who have to live alone get a worse deal for their money than anybody in the city," Shaw said.

I asked Elizabeth Knight why she didn't move to another hotel, instead of fighting the Cold War in this one. She shrugged and the despair of age ran through her shoulders like an earthquake tremor. "There's no sense to moving hotels in the Tenderloin," she said. "You just change one Patel for another."

[*San Francisco Chronicle*, December 6, 1982]

San Francisco Cops Get Their Man

A FUNNY THING HAPPENED TO ME LAST NIGHT after I finished a column saying the chief of police should be fired. Two cops arrested me outside the *Chronicle* building and hauled me off to the clink.

"You Hinckle?" one of the cops asked me on the sidewalk. I allowed I was. It's hard to hide if you're fat and wear an eye patch. "You got any warrants?" the cop asked. I said not that I know of. "They told me you got warrants," the cop said. "You'll have to wait here while I check the computer."

The two cops were patrolling in front of the Old Mint Building directly across the street from the paper. Both sported mustaches and carried walkie-talkies. I said I was on my way to get a beer and I'd be right back while they checked. "You're not going anywhere," said the cop with the bigger mustache. "You're being detained. You stand right here." The walkie-talkie squawked. "You got two warrants against you. You'll have to come with us," the cop said.

How sweet it is. I've been on the cops' backs for two weeks for the numbskull arrest of Marilyn Chambers. Earlier this week I wrote that the force resembled a bunch of jackasses led by jackals. Now they were busting me in front of the newspaper. The Irish call that tit for tat. Fair's fair. This was just another comedic event in the continuing Chambers how-de-do that has seen the force take almost entire leave of senses dispatching a couple of dozen cops to bring the majesty of the law to bear against a 126-pound nude female dancer.

The cops followed me into the newsroom to get my coat. The city editor told a photographer to take my picture. The last time I saw uniformed cops inside a newspaper was in the classic fifties newspaper movie *Deadline USA* when gangsters dressed as cops dragged the stoolie out of the office of Humphrey Bogart, who played the editor. They machine-gunned him down in the pressroom and he fell into the presses and got gobbled up.

Last night a Black Maria with the light flashing on top was waiting outside. The two cops got in and another cop was driving. That made three cops that took me off. What the hell, they used almost ten times that to get Marilyn Chambers. On the way to the Bastille I asked the cop who arrested me, whose name was Marty Sacco, how he heard about my warrants. "It was posted on the bulletin board a few days ago with a list of warrants," he said. I said that was kind of funny timing, what with me blasting the vice squad the last two weeks for the Chambers thing. He said he didn't know anything about Chambers. He said he didn't read newspapers. I explained that the whole town was laughing at the cops for their stupid little adventure and that I'd been the least restrained of the critics. "Well, isn't that ironic," he said. He smiled for the first time.

At the Hall of Justice the computer took twenty minutes to cough up my warrants. Sure enough, they were right. The law always is. I had neglected to pay a four-year-old Marin County charge for having an out-of-date license sticker on my car ($80) and a patrol ticket from the SPCA for walking my late dog without a license (a total of $98 for ignoring successive tickets for this offense). I remember tearing up the $98 ticket that came for the dog-walking charge. I am by inclination a scofflaw.

There at the Hall of Justice, surrounded by San Francisco's finest, I coughed up the $178 and they released me. But in the receipt they gave me there was an additional charge. It said 215 MPC. MPC stands for Metropolitan Police Code. I asked the cops what 215 MPC was. Sergeant Glover looked it up in a fat narrow book with a leather cover. "That's a lewd charge," he said. I said I had never been arrested, let alone for lewd. I took it as a slur against my dog. The sergeant checked the computer again. "Nope, you're in there for a 215 MPC," he said.

"Hey, that's the same charge that Marilyn Chambers was arrested on," said one of the many cops standing around. I think some of the fun-loving vice cops I'd been criticizing had hacked into the computer.

Oh, yes. The reason I wrote a column saying that the chief should be fired: Instead of kicking the vice squad's ass for acting like classic bozos busting a bimbo, Con Murphy said on the Ronn Owens radio show that the Mitchell brothers had "set up" the nefarious incident to make the department look silly. That the department looks silly is an undisputed proposition. But that the cops could be stupid enough to let two porn czars entrap almost the entire vice squad is a wholly new idea. If anyone but the chief himself said it, he'd be considered anti-cop.

Me, I'm not anti-cop. I liked the guys who arrested me.

[*San Francisco Chronicle*, February 14, 1985]

Save Us from
"I Left My Heart in San Francisco"

*T*HIS IS THE CASE FOR MAKING the rousing and wonderful "San Francisco" the city's official song, replacing the flatulent and dopey "I Left My Heart in San Francisco." We begin, properly, with the Earthquake: At approximately 5 a.m. on April 18, 1906, in the last fun-filled minutes before the super-duper leveled Frisco, Jeanette MacDonald, a choir singer with a bedeviling bodice, brought down the roof at the Chicken's Ball by belting out the greatest song ever written about San Francisco. Five in the morning was then a normal hour for song. In the champagne days of San Francisco, gentlemen dined at dawn and breakfasted in the afternoon. "Saaaaan Fraaaaan-cisco, open your Gol-den Gate," sang the cow-eyed redhead in the final rousing chorus of "San Francisco," and the dance hall crowd of Barbary Coast geeks and Nob Hill swells, their voices hoarse from drink, roared a final berserko hurrah. This riled Clark Gable, who threw a solid silver cup full of gold coins at her petite feet and stomped off in a snit as a loud and terrible rumbling was heard, chandeliers swayed, walls groaned, and the whole town crashed down around the happy sinners.

We are talking movie-movie here, the best disaster flick of all time, the memorable 1936 earthshaker *San Francisco*, which also gave us the title song of the same name—a robust, rinky-dinky, sock-it-to-'em warbler that perfectly captured the spirit of the rowdy and independent and optimistic place that is everybody's favorite city. Whenever "San Francisco" is sung today it can bring tears of pure joy to even cynical eyes. Judy Garland wowed the Eastern Seaboarders by belting out "San Francisco" at her famous Carnegie Hall concert; audiences love it when Charles Pierce memorably mimes it; people jump up and tear the seats apart when "San Francisco" is done near the finale of *Beach Blanket*

Babylon; and to hear the Gay Men's Chorus singing "San Francisco" is the stuff of gooseflesh, like "Dixie" to a Southerner. "San Francisco" is the true-grit song of San Francisco, a splendid city once as magical as a Shakespearean forest, that has lost some of its luster in recent decades but still has a great song to remember the glory days by.

But when the klieg lights come on for the Democratic boxing match here this summer, what song is the watching world likely to hear over and over? Not the great "San Francisco." No sir. The world will hear a smarmy, deliberately sentimental piece of musical garbaggio called "I Left My Heart in San Francisco," with its infantile drool about little cable cars climbing halfway to the stars. When you hear "San Francisco," it brings to mind the quintessential image of San Francisco manhood, Clark Gable as nightclub owner Blackie Norton, slugging a buttinski priest and locking a parson's daughter into his bedroom. When you hear "I Left My Heart in San Francisco," the image that comes to mind is of some wimpy traveling salesman tidying up his sock drawer. "I Left My Heart" is a song barely suited for elevator music. It is as much San Francisco as bathtub chablis.

It is not the crass taste of the nation at large that has forced this schmaltzy, objectionable song on our town. San Francisco has brought this on itself. "I Left My Heart in San Francisco" is the official song of the City and County of San Francisco. For this you can thank the cabbage heads on the Board of Supervisors who voted it so back on October 6, 1969, a day that will live in infamy. No politician has since been man or woman (then-supervisor Dianne Feinstein voted for it) enough to correct this blot on the town. Voting for "I Left My Heart in San Francisco" in 1969 is susceptible to the analogy of selling scrap metal to the Japanese in 1939. "Tourists are the only people who ever request 'I Left My Heart in San Francisco,' said pianist Peter Mintun, who holds court at L'Etoile. "If it's sung, it should be sung away from San Francisco so we don't have to hear it." He favors making "San Francisco" the official song.

San Francisco music historian Bob Grimes lays the unfortunate official enshrining of the offending song to a plot by the incurable boosters who lurk in the closets of the Convention and Visitors Bureau. As Grimes reconstructs the shameful events of October 6, 1969, the tourist-bureau types wanted for a city song something sappy and unoffending that would lure the mindless to San Francisco. "They were afraid of 'San

Francisco'—they're afraid to promote anything attached to the earth-quake because it might scare off tourists," Grimes said. The booster-boys even made a film of Tony Bennett in front of a cable car singing this piece of musical macaroni and showed it to the supervisors, who have never been accused of having good taste, and they voted in the dingbat ballad. One of the selling points was that "I Left My Heart in San Fran-cisco" had been "adopted by American forces in Vietnam as their own war anthem," the then head-tourist-catcher for the city told the board, so help me God. One feels sorry for poor Tony Bennett, who got rich off this idiot song but is forever condemned to carry its baggage while people forget the really great Tony Bennett, the balladeer of "From Rags to Riches."

So San Francisco, famously a city of song, where a century ago the naughty Lottie Collins made "Ta Ra Ra Boom De Ay" famous, is saddled with a song that a right-thinking canary wouldn't sing. "It doesn't make any sense as an official song," said Grimes. "You should be able to play a city song in any manner of styles. 'San Francisco' plays equally well as ballad, honky-tonk, march, or even symphonically. But people have tried to play 'I Left My Heart' different ways and it just doesn't wash. It has no elasticity. It comes off sounding like merry-go-round music." Grimes, who works at Patrick and Co. stationers, lives in a three-room apartment surrounded by over twenty-one thousand pieces of sheet music he has collected. Hundreds of them are songs about San Fran-cisco. He lovingly examined titles such as "I'm Always Drunk in San Francisco" and "Frisco You're a Bear," but said that the all-time show-stopper about the town was "San Francisco."

If "I Left My Heart, Etc." were a racehorse it would never be put out to stud. It is the only song written by the late songwriting team of George Cory and Douglas Cross that became famous. The melody for "San Francisco" was written by Bronislaw Kaper and Walter Jur-mann. The lyrics came from Gus Kahn, who wrote such bouncy oldies-but-goodies as "Pretty Baby," "Side by Side," "I'll See You in My Dreams," "It Had to Be You," "Toot Toot Tootsie, Good-by," and "Yes, Sir, That's My Baby." The song "San Francisco," like a lot of old things in this city, comes from good family.

The motion picture *San Francisco,* which spawned such memorably chauvinistic lines in the song as "Other places only make me love you best / Tell me you're the heart of all the golden west," was written as a sort of love offering to the city by the great screenwriter Anita Loos, a transplanted San Franciscan who was suffering the pangs of separation in Hollywood. Ms. Loos was particularly proud of the scene where a drunk teasing a singer in Blackie Norton's nightclub is asked, "Where are you from?" The drunk says, proudly, Los Angeles, at which point the bouncer says, "I thought so," and decks him.

Grimes has been busy contacting people in the music world to seek musical redress from the politicans and make "San Francisco" the official song of the city before the onset of the Democratic Convention. "Everyone who's ever heard the song just loves it," Grimes said. "It's earthshaking." I'll say. What if we had another earthquake? Can you imagine anyone standing in the ruins singing "I Left My Heart in San Francisco"?

[*San Francisco Chronicle*, April 18, 1984]

The Last Night of Freedom
for Fugitive Black Artist

*A*BOUT 5 A.M. TUESDAY MORNING, under circumstances very strange and in setting very spooky, I became a collector of the art of Akinsanya Kambon, formerly Mark Anthony Teemer, formerly a Sacramento street fighter, formerly a very tough Marine known as Popeye, formerly a badass Black Panther, currently a fugitive from justice for whom the FBI was searching even as I paid.

Kambon is the black artist who first popularized the image of cops as pigs back in 1968. The cops, who have a long tribal memory for such things, have been on his case ever since. He has been living underground with his two teenage boys in an abandoned house in a rundown beachfront area on Chicago's South Side since fleeing Sacramento a year and a half ago after his conviction on a drug charge. This was the latest in a series of charges, including murder, filed against him by the Sacramento police, who have been sticking closer than a shadow to the black revolutionary for almost twenty years since he created the *Black Panther Coloring Book*, which taught ghetto kids that shooting pigs was a good indoor sport. Now the fugitive artist wishes to return to California and surrender to the very cops who he says in the warlike past have beat him and chained him up and kicked his teeth in and smashed his statues and slashed his paintings. His attorney is William Kunstler, the famed civil rights lawyer, who, of course, wants to put the cops on trial, and there will be a battle royal in Sacramento. Kambon is bringing the artwork back home to Sacramento and he wanted someone to see it while he was still in hiding lest it vanish in the black hole of a police evidence room.

The Chicago taxi driver refused to take me down the darkened dead-end street where the revolutionary black art professor was hiding. I walked past two parked cars where the passengers seemed more concerned with needles than necking. The only light was from a wan Midwestern moon. Kambon's house was at the end of the street where the sidewalk trailed off into tufts of wild grass and Lake Michigan lay vaguely luminous and still in the distance. The house was gabled and turreted and decaying. The doorbell was taped over with black electrical tape and when I knocked on the screen door it fell off one hinge. Two minutes passed before the door was opened by a big man with silky black skin and magnificent dreadlocks that hung down over his forehead like ragdog curls. His large brown eyes stared out from behind thick black glasses. "Come in, man," said the man at odds with white America.

I walked into a scene as strange as any I have encountered in many years of covering the vicissitudes of urban warfare. The ground floor of the house had been transformed into a secret African art gallery. Hundreds of paintings—mostly primitives done in oil and watercolors—hung on the walls over the decaying wallpaper. There were paintings of slave markets and paintings of starving black women staring hollow-eyed as their dying children suckled at their dry breasts. There were statues—hundreds of statues of proud African heads with patinas of bright green and black and red. There were unfinished statues—clay molds in the making—and broken statues, statues Kambon says the cops smashed, which he was repairing in one corner of the two large rooms turned into a gallery of his work—an art gallery that had never had, until now, a visitor. The ceilings were crumbling and the light fixtures removed. Cords tied off with electrical tape cast shadows on the stained green carpet in the illumination from occasional naked bulbs along the walls.

He picked up a statue of a Zulu warrior. "They broke the head right off this one," he said. "I'm going to glue it back on." He picked up a casting of the African continent—one part of it was broken off like a pizza with bites out of one side. "They did this, too," he said. Kambon said most of the damage to his art occurred when the cops broke into his home "with a battering ram" to arrest him on the possession-of-cocaine-for-resale charge he has fled. After they took him off, he said, the police left the doors open so people could walk in from the street and make off with his art.

Kambon fled Sacramento with more than seven hundred works of art—mostly the African sculptures and primitive paintings I saw in

Chicago—that he has created since 1968 during his almost twenty-year war with the Sacramento police, a war in which neither side seems inclined to take prisoners. He has admitted that he has been shot at and shot back in the Sacramento urban battles. Kambon was found not guilty in the murder trial of a policeman in the early seventies, but was later convicted of assault on the driver, whom he said attempted to run down one of his children.

The political battle over his art is a continuation of the war begun with the *Black Panther Coloring Book*, a star exhibit at the hysterical Senator John McClellan committee hearings on urban terrorism. Drawings of ghetto kids shooting at oppressor-cops dressed as uniformed pigs did not go over too well in the late sixties, and I do not think they will go over too well with the Sacramento cops in the late eighties. Kambon said when he was lecturing in an art class at Long Beach State College a few years ago the local police came into the classroom and dragged him off in front of his students on a warrant, later dropped, from Sacramento. "Look, I don't know the truth about every allegation of Kambon's, but it's clear that the Sacramento cops have been out to get him for a long time," said a former *Sacramento Bee* reporter who is now an aide to a state senator. "There used to be a joke around town that if the cops had their choice between an ax murderer and Kambon, they'd let the ax murderer go and take him."

Kambon was convicted on the drug charge only after a third trial— this with an all-white jury, his attorneys say—and says he is tired of "looking over his shoulder" hiding in Chicago and will chance beating the charges once again. "The long harassment of Kambon is a clear example of the persecution of revolutionary artists by local police authority and we welcome the chance for him to return to Sacramento and confront the police," said Kunstler. "We think there are excellent grounds to seek a new trial and that his name will be cleared."

The black art professor has been supporting his sons, who are returning to Sacramento with him, by painting on the streets of Chicago and taking donations from the rubberneckers. Occasionally someone will purchase an oil he's whipped out on the street, he said, but he couldn't dare bring customers to his gallery because "the FBI is always going around asking questions. They seemed to have guessed that I'm in Chicago somewhere." Since I was the only visitor to this eerie art exhibit that he was preparing to pack into crates and return with him to California, I bought an oil painting—a slave market scene—from him. Tears of gratitude came into this tough man's eyes.

"You hang onto that," the revolutionary artist said. "It's going to be worth money some day."

A PORTRAIT OF THE ARTIST AS FUGITIVE: That night, before he turned himself in, Akinsanya Kambon lay in a strange bed in the town he knew so well and counted his blessings. It was a short count.

The cops in his old hometown seem to love to bust the controversial artist and former Black Panther leader who first drew cops as pigs, an image not universally attractive to them, and seem to love almost as much to bust up his art. After seemingly hundreds of encounters with the Sacramento cops over two decades—some of them shoot-outs, some of them revolutionary art bust-ups—Akinsanya fled Sacramento with all his art, seven hundred pieces of sculpture and paintings in the African mode, and went underground in Chicago a year and a half ago.

Last Thursday he surrendered here with two of his teenage children who had been the run with him on drug charges of which he was convicted by a jury not of his peers, said jury being all white. He faces an uncertain future hinged on the amenities the law traditionally offers a black fugitive revolutionary and the courtesies hometown cops—why should Sacramento be an exception—show to bad-news black activists they suspect to be cop killers. (The jury in a 1970 case where Akinsanya was charged with the sniper killing of a Sacramento cop found him innocent, but the cops' suspicion and anger hangs on.)

America is a great country, but not the greatest to bring kids up in on the lam, the fugitive artist told me when I met him underground in Chicago two weeks ago. He said he was going to turn himself in for the sake of his children. Nothing like that is simple, and last Wednesday night in Sacramento the haunting waves of memories came back to him as he sleeplessly awaited the dawn of the day he has come to call "D-Day" in his life. That hot, sleepless night in Sacramento, Akinsanya Kambon daydreamed the situations of growing up in the ghetto that contributed to his political and artistic education and got him into his current sticky situation.

He was brought up in an abandoned railroad car placed on cinder-blocks on a lot his mother owned but couldn't afford to build on. He was reared by a snuff-chewing grandmother who first introduced him to the reality of race relations in these United States by yanking his ear and marching him down the street away from the white picket fence and the friendly greeting of a young white girl, blond with curly locks, in his third-grade class. "My grandmother got my ear hard and said, 'Boy, that's fire and rope, fire and rope! You get away from that.'"

Akinsanya joined the Boy Scouts at age twelve. He and a couple of friends from the Oak Park section of Sacramento were the only children of color in the scout unit. They were also distinguished from the rest of the troop by benefit of the lack of uniform, which their families could not afford. Akinsanya recalled sitting in the back of a troop meeting room, being proud to be a scout, listening in awe to the instruction of a fat man from Arkansas who was a national scout leader instructing the good-deed faithfuls in the fine art of tying knots. "Now I'm going to show you a special knot," Akinsanya recalls the scout leader telling the class. It was the hangman's knot. Akinsanya recalls faithfully learning to make the knot—all thirteen loops—"You have to let it slide loose to get the neck right," the instructor said. When he finished showing the class how to make a noose, the scoutmaster said, "I'll show you what it's used for." He walked to the back of the room and motioned to young Mark Teemer (his name before he adopted an African name ten years ago) to come forward. Akinsanya said he was at first thrilled to be selected from the crowd to participate, him being without a uniform and all. He was happy even when the good scout from Arkansas brought him to the front of the room and put the noose around his neck and tightened it. Everyone was laughing and it all seemed a matter of good fun until the knot got so tight he couldn't breathe. And all he remembers as he passed out was scouts running up to the scout leader and trying to get him to loosen the hangman's knot.

When he told his grandmother about the incident, she said, "Just shut up, and don't you ever let white folks see you cry."

Before he became a Black Panther, Akinsanya recalled during that sleepless pre-surrender night, he joined another famous American insti-tution, the U.S. Marines. He said he was torn between James Brown's 1965 song "Say It Loud—I'm Black and I'm Proud" and his earnest desire to be "the best patriotic warrior the USMC had ever seen." He was warrior material. Crippled early in life by polio and growing up as a street fighter in the Sacramento ghetto he learned how to use his fists when other kids made fun of the left side of his face, which remained partially paralyzed from polio. In the Marines he earned the nickname "Popeye" because of the half-opened left eye on the paralyzed side of his face. Ridiculed there, he fought his way through the cracker-patriots. "I was a two-hit fighter—I would hit the man and he would hit the ground," he said. Akinsanya said the thing that disturbed him about the Marines—this from a man who now has sixteen children—was that his Marine instructor told the boys how to "cut a pregnant woman open—turn the blade skyward between the navel and the crotch," and remove the fetus she was carrying for the military purposes of stomping it. "Don't give the little sonofabitch a chance to grow up and kill us," he said the instructor told him.

In Vietnam, Akinsanya because of his graphic talents was made a Marine combat illustrator. He traveled all over the war zones. There were scenes he dared not draw till he returned to the states, he said. "I went into this village where the Marines had raped a nine-year-old girl, after killing her family for their VC sympathies. After they were finished with her they shot her in the head and then—there are some things you just can't forget—they tried to wrap her little hand around a grenade. We had been told that when you kill a civilian without good reason to wrap a grenade around their hand and say they were attacking you. But this girl was so little they couldn't get her fingers around it. They just weren't big enough. I'll never forget that moment."

Akinsanya said after experiencing racial segregation in R&R areas in Okinawa and elsewhere that he came to view his years in the Marine Corps as those of "Europeans [whites in his vocabulary] looking out for Europeans and Africans looking out for Africans." Black members of the Marine Corps took to wearing their tribal African emblems on their helmets, and when he left the Marines they were black and white at war against themselves, he said.

These memories were among the night sweats of Akinsanya Kambon before he surrendered last Thursday to the cops on a drug conviction—an unprecedented third trial—that many in Sacramento believe is only another leg in a continuing vendetta to nail the offending black artist-activist on the part of Sacramento law enforcement, a charge the cops indignantly denied. The unusual situation of a political artist fleeing— and returning—to his hometown with his art has led to Akinsanya being represented by veteran civil rights attorney William Kunstler and Sacramento civil rights attorney Mark Merin. Merin surrendered Akinsanya at the Sacramento sheriff's office last Thursday under circumstances of strained politeness. Merin said there would be a bail hearing later this week at which the unusual circumstances of the artist's flight and voluntary reappearance would be discussed in hopes of the court granting him some degree of freedom.

Akinsanya surrendered at the Calvary Christian Center Church on Del Paso Boulevard. His artwork was spread around the chapel, a proud African sculpture propped on the brick pulpit. To the fugitive's surprise, his latest son—child No. 16—was presented to him for the first time at the church by a proud mother. "He's less than a year old—I've been running a year and a half; no wonder I haven't seen him," he said. He carried his new baby with him on his shoulder to jail.

The pastor of the church, the Reverend Phillip Goudeaux, was resplendent in a brown preacher suit and modest Afro hairdo. Pastor Goudeaux was restrained and parsonally formal in answering questions put to him by the mass media as to why his church had been picked for the surrender. I got him off to a side of the chapel. "Hey, man, weren't you in the Panthers with this dude?" I asked him. A gigantic smile full of memories came across Pastor Goudeaux's formally firm face. "Yeah. I used to be in there with him," he said with a beatific smile.

What goes around. It was Akinsanya's temptation with the pen that got him into trouble in Sacramento in the first place. Now it may be his large collection of Amer-Afro art—"powerful work related to life experiences," said Alan Gradon, chairman of the art department at Sacramento State College—that may bail him out. Perhaps literally. Attorney Merin says that it will cost a minimum of $10,000 to prepare a transcript of Akinsanya's controversial third trial for an appeal. Perhaps ditto for bail money. The fugitive artist hopes that he can sell his art, now sequestered in the church on Del Paso Boulevard, to save his life. Somehow, if this happens, it would seem appropriate.

[*San Francisco Examiner*, May 3 and 11, 1987]

Huey's Death Quickly
Ended Sixties Rebirth

*T*HE REBIRTH OF THE SIXTIES WAS MERCIFULLY BRIEF. It started with the mawkish outburst of aging hippie sentimentality for the twentieth anniversary of Woodstock, which made us a nation once again. It ended last week when Huey Newton was gunned down by a crack dealer on the same West Oakland streets that put him into revolutionary orbit in 1966. Black Panther Supreme Commander Huey Newton—radical icon, dope fiend, Kantian scholar, baby-faced muscleman, alkie, Hollywood darling, thug, revolutionary theorist, silk-suiter, Kools smoker, bad dude, recidivist ex-con, writer of books, poster boy, FBI psy-war victim and, finally, pipehead—held, in one mystery personality, all the contradictions and accomplishments of the century's most contentious decade. After the shooting was heard at dawn in Oakland on Tuesday, a mute inglorious taps was played for the sixties; this time the stake had been put through the heart of the vampire.

The Panthers contributed the lion's share of sixties political iconography—the clenched-fist Black Power salute, free breakfasts for ghetto kids, the coloring-book symbolism of cops as pigs, the slogan "Power to the People," images of blacks with the guns that the NRA thought were its alone. Theirs was everything except "We Shall Overcome." Whatever may be said of Huey in the rhetorical heights of bereavement at his funeral Monday, he was no Martin Luther King Jr. His mind soared to the heights of Mao, but his heart was never far from the street. Although at times he formally disavowed violence, he never disowned it; rather, it seemed more to own him, the way dust clings to the cowboy. He used violence, not fiat, to expel cofounder Bobby Seale from the Black Panther Party, and violence in one unappealing form or the other followed his descent into the eighties until the hour of his death. It is not to excuse government violence against the Panthers—there was plenty of that, from covert dirty tricks to outright murder, altogether more violence than the Panthers gave back—to say that Huey had his own private demons.

I knew the Panther triumvirate—Eldridge, Bobby, and Huey—when I edited *Ramparts* magazine during the sixties. *Ramparts* welcomed the Panthers to the political turbulence as, believe it or not, a peacekeeping force. The party's bold assertion of blacks' constitutional right to bear arms drove the occupying army of Oakland, i.e., the cops, to a malicious recklessness that provoked many shoot-outs and many fatalities. But in terms of the strains pulling black power politics in two extremist directions—guerrilla warfare against whites on one hand, anti-Semitism and black separatism on the other—the Black Panther Party exerted a powerful centrist force. The Panthers dashed the Weathermen's romantic white hopes of going underground with blacks with guns to fight a guerrilla war against the mother country and opted instead for a traditional, multiracial united front on the left. For all their rhetorical violence, the Panthers got heavily into the sort of electoral and coalition politics that led to the election of progressive black politician Ron Dellums to Congress.

Huey Newton always insisted that the Panthers were politically internationalists, not Pan-Africanists, and he rebuked Stokely Carmichael's black separatist notions, which Huey suggested were put in Stokely's head through radio beams from the CIA. In a sensate political history of the sixties, if ever one is written, Newton will be remembered for the surprisingly moderate political line of the Panthers, which may have been the only moderate thing in his life. "Huey loved his Courvoisier, which he called 'Vas,' and he could handle that all right, and just cocaine made him mellow, but when he combined the two it was deadly. "He became really crazy," said Oakland's Ken Kelly, who did much bonding with Newton during Kelly's sixties incarnation as information minister of the White Panther Party. Kelly was theorizing about Huey's end among the crackpots of Oakland.

However, the links of his alleged killer with the Black Guerrilla Family lend weight to what Charles Garry, the great radical attorney and Newton's longtime defender, told me about Huey's death—that it was anchored in wars past. The BGF vowed to kill Newton and, among others, attorneys Garry and Fay Stender. They got her because the attorneys continued to defend Newton after the BGF had signed his death warrant. The prison gang claimed the Panthers had agreed to provide backup for George Jackson's 1971 escape attempt, but that Huey called off his troops. If he did he was being, once again, sensible, because Jackson's escape plan had the unsavory smell of a government setup about it. The genocidal drug war that finally engulfed Huey Newton resulted from failure of the system, a failure that institutionalized a nation's racism and led to the upheavals of the sixties, which saw the breech birth of the Panthers.

Huey Newton's life was, in its strange way, one long act of revolutionary suicide.

[*San Francisco Examiner*, August 27, 1989]

Q: What's Wrong with
San Francisco Politics?
A: Money

*O*N THE AFTERNOON of November 6, 1987, the Friday after the election, a crisp and cool San Francisco day without a sunbeam of hope piercing the dark electoral cloud gathered over his head, Supervisor John Molinari was secluded in his second-floor City Hall office, receiving no visitors but the intimate and the anointed. Molinari's new campaign manager, Jack Davis, knocked on the door and went in without waiting, as was his custom. He stopped short at the scene inside. John Molinari was seated behind his desk in what seemed to be a state of shock. In a supplicant pose before the supervisor was the Reverend Cecil Williams with his arms outstretched in prayerful entreaty, looking for all the world like an ecclesiastical Al Jolson doing "Mammy." The black pastor gave Davis the annoyed glance of one who is interrupted during a sacramental process. Molinari waved the campaign manager off. Davis closed the door softly. The moment had the sanctity of the confessional. Indeed, it was a bizarre religious tableau of the type not seen in American politics since the conniving Kissinger knelt with the besotted Nixon in the bunker hours of Watergate.

The Reverend Williams, playing the rat to Molinari's mole—even his friends call Molinari "the Mole"—told him that he was jumping ship to join Art Agnos, who had just come within a few thousand votes of burying the Mole, the former frontrunner, in his own campaign mistakes. And Williams had the chutzpah to urge the Mole to quit the race while Agnos was soaring ahead. Molinari, who had just slam-dunked $1.4 million of his friends' money down the political sewer, was stupefied; the smiling clergyman wanted to turn the election into a coronation. Williams is the boss of Glide Memorial United Methodist Church, the

Notre Dame of the Tenderloin. He is also one of the face cards of San Francisco politics.

A savvy ecclesiastic who receives $800,000 a year from the city to feed the hungry in his Tenderloin tabernacle, Williams was a premature supporter of Molinari. That was back in the good old days when Jack took an early lead in the polls after raising over a million dollars from garbagemen (the supervisor's grandfather was a pioneer San Francisco scavenger), real estate developers, and others doing business with the city and county of San Francisco. When Molinari came in a distant second in the November 3 primary, Williams was quick to apprehend an apparent change in divine will; God, after all, is on the side of the winners. The mercurial minister was the first of many longtime Molinari supporters to jump ship, citing what he saw as the candidate's move to the right; many of the others deserting were men of capital who simply could not afford to back a loser.

The shock effect of Agnos' dramatic showing against the previously heavily favored Molinari affected many in the city, not the least Agnos himself. "[Dianne] Feinstein is going to go to pieces," he said. "She won't be able to handle re-entering ordinary life without the policemen and the limos on hand. You can't imagine the incredible power it gives you being mayor, but you've got to be able to handle the power. I'm tough. I'll be able to handle it. I'll stand on the steps of City Hall like Feinstein never did and let the ordinary people come up to me and ask me questions, call me an asshole. The power won't get to me."

Agnos told me that the night Williams did his Al Jolson routine in Molinari's office, Agnos seemed adrenalated and his eyes were glistening with the otherworldly look of a messiah. He was in the state of political rapture that once moved his fellow Democrat Lyndon Johnson, high from peacemaking, to boast, "I've got doves coming out my armpits."

I know these things because I was a candidate for mayor; not a journalistic observer, but a participant. I crossed the line dividing citizen and politician and entered the twisted world of San Francisco electoral politics, analogous in every way to the Twilight Zone. It is a world closer to the double-dealing of the Middle East than to the values of middle America—a world where money is regent and the commitments that count are the ones that ring the cash register. And yet it's an amazingly personal world where the loyalties and hatreds that shape the campaign come from real, or imagined, hurts of years past. Just say no, I reply, when people ask me why anyone would run for mayor.

My decision to run had a lot to do with being born and raised in this town and thinking that the vision of the old city was being dirtied and chiseled by the politicians. There was a pervasive feeling, shared by many, that San Francisco deserved better than it was being offered in this election, or, perversely, that it was getting just what it deserved. I thought the city was getting short-sheeted, and that in the last free-for-all election we will see in many a year, some idiot had better jump in there and give the politicians what for. As it turned out, I was that idiot.

Yet this mayoral race, for all of its nightmarish big-bucks elements, has brought a few real changes. Who would have imagined a year ago that the election of 1987 would see:

- The nationally hyped Feinstein regnant go out with a whim-per, the city busted financially and Madame Mayor unable to deliver for either Molinari or the Giants stadium, her two final lost causes.

- Herb Caen losing it by putting his healthy cynicism aside and his fifty years of power on the line for a dice-playing buddy named Jack "Millionari" Molinari. Meantime, the young colum-nist for the afternoon paper went for Agnos, making Mr. San Francisco look like Mr. Milpitas.

- Political control of San Francisco shifting from the Feinstein/Molinari lazy bucks, let-'em-build-skyrises clique to the Sacra-mento moneybags machine headed by Assembly Speaker Willie Brown, the new power behind the Agnos throne.

- The entrance fee for any serious run for mayor of San Fran-cisco becoming a cool million bucks.

Running for mayor of San Francisco was an exhilarating, exhausting, dreadful, extremely informative, and sometimes hilarious experience. At a party thrown by a left-wing Valencia Street bookstore, a worker at McAuley Neuropsychiatric Institute came up to me and said he had great news. He had polled six people at the hospital and all six had said they were going to vote for me as the candidate who cared most for the poor and the homeless. That was encouraging, I said. Were these six of his coworkers? No, he said, crestfallen, they were inmates.

When you don't have a million bucks like your rivals, you have to think up gimmicks to draw attention to your candidacy. That's why we developed the official "Hinckle for Mayor" condoms. They were produced in faraway Thailand and packaged in Tempe, Arizona (sorry, no union bug), in covers cleverly resembling traditional campaign matchbooks. We gave away thousands for educational purposes here in the AIDS capital of the country.

Good news travels. During a stuffy black-tie fundraiser at the Players Club in New York, I gave one of the campaign matchbook/condoms to Tom Wolfe, the writer. Tom used to live in San Francisco and thought this great sport. He bounded across the room to former New York mayor John Lindsay and handed him the little package, saying this was from his candidate for mayor. Lindsay began to slip it politely into his pocket, as one would with matches. Wolfe said, "Wait a minute, Your Honor, these aren't regular matches, these are from San Francisco." Lindsay looked down and opened the cover. His tanned chin dropped in horror.

> "The Hinckle voters are an interesting collection—very, very liberal and very, very conservative."
>
> —District Attorney Arlo Smith

QUENTIN KOPP GOT HIMSELF A NEW HAT for his bachelor party. It was a moose-head cap with Bud cans dangling from the antlers and a mild obscenity scrawled across the visor. It gave the bespectacled state senator the slightly addled look of Danger Mouse. His high-rolling friends among the city's conservative elite, in an attempt at damage control, had herded themselves into the basement of the North Beach Restaurant to hoot at their hero on his last night out as a swinging single. The floor was wet with spilled wine when I walked in. "The candidate is here," Kopp boomed, in the voice he uses to break sound barriers. Senator Kopp, whose obsessive troublemaking is often mistaken for curmudgeonliness, had signed on, to the mystification of many, as a ballot sponsor for my eleventh-hour mayoral candidacy. This led to some confusion in the ranks of right-wing faithful as to whom, precisely, Kopp was backing, since he had previously announced for Roger Boas. That lack of precision elicited from Boas one of those blue streaks of language for which he was to become famous during the campaign—the former city chief administrative officer who had solved the city's garbage crisis was a garbage mouth.

Rare were the Boas supporters in the basement of the North Beach Restaurant that evening in early October. In their political prism, Roger Boas was pink, John Molinari was yellow, and Art Agnos red all over. This was a gathering of the Old Town—mostly third- and fourth-generation San Franciscans, judges, lawyers, retired military types, and mossbacked successful businessmen. They would take no prisoners and wanted as mayor only their St. Joan in a moose cap, Quentin Kopp, or possibly someone further to his right. I was there on a mission: to lift the veil from the tabernacle of San Francisco conservatism and see if I could partake of some of its electoral fruits. An old political pro had told me that you cannot win an election in this town without getting votes from the side opposite your ideological compass bearings. The liberals, radlibs, and lefties will split their votes, I was told, but the conservatives tend to vote en masse. My assignment was to slice off a piece of the right-wing pie.

The all-male crowd was well-dressed, and well-deported in the manner of *Hogan's Heroes* pranksters. I worked the tables, shaking hands, saying "How you doin'?" *in serium* and handing out miniature "Hinckle for Mayor" black eye patches. I had a fistful of campaign condoms in my pocket, but this was not the crowd for those. Instead I told growing-up-in-Catholic-school stories, which in Old Town Frisco qualifies you as one of the boys. But when I told a fanciful bad-taste bachelor-party gag about Kopp mating with one of the Mitchell brothers and bringing more little pornographers into the world (the senator cackled at this like a hen with lower intestinal problems), I was scolded for the naughty words by the maharajah of west-of-Twin-Peaks, John Barbagelata. I remembered the former mind-your-manners supervisor once had written a Savonarola-like law that put pasties on the neon nipples of Broadway strip-joint signs.

A candidate does not wish to fall into Barbagelata's disfavor, as he still carries considerable clout in the cautious, vote-rich area west of Twin Peaks. It is an axiom of practical politics in San Francisco that you cannot win in the liberal east side of the city alone but must cross the great divide into the more right-thinking western quarter of Baghdad-by-the-Bay. An amateur political geographer, Barbagelata staked out as his turf the "Golden Crescent"—a serpentine half-moon rising in the Republican tip of Pacific Heights and extending across the outer Richmond, the Inner Sunset, and the Outer Mission. This is the largely middle-class, homeowning, fed-up-with-the-tax-eaters-of-City-Hall constituency that doesn't fit the national media profile of wacko San Francisco. Their stalwart support had brought the bantam-sized realtor/politician to within a whisker of defeating George Moscone, the old Democratic machine's liberal candidate, in the 1975 mayoral election.

I was flattered when Barbagelata—known as "Barbo" by his political intimates—asked me to his West Portal aerie to discuss my campaign. He allowed as how he was so personally disgusted with Molinari and Boas—Agnos he considered backed by "socialists and communists"—that he would consider even a radical wanker like myself for mayor. "Politics in this town is a lot of crap," said Barbagelata. "And besides, I know your mother. She's all right even if you aren't," he added.

THE INNER SANCTUM OF CONSERVATIVE SAN FRANCISCO is not without its links to permanent adolescence, including verbal pie-throwing and arcane nicknames for key players: Kopp is affectionately known as "Pin," which is short for "Pinhead." Appellate Court Justice William Newsom answers to "Fit," short for "Tightfit" (an allusion to his suits); Kopp's chief of staff, Jack Davis, is called "Chiefie"; attorney Jeremiah Hallisey, Kopp's longtime finance chairman, is called variously "the Bag" or "Lace," a reference to his Boston Irish ancestry; Lorenzo Petroni, one of the proprietors of the North Beach Restaurant, where the city's conservative kitchen cabinet meets in rump session, is called simply "the Greed."

Barbo wasn't the only old pol holding old grudges. Ghosts of battles past haunted the mayor's race. One is the bitter 1986 battle between then-supervisor Kopp and then-assemblyman Lou Papan for the state Senate seat that Kopp now holds. Jack Davis managed Kopp's campaign and Richie Ross, now Agnos' campaign manager, was running Papan's. According to Davis, Agnos, a Papan supporter, mau-maued him at a gay

Democratic club meeting. "He came unglued; he rushed up and grabbed my tie and put his nose right in my face and began pounding his finger on my chest and told me that I never run a campaign of any integrity." Davis took a leave from Kopp's Sacramento staff for the seemingly thankless task of taking over the Mole's faltering campaign in its Waterloo period largely because of that personal bit of high intensity.

Kopp's refusal to back the more conservative Molinari against Agnos was not unrelated to Molinari's alliance of convenience with Kopp's favorite enemy, Her Honor Dianne Feinstein, who was backing the Mole for mayor. The history becomes ancient here. Kopp has never forgiven Di-Fi for going back on what he says was a handshake deal engineered by Barbagelata in 1978 for Dianne to become president of the Board of Supervisors and Kopp to run for mayor in 1979. Feinstein never endorsed Kopp, and when George Moscone was assassinated in November of 1978, she took over the mayor's chair and sat there for another nine birthdays.

This town is living proof of the old saw that the personal is political. Bernie Orsi, who is as conservative as an undertaker's suspenders, backed the liberal Agnos early in the game because he has an old grudge against Molinari. Lorenzo "the Greed" Petroni is known to have turned the shade of pesto and jumped around like Rumpelstiltskin upon hearing the Mole's name because he blames the supervisor for a city mental health clinic going in next door to his restaurant.

"LET ME ASK YOU ONE THING. Are you really a communist?" Barbagelata asked me when I visited him in his West Portal real estate office. "I really hate communism," he said. I passed Barbo's loyalty check by telling him that as far as I was concerned, communists were too conservative and I could never be one of them. Barbagelata peered at me over his steel-rimmed aviator glasses. The bantam-sized former supervisor weighs about as much as a bag of unsalted peanuts and is always having little heart attacks because, as his wife Angie will tell you, he worries too much. When he isn't worrying about the tax eaters in City Hall he's worrying about the Reds in Managua. "I'll let this go, but I've got to ask you—do you know how close Nicaragua really is? Do you know how many miles?"

We were in the Barbo's private office, which closely resembled an FBI file room. He handed me the Feinstein dossier, which he described as though it had powers against the woman akin to kryptonite—actually, it contained a bunch of press clippings. "If you write leaflets against Feinstein in your campaign, I'll get the Republicans to give you some money and they'll mail it out statewide. They're afraid she might get to be governor," he said.

To talk to Barbagelata about money is enough to make anyone a fiscal conservative. The city wastes it like water overflowing a tub. In 1969 the Board of Education talked about floating a $150 million bond issue to earthquake-proof the schools. Barbagelata asked some embarrassing questions and discovered that the geniuses at the San Francisco Unified School District had come up with that figure by taking one school, guesstimating the cost to earthquake-proof it, and then multiplying that figure by the total number of schools. The figure quickly came down to $56 million. When Barbo screamed again, the job was finally approved at $38 million. "That sort of hidden crap goes on all the time," Barbagelata said. "This city is a walking scandal."

The real estate man gave me one of the printing presses on which he had printed his campaign literature when he ran for mayor and convinced me that I could run a campaign for practically nothing if I used odd-lot paper to print on—"they throw it away and it's perfectly good"—and got volunteers to distribute the literature and run the headquarters. This was comforting news, because practically nothing was what my campaign had raised. We opened the doors of our headquarters on Valencia Street to the homeless, who slept in the building and answered the phone and tinkered with the printing press.

Things seemed to be going swimmingly for an operation with practically no money, until I received a call from my campaign treasurer, Bob Mulcrevy. There was a lot of music blaring over the line. It didn't sound like he was calling from someplace a treasurer should be. "I'm in the bar," Mulcrevy said. "I've got news." The bar next to the headquarters was a former gay cowboy bar now called Zeitgeist and catering to straight bikers. "I ordered a drink and they asked me if I wanted to put it on our account."

"What account?"

"Your homeless supporters have opened up a tab," he said.

ART AGNOS GAVE ME A LOOK that would neuter a cat. We were on television, smack in the middle of a live-at-eight mayoral debate. On my left was the Mole. He was wearing one of his dress-for-success suits and he had a set, silly grin screwed onto his face. On my right, rigid as a penny gum machine, was Roger Boas in his double-breasted blazer. His chin stuck out like he was waiting for a clown to come up and smack him with a pie. Agnos was standing stage right in a First Communion suit, glaring at me.

Agnos had tweaked my proposition to put a gambling casino on Alcatraz, and I had shot back that the assemblyman was a captive of his big donors in the horse-racing lobby in Sacramento. What the hell, it was a debate. Agnos shot me his Darth Vader look. I had violated the unwritten rules by bringing up the unclean subject of where politicians get their bucks. That is simply not done in polite campaign society. The last thing politicians want to talk about, onstage, is money. Offstage, money is the first thing they talk about. Most nights on the campaign trail, after the set speeches were over and the gossip lamp was lit, money was the only thing they talked about.

"Now, you take Mo Bernstein, there's a great bag man for you, all smoke and mirrors," a Molinari staffer was telling me at the bar at Miz Brown's Country Kitchen on Mission Street, where voters and pols alike were mixing after a community meeting in the back room. He was speaking about the esteemed president of the San Francisco Airport Commission and senior political citizen. "Mo is a somebody-else's-check expert. You won't get his money, but he's great at asking other people for a check and getting it out of them. He's always showing up with a fistful of checks—that's where he gets his reputation as a big money man. Most of those people would give you money anyway, but Mo's there first to put it together. And he's all over the board. Smoke and mirrors. Mo's great," he said. There was a faint *tee-hee* in his voice as the Mole's operative discussed what sounded to me like perfidy with genuine admiration. After you hang around politicians for a while you get used to this; they really are different from other people.

Elections make all politicians crazy, and the mayoral election of 1987 had them running around at high speed, like a bunch of dirt farmers drunk on flea-killing vodka. The impetus for the special frenzy of this exercise in the art of democracy was that the Mole had sucked up almost all the available dough in town. This was no small feat, given the $500 individual donation limit that then–San Francisco supervisor Quentin Kopp had passed into law in 1986. Kopp's brave new law turned out to be a joke as Molinari became Millionari, using his position as political heir apparent to the Dowager Empress, toiling the fields of firms doing business with the city and harvesting $500 checks in bushels like wheat.

The Mole has a long reach. Some garbage guys were planning a little lunch for my campaign in the basement of Gino & Carlo, the North Beach saloon, to which a handful of scavengers were invited to kick in fifty bucks each. Alas, the lunch was aborted, I was told, when orders came down from the High Arctic of the removal business that the lunch Must Be Canceled. The Mole had an iron lock on the garbage money, and he was enforcing his due.

I did get some offers of scratch from rival camps. A fellow who described himself as close to the Boas money said he could get me $40,000 from the Boas gang if I agreed to drop out of the race in the last week and endorse old Rog. Although I liked Boas personally the best among the candidates, I declined. A high roller from the Molinari campaign offered me $10,000 to pay for a mailer to the liberal east side of the city attacking Agnos from the left. They wanted me to print bills from Agnos' slush fund, such as $289 for "beverages for legislators," but I was not inclined to throw glasses around that stone house.

Boas wrote his own election a handsome check and financed much of the rest off the silver tea platter of Ann Getty, who hosted many a fundraiser for him. Meanwhile, Agnos went out of town in search of his million. He gathered his dough from Greek friends and associates who had helped make him wealthy on an assemblyman's salary. Some Agnos partisans argue that Willie Brown could have helped him more in the pre–November 3 period. But other more cynical observers believe that, unless Agnos suddenly changes his political religion and breaks with the Sacramento-based Democratic money/power machine that helped raise him so much dough, Willie Brown will be the Cardinal Richelieu of the Agnos administration.

Financing a San Francisco mayoral race from the unbending river of Sacramento special-interest money seemed like a risky gambit to me. The big boys are used to getting some bang for their buck. The local media did not seem to share my alarmist concerns about *ausländer* money buying heavily into a San Francisco politician. However, Agnos knew what I meant when I twitted him about his horse-racing contributors influencing his opinion of a casino on Alcatraz. (You mean there would be betting without going to the track? Agnos, get in here!)

Thus the evil eye he gave me on TV.

IT GETS REAL MEAN OUT THERE: From the Agnos partisans I heard about Molinari's kick-'em-around nature. The staff at the Golden Gate Bridge District used to call him "Bully Boy." From Boas' people I heard about Agnos' revenge syndrome (then I read in Rob Morse that the job in Agnos' administration that Richie Ross, his campaign manager, wanted was Minister of Revenge). From Molinari's people I heard about Boas' garbage mouth. From other candidates I heard that Agnos and Boas people were saying I was some kind of a monster who eats his young and a card-carrying dipsomaniac, a perception possibly grounded in my longstanding habit, taken from the work ethic of Gogol, of writing in taverns.

"I bet you really hate politicians now, huh?" a cabbie asked me the day after the election.

"Politicians and the press, too. The whole lot can go sod off as far as I'm concerned," I said. Then I remembered that Jimmy Breslin, the New York columnist, had predicted before I decided to run for mayor that this would be how I'd feel. Breslin ran for New York City Council president in 1969, the same year that Norman Mailer ran for Big Apple mayor. (In addition to Breslin and Mailer, the ranks of journo/writers who have stood for elected office in this country include Bill Buckley, Marvin Kitman, James Michener, and Gore Vidal. All of them lost. There may be a lesson there.) "The newspaper and television reporters—the stupidity of the people asking you questions. As you see it unfold, the ignorance is unbelievable. They fawn, they're gullible, they jump to conclusions. It's a tremendous lesson in reporting—from the other side," Breslin told me. The man was a prophet.

At the time—late July—I was enmeshed in an intramural flap at the *Examiner*. Journos are at once the most narcissistic of beasts and hypochondriacs who cannot resist writing about the symptoms of their own illnesses. The flap was over whether I should continue to write my column while running for mayor. I took the position that obeisance to the First Amendment didn't require you to forfeit the rest of your civil rights—such as standing for elective office. If Boas could keep selling cars and Molinari and Agnos could continue eating out of the taxpayer's trough while running for mayor, there was no reason I couldn't continue writing my column. If a rival candidate thought that unfair, let him write a column in rebuttal. And after seeing these geezers close up, I knew that would mean a windfall make-work program for ghostwriters. Breslin was in my corner. "Of course you should write the column. You should go out there and ring doorbells and report what people are really saying and write about the whole insane process of running for office," he advised. He offered wisdom learned on his own campaign. "There are no votes after nine o'clock at night. Stay out of the bars. They're all drunk and they'll promise you anything."

Other journalists, including about half the *Examiner* staff, felt differently. They were in a state of agitation at the prospect of covering one of their own running for higher office. Finally the paper succumbed to what *Newsweek* has called "the wimp factor" and announced that I would not write my column while running for mayor. I would be covered like any other candidate. When people invariably asked me if I was seriously running for mayor, I would reply that I was the only candidate who had given up his job to run.

After announcing, I fell through a black hole as far as the newspapers were concerned. The *Chronicle*, where I used to work, treated me as a nonperson; I couldn't get in the paper if I got run over by the Wright Brothers. The *Examiner* assigned a veteran reporter, Harry Jupiter, to cover me. The next three months became a comedy of kvetching with Jupiter—who is a good kvetcher—bugging the city desk to put Hinckle stories in the paper and hitting maybe one in four. "I'm the Hinckle reporter," said Jupiter, "except when I try to write about Hinckle."

The experience of being interviewed as a candidate by newspaper editorial boards was also enlightening. At the *Bay Guardian*, the radicchio eater's weekly, I got into a classic sixties liberal tussle with publisher Bruce Brugmann. He was dressed like a man of the people in a Dan Rather sweater and fumed over my proposal to get the army out of the Presidio and transform it into senior citizen housing and childcare facilities. Brugmann was horrified at the idea of the army leaving the Presidio.

He said the army protected the Presidio not from invading troops but from...real estate developers. "If the army goes, the developers will be building high-rises there within a few years," he said.

I told the liberal publisher not to worry, that we'd pass legislation to require a two-thirds vote of the people of San Francisco to change its use from senior housing and childcare. Brugmann pessimistically maintained that the developers would get in. "They'll put something on the ballot and bamboozle the public and the *ExChron* will go along," he whined. I told Brugmann that his problem was that he was so elitist he didn't trust the people to make up their own minds. Did he really think San Franciscans would vote to tear down the Presidio for developers? Brugmann insisted that only the army could keep the Presidio safe for trees. Well then, I told him, why don't you write an editorial calling on the army to invade Golden Gate Park and occupy it so they could protect the park, too?

At the *Chronicle* editorial board, I was waxing blissful about shaking up the idiotic planning department and encouraging in-law units to be built in homes to ease the housing crisis. I talked about how revenues from a casino on Alcatraz would ease the city's financial crisis, how the income from a municipal golf course in the Presidio on the site of the Army's VIP course would bring the city sufficient revenue to maintain senior citizen housing there. Then a *Chronicle* editorial writer had a question. "Let me get this straight," he said. "You're proposing that the city take two properties, Alcatraz and the Presidio, away from the federal government and turn them over to the city's control?"

"That's right," I said.

"But that's never been done," said the *Chronicle* man. In this city, which still basks in the bold legacy of its Ralstons, Gianninis, Sutros, and Crockers, this is the voice of the morning newspaper.

If the election of 1987 was not the press's finest hour, other major institutions of the city performed in a sad-sack and barbaric manner. Organized labor, once the pride and muscle of San Francisco, fulfilled the prediction of one of my campaign cochairmen, George Evankovich of the laborers' union: "The labor movement in San Francisco," Evankovich said, "couldn't knock a sick whore off a bedpan."

The comintern that runs the San Francisco Labor Council endorsed both Molinari and Agnos, spacing out the obnoxious role Molinari played in the city workers' strikes in the 1970s and going amnesiac on Agnos' anti-labor stands for Proposition M and against the homeporting of the USS *Missouri*. The brokered dual endorsement was already writ in stone before mayoral candidates were even invited to address the Labor Council. I tried to rouse the delegates from their stupor by denouncing the boss system. When delegates from some unions demanded the freedom to vote for the candidates of their choice, the union bosses sat on them. So much for union democracy in the city and county of San Francisco.

One Establishment lesbian and gay Democratic club made itself an object of hilarity by realizing too late that its endorsement system allowed the club's blessings to be "bought" by politicians sending in designated hitters to purchase memberships. One of the privileges of membership, as American Express says, was to vote to endorse a candidate for mayor. The Harvey Milk club went for Agnos early in the campaign. The Mole got the endorsement of the more conservative Stonewall club. But it was the Alice B. Toklas club, boosted by memberships purchased by the Agnos and Molinari camps, that ballooned from about three hundred to eleven hundred members in the final days of the campaign, though neither candidate got a clear majority. In the beginning, the daily press reported these venal endorsements straight, if you will pardon the expression, as if grassroots democracy were in action in the Castro. After the fact, the clubs all looked to their endorsement rules, and the Alice B. people promised to do better next time.

THE COPS MAY HAVE PUT THEIR FEET in deep doo-doo by attempting to mess with the mayoral election. To many, it appears that furtive elements within the local constabulary savagely violated the rules of policely deportment by stealing—copying—court-sealed information from the Hall of Justice records room and dropping it off at the local dailies in the Frisco flatfoots' equivalent of a plain brown wrapper. The aim was to destroy the reputation of a candidate for mayor. The target of the smear attempt was John Molinari, the main opponent of the candidate endorsed by the powerful San Francisco Police Officers Association, Art Agnos.

The year 1987 was the one when character became an issue in politics. The stories of why senators Gary Hart and Joe Biden dropped out of the Democratic presidential race are well known. Not so well known is that two public figures in 1987 withstood concentrated rumor campaigns against them alleging defects of character. One was Governor Mario Cuomo of New York, who faced a barrage of rumors earlier this year that he was somehow connected to the Mafia. Even though many politicians' reactions would be otherwise, Cuomo chose to go to the press and confront the rumors. He said that false information was being spread about him, and his statement sparked a disclosure that the Republican counsel to the New York State Senate Crime and Correction Committee had been sending anonymous packages of "documents" to the press alleging Cuomo's links to organized crime. When Cuomo went public the malefactor was exposed and punished and the rumors ended.

Another attempt at character assassination was made in the San Francisco mayoral race against John Molinari. Molinari anguished over it but chose not to go public and confront the rumors, which continued even after the election. The purloined information involved a family matter. Under the confidentiality provisions of state law, a part of the police file had been sealed and could legally be released only by court order. But some slime-minded person stole the report and tried through innuendo to sell the press on the idea that he had something on Molinari. The dropping of the report was followed by anonymous telephone calls to the papers, hinting there was more to the "story" than met the eye. As the rumors spread around town this summer, both daily newspapers—and eventually other media—investigated the allegations. They were found to be false. When nothing was printed, the anonymous calls to the press began anew, this time with a claim that an additional police report on Molinari had been stolen from the record room by Molinari's friends in a coverup. This was a lie.

The attempt to smear Molinari was Topic A during the mayoral campaign. Every candidate, and every candidate's aides, talked about it. The responsible parties—who, police chief Frank Jordan made clear, could have been either civilians or police officers—tried to flog the story as far away as Fresno. "It was all so blatant," said a clearly upset Jordan, when I asked what he intended to do about the mess. "They took the report and shoved it under the door of the major dailies. They did it deliberately in an attempt to antagonize this election. They tried to hurt the man and destroy his family. We can't have sensitive records walking out of the Hall of Justice to be used for partisan political purposes," he said.

Intimates of Molinari told me that the smear attempt had shattered the supervisor and thrown the whole campaign off. Said a relative: "They really knew how to get to John. They were driving him crazy with these lies." I remembered that Molinari had earlier in the campaign made a controversial statement that he was considering replacing Jordan with another chief if he got elected. He said the chief wasn't going after double-parked trucks energetically enough. That sounded a little strange at the time. I wonder now if Molinari's public musings on changing chiefs might have been part of his private agony over the police smear.

Who did it? "If I knew that, they would be up on charges," the chief said. There are no fingerprints on photocopies—"we may never find out who did it." Jordan said he had instituted new security procedures in the records room to head off a similar incident. "If these people would dare do this to a powerful politician," the chief wondered aloud, "who else would they do it to?"

"What a sick thing, eh? Did you ever think it was as bad as this?"

—campaign manager Jack Davis

IT WAS AFTER MIDNIGHT AT MUMM'S, the Taj Mahal of Frisco discos, and a banker in a velvet blazer was talking politics. "Now I don't think that Willie Brown fellow—I saw him here the other night—has done all that well financially in Sacramento. He puts all his money in his cars and his clothes. So I figure being in Sacramento doesn't get you all that rich." At Mumm's, the private lives of public persons are dissected like a biology-class frog, especially the lives with the finely tailored cut of Speaker Brown's and Herb Caen's, another Mumm's familiar face. This was the evening after the November 3 election. Artie Mitchell, the caring por-nographer, had dragged me from the Tosca Café, where I was drown-ing my election sorrows in cappuccinos, and whisked me to Mumm's to conjugate the sorrowful dative of how our $31,000 had gathered

3 percent of the vote against the $3 million of my opponents. In the real world there are no electoral Davids against million-dollar Goliaths.

I wasn't so sure that the velvet-chested banker was right. The state legislature seems at times an ample way to make one's fortune. Consider the wretched Ed Meese, who, after decades of hanging around the executive branch of government with Ronald Reagan, remains reduced to the finances of a riverboat gambler. The legislative branch, in contrast, is a cheery place. While in the state legislature Art Agnos' friend, former assemblyman Lou Papan, became a millionaire and Agnos himself managed, with a little help from his developer friend Angelo Tsakopoulos, to turn himself into a wealthy man, which is not exactly hind tit on a salary of $37,000 a year. The irony of the 1987 mayoral race was that John Molinari, the insurance executive who was nicknamed Millionari for his relentless fundraising, is much further from being a millionaire than his ex–social worker opponent is.

Politics is all perceptions. While the perception grew among the voters that Molinari was not a dear old peanut at all but a money machine sitting on a molehill of cash extracted from developers, lawyers, accountants, contractors, and others doing earnest business with the city, there was little public perception of the fact that Art Agnos was raising about as much as Molinari. The potential conflicts of interest in the source of Molinari's funds were clear to all. But no inquiring reporter flicked out a Bic in serious speculation about any problems inherent in the sources of Agnos' financing.

The fact that Art Agnos' campaign money came from out of town was partially obscured by the unseemly rush of Molinari's contributors after their candidate's November 3 electoral meltdown to the lifeboat of Art Agnos' treasury. The developers, bankers, and businessmen who thought they had bought a sure thing with the Mole kicked women and children out of the way to cover their bets with the previously unacceptable Agnos. Typical of the midstream-switch artists was liquor tycoon and San Francisco Fire Commission president Henry Berman, who kept his principles liquid enough to give Molinari more than $1,000 ($500 from Mr. B, $500 from Mrs. B) before November 3 and Agnos more than $2,000 (individual and business contributions) immediately thereafter. Molinari rudely learned from the papers that his soul mate Berman had deserted him and became furious when Berman claimed that he had tried to telephone Molinari to tell him that he was switching to Agnos but couldn't get through.

That a heaping portion of Art Agnos's $1.4 million in contributions came from the big bubbling Democratic-money/special-interest pot is beyond dispute among political pros. And it is a well-known fact of political life that major contributions do not flow southward from Sacramento to local politicians without the blessing of the all-powerful Willie Brown. This raises the unavoidable question: not of potential local conflicts of interest but of foreign pressures on the independence of the mayor's office, and how a new mayor beholden to out-of-town dollars is going to govern hassle-free of those interests. Speaker Brown's firm, for instance, represents the Southern Pacific Realty Corporation. The SP is a major partner in the huge Mission Bay development project, controversial details of which the next planning commission must approve.

The 1987 mayoral race, when all the bills are paid and the deficits raised, will cost over $4 million. This must be a world record for a local municipal election in a city the size of San Francisco. "There's only one source for that kind of money—from the people who want something from you," said Walter Zelman of Common Cause, the citizen's lobbying group that is pushing for public financing of statewide elections in California. The case for public financing of Assembly and Senate posts in Sacramento is manifest; the lobbyists have made it clear that they are willing to buy any vote in Sacramento that is even obliquely for sale.

The case for public financing of mayoral elections in San Francisco is developing in front of us. It is becoming a national cliché—on the cutting edge of a joke—that the system of financing and electing major candidates for office in these United States is perfectly wacko. In the state of California alone, the cost of running for public office has risen by more than 3,000 percent since the 1950s. In terms of the cost of San Francisco municipal elections, the cow has gone right over the moon.

The cost of the fundraising arms race is more than just political. The issue is not merely whether a politician must pay the piper; no one with special-interest big dollars gives a candidate money without demanding at least the right to plead his special cause in chambers. The larger problem is the personal drain on politicians—the almost collegiate hazing system of collecting campaign funds. A friend of Molinari's told me that the candidate went into the mayoral race exhausted because for almost a full year before he announced "there was a fundraiser every night." This is not a local problem. "The campaign never stops," said U.S. Senate Democratic majority leader Robert Byrd (D-West Virginia), making the argument for electoral reform that most senators end up as full-time fundraisers rather than legislators.

Legislation is pending before the New York City Council that would create the option of public funding for municipal elections—the candidates raise a maximum amount, the public matches it. By one estimate, such a scheme would require about $4 million of public money for the Big Apple mayoral race every four years—at election time—to give the scandal-ridden city the vestiges of clean government. Public financing laws, though not binding, tend to be accepted by candidates (the last two presidential winners, for example, played within the national public-financing rules). In San Francisco, the cost would be perhaps $1 million every four years. When you're electing a mayor who presides over San Francisco's nearly $2 billion annual budget, the cost of municipal financing seems on the cheap side.

The way it stands now, if my basset hound, Bentley, raised a million dollars, he could be mayor. Of course, there are always two sides to every argument.

[*San Francisco Examiner, Image* magazine, January 3, 1988]

Index

WARREN JAMES HINCKLE III was born October 12, 1938, in San Francisco
and graduated in 1961 with a degree in philosophy from the University of
San Francisco, a Jesuit institution. After college, he started a public relations company and ran, unsuccessfully, for the county board of supervisors
before joining the *San Francisco Chronicle* as a city reporter. Later, as editor
of *Ramparts* magazine (1964–1969), he received the Thomas Paine Award
in 1967 for his work exposing the CIA's infiltration into American domestic institutions. He was also the recipient of the George Polk Award in
1966 for his "explosive revival of the great muckraking tradition," and the
H. L. Mencken Award in 1988 for America's best newspaper columnist.
The cofounder of *Scanlan's Monthly* and later editor of *City of San Francisco*
magazine, the semi-monthly *Frisco*, and the journal *The Argonaut*, Hinckle
also wrote weekly columns for the *San Francisco Chronicle*, the *San Francisco
Examiner*, and the *San Francisco Independent*. The father of three children, he
was the author of numerous books and pamphlets, including *If You Have
a Lemon, Make Lemonade: An Essential Memoir of a Lunatic Decade*; *The Fish
Is Red: The Story of the Secret War Against Castro*; *Gayslayer! The Story of How
Dan White Killed Harvey Milk and George Moscone & Got Away with Murder*; and
the editor of *Who Killed Hunter S. Thompson? The Picaresque Story of the Birth
of Gonzo*. He died in San Francisco from complications of pneumonia on
August 25, 2016, at age seventy-seven.

A NOTE ON TYPE

PERPETUA is a serif typeface designed by English sculptor and stonema-
son Eric Gill for the British Monotype Corporation in the first quarter
of the twentieth century. Based on the designs of old engravings, the Perpetua font recalls a classical impression due in no small measure to its
small, diagonal serifs and its medieval numerals, while embodying a crisp,
contemporary feel. Perpetua is named for the Christian martyr Vibia
Perpetua.